From Access to Success

 A Book of Readings on College Developmental
Education and Learning Assistance Programs

Edited by Martha Maxwell, Ph.D.

H&H Publishing Company, Inc.
1231 Kapp Drive
Clearwater, FL 34625

H&H Publishing Company, Inc.

1231 Kapp Drive
Clearwater, FL 34625
(813) 442-7760
(800) 366-4079
FAX (813) 442-2195

FROM ACCESS TO SUCCESS
A BOOK OF READINGS ON COLLEGE DEVELOPMENTAL
EDUCATION AND LEARNING ASSISTANCE PROGRAMS

Edited by Martha Maxwell, Ph.D.

Production Editing
Karen H. Davis, Priscilla Trimmier

Production Supervision
Robert D. Hackworth

Business Operations
Mike Ealy, Sally Marston

Copyright © 1994 by H&H Publishing Company, Inc.

ISBN 0-943202-47-7

Library of Congress Catalog Number 94-079104

Printing is the lowest number: 10 9 8 7 6 5 4 3 2 1

Introduction

Today's colleges are characterized by diversity — both institutional diversity and student diversity to a greater extent than ever before. Students differ in many ways from those whom college professors expect to teach — the traditional middle-class white students who are becoming the minority in many classrooms. Current students differ not only in ability and academic preparation, but in age and maturity, social background, ethnicity, language, and in psychological preparation for college. Increasing numbers have physical and learning disabilities as well. However, after thirty years of including non-traditional students in college classrooms, today's institutions of higher education have clearer goals and should be more familiar with strategies that work with these students. We now know that those who need skills courses the most do *not* volunteer, and that high risk students do not learn from lectures even when taught by outstanding instructors. We have finally recognized that most students need some academic support and some students need a great deal of support to succeed. Furthermore, many of the teaching techniques and strategies that help non-traditional students are equally effective with traditional, well-prepared freshmen.

This book is intended to give an overview of college learning assistance programs and developmental education for those who are new to the field as well as for interested administrators and faculty members from other disciplines. College skills experts were asked to nominate articles in their specialities that they considered seminal articles dealing with crucial concepts in the field — articles that they felt would give the reader the best introduction to the history, issues, theory, current practice and research. Since it was not possible to reprint all of the articles recommended, we cited many of them in the bibliographies following each section.

What's in a Name?

College learning skills services are called by many names. Programs for underprepared college students have long been termed remedial — a term borrowed from medicine implying that the course will fix some weakness in the student's academic background; and, according to Clowes (1980), "In its most restricted sense, (remedial) refers to work with academically backward and less able students." This negative connotation would, he felt, be also applied to the student who was viewed as a patient to be diagnosed, prescribed for, treated, and then retested. Current examples of remedial programs include the many required courses in basic reading, mathematics, and writing that are mandated by a number of states for entering students in public institutions who have failed college-level skills placement exams. Until a student completes the required remedial course(s) (and/or passes the post-test), he/she cannot enroll in further college courses.

Clowes further differentiated between compensatory and developmental education. Compensatory education, Clowes states, is of more recent origin, having been introduced in the period following WWII, when federal legislation for elementary and secondary education formalized school efforts to make up for the debilitating consequences of discrimination and poverty. In other words, compensatory education was associated with cognitive deficiencies that were thought to be environmentally induced as exemplified by President Johnson's War on Poverty. TRIO programs are compensatory programs with Special Services programs addressing the needs of college age students. In addition to providing help in basic skills (reading, writing, mathematics) compensatory education tries to counterbalance a non-supportive home environment by providing a cultural enriching experience. The traditional black colleges provided a compensatory model of education in which the college assumed a strong in loco parentis role.

The term, developmental education, emerged from the student personnel movement's attempts to merge academic and student affairs personnel to support student learning. As opposed to the negative connotations of remedial and compensatory education which view the learner as inadequate, the programs of the 1970s stressed the value and worth of each individual and focused on the potential of continuing growth and change. The goal is to have everyone involved master increasingly complex developmental tasks, achieve self-direction and become interdependent. This establishes developmental education as a series of major life choices and processes through which all students must pass rather than programs that are appropriate only for the weakest students. Learning centers which offer academic support services to all students epitomize the developmental viewpoint. Clowes points out that all three of these types of programs, remedial, compensatory, and developmental, exist in colleges and universities today and often the same institution offers all three programs, yet the tendency is to consider them as the same. It is important to understand the differences between these approaches in order to articulate purposes and goals and to be clearer about expectations and desired outcomes.

More recently the term learning assistance has been associated with the learning center movement and with services to students at all levels. Unfortunately, remedial and developmental are often used interchangeably to describe programs so that developmental education at the college level is regarded by some as having the same pejorative connotation as does remedial work. As a result, many practitioners prefer to refer to their services as college learning assistance offered to all students rather than using the term developmental or remedial.

Mary Rubin (1991) reported the attempts of a CRLA (College Learning and Reading Association) committee to clarify terminology in the field and observed that the term REMEDIAL suggests that skills have been taught, but not learned (or not learned correctly) and that therefore, the student must be retaught. Developmental education she considered the normal expected sequence of learning, usually used in contradistinction to accelerated and/or remedial learning. Referring to college courses as developmental, assumes or takes cognizance of the fact that there is a gap between high school and college that needs to be filled for many students. The claim is that developmental students need to learn skills they have not previously been taught in high school and that the fault is not with their ability, but with their preparation. Also she concludes that remedial instruction may be a tool used in a developmental program.

When program directors were asked what term they used to describe their program in budget requests, Rubin (1991) reported "academic skills courses" was the most frequent term used; developmental courses ranked fifth. This suggests that there is still some confusion about the term developmental as it is applied and understood in academe.

I have chosen to use the title "learning assistance programs" in this book, feeling that the topics it addresses will be of interest to those who see their programs as developmental, remedial, compensatory, or student support services. I'm using learning assistance in a generic sense to mean a program that helps all students and is based on a developmental philosophy — i.e., as a field of research, teaching, and practice designed to promote academic performance and as a process of utilizing principles of developmental theory to facilitate learning that employs the principles of cognitive and affective development in designing and delivering instruction (Rubin, 1991). The designation, learning assistance programs, I feel, includes both remedial and compensatory programs but is not limited to them, for it provides a variety of other services to other student clients including advanced undergraduates as well as graduate students and is not restricted to entering freshmen.

The audience to whom this book is addressed includes the following:

1. The many hundreds of instructors who enter the field of college developmental education each year with minimal formal training or experience in college skills work.

2. Skills specialists attending inservice workshops, courses, and institutes in developmental education and learning assistance.

3. Students in graduate courses in learning assistance and developmental skills.

4. Interested faculty and administrators in other disciplines who want to learn about learning assistance programs.

5. Our international colleagues to help them learn about and understand what's happening in access education in the United States.

It is not the purpose of this book of readings to be all inclusive, but rather we have chosen to present articles that provide an overview. Therefore we have restricted topics to the following:

1. History of Developmental Education & Learning Assistance

Starting with a brief history of how higher educational institutions have dealt with underprepared students in the past, Boylan and White describe how this problem existed from the founding of American colleges, reappearing whenever a new population was targeted for college admission. Clowes explains that despite the fact that college remedial programs have existed throughout our history, scant attention was paid to them by researchers until the

1960s. Furthermore, he notes that the past few decades have marked the emergence of remedial/developmental education as a profession. Further evidence of this change can be found in the selections on professional standards and research on outcomes in the last section of this book.

Hardin's article presents a rationale for the importance of programs to help developmental students in colleges and describes six types of students who are served by these programs. Starks reviews the research on the impact of developmental programs on the retention of college students.

2. Learning Assistance Centers – Organization and Functions

As Enright points out, learning assistance centers first appeared in the late 1960s in response to technological changes and the open admission policies that brought larger numbers of underprepared students to college. Reading and study skills laboratories had existed in many colleges and continued to serve regular students as they expanded to include the newer high risk students and became learning centers. The philosophies and policies of learning centers varied with the institution they served, and Christ, Maxwell, and Reed describe some of the contrasts. Enright and Kerstiens propose some future directions for learning centers and Van's paper summarizes the criteria by which professionals judge learning assistance programs.

3. Tutoring

Peer-tutoring has become an integral part of learning assistance programs in almost all higher education institutions and studies indicate that tutor training makes a significant difference between successful and unsuccessful developmental programs. Tu-

tor training programs vary widely too — some are brief and intense such as Condravy's; others are semester length tutoring for credit programs like Hawkins'. Some emphasize metacognitive training as Gourgey describes, others emphasize counseling skills (Hancock and Gier, and Winnard), while still others train tutors to understand basic principles of learning (Stahl, et al.). Maxwell summarizes the research on peer tutoring and discusses some of the reasons why, despite its great popularity, studies often fail to show that tutoring improves student grades.

4. Assessment

Assessing and placing students in college courses has become one of the most important functions involving learning assistance professionals, admissions officers, and college faculty as well. Moranti discusses the dilemma of colleges admitting underprepared students and argues that all students should be tested, and those whose skills are weak should be required to take appropriate remedial courses. Simpson and Nist's article describes a comprehensive testing and teaching program in basic college reading skills. Smittle describes how a computerized testing program can reduce time spent administering and scoring tests and increase instructional time for both teachers and students.

Basic Skills Courses & Programs Including:

5. Reading and Study Skills

Stahl, Simpson, and Hayes summarize the findings of research and their own experience to make recommendations on better ways to teach high risk students. Their paper mainly concerns reading skills, but the same recommendations are equally applicable to mathematics and writing courses as well.

Maxwell reviews some recent research in learning and study skills and asks whether the age-old techniques and learning strategies we teach are still applicable to today's college student. Nist and Hynd describe a unique reading lab where poor readers receive individual instruction from the teacher and are not just assigned individualized exercises and workbooks.

6. Writing

Hughes describes a model writing center for improving writing across the curriculum — a service that the University of Wisconsin-Madison provides for any student from freshman to graduate level.

Two articles present some recent research on teaching basic writing and writing for ESL students. First, MacDonald explains why poor writers often ignore teacher's comments on their papers and what can be done about it and second, Whimbey and others explain the research underlying two successful methods for teaching writing to basic writers: sentence combining and text reconstruction. Finally, Hawkins looks at a common problem of student writers in not recognizing the audience whom they are supposed to address and shows how peer-tutors can help them strengthen their compositions in this important area.

7. Course Related Skills Services

(Adjunct Skills and Supplementary Instruction). These refer to services that teach students to apply effective learning skills to their work in a particular course (as contrasted with general study skills courses). Dimon details the theoretical and pedagogical principles that underlie adjunct skills courses and explains their success in living up to their claims to improve students' course grades. Burmeister describes the Supplemental Instruction (SI) Program,

a program developed at the University of Missouri-Kansas City that has been a prototype for similar programs in over 300 colleges and reviews the research on SI.

Visor and others report on a study in which students who volunteer for SI are compared on affective characteristics with those who don't volunteer and/or don't continue to attend SI sessions. Their report contains suggestions about how to encourage more students to attend SI.

8. Technology

Three articles on using computer software in developmental programs by Broderick and Caverly give specific and practical suggestions on choosing and purchasing software, using the computer as a tutor and as a tutee.

9. Mathematics

Hackworth presents an overview of teaching mathematics and explains how it can be improved to help reduce the increasing numbers of college students who need basic mathematics skills. Goolsy and others report on a study involving attitudinal and anxiety factors in learning basic college mathematics and depict a college math program that emphasizes the affective factors. Darken explains the factors that cause so many college students to be weak in basic arithmetic skills creating instructional dilemmas for college math instructors.

Hartman outlines some cooperative approaches to learning mathematics that have been widely adopted in high schools and more recently in college courses and discusses their strengths and limitations. Stine and others present an idealized model of Math-X, a self-paced, self-help mathematics course at the community college level.

10. Evaluation and Outcome Research

In this section, we examine program evaluation, especially the work by Akst and Hecht describing the advantages and disadvantages of different evaluation models for remedial courses. Then Thayer and Maxwell look at how the standards and guidelines developed for Learning Assistance Programs by the Council for the Advancement of Standards and the NADE guidelines for program components including tutoring, adjunct skills programs, teaching and learning and developmental courses can help both in the planning and development of programs as well as in their evaluation. An institutional case study by Roueche and Baker shows how an open admission institution can assure the excellence of its programs and the quality of the students who complete them.

The reports by Boylan, Bliss, and Bonham from the long-term follow-up study funded by the EXXON Foundation reveal that students who complete developmental courses do go on to succeed in college and describe the differences in the success rates of minority students depending on the type of institution they attend.

The articles and topics chosen for this book are not intended to be an exhaustive list, but were meant to give the reader an overview of the issues, ideas, research and practice in the field of college learning assistance. Space limitations compelled us to condense some articles and exclude some topics. For example, we might have included more detailed selections on critical thinking, learning styles, programs for the special groups such as the learning disabled, students for whom English is a Second Language, GED programs to help students complete high school and many others that today's college learning assistance programs often include. We leave these and other topics for editors to collect and distribute in future publications.

The editor wishes to express her deep appreciation to the following experts who recommended articles for this book and cooperated in many other ways.

David Arendale, University of Missouri-Kansas City

Geoffrey Akst, Borough of Manhatten Community College

Barbara S. Bonham and Hunter R. Boylan, Appalachian State University, Boone, NC

Sandra Burmeister, Cazanovia College, NY

David C. Caverly, Southwest Texas University

Frank L. Christ, Director – Winter Institute for Learning Assistance Professionals, University of Arizona-Tucson

Darrel A. Clowes, Virginia Polytechnic & State University

Gwen Enright, San Diego Community College

Missy Garrett, Slippery Rock State University, PA

Tom Gier and Karan Hancock, University of Anchorage, Alaska

Hope J. Hartman, City College of New York

Sue Hashway, Grambling State University

Thom Hawkins, University of California, Berkeley

Bradley Hughes, University of Wisconsin, Madison

Gene Kerstiens, Director Andragogy Associates, College/Adult Learning Specialists, Rancho Palos Verdes, CA

Ross B. MacDonald, Los Medanos College, CA

Sherri L. Nist, University of Georgia

Karen Quinn, University of Illinois at Chicago

Michele L. Simpson, University of Georgia

Norman A. Stahl, University of Northern Illinois

William G. White, Jr., Grambling State University, LA

The editor also wishes to thank the following publishers who generously permitted us to reprint their works: *The Journal of Developmental Education, Research in Developmental Education, The Journal of Reading and Learning, Research and Teaching in Developmental Education, Journal of Reading, College English, Illinois English Bulletin, The Educational Facility Planner*, Jossey-Bass Publisher, Agathon Press, and Kraus International Publications.

Hopefully, you'll find many different uses for this book — as a general orientation for new professionals or for updating experienced staff, and as a way to inform others in your institutions about what it is that you do for students.

This book is dedicated to Perry Perretz.

**Martha Maxwell, Editor
1994**

References

Clowes, D. A. (1980). More than a definitional problem: Remedial, compensatory, and developmental education. *Journal of Developmental & Remedial Education*, 4(1), 8-10.

Rubin, M. (1991). A glossary of developmental education terms compiled by the CRLA Task Force on Professional Language for College Reading and Learning. *Journal of College Reading and Learning*, xxxiii(2), 1-13.

From Access to Success
Table of Contents

Part I

History
&
Philosophy

From its inception, American higher education has found many of its entering students underprepared, so efforts by colleges to help students make up their deficiencies go back a long way.

Educating All the Nation's People:
The Historical Roots of Developmental Education

By Hunter R. Boylan and William G. White Jr.

(Condensed from Hunter R. Boylan and William G. White, Jr., "Educating all the nation's people: The historical roots of developmental education - Part 1," *Research in Developmental Education*, 4(4), 1987 and Hunter R. Boylan, "The historical roots of developmental education - Part 3," *Research in Developmental Education*, 5(3). Reprinted by permission of *Research in Developmental Education* (Appalachian State University, Boone, NC 28608) and Hunter R. Boylan & William G. White, Jr.)

On most American college and university campuses developmental educators are regarded as the "newest kids on the block." To most professionals in academe, developmental programs and the students they serve are of relatively recent vintage — a phenomenon that results from 1960's egalitarianism and the subsequent "open door" admissions policies of public colleges and universities. College administrators, legislators, and the public believe that the problem of underpreparedness that developmental programs are designed to resolve is a recent one — one that results from all the shortcomings of American public education that a spate of recent reports has so eloquently pointed out.

A more accurate view would be that developmental education programs and the students they serve, are not new to higher education. They have been present on college and university campuses in one form or another since the very beginnings of American higher education. The field of developmental education is simply the modern version of past efforts to respond to the fact that, at their point of entry, many college students are unable to succeed without some sort of special assistance. It also represents the most recent version of American higher education's long standing commitment to proving access to college for all the nation's citizens who might profit from it.

17th Century Precedents for Developmental Education

America's first college was founded as a result of an act by the leaders of the Massachusetts Bay Colony which provided for the establishment of a college that would train clergymen for the colony, " . . . once our present generation of ministers has passed from this Earth" ("Old Deluder Satan Act" of 1624).

The institution that was founded as a result of this act, Harvard College, did not open its doors until several years later — 1630 to be exact. When it did open, it was immediately confronted with a need for remediation among its students, a result of the fact that the language in which most learned books were written was Latin. Furthermore, following the European model of the time, Latin was also the language of instruction for most courses. It is worth noting that the King James Version of the Bible was one of the first books written in common English so that all the citizens of England might be able to read it. And the King James Version of the Bible was not published until the early 17th century. Few books, particularly scholarly works, were available in any language other than Latin. Unfortunately, the learning of an academic language was not a high priority for colonists attempting to carve a homeland out of the wilderness. Consequently, it was necessary for those who wished to attend Harvard college to study Latin before they could be successful in their studies. Harvard, therefore, provided tutors in Latin for incoming students (Brubacher and Rudy, 1976). The provision of such tutoring assistance may rightly be regarded as the first remedial education effort in North America — the earliest antecedent of developmental education in American higher education. The use of books written in Latin and the use of Latin as a language of instruction persisted well into the 18th century in American colleges. It was not until after the American Revolution that English language texts and English language instruction became available on a widespread basis (Brubacher and Rudy, 1976). Until this happened, tutorials in Latin were a predominant feature of American colleges.

Developmental Education in the 19th Century

One of the major political and philosophical forces in the United States from the early-to-mid nineteenth century was "Jacksonian Democracy," a movement based on an appreciation of the common man combined with an effort to serve his needs and aspirations through government. The "Jacksonian Period" is generally regarded as falling between 1824 and 1848, the period between the election of Andrew Jackson to the presidency and the election of Zachary Taylor — when Jacksonian ideas began to decline.

Spanning more than two decades, Jacksonian Democracy impacted on all facets of American life. During this period, suffrage was extended, the lot of workers was improved, the middle class of merchants and tradesmen grew rapidly, and education at all levels was provided to an increasing number of citizens. One area in which educational access was expanded during this period was in higher education. In an effort to improve the lot of the common man, to provide training for merchants and tradesmen, and to expand the pool of engineering, agricultural, and scientific talent in the developing nation, new colleges were established in practically every state in the union (Van Deusen, 1986). But because education had, heretofore, been neither mandatory nor universal, there were few people available who had much preparation for college. Yet, if the new colleges were to remain open, they would have to collect fees from students.

> Colleges in the early 1800's were largely self-sustaining operations. This meant that anyone who had the money to attend college was able to do so without regard to preparation.

It should be noted that the colleges of this period were largely self-sustaining operations. While they were sometimes funded by land sale, such as those provided by the Ohio Land Grant Act of 1802, more often than not, they were funded by private donations and student fees. Thus, a major criterion for admission to college was the student's ability to pay his own (the masculine gender is used here purposefully since women were not generally admitted to college in the early 19th century). In essence, this meant that anyone who had the money to attend college was able to do so without regard to prior learning or preparation (Brubacher and Rudy, 1976).

As a result, the colleges of the time were confronted with substantial numbers of students who were unprepared to do college level work. Most efforts to respond to this problem consisted of individual tutoring of students. As enrollments grew, however, the number of individual tutors became insufficient to meet the demand. As Brier (1984) points out, many colleges had more people involved in giving and receiving tutoring than were involved in delivering and taking classes.

> The University of Wisconsin established the first college preparatory department in 1849 offering remedial courses in reading, writing, and arithmetic.

At the University of Wisconsin, the problem became so severe that the institution established the nation's first college preparatory department in 1849 (Brier, 1984). This department functioned in much the same way as a modern developmental education program. It provided remedial courses in reading, writing, and arithmetic to students who lacked sufficient background to succeed in more advanced college courses. Soon, the college preparatory department model was adopted by other institutions across the country. In fact, by 1889, more than 80 percent of colleges and universities in the United States offered college preparatory programs (Brier, 1984).

The growth of college preparatory programs was stimulated not only by an influx of underprepared students but also by a further expansion of the number of colleges and universities. While a combination of economic and political conditions stifled the growth of higher education in America in the years immediately preceding the Civil War, the Morrill Act of 1862 stimulated another period of growth for higher education institutions following the Civil War. Furthermore, the Morrill Act (1862), or the

Land Grant Act as it is commonly known, also made it clear that institutions established as a result of this act should serve "the industrial classes" of America. The act was designed not only to expand the number of qualified engineers and agricultural, military, and business specialists, it was also designed to promote access to higher education for a greater variety of citizens.

During the latter parts of the 19th century, an unprecedented period of growth took place in the number and variety of higher education institutions. State land grant colleges were not the only institutions that expanded in number following the Civil War. Colleges for women, agricultural colleges, technical colleges, and colleges for blacks also expanded. And, as the number and variety of institutions grew, so did the number of college students who were underprepared for college.

Women's colleges, which first appeared in the late 1830's, were an outgrowth of a great reform movement that sought legal, political, and social and educational equality for women, and which was, in many ways, linked with Jacksonian Democracy. With every college of the early nineteenth century except Oberlin refusing to accept women, a number of institutions were established exclusively for women.

> The women admitted to early women's colleges were underprepared for college because they were unable to obtain an adequate secondary education.

Those opposed to admitting women to college argued that they were mentally unsuited for higher education. While that certainly was untrue, it was true that most women were underprepared for college because they were unable to obtain an adequate secondary education. The early women's colleges were thus forced to keep the age of admission low, and the curriculum provided was understandably more akin to secondary than higher education. The baccalaureate degrees granted by women's colleges were not regarded as equal to those granted by other institutions.

The Civil War, in addition to settling a number of constitutional issues, also settled a number of social ones, including the question of whether women should attend college. Following the war, the question changed from "if" to "where."

In the northeastern states the dominant pattern became superior but separate women's colleges with independent institutions such as Vassar, Wellesley, Smith, Bryn Mawr, and coordinated women's colleges affiliated with several "Ivy League" schools. But even in these efforts, preparatory schools were still necessary.

One of the earliest women's colleges, Vassar, had a college preparatory program from its very beginnings. But, in spite of the fact that Vassar was founded for the purpose of including those who had previously been denied access to higher education, there were those who questioned the presence of underprepared students, and the question of whether or not underprepared students should be admitted at all to the institution became a major issue for the college during the late 1800's (Report to the Trustees of Vassar College, 1890). Nevertheless, Vassar continued then and continues now to admit women who have inadequate secondary preparation (Boylan, 1986).

The trend to establish separate colleges for women was not, however, a universal one. In the newer universities of the East and in colleges throughout the Western states, where coeducational secondary schools were preparing young people for college,

coeducation became the pattern (Brubacher and Rudy, 1976).

The increase in the number of students going to college following the Civil War was not only the result of a democratic movement but also of a greater demand by men and women for higher training to prepare them for an increasing number of professions, trades, industries, and businesses that required specialized preparation. Two other efforts to provide postsecondary education for students who were either uninterested in or underprepared to pursue the traditional classical/liberal arts curriculum centered in technical institutes and scientific schools. Technical institutes had first appeared in the 1820's and were the first to offer extension programs and evening courses which made higher education accessible to non-traditional students. These efforts were the precursors of the modern adult education programs.

Technical institutes were soon followed by scientific schools, established alongside a number of leading colleges, to care for "practical minded students" who in many cases were not prepared to complete the classical curriculum (Butts, 1939). In many respects, the early technical and scientific schools faced challenges and opposition analogous to that faced by junior and community colleges in the twentieth century.

Another major precedent for developmental education was the establishment of colleges for blacks during the early part of the twentieth century. Following the Civil War, it was apparent that Black Americans would become part of the social, political, and economic system of the nation. Yet the institution of slavery had systematically denied most of these citizens access to all but the most rudimentary forms of education.

In response to this, postsecondary institutions for Black Americans were established through a number of channels. The American Missionary Society set up a number of institutions in the South for the purpose of educating freed slaves (Brubacher and Rudy, 1976). The Second Morrill Act (1890) also provided for the establishment of land grant colleges for Black Americans. In addition to these, Black Americans also established several colleges through their own efforts.

> The early black colleges were extraordinarily successful in providing remedial and developmental education to their students in the face of overwhelming odds.

All of these institutions were confronted with the enormous problem of providing the training necessary to prosper in a modern industrial society to a generation of people who had been denied access to education in any form. In fact, the contribution of historically black colleges in delivering a massive, remedial and developmental education effort has largely been ignored in the field of developmental education. For many of these institutions, their entire mission might be defined as remedial and developmental. And it should be noted that the early black institutions were extraordinarily successful in the face of overwhelming odds. The fact that so many of the black leaders, scientists, legislators, doctors, and attorneys of the late 19th century and early twentieth centuries, as well as today, were trained at these institutions attests to their effectiveness. It could well be argued that some of the most amazing feats of developmental education were accomplished at historically black institutions in the United States.

References

Boylan, H. (1983). The growth of the learning assistance movement. In H. Boylan (Ed.), *Forging new partnerships in learning assistance.* San Francisco: Jossey Bass.

Brier, E. (1986). Bridging the academic preparation gap: An historical view. *Journal of Developmental Education,*8(1).

Brubacher, J. S., & Rudy, W. (1976). *Higher education in transition.* New York: Harper & Row.

Canfield, J. H. (1889). *The opportunities of the rural population for higher education.* Nashville, TN: National Council on Education.

Carnegie Commission on Higher Education (1990). *Three thousand futures.* San Francisco: Jossey-Bass.

Enright, G., & Kersteins, G. (1980). The learning center: Toward an expanded role. In O. Lenning & R. Nayman (Eds.,) *New roles for learning assistance.* San Francisco: Jossey-Bass.

Jencks, C., & Reisman, M. (1969). *The academic revolution.* San Francisco: Jossey-Bass.

Maxwell, M. (1979). *Improving student learning skills.* San Francisco: Jossey-Bass.

Richardson, R., Martens, K., and Fisk, E. (1981). *Functional literacy in the college setting.* (AAHE/ERIC Higher Education Research Report No. 3). Washington, DC: AAHE.

Roueche, J., and Snow, J. (1977). *Overcoming learning problems.* San Francisco: Jossey-Bass.

Wright, D., & Cahalan, M. (1985, April). *Remedial/developmental studies in institutions of higher education: Policies and practices.* Paper presented at the American Educational Research Association Convention, Chicago, IL.

Hunter R. Boylan is Director of the National Center for Developmental Education at Appalachian State University (NC) and William G. White, Jr. is Associate Professor of Educational Leadership at Grambling State University (LA).

Although remedial programs have existed in American colleges and universities since their beginnings, they have largely been ignored by historians and have attracted little attention from researchers. Clowes describes how the field has changed since the open-admission policies of the 60s and 70s ushered in the current movement toward professionalization of remedial educators.

Research, Respectability, and Legitimation of Postsecondary Remedial Education

By Darrel E. Clowes

(Excerpted from Darrel E. Clowes, "Remediation in American Higher Education." In Smart, J. C. (Ed.) *Higher Education: Handbook of Theory and Practice Volume VIII*, Bronx, NY: Agathon Press, 1992, (462 - 465). Reprinted by permission of the publisher and Darrel E. Clowes.)

Remediation has been an area of "benign neglect" for much of American higher education's history. Remediation activities have been largely ignored in the literature on higher education and the function has been little studied. Recently, since the movements toward increased access to higher education of the 60s and 70s, remediation has emerged as a significant factor in the curriculum and social agenda of American higher education. However, the kinds of students who are considered remedial have changed significantly over time and the social agenda undergirding remediation efforts in higher education has also changed. These factors as well as the shifts in program design and assessment criteria over the past decades make comparison over time difficult and complicate our understanding of the pedagogic and policy issues enmeshed within remediation.

State Of The Field

Research on remediation in American higher education has been modest at best. During the periods Cross (1971) labels as the Period of Aristocracy (colonial times to the Civil War) and the period of Meritocracy (from the Civil War to the Civil Rights movements of the 1950s), little serious research was done. There is trace evidence that programs existed, but little evidence of serious studies of the design or effectiveness of these programs has survived. Rudolph's (1977) history of the undergraduate curriculum does not discuss remediation as a curriculum issue, and Reynold's (1969) study of the junior college curriculum discusses remediation as a form of skill building he predicts will become important for junior colleges of the future.

The 1960s began the Period of Egalitarianism as numbers of students entered higher education who scored in the bottom third on nationally normed tests of academic ability: Cross's (1971) "new" students. As remediation programs multiplied in higher education, first calls for studies of remediation came and then the studies themselves began to emerge. Roueche (1968) responded to the volume of descriptive material on remediation coming to the ERIC Clearinghouse for Junior Colleges by calling for recognition of remediation as a significant function of higher education and especially the junior college. There was little response until Roueche responded to his own call with a series of descriptive studies (Roueche and Kirk, 1973;

Roueche & Snow, 1977, Roueche, Baker, and Roueche, 1984).

These studies and others established clearly that remediation programs were increasing in higher education and were a prominent part of the curriculum of higher education. Despite this, remediation was not a respectable or legitimate aspect of the undergraduate curriculum. A publication by the Carnegie Foundation for the Advancement of Teaching (1977) states: "College curricula must be planned on the assumption that all of the new students on campus each year have acquired a certain minimum amount of learning skill and knowledge" (p. 221), but the report adds: "Once students have been admitted, a college has an obligation to give any support it can to help them succeed in meeting educational goals" (p. 222). The thrust of the Carnegie argument is that secondary schools have responsibility for basic skills preparation, and colleges and universities have a supportive but secondary role in that endeavor. Recent content analyses of the professional literature underscore the marginal nature of remediation in higher education. Kuh, et al., (1986) analyzed the research literature on college students between 1969 and 1983. Eleven hundred and eighty-nine articles were reviewed and the primary and secondary topics covered were identified. Of a possible incidence of coverage of just under 2,400 articles, there were only 215 instances of topics being covered that might possibly be related to remediation.

On the 215 articles (11 percent of the total), 91 were instances of coverage of "minority" students, 49 covered "learning styles," 42 focused on "study skills," 22 on "educationally disadvantaged," and 11 on "handicapped" students. No topic related to remediation received "considerable" attention (100 or more incidents of coverage) as defined by the authors. Clowes and Towles (1985) analyzed the contents of the journal published by the American Association of Community and Junior Colleges (currently the *Community, Technical, and Junior College Journal*) from 1930 to 1980. They found remediation the least addressed of all curriculum areas and even detected a decline in coverage during the last 20 years. With scant attention from major journals covering research on college students or the major issues of the community colleges, remediation must be considered a marginal enterprise.

Legitimation

The legitimation of remediation, a movement away from benign neglect and marginality toward acknowledgment as an accepted activity and object of research in higher education, has been underway for sometime and may be close to attainment. In 1977 the National Association for Remedial/Developmental Studies in Postsecondary Education held its first annual conference. The Association, now the National Association for Developmental Education, has remained active and continues to sponsor a national conference and a variety of state and region organizations and conferences on developmental education in higher education. A Center for Developmental Education was established at Appalachian State University with assistance from the Kellogg Foundation. The Center has sponsored a journal since 1977, now the *Journal of Developmental Education*, and sponsors training institutes and graduate study for practitioners in higher education. Jossey-Bass established (in 1980) a New Directions for Learning Assistance Centers Series. These activities provide an academic legitimacy for remedial education. Recent surveys have again documented the strong presence of learning assistance centers, remedial programs, and remedial courses in higher education (Abraham, 1987;

Lederman, Ryzewic, and Ribaudo, 1983; Sullivan, 1980; Wright and Cahalan, 1985). This continued documentation of the presence of remedial activities has gone a long way to establish the fact of remedial activities in higher education. It has not made them desirable or truly respectable.

Respectability may be a function of the role remediation can play in supporting the open admissions policies of community colleges and many four-year institutions. Open access is a cornerstone of the community and junior college mission. It is also a cornerstone for a significant number of four-year institutions' missions since the promise of equal opportunity finds expression at the state level in public policy supporting access to higher education for all our citizens.

The need for remediation has perhaps been best documented in New Jersey through the continuing activities of the New Jersey Basic Skills Council. In a series of reports beginning in the late 1970s, assessment of the skills levels of first-time students entering New Jersey's public colleges are reported (see Morante, Faskow, and Menditti, 1984a, 1984b). Carefully developed measures are a strong point of the Basic Skills Council's work, and the levels of remediation needed by students at all levels of the higher education system are eye-opening. Among full-time students entering all levels of public higher education in New Jersey, 30 percent needed remediation in writing, 30 percent in basic computation, another 31 percent in basic algebra, and 34 percent in reading; the authors believe the rates for

part-time students would be even higher (Morante, Faskow and Menditti, 1984b, Martin Trow, 1982-1983) summed up the situation well:

American colleges are not strangers to underprepared students or remedial instruction. And today, our problems, and indeed many of our responses, are remarkably similar to those of the 19th century college. We share with our academic forebears a powerful democratic ethos, weak secondary education, the pressure of the market felt through enrollment-driven budgets, and the absence of any central agency for setting or enforcing high school curricula or standards for college entry. Today, as in the past, all these and other forces are bringing to our public colleges and universities, many students who are not, on entry, prepared to do work at a standard which those institutions define as "college level" (p. 17).

Concern for the competing demands for providing access to higher education while also maintaining appropriate levels of quality within higher education has moved remediation activities out of the shadows and into the mainstream of academic life. The emergence of community colleges as a potential institutional base for remediation within higher education, has also made remediation more acceptable to higher education practitioners and to public policy makers. The formation of professional associations, institutes housed in academic institutions, and the emergence of journals specific to the field have all contributed to the legitimation of remediation in higher education.

References

Abraham, A. A., Jr. (1987). *Readiness for college: Should there be statewide placement standards? (A Report on College-Level Remedial/Developmental Programs in SREB States).* Atlanta, GA: Southern Regional Education Board. (ERIC Document Reproduction Service No. ED 280 369).

Clowes, D. A., & Towles. D. (1985). Community and junior college journal: Lessons from fifty years. *Community, Technical, and Junior College Journal,* 56, 28-32.

Cross, K. P. (1971). *Beyond the open door: New students in higher education.* San Francisco: Jossey-Bass.

Kuh, G. D., Bean, J. P., Bradley, R. K., Coomes, M. D., & Hunter, D. E. (1986). Changes in research on college students published in selected journals between 1969 and 1983. *Review of Higher Education,* 9, 177-192.

Lederman, M. J., Ryzewic, S. R., & Ribaudo, M. (1983, September). *Assessment and improvement of the academic skills of entering freshmen: A national survey.* (Research Monograph Series, report No. 5). New York City: University of New York. (ERIC Document Reproduction No. ED 238 973).

Morante, E. A., Faskow, S., and Menditti, I. N. (1984a). The New Jersey basic skills assessment program. Part I. *Journal of Remedial and Developmental Education,* 7(2), 2-4, 32.

Morante, E. A., Faskow, S., and Menditti, I. N. (1984b). The New Jersey basic skills assessment program. Part II. *Journal of Remedial and Developmental Education,* 7(3), 6-9, 32.

Reynolds, J. (1969). *The comprehensive junior college curriculum.* Berkeley, CA: McCutcheon Publishing Co.

Roueche, J. E. (1968). *Salvage, redirection or custody? Remedial education in the community and junior college.* San Francisco: Jossey-Bass.

Roueche, J. E., and Kirk, R.W. (1973). *Catching up: Remedial Education.* San Francisco: Jossey-Bass.

Roueche, J. E., and Snow, J. J. (1977). *Overcoming learning problems: A guide to developmental education in college.* San Francisco: Jossey-Bass.

Roueche, J. E., Baker, G. A., & Roueche, S. D. (1984). *College responses to low achieving students: A national study.* Orlando, FL: Media Systems Corporation.

Rudolph, F. (1977). *Curriculum: A history of the American undergraduate course of study since 1636.* San Francisco: Jossey-Bass.

Sullivan, L. L. (1980). Growth and influence of the learning center movement. In K. V. Lauridsen (ed.), *New Directions for college learning assistance: Examining the scope of Learning Centers,* No. 1. San Francisco: Jossey-Bass.

Trow, M. A. (1982-83). Underprepared students at public research universities. In Cross, K. P. (ed.), *Current Issues in Higher Education: No. 1, Underprepared learners,* Washington, DC: American Association for Higher Education.

Wright, D. A., & Cahalan, M. W. (1985, April). *Remedial/developmental studies in institutions of higher education: Policies and practices, 1984.* Paper presented at the annual conference of the American Educational Research Association, Chicago, IL. (ERIC Document Reproduction Service No ED 263 828).

Darrel A. Clowes is Professor of Higher Education at Virginia Polytechnic Institute and State University, Blacksburg, VA.

Students entering college today who need developmental/remedial courses are a diverse group. Carlette Hardin describes six types of developmental students.

Access to Higher Education: Who Belongs?

By Carlette J. Hardin

(From the *Journal of Developmental Education*, 12:1, 2-6, 19, (Fall 1988). Reprinted by permission of Carlette J. Hardin and the *Journal of Developmental Education*, Appalachian State University, Boone, NC 28608.)

Abstract. Research indicates that 82% of all institutions and 94% of public institutions offer at least one course considered to be remedial or developmental in nature (Abraham, 1987). However, there are those who still ask, "Can we justify allowing students needing remedial or developmental courses to enter institutions of higher learning?" To provide an answer to this issue, six categories of students requiring remedial or developmental courses are identified. These categories are: The Poor Chooser, The Adult Student, The Foreign Student, The Ignored, The Handicapped, and The User. Characteristics and needs of these six groups are provided.

It happened again today. A colleague was explaining Tennessee's Developmental Studies Program to a group of secondary teachers. When it came time for questions, someone in the audience asked, "How can you justify allowing into the university students needing this kind of help? These students just don't belong in college. If you know they can't make it, you shouldn't allow them to enter." The session ended without a satisfactory response to the question, and I have been wrestling with the issue all day. I have heard this question before. It's just that after six years as a developmental educator, I am surprised that there are those who still maintain

that the opportunity to learn should be limited to those who have demonstrated that they can learn. However, I must admit that the statement makes sense. If, as Roueche (1968) points out, developmental students are admitted to institutions of higher education with little hope of success, then the open door policy of many institutions becomes a "revolving door policy." If we know that a student has no chance of earning a college degree, then we are certainly doing the student an injustice by allowing him or her to enter the university. The problem is how to determine if a student will make it or not. I have taught many students who should not be in a college setting if we considered background alone. Some of these students left college after a few weeks.

The formation of the preceding assumptions caused me to take a closer look at the backgrounds, needs, and goals of my students. In doing so I realized that developmental students typically share one or more of the following characteristics.

> **The developmental student has made a decision or decisions which adversely affected his/her academic future.**

The "poor chooser" is in need of remedial or developmental work because, at some point in life, the student chose an academic curriculum which did not prepare him or her for college-level work. Maxwell (1979) suggests that such students might be labeled "misprepared" rather than underprepared. There are hundreds of examples where students made a poor choice about their academic future, but poor choosers are typically one of two types.

The first type of poor chooser selected something other than a college-prep curriculum while in high school. Research by Abraham (1987) indicates that only one-third of today's high school students are enrolled in a college-prep program. However, the number and percentage of high school graduates enrolled in higher education have increased dramatically.

The decision to choose something other than a college-prep curriculum might have been made for a number of reasons. It may be that the students had no intention of pursuing a college degree and saw no reason to subject themselves to the work required in a college-prep curriculum. Or, based on the student's past academic record, a teacher, counselor, or parent suggested that the student wasn't college material and, therefore, should pursue a less demanding curriculum. In some cases, students do not understand what is required in college. As a result, they may often take courses which will protect their GPAs and help secure financial backing for college, but they enter without the necessary skills to succeed.

The second type of poor chooser dropped out of high school. Again the reasons for such a decision are numerous and vary from boredom to pregnancy. At a later time, usually when the student has matured and has come to understand the value of an education, the poor chooser decides to return to an academic setting.

Two important points should be made about poor choosers. First, most poor choosers made their decisions while between the ages of 14 and 18. Should the poor chooser be penalized the remainder of his or her life for a decision made as a teenager? Second, poor choosers need help because they lack background, not ability. They are playing a catch-up game and, once this has been done, they do remarkably well throughout their collegiate careers.

> The developmental student, in many cases, is an adult learner who has been away from an academic setting for an extended time.

One of the fastest growing populations in colleges across the United States is the "adult learner." Between 1972 and 1982, the percentage of adults (age 25 to 34) attending college increased 69.8% (King, 1985). For those adults over the age of 34, the percent of increase was an astounding 77.4%. Hodgkinson (1985) notes that of the 12 million college students in the United States, only about two million are full-time, living on campus, and aged 18 to 22. The image of the typical college student is quickly changing, and adult students bring to campuses a set of unique problems.

The adult learner is often in need of either remedial or developmental help. Many are former poor choosers who left high school without acquiring the skills needed to succeed in college. Other adults had a solid college-prep program in high school but haven't been required to use the knowledge they possess in a formal academic setting for a number of years. For this last group, it is not a matter of acquiring skills but rather one of brushing up on skills which have been dormant for a number of years.

When adults are thrown into the regular college environment without the help provided in a remedial or developmental program, they may quickly become discouraged and decide they were wise to avoid the college environment for such a long time.

The existence of programs to meet the needs of developmental students is often defended by pointing out that everyone deserves a second chance. For adult students, developmental studies offer not a second chance but a first chance. For many, it may also be their last.

> The developmental student frequently has academic or physical weaknesses which were never detected while attending high school.

Numerous students spend their academic lives staying out of the teacher's way and, in the process, have academic and physical problems ignored. These "ignored students" expend a great deal of energy becoming anonymous. Of course, while being anonymous eliminates the possibility that they will be corrected or embarrassed in the classroom, it also limits what they will learn. Later, when they decide to give teachers and the educational system another try, they have fallen behind their classmates in what they can do. The habits they acquired in elementary and high school also make it very difficult for the ignored to ask for help. Like the "new student" described by Cross (1971), the ignored student has been failed by the traditional educational system and, unless the student can develop new perceptions of how learning takes place, higher education will also fail this student. In addition, the ignored's passive involvement in classes often allows physical problems to go undetected.

These physical problems can limit the student's ability to achieve academically. For example, students in the Developmental Studies Program at Volunteer State Community College recently participated in a vision and hearing screening (Hiett, 1987). Of the 128 students tested, 65.6% had vision problems which would interfere with the learning process. Fifty-four percent had a hearing loss in at least one ear. Fifty-three students (41.4%) had both vision

and hearing difficulties. Is it any wonder that these students also had academic problems?

Obviously, the ignored need more than academic intervention during their college experience. In addition to having physical problems which may need to be corrected, these students must learn to interact with classmates and instructors. They have to learn how to ask for help. They have to discover that learning requires more than passive observation. If those of us who work in a developmental studies program can help the ignored learn such lessons, a new world of learning can develop for many of these students.

> The developmental student sometimes acquired his or her elementary and secondary education in a foreign country.

"Foreign students" who need remedial or developmental assistance typically require help in reading or writing. Since mathematics seems to use an international language of symbols, foreign students normally do well in mathematics. But, as Ross and Roe (1986) note, even very intelligent foreign students often have inadequate English communication skills. This causes these students problems as they try to communicate. English expressions used in texts and classroom lectures frequently puzzle foreign students. Many times, foreign students lack the background to understand textbooks which are written with the assumption that the reader grew up and was educated in America. Foreign students must also learn how to deal with American professors. The more relaxed interchange between college student and instructor in the United States often confuses the foreign student. Afraid to let their instructors know that they do not understand, foreign students nod and smile when the teacher tries to determine if they understand the lecture or textbook material.

> **The developmental student, in some cases, has a physical or learning disability.**

The "handicapped student" who is placed in remedial or developmental classes is generally either physically handicapped or learning disabled. The physically handicapped student needs assistance for a variety of reasons:

1. The handicap may have prevented the student from being part of mainstream secondary education and acquiring a college-prep background. If so, the handicapped student is likely to enter college with academic deficiencies.

2. The handicapped student may have been taught in isolation with only the teacher present. Under these circumstances, the student may not have learned to interact with fellow students nor been exposed to a variety of teachers and/or teaching styles.

3. Previously learned material may have been lost if the handicap was the result of an injury. Relearning often becomes a frustrating experience.

Most handicapped students are not only faced with learning new material, they also must learn to deal with hearing aids, wheelchairs, braille texts, typewriters, and other learning aids, and this process can be time-consuming. For the handicapped student, every task is more difficult, and each hurdle is higher. Yet, for physically handicapped students, the stakes are also higher. A college degree may be viewed as their only chance to be self-sustaining. The pressure to succeed adds to their frustrations.

The difficulties learning disabled students encounter in learning are often viewed by teachers, peers, and even parents as the result of laziness and lack of motivation.

College professors are usually eager to help students who are physically handicapped. They can readily see the need for extending standard time limits on assignments or exams and providing such teaching aids as notetakers, interpreters, tape recorders, and typewriters. This, unfortunately, is not true for those students classified as learning disabled. Because theirs is a "hidden handicap," the learning disabled may not get the sympathy and understanding received by their physically handicapped counterparts. The difficulties they encounter in learning are often viewed by teachers, peers, and even parents as the result of laziness and lack of motivation. These perceptions can be further reinforced by learning disabled students' lack of self-confidence. Knowing that they are weak in a particular area, they may avoid any attempt to learn, are often adamant that they cannot learn, and have their perceptions repeatedly validated by failures.

It is the learning disabled student who may cause the developmental educator the most frustration. As both Roueche (1972) and Moore (1970) point out, all too often developmental educators are subject area specialists and have not had pedagogical training. When faced with students who cannot learn through traditional college classroom techniques, teachers can feel powerless to help these students.

Learning disabled students may feel as helpless as their college teachers. These students have often spent their high school years in classes where the teacher/student ratio was very low. When confronted with the typically large lecture sections in many lower division courses, they often feel helpless and frustrated. Cordoni (1982) stresses that facing college without the support systems which were available to them in secondary education can be a terrifying prospect for learning disabled students.

Not only must handicapped students be given access to college, but colleges must also provide academic assistance for handicapped students.

The number of disabled students in college has increased from 2.6% in 1978 to 7.41% in 1985 ("More disabled," 1987). As these numbers rise, pressure on students and difficulty increases concurrently. These students bring other problems to campus as well as their disability. One study mentioned in the article found that handicapped students are older, are less academically prepared for higher education, rank lower in high school class standing, possess a lower level of self-confidence, and are dependent to a greater degree on outside funding.

Developmental educators need to become more skilled in meeting the needs of the handicapped. According to Section 504 of the Rehabilitation Act of 1973, not only must these students be given access to college, but colleges must also provide academic assistance for handicapped students (Vogel, 1982). It is no longer a question of "IF" we should serve these students but of how to effectively serve the handicapped.

> The developmental student frequently lacks clear cut academic goals and intends to use the educational system for his or her own purposes.

The "user" is not going to college to acquire an education but to reap the benefits of being classified as a college student. Many times these benefits are monetary as students receive financial aid, veterans' benefits, etc. Sometimes these students are simply attending college as a means of avoiding acquiring a job or facing their parents' wrath. Athletes may see college as a place to hang out and play sports until spotted by a professional team.

Users assess the academic climate and determine what is minimally acceptable for continued enrollment. If they must maintain a 2.0 average, they will earn a 2.0 and no more. If they are allowed three absences, they see these as three days of vacation and somehow feel cheated if they don't take the holiday. Once they know the ground rules, they may become the most vocal in their dislike of subject matter and university requirements, lending to the creation of an atmosphere which makes it difficult for classmates or dorm-mates to learn.

Users need much more than mere academic assistance. They need counseling to overcome their myopic view of life. Career counseling is also needed as users have planned only for the immediate future and have not considered what they will do when they slip below the minimum requirements and are suspended.

Of all the categories of students described thus far, it is the user that most readily comes to mind as an appropriate candidate to bar from the "open door." However, once users become excited about the prospect of learning and decide that earning a degree is a priority in their lives, they make rapid academic progress and often discover that they have talents they were not even aware they possessed.

In the past, many labels have been used to describe developmental students. Roueche and Snow (1977) identified over 12 such labels which included disprivileged, disadvantaged, nontraditional, new, and high-risk. Most of these labels focus on weaknesses rather than strengths. It is not my intention to add new labels by listing the above characteristics. However, I hope that by focusing on these characteristics, one can see that the backgrounds and needs which put developmental students at a disadvantage can be overcome.

There will always be at-risk students who do not make it. But, rather than close the open door to all these students, we should remember: with good teaching and good support systems, there will be many who do make it. We have an obligation, especially those of us in public education, to provide access to higher education to all citizens who can benefit. We have a further obligation to provide assistance to those who need it. As Soldwedel (1971) so beautifully puts it:

. . . higher education shall not be higher by virtue of serving the rich, the well-born, the academi-cally able and advantaged, or those destined to fill the academic ranks; rather, it shall be "higher" because it takes an adult or near adult beyond his present level toward a fuller realization of his powers to be (P 107).

If developmental studies programs can help produce individuals who are open to their fellow citizens who can communicate effectively, and who can make wise consumer decisions, we will add much to the lives of these students.

References

Abraham, A. A. (1987). *A report on college-level remedial/developmental programs in SREB states.* Atlanta: Southern Regional Education Board.

Cordoni, B. (1982). Postsecondary education : Where do we go from here? *Journal of Learning Disabilities, 15,* 265-266.

Cross, K. P. (1971). *Beyond the open door.* San Francisco: Jossey-Bass Publishers.

Cross, K. P. (1976). *Accent on learning.* San Francisco: Jossey-Bass Publishers.

Hiett, J. (1987). *Results of vision and hearing screening.* Gallatin, TN: Volunteer State Community College.

Hodgkinson, H. L. (1985). The changing face of tomorrow's student. *Change, 39,* 8-39.

King, R. C. (1985). The changing student. *National Forum, 65,* 22-27.

Maxwell, M. (1979). *Improving student learning skills.* San Francisco: Jossey-Bass Publishers.

Moore, W. (1970). *Against the odds.* San Francisco: Jossey-Bass Publishers.

More disabled attend college. (1987). *Clarksville Leaf Chronicle, 179,* 8A.

Ross, E. B., & Roe, B. D. (1986). *The case for basic skills programs in higher education.* Bloomington, IN: Phi Delta Kappa.

Roueche, J. E. (1968). *Salvage, redirection, or custody?* Washington, DC: American Association of Junior Colleges.

Roueche, J. E. (1972). *A modest proposal – students can learn.* San Francisco: Jossey-Bass Publishers.

Roueche, J. E., & Snow, J. J. (1977). *Overcoming learning problems.* San Francisco: Jossey-Bass Publishers.

Soldwedel, B. J. (1971). Whoever wants it needs it. In W. T. Furniss (Ed.), *Higher education for everybody.* Washington, DC: American Council on Education.

State Board of Regents. (1984). *Developing a plan to educate underprepared post-secondary students in SBR institutions: A white paper.* Unpublished manuscript. Nashville, TN.

Vogel, S. (1982). Developing L. D. college programs. *Journal of Learning Disabilities, 15,* 518-527.

In this essay Gretchen Starks surveys the research on the components of developmental skills programs that impact on college retention.

Retention and Developmental Education: What the Research Has to Say

By Gretchen Starks

(Condensed from *Research and Teaching in Developmental Education* (Fall, 1989), 6(1), 21-32. Reprinted by permission of Gretchen Starks and *Research and Teaching in Developmental Education*.)

In order to fully understand the effect of developmental education upon student retention, one must first review current models of student departure and determine how developmental education intersects with these models. After this framework is established, then one can examine program and pedagogical components within developmental education that are successful in retaining students and improving grade point averages. Therefore, this paper will first summarize four models of institutional departure. Next, various program and pedagogical components of successful developmental programs will be enumerated as they relate to the characteristics of student retention models. It is the opinion of the author that models supporting more interaction among all components of the institution and less isolation of developmental educators are the most worthwhile.

Student Retention Models

There are primarily four types of student retention models identified in the research literature: (1) psychological, (2) economic, (3) organizational, and (4) interactional. Some are more relevant than oth-

ers for the purpose of designing successful developmental education programs.

1. Psychological Models

Psychological models claim that leaving is a response controlled by the students (Rose & Elton, 1966) and that students make this decision because they are unable to adjust to college (Heilbrun, 1965; Rose & Elton, 1966). The primary source of leaving is found by looking at the personality of individuals. Studies relying on personality traits find that dropouts tend to be less mature, less serious, and less dependable than persisters. The assumption is that the student is dissatisfied with school and is "maladjusted" to it (Rose & Elton, 1966).

It would not be appropriate to utilize this model when designing programs in developmental education because it presupposes that the institution can do little to prevent students from departing. Personality is set before the student even arrives in college, and thus intervention strategies such as a developmental program would have little impact. This model does not take into consideration the interactive process of the college environment that may have a positive influence upon students' personalities and cause them to change and become more mature, more serious about studying, and more dependable.

2. Economic Models

The economic models assume that students weigh the costs and benefits of an education and decide to stay or leave based on their conclusion. Relating to this model, Zwerling (1980) found that commuting students who have part-time work on campus are more likely to stay. Scholarships and work-study programs have proven a more viable avenue of student aid than loans for promoting student retention (Lenning, Sauer, & Beal, 1980).

> **Research has shown that if students are satisfied with college, they will suffer great economic burdens to continue.**

The shortcomings of these models is that they look at monetary benefits and neglect the intrinsic, social and intellectual rewards of college, rewards that are encouraged through comprehensive developmental education programs. Research has shown that if students are satisfied with college, they will suffer great economic burdens to continue (Tinto, 1987, p. 81). Developmental education can foster this satisfaction.

3. Organizational Models

Bean (1983) is a well-known proponent of the organizational model. These models study the impact that the organization has upon the academic and social integration of students. Bureaucratic structure, institutional size, faculty/student ratio, resources, goals and missions, and rewards of grades are some of the variables studied. The premise is that if institutional policies increase student involvement, they will lead to better persistence rates.

Studies conducted from the organizational perspective account for less than one-quarter of the variance in dropout (10-20% in Bean's 1980 study; 25% in his 1983 study). They do not study the process by which organizational factors can impact upon students' decisions since they leave out the variables of external forces and of patterns of student-faculty interactions. These variables, in fact, may help account for substantial portions of the remaining variance. Developmental educators are particularly interested in the impact of student-faculty interactions and these models do not include this factor.

4. Interactional Models

Interactional models view departure from college as a function of the interaction between individuals and their environment. Decisions are impacted by a myriad of factors that include individual attributes, the organization of the college, the college environment, the economic situation of the student, academic integration, social integration, and pre-enrollment characteristics. These variables and interactions among these variables determine whether students persist or leave. These models are student-centered in that they stress how students perceive themselves and their surrounding. The consequences of these perceptions determine how students define success and failure and how they ultimately make decisions. These models are also situational in that each student and each situation is unique and circumstances along a time continuum can influence decisions (Tinto, 1985).

Tinto's model (1975) is longitudinal, involving a complex series of socio-psychological interactions between the student and the institutional environment. Students bring to college certain characteristics such as family background (socio-economic status, parental values), personal attributes (sex, race, academic ability, personal traits), and experiences (pre-college, social, and academic achievements). They also bring a predisposition to goal commitment and institutional commitment or loyalty to the college. These in turn interact with formal and informal attributes of the college environment which lead to integration into the social (peer group and adult interactions) and academic (grades, faculty interactions, and intellectual developments) system of the college (Terenzini & Pascarella, 1978, p. 348; Weidman, 1985, p. 7). "Other things being equal, the higher the degree of integration of the individual into the college systems, the better the chances of persistence in college" (Tinto, 1975, p.96).

Tinto has recently revised his 1975 model and expanded his concept of academic and social integration (Tinto, 1987, p. 114). Academic integration is derived from the interaction of pre-enrollment attributes, goal and institutional commitments, intentions to graduate, academic performance (formal) and faculty/staff interactions (informal). Social integration builds upon the interaction of pre-enrollment attributes, goal and institutional commitments, intentions to graduate, extracurricular activities (formal) and peer group interactions (informal). "Other things being equal, the lower the degree of one's social and intellectual integration into the academic and social communities of the college, the greater the likelihood of departure. Conversely, the greater one's integration, the greater the likelihood of persistence" (Tinto, 1987, p. 116).

In the research, academic integration is sometimes referred to as "institutional fit." If students are in the proper academic program according to their goals and abilities and have adequate support services, they are likely to graduate (Lenning, Sauer, & Beal, 1980). Informal contacts with faculty and other students while at college are also significant. "Simply put, the more time faculty give to their students, and students to each other, the more likely are students to complete their education" (Tinto, 1982, p. 697).

Interactional models which take into consideration faculty/student interactions and student/student interactions have the most potential for contributing to successful developmental education programs.

The effect of social integration is also recognized in the research. Student involvement factors include friends, clubs, extra-curricular activities, tutor and mentor relationships, work-study assignments and living close to campus. Integration into the social milieu often has a positive effect on student retention (Lenning, Sauer, & Beal, 1980). In community colleges, where students usually commute and have fewer social interactions on campus, faculty interactions appear to be even more important (Halpin, 1983).

Interactional models, which take into consideration faculty/student interactions and student/student interactions, have the most potential for contributing to developmental education constructs. They postulate that the institution can make a difference by providing academic support for students and thus influencing their commitment to graduation. Developmental educators should examine interactional models when planning programs and when developing teaching strategies.

Program Components

Much of the literature in developmental education reveals that interdisciplinary programs have a more lasting effect on students (Spann, 1977; Hill, 1978, Palmer, 1983; Keimig, 1982; Morante, Faskow & Nomejko-Menditto, 1984). Keimig (1982) identified four levels of developmental programs: 1) developmental courses; 2) courses and learning center services; 3) mastery learning with competency-based courses and comprehensive support services; and 4) developmental programs that foster involvement of staff in all disciplines and at all levels (p. 39).

> **Isolated remedial courses were the least effective of all remedial efforts.**

1. **Level One** programs most often include credit and non-credit bearing courses in reading, writing, mathematics, and study skills. Boylan (1983) indicates that such courses should bear credit or at least apply towards financial aid allocation.

   Research at Miami-Dade Community College showed that there was a decrease in persistence rate as fewer courses were completed (Losak & Morris, 1985, p. 3). Successful students in this developmental program took longer to complete their college education, but their persistence rates were the same as those students who needed no developmental program (Losak & Morris, 1985).

   Basic skills courses alone, however, are limited in their effectiveness. Looking at developmental programs as a group, Keimig noted that "isolated, remedial courses did not make much difference in overall student success or retention and were the least effective of all remedial efforts" (Keimig, 1982, p. 11).

2. **Level Two** programs include courses and learning center services. Some of the services are peer tutoring, professional tutoring, learning disabilities services, computer-assisted instruction and audio visual programs. The author was unable to find any recent retention research on developmental programs that included these program components exclusively.

3. **Level Three** programs included courses, learning center services, personal and academic counseling, career counseling, early warning systems, placement testing, and library skills orientation. These programs meet with success because they are comprehensive: they integrate students' affective and academic needs and they provide diagnosis of students' strengths and weaknesses as well as ongoing evaluation of their progress (Maxwell, 1979). They embody the concept of interactive retention models that stress the importance of academic integration of students in college.

A number of Level Three types of program with comprehensive services, diagnostic testing, and competency-based education have been successful in retaining students (Hechinger, 1979; Herscher, 1980). Two other illustrations follow: (a) Western New Mexico University was concerned with their 65% attrition rate with freshmen and a subsequent 35% attrition rate with sophomores. They had a developmental education program but found that students did not take advantage of the services, so they instituted what they called an "Intrusive Advisement" program based on the philosophy that the university should call students in for advising numerous times during the year (Glennen & Baxley, 1985, p. 12). They gave ten faculty members released time to meet with high risk students during weeks one and two, other students during weeks three through seven, students with mid-term deficiencies during weeks eight to ten and other students for pre-registration for the next semester during the remaining weeks. Their freshmen attrition dropped to 25% and the retention for high risk students increased by 27% (Glennen & Baxley, 1985).

(b) Career counseling coupled with developmental education was found to help students complete training and degree programs at the University of California-Los Angeles (Healy, Mourton, Anderson & Robinson, 1984). This program is still in existence because of its effectiveness.

4. **Level Four** programs demonstrate the current trend of including an interdisciplinary approach along with comprehensive student-help services. The programs include all of the Level Three services with a focus on the content areas. Level Four programs include orientation courses or freshman year experience programs, supplemental instruction, paired courses, blocked courses, and team teaching. Some successful Level Four programs follow: (a) Western Kentucky University paired English, reading and history. Essays, study techniques, research papers and tests revolved around a history theme. An outside task force found gains of 90% on pre- and post-history tests, improved writing ability and a higher average grade than the regular history class (Wallace, Washington & Thompson, 1980). (b) Porterville College in California initiated a Basic Skills Project with English, speech and math. Students got eight credits towards a degree. The instructors met weekly to plan instruction. Eighty-one percent remained in college after the first semester. "Preliminary results indicate that an intensive comprehensive and integrated course of basic skills is superior to separate non-integrated courses" (Rank, 1979, p.7).

There are many other examples of successful retention programs as colleges have incorporated orientation, mentoring, and freshmen seminars with comprehensive learning support programs.

Pedagogical Components

Beyond program characteristics, there are a number of pedagogical considerations to address when evaluating successful developmental instruction that fosters retention. The following are eight vital components:

1. **Cooperative or collaborative learning** through small group sessions where students teach each other initiates involvement in learning, enhances peer group interactions and encourages students' academic commitment to the college. Collaborative learning forces frequent faculty/student contact by allowing students to actively share their learning process with the instructor and with their peers. This interaction is a necessary characteristic of effective retention rates (Boylan, 1983; Long & Long, 1987; Morgan, 1988; Carpenter & Doig, 1988).

    An example of cooperative learning is explained by one of its proponents, Claire Weinstein, professor of educational psychology at the University of Texas, who stresses the importance of active learning: "Students learn to set specific goals and to develop a variety of learning strategies to help them reach these goals. For instance, a student who has trouble understanding a chapter of text might not get anywhere if he simply rereads the chapter. Another approach, like discussing the material with a classmate, might be more effective" (Mangan, 1988, p. A3).

2. **The use of electronic media**, including computers, interactive video, and telecommunication to encourage student participation is also recommended (Carpenter & Doig, 1988). A number of studies have shown that teaching

writing through word processing is successful in developmental programs (Schwartz, 1982).

3. **A focus on metacognition** or thought processing is also important to include in developmental courses (Long & Long, 1987). One way to do this is to provide supplemental instruction sessions for students. Supplemental instruction is designed to assist students in mastering course concepts and to increase competence in the basic skills at the same time. Learning specialists attend the course lectures where they take notes and complete assigned readings. The specialists schedule sessions outside of class for students to discuss the course and share learning strategies. One of the reasons for the success of supplemental instruction is that "it is designed to promote a high degree of student interaction and mutual support" (Blanc, DeBuhr, & Martin, 1983).

Many developmental educators now provide activities that foster thinking skills in the classroom. Narode, Heiman, Lochhead and Slomianko (1987) recommend paired problem solving to create a learning environment with the listener and the problem solver working together and the teacher acting as a coach or facilitator. They claim that this method builds trust among students and faculty (Narode & others, 1987, p. 8).

Protocol writing is another form of providing opportunities for sharing information processing with papers, homework and examinations. In this approach, students' summaries of notes and written reasons for their answers on tests encourages them to think about how they learn. Faculty then provide comments for positive reinforcement of learning (Narode & others, 1987).

4. Roueche and Snow (1977) have recommended **small classes for individualized learning**. Individualizing instruction provides opportunities for interaction, both social and academic. This interaction fosters retention.

5. **Frequent student/faculty contact in the classroom setting** fosters involvement for students. An example of this type of interaction would be class conferencing with individual students (Donovan, 1975; Bizarro & Warner, 1985).

Another development is represented in a program at Cook College in New Jersey. The program is designed for underachievers and provides workshops for students on study skills and career planning with supplemental instruction, freshman orientation, and academic and personal advising as program components. It is successful because the focus is on "small group sessions with high levels of interactions between students and staff" (Levitz, 1988, p. 5-6).

6. It is important to pay **attention to a student's personal style of learning**. Guenther and Anderson (1988) conducted a recent study where Guenther took a geography course along with students. Rather than teaching the "tried and true" SQ3R study technique, he helped students select what information to study and then to develop their own study style based on the instructor's teaching style. His conclusions stressed the importance of adopting study strategies which work for each "unique individual." Process and awareness of process are important for students in order to succeed (Guenther & Anderson, 1988).

7. **Evaluation of students and continuous and frequent feedback on progress** keep students involved and gives them constant reinforcement (Coda-Messerle, 1981). Frequent evaluation through testing is also recommended by Cross (1976) to, again, provide feedback and reinforcement.

8. **Evaluation of teaching by students** provides significant feedback for planning, monitoring, and revision of program activities, and it keeps the instructor current while allowing input by students into course content and its relevance to their lives. This involvement of students in evaluating teaching fosters commitment and the feeling of "I am important" on the part of students (Cross, 1976).

In essence, these pedagogical components provide strong links between a student's experiences inside and outside the classroom. If the goal is a college degree, this commitment can give students the motivation to remain in college to graduation. From an academic perspective it enhances their skills which in turn increases confidence within each individual. This boost in self-image serves to strengthen commitment to college and ultimately impacts upon student retention.

Conclusion

The most promising models of retention take into consideration the interaction of events, perceptions, environment, and student experiences to explain the process of staying or leaving. As Cope and Hannah (1975) so aptly state: "Attrition is the result of an extremely intricate interplay among the multitude of variables" (p. 96). These models support the contention that the college can make a difference and that developmental education, working closely with faculty across the disciplines, can intervene to retain students. As Keimig (1983) reiterates, "The interaction among academic and developmental educators and their shared problem-solving is the fundamental dynamic in successful learning improvement programs, producing gains in GPA and retention that cannot be delivered by remedial/developmental personnel working alone in remedial settings" (p. 6).

> Developmental programs that include comprehensive and/or interdisciplinary approaches are most successful in retaining students because they support academic and affective needs.

To be successful, developmental programs can no longer remain as isolated entities within the college structure. They must reach out to involve the total college. Developmental programs that include comprehensive and/or interdisciplinary approaches are most successful in retaining students because they support academic and affective needs. They allow numerous avenues for students to relate to college and to receive assistance.

In the pedagogical domain, teaching techniques and settings that provide for maximum student interaction and for processing of ideas and learning modes also lead to a level of student involvement that encourages retention. Although there are a myriad of programs and teaching situations, those programs and instructional techniques that involve students, allow for frequent faculty-student contact, and encourage students to learn from each other, meet with the most success.

References

Barchis, D. (1979, November). *The Loop College individual needs (IN) program.* (ERIC Document Reproduction Service No. ED 181 946).

Bean, J. P. (1980). Dropouts and turnover: The synthesis and test of a causal model of student attrition. *Research in Higher Education, 12,* 155-187.

Bean, J. P. (1983). The application of a model of turnover in work organizations to the student attrition process. *The Review of Higher Education, 6,* 129-148.

Bizzaro, P., & Werner, S. (1985). Group identity: Faculty-counselor collaboration. *Research & Teaching in Developmental Education, 1,* 40-47.

Blanc, R. A., DeBuhr, L. E., & Martin, D. C. (1983). Breaking the attrition cycle: The effects of supplemental instruction on undergraduate performance and attrition. *Journal of Higher Education, 54,* (1), 80-89.

Boyer, E. (1987). *College: The undergraduate experience in America.* New York: Harper and Row.

Boylan, H. R. (1983). *Developmental education programs: Are they working? An analysis of the research. NARDSPE Research Report No. 2,* Chicago: National Association for Remedial/Developmental Studies in Postsecondary Education.

Carpenter, C. B., & Doig, J. C. (1988). *AAC report urges colleges to stress how to learn.* Washington, DC: Association of American Colleges.

Cope, R. G., & Hannah, W. (1975). *Revolving college doors.* New York: Wiley & Sons.

Cross, K. P. (1976). *Accent on Learning.* San Francisco: Jossey-Bass.

Davis, B., & Luvaas-Briggs, L. (1983, March). *It's not my job: Basic skills development in a sociology class, a shared solution.* (ERIC Document Reproduction Service No. ED 231 496).

Donovan, R. A. (1975). *National Project II: Alternatives to the revolving door.* New York: Bronx Community College.

Glennan, R. E., & Baxley, D. M. (1985, Winter). Reduction of attrition through intrusive advising. *NASPA Journal, 22,* (3), 100-114.

Grant, M. K., & Hoeber, D. R. (1978). *Basic skills programs: Are they working? AAHE/ERIC Higher Education Research Report, No. 1,* Washington, DC: American Association for Higher Education.

Guenther, J. W., & Anderson, T. H. (1988, Spring-Summer). Studying hard for a college level geography course: A case study. *Forum for Reading, 19(2),* 7-18.

Halpin, R. L. (1983). *Student integration in relation to freshman persistence and exit at a community college.* Dissertation Abstracts International, 44, 366A. (University Microfilm No. 83-15068).

Healy, C., Mouron, D., Anderson, E., & Robinson, E. (1984, July). Career maturity and the achievement of community college students and disadvantaged university students. *Journal of College Student Personnel, 25,*(4), 347-352.

Hechinger, F. M. (1979, October). Basic skills: Closing the gap. *Change, 11(7),* 29-33.

Heilbrun, A. B. (1965). Personality factors in college dropouts. *Journal of Applied Psychology, 49,* 1-7.

Herrscher, B. (1980, Fall). Competency-based education: A viable framework for developmental studies program design. *Journal of Developmental and Remedial Education, 4(1),* 18-21.

Hill, A. (1978, Fall). Developmental education: Does it work? "An ERIC review." *Community College Review, 6(2).* 41-47.

Keimig, R. T. (1982). Improving learning and retention: The decision guide for effective programs. Unpublished manuscript.

Lenning, O. T., Sauer, L., & Beal, P. (1980). *Retention and attrition: Evidence for Action and Research.* Bolder, CO: National Center for Higher Education Management Systems.

Levitz, R. (1988, October). H. E. L. P. is on the way. *Recruitment and retention in Higher Education*, 2(10), 5, 6.

Long, J. D., & Long, E. W. (1987, September). Enhancing student achievement through metacomprehension training. *Journal of Developmental Education*, 11(1), 2-5.

Losak, J., & Morris, C. (1985, December). *College preparatory analyses Part I, first time in college students,* Fall, 1982. (ERIC Document Reproduction Service No. ED 264 921).

Luvas-Briggs, L. (1984, Winter). Integrating basic skills with college content instruction. *Journal of Developmental and Remedial Education*, 7(2), 6-9, 31.

Mangun, K. S. (1988, September 14). A pioneer in teaching "learning to learn." *Chronicle of Higher Education*, 35(3), A3.

Maxwell, M. (1979). *Improving student learning skills.* San Francisco: Jossey-Bass.

Morante, E. A., Faskow, S., & Nomejko-Menditto, I.(1984, Winter & 1984, Spring). The New Jersey basic skills assessment program: Parts I & II. *Journal of Developmental and Remedial Education*,7(2,3), 6-9, 2-4, 32.

Narode, R., Heiman, M., Lochhead, J., & Slomianko, J. (1987). Teaching thinking skills: *Science.* Washington, DC: NEW Publication.

Palmer, J. C. (1983, September). Interdisciplinary studies: An ERIC Review. *Community College Journal*, 11(1), 59-64.

Pascarella, E. T. (1980). Student-faculty informal contact and college outcomes. *Review of Educational Research*, 50, 545-595.

Rank, J. (1979, April). *One that works! An integrated program of basic skills.* (ERIC Document Reproduction Service No. ED. 173-762).

Roueche, J. E., & Snow, J. G. (1977). *Overcoming learning problems.* San Francisco: Jossey-Bass.

Schwartz, M. (1982, November). Computers and the teaching of writing. *Educational Technology*, 22(11), 27-29.

Spann, M. G. (1977, Winter). *Building a developmental education program. New Directions for Higher Education, #20,* San Francisco: Jossey-Bass, 23-29.

Terenzini, P., & Pascarella, E. (1978). The relation of students' precollege characteristics and freshmen year experience to voluntary attrition. *Research in Higher Education*, 9, 347-366.

Tinto, V. (1975). Dropout from higher education: A theoretical synthesis of recent research. *Review of Educational Research*, 45, 89-125.

Tinto, V. (1982). Defining dropout: A matter of perspective. In E. T. Pascarella (Ed.), *New directions for institutional research: Studying student attrition Number 36* (pp. 3-16), San Francisco: Jossey-Bass.

Tinto, V. (1985). *Defining Dropout: Varieties of student departure from higher education.* Unpublished manuscript.

Tinto, V. (1987). *Leaving college: Rethinking the causes and cures of student attrition.* Chicago: The University of Chicago Press.

Wallace, H. L., Washington, M., & Thompson, J. S. (1980, April). *An interdisciplinary mastery learning program for "high risk" students.* (ERIC Document Reproduction Service No. Ed 181 103).

Weidman, J. C. (1985). *Retention of non-traditional students in postsecondary education.* Paper presented at the 1985 annual meeting of the American Educational Research Association, Chicago, Illinois.

Zwerling, J. L. (1980, Fall). Reducing attrition at the two-year colleges. *Community College Review*, 8, 55-58.

Gretchen Starks Martin is Academic Dean at Jefferson Community College, Watertown, NY 13601.

Further Readings on the History and Philosophy of Learning Assistance

Boylan, H. (1983). The growth of the learning assistance movement. In H. Boylan (Ed.), *Forging new partnerships in learning assistance*. San Francisco: Jossey Bass.

Brier, E. (1985). Bridging the academic preparation gap: An historical view. *Journal of Developmental Education*, 8(1), 2-5.

Bullock, T. L., Madden, D. A., & Mallery, A. L. (1990, Spring). Developmental education in American universities: Past, present, and future. *Research & Teaching in Developmental Education*, 6(2), 5-74.

Clifford, G. J. (1987, September). *A sisyphean task: Historical perspectives on the relationship between writing and reading instruction. Technical Report #17*. Berkeley, CA: Center for the Study of Writing, UC Berkeley, (also in Dyson, AH. (Ed.) *Writing and reading: Collaboration in the Classroom*). Note: Traces the history of how reading and writing instruction became separated in elementary, high schools, and colleges.

Clowes, D. A. (1980). More than a definitional problem: Remedial, compensatory, and developmental education. *Journal of Developmental Education*. 4(1), 2-5.

Clowes, D. A. (1992). Remediation in American higher education. In J.C. Smart (Ed.) *Higher Education: Handbook of theory and research*. 8, Bronx, New York: Agathon Press, 460-493.

Cranney, A. G., & Miller, J. S. (1987). History of reading: Status and sources of a growing field. *Journal of Reading*, 30 (5), 388-398.

Enright, G., & Kersteins, G. (1980). The learning center: Toward an expanded role. In O. Lenning & R. Nayman (Eds.), *New roles for learning assistance*. San Francisco: Jossey-Bass.

Jones, H., & Richards-Smith, H. (1987). Historically black colleges and universities: A force in developmental education. Part II. *Review of Research in Developmental Education*, 4 (5), 1-3.

Kerstiens, G. (1993). Postsecondary student assessment and placement: History, status, direction. *Proceedings of the Winter Institute*, University of Arizona, Tucson, AZ.

Maxwell, M. (1976). *Remedial Education at Berkeley: Why do we still require it?* Student Learning Center, UC Berkeley. ERIC/RCS.

Maxwell, M. (1979). *Improving Student Learning Skills*. San Francisco: Jossey-Bass (Chapter 1).

Mickler, M. L., & Chapel, A. C. (1989, September). Basic skills in college: Academic dilution or solution? *Journal of Developmental Education*. 13(1), 2-4,16.

Miles, C. (1984). Developmental education: Speculation on the future. *Journal of Developmental Education*. 8 (1), 6-9, 27.

Richardson, R., Martens, K., & Fisk, E. (1981). *Functional literacy in the college setting*. (AAHE/ERIC Higher Education Research Report No. 3). Washington, DC: AAHE.

Richardson, R. C., Fisk, E. C., & Okun, M. A. (1983). *Literacy in the open-admission classroom*. San Francisco: Jossey-Bass.

Roberts, G. H. (1985). *Developmental education: An historical study*. (ERIC Document Reproduction Service No. 276 395).

Roueche, J., & Snow, J. (1977). *Overcoming learning problems*. San Francisco: Jossey-Bass.

Walvekar, C. C. (1987). Address: Thirty years of program evaluation: Past, present, and future. *Journal of College Reading and Learning*, 20, 155-161.

Van, B. (1992, June). Developmental education: Its past and future. *Journal of Learning Improvement*. 1(2), 21-28.

Wyatt, M. (1992, September). The past, present, and future needs for college reading courses in the U.S. *Journal of Reading*, 36(1), 10-20.

Part 2

Learning
Centers

With the advent of new technology for improving learning, many colleges implemented learning centers in the early 1970's as one way of responding both to increases in student enrollment and the influx of non-traditional students.

College Learning Skills: Frontierland Origins of the Learning Assistance Center

By Gwyn Enright

(Reprinted from *College Learning Skills: Today and Tomorrowland, Proceedings of the Eighth Annual Conference of the Western College Reading Association*, Volume VIII, pp. 81-92, (August, 1975) by permission of Gwyn Enright and the College Reading and Learning Association.)

No one is as critically aware of the youthfulness of the Learning Center movement as those caught up in it. That the reading or learning practitioner is a forward thinking zealot thriving on a diet of innovation is illustrated by the theme of this conference, "College Learning Skills — Today and Tomorrowland."

However, before rushing into Tomorrowland, I recommend a stroll through Frontierland. In carving a frontier, as in forging any new field, an interlude for integrating past occurrences, accomplishments, and hazards promotes continued, but directed, progress. In the Learning Center movement, where the formalized Learning Assistance Center concept is four years old, where 57% of the Learning Centers in the country have become operational since 1970 and where a Learning Assistance Center director is considered a mature practitioner after only four years in the field, a glance at where we have been and how we got here is, at least, an antidote for Disneyland and high-speed vertigo.

Using a composite definition of the Learning Assistance Center as a place concerned with learning environment within and without, functioning primarily to enable students to learn more in less time with greater ease and confidence; offering tutorial help, study aids in the content areas and referrals to other helping agencies; serving as a testing ground for innovative machines, materials, and programs (Christ, 1971, p. 35); and acting as a campus ombudsman (Kerstiens, 1972), I reviewed the professional literature for evidence of the early origins of the Learning Assistance Center. Sources included, but were not limited to ERIC, the Minnesota Retrieval System, NRC Yearbooks, WCRA Proceedings, and nationally disseminated education and media periodicals. Since most articles, monographs, and books relevant to College Learning Centers were primarily descriptions and statements rather than research reports, criteria for consideration was unsophisticated and threefold. What was the publication date? Is the program conceptualized or actualized? Are Learning Assistance Center components identifiable?

Categorized by decade, the literature selected falls into four separate periods. If we assume literature records what is happening in the field and if we disregard some overlap, we can discern general trends which characterize each age of development. Seen cynically, the stages might appear cyclical, however, the development of the Learning Assistance Center viewed retrospectively can be considered evolutionary and, in some respects, revolutionary.

Age Of Clinical Aspiration: Programs Become Scientific 1916-1940

Early programs and practices in the nineteen twenties and nineteen thirties would later become woven into the Learning Assistance Center fabric. The idea that a student could study to become a student can be traced to a student skills guide first published in 1916 (Whipple, 1916). Although this guide instructed both high school and college students, a study procedures handbook published in 1929 was addressed to college students exclusively (Von Kliensmid & Touton, 1929). Learning skills covered in these guides included textbook reading, listening and notetaking, studying for and taking exams, concentration and memory, study environment and time management, library skills, vocabulary skills, critical thinking, lab procedures and study procedures in the content areas.

The issue of a college or university involving itself in an organized effort to save students with less than adequate academic etiquette is alive by the late twenties. Most authors justify the skills programs, noting a student's skill must be learned as a doctor's or lawyer's, a swimmer's, or an apprentice's skill is learned. One team states that the college study skills course is more of a service to society than to the college and recommends that, if the college can afford to pick and choose, the college should not admit students who are poor risks (Jones & Eckert, 1935).

Study skills courses, called "how to study" courses in the late nineteen twenties and thirties, were offered to entering freshmen and to freshmen on probation as ten-week or one-semester orientation courses. At the University of Buffalo, beginning in 1926, admission for underachieving high school students was contingent upon successful completion of a three-week summer skills course (Jones & Eckert, 1935). Materials used in the "how to study" classes were assignments from the freshmen courses. Time management, library skills, outlining, notetaking, studying for tests, and reading efficiency were treated; the format was mainly lecture and discussion. Evaluation was in terms of grades, persistence, pre/post tests, efficiency ratios (number correct/time), and subjective questionnaires. By 1934, "how to study" classes were organized as study methods laboratories (Behrens, p. 195).

The need for a more specific, systematic, and scientific approach to study skills instruction surfaced through the "how to study" courses. Reading was singled out as the most important skill and remedial reading was discussed in approving tones as the scientific panacea. A 1927 study by Bock and a 1929 survey (Parr, 1930) point out that remedial reading was not a course in itself, but only a topic in a "how to study" course. Of the nine schools out of forty in the United States identifying poor readers, seven included reading in the "how to study course" (Parr, 1930). In his discussion of college remedial reading, Parr pointed to a particularly progressive program which boasted instrumentation and instruction regarding eye movements and vocal processes. The college adult reading program would develop as the bastard child of the psychology laboratory, where technologically naive reading teachers would go to borrow devices like the tachistoscope. In this way, the art of study became the science of study. The idea of skills instruction, the relation to professionalism, the need for specificity or treating a problem in small parts, the seductive power of hardware, of mobilizing all available resources are concepts which would later reappear in the Learning Assistance Center model.

The Age Of Disenchantment: Remedial Reading Is Not The Anwser 1940-1950

In the nineteen forties, remedial reading programs gained wide support. One survey of California programs reported that 10 out of 22 respondents stated they believed remedial reading should not be part of every junior college curriculum, and the remaining 12 did not answer the question (Zerga, 1940, p. 195). Courses were held in laboratories instead of classrooms, and programs were characterized by instrumentation (Simpson, 1942). Individualization, though preferred, was dismissed as too expensive, but a combination of group and clinical work seemed a fair compromise (Triggs, 1942). A program planned at the University of Minnesota provided for diagnosis of reading difficulties. After a remedy was prescribed, outlined, and placed in the student's file, the student would then report for supervised practice by appointment "where it is felt this work can be done more expediently by him alone than in the group" (Triggs, p. 376). When more appropriate, group work was planned.

Weekly individual conferences in a remedial reading course with a ratio of one counseling intern to four reading students afforded a second compromise to total individualization (Robinson, 1945). The private conference, scheduled for seriously deficient students (Triggs, 1942) or for orienting freshmen (Andrews, 1932), had been reported in the literature since the thirties, but the Brooklyn College program combined two hours in class with one hour in a regularly scheduled conference (Shaw, 1950). Another provision for individual differences was to offer clients three different courses or to give clients the choice between group work and personal counseling. Yet, for all the flexibility of the remedial reading and study skills laboratory courses, only one out of 67 college and university programs claimed to be individualized according to a 1950 survey (Barbe, 1951, p. 7).

In addition to the frustrating inability to realize a truly individualized program, the inclusion of upper division students in study methods courses (DeLong, 1948) rendered the term "remedial" completely unsatisfactory. At this time the term "developmental" was popularized to mean a higher level reading course, but one author predicted abandonment of both terms (Walker, 1964). Since achieving maximum efficiency was the newly stated goal of the reading and study methods programs, the term "remedial" was deemed inappropriate, and a "remedial emphasis" was to be avoided at all times.

A third factor paving the way for the advent of the Learning Center and contributing to the Age of Disenchantment was the recognition that reading remediation alone was not enough, that other difficulties interfering with student achievement must be treated and that "if one way of handling the student's problem does not seem to yield results, another way must be attempted" (Simpson, 1942, p. 623).

The Age Of Integration: Programs Treat The Whole Student 1950-1960

The question receiving attention at the beginning of the nineteen fifties was "Why do study skills reading programs treat only one facet of the student's skills when many factors work together to insure his academic success and when all students do not learn the same way or share the same weaknesses?"

When they reviewed the literature in 1951, Tresselt and Richlin credited only Robinson's program at Ohio with considering both the student's affective side and his academic side. Describing their New

York University two-credit "how to study" course, Tresselt stated that of the three variables categorizing students — ability, personality, and study techniques — personality played the most important role in terms of academic achievement (Tresselt and Richlin, 1951, p. 64). While it was felt study techniques could be handled in the class, more "basic problems" such as personal adjustment were felt best treated in individual interviews. Students enrolled in the University of Michigan's program were screened diagnostically to determine their reading ability, vision, and personality structure; if indicated, referrals to other campus services were also made (Spache & others, 1959). Personal adjustment and attitude were examples of the "non-writing" areas considered in a remedial writing program (Weber, 1954, p. 291).

In addition to the student's feelings being integrated with his academic performance, his course content was also seen working together as a total learning experience during the Age of Integration. "Reading, writing, speaking and listening are aspects of the single process of communication" (Blake, 1955, p. 165) was the thought of the period and those aspects were integrated into combined communication courses. Though not unopposed, "fusion courses" were operating in a large percentage of California remedial reading programs (Miklas, 1954).

Administrative diversity resulted from the belief to be inherited later by Learning Assistance Center practitioners that the reading and study skills client needed more alternatives than the tachistoscope and workbook exercises alone could provide. Although psychology departments, educational psychology departments, and English departments administered programs up to this time, most programs developed under student services, and Bamman's survey, published in 1954, showed counseling services leading

other departments in administering programs (Bamman, 1954, p. 580). That the college reading and study skills program was not becoming just another content course or General Education requirement is seen in the frequent use of the term "service function" in the program descriptions.

The service orientation of college reading and study skills programs allowed a broad base from which to help students who had multi-faceted and interrelating scholastic problems, and the laboratory organization allowed the flexibility needed for individualized endeavors. An early form of learning modules (Kingston, 1959, p. 23) and the drop-in clinic (Simpson, 1942) contributed to meeting the needs of a student viewed as an individual and as a whole. In 1956, a program was outlined which combined lecture/lab sessions with content tutoring, remedial instruction, and individual counseling (Blake, 1955).

Tenets for the nineteen fifties were outlined by Blake: diagnosis, individualization, integration, developmental (as opposed to remedial), and "student centered rather than content centered" (Blake, 1955, p. 165). Thus, the schema for skills development was set with students visiting labs on the recommendation of other students and finding a program outlined for their specific needs as academic citizens trying to achieve maximum efficiency (Wittenborn, 1944).

The Age Of Actualization: Good Ideas Become Realities 1960-1970

By the nineteen sixties, many of the philosophies and theories that previously could only be lauded could now be realized. Self-paced, individualized learning became an actuality with the implementation of programmed instruction. In 1966, a California junior college survey called for "modern materials" to increase the efficiency of self-instruction

Origins of the Learning Assistance Center

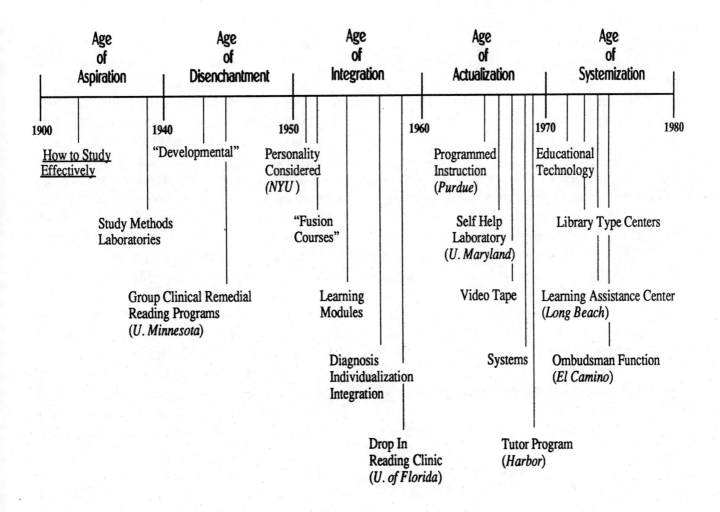

Age
of
Aspiration

Age
of
Disenchantment

Age
of
Integration

Age
of
Actualization

Age
of
Systemization

1900   1940   1950   1960   1970   1980

How to Study
Effectively

"Developmental"

Personality
Considered
(*NYU*)

Programmed
Instruction
(*Purdue*)

Educational
Technology

Study Methods
Laboratories

"Fusion
Courses"

Self Help
Laboratory
(*U. Maryland*)

Library Type Centers

Group Clinical Remedial
Reading Programs
(*U. Minnesota*)

Learning
Modules

Video Tape

Learning Assistance Center
(*Long Beach*)

Diagnosis
Individualization
Integration

Systems

Ombudsman Function
(*El Camino*)

Drop In
Reading Clinic
(*U. of Florida*)

Tutor Program
(*Harbor*)

(Newman, 1966), but these materials were reportedly being put together at the University of Minnesota since 1958. Raygor wrote that the key to individualizing the University of Minnesota program was the development and availability of self-instructional materials (Raygor, 1966, p. 170). The program there was four part; after diagnosis, the student would participate in an interview where he would help determine his schedule and his learning activities. Then the student would work to improve his weak areas in monitored practice sessions. Ideally, evaluation would then follow. In two studies comparing methods of course organization, self-paced or programmed courses were shown especially beneficial for the freshmen and upperclassmen with lower ability (Lewis, 1964) and for the student who might otherwise drop out of a study skills program (Maxwell, 1966).

Programmed, self-instructional materials allowed the reading and study skills programs to meet the changing needs of their more sophisticated clientele. Graduate students were enrolled in Stanford's program (Bamman, 1954) and 44% of the applicants to another program recorded college board scores in the upper half of a distribution of university students. The subjects in nine out of twenty-two studies reviewed by Entwisle were "college students" instead of "freshmen" (Entwisle, 1960).

Another reason individualized instruction became affordable in the nineteen sixties was innovations in the field to be later called Instructional Technology. As early as 1958, instructional television was well received by State University of Iowa students (TV Retention and Learning, 1958). Videotape was incorporated in skills instruction and the computer was put to work efficiently and humanly. From technological modes of thought came the application in 1967 of the systems approach to reading and study skills programs (Williams, 1967). Systems provided an answer to meeting the student's individual needs "since the strength of learning systems rests in the analysis of alternate pathways through which desired terminal objectives may be obtained" (Williams, 1967, p. 109). Christ's SR/SE Laboratory was a usable system for learning assistance based on diagnosis, referral, follow-up and modification (Christ, 1969, p. 214) while offering alternatives to students having individual learning styles.

The lab was the stage for the events of the Age of Actualization, and as the term "laboratory" gave ways to the term "center" in the later nineteen sixties, a wide diversity of center names developed. The Instructional Resources Services planned for the St. Louis Junior College District consisted of an Instructional Materials Center and a language lab and made the claim that the program was "effective in bringing students up to an acceptable level of performance" (Jones, 1955, p. 13). The Learning Center at Stephens College was designed primarily for convenient hardware sharing (Balanoff & Wood, 1963). The Fundamentals Learning Laboratories in North Carolina colleges were primarily adult education centers to assist students preparing for high school equivalency exams, but they also served students interested in their own "educational improvement" and students needing academic assistance to complete their college requirements (Brown, 1965, p. 80). The Study Skills Center at Lane Community College was unique in the nineteen sixties because it, like the College Reading Laboratory at the University of Maryland, was not a library-oriented arrangement nor an expanded adult education program. It is described as a programmed materials center supplementing and reinforcing the general curriculum in addition to offering reading and study skills assistance (Ellison, 1970). The educational

educational breakthroughs characterizing the Age of Actualization were quickly implemented, and by 1970, at least fifteen different center titles could be found in the literature.

The Age Of Systematization: The Learning Assistance Center Is Organized (1970-1980)

By the nineteen seventies, the confusion of center names mirrors the diversity of center origins and center functions. Many hybrid centers had been developing in semi or total isolation from one another. In 1970, four main center categories of Instructional Materials Center, Reading Laboratory, Study Skills Center, and Audiotutorial System were determined (Carmen, 1970). Another attempt at categorization in 1975 (Devirion, Enright, & Smith, 1974) distinguished between the library type of center which developed in a hopeful effort to reevaluate non-print media and to reembrace the audiovisual department, the reading and writing laboratory which was nurtured under the wing of the English department, and the Learning Center, which integrated a wide diversity of functions — all geared to buttressing the student for the academic challenge while dedicating itself to improving higher education. The Learning Assistance Center concept, formulated by Frank Christ, is composed of many of the center characteristics organized systematically as one support service honoring the marriage of instruction and technology (Christ, 1971).

Factors influential in the continued growth of the center through the seventies include decelerating enrollments, changes in admissions policies, reinterest in teaching students to learn, endangered financial support, and the belief that learning continues beyond formal education. The issue of student rights, the more frequent appearance of the non-traditional, non-initiated student, and the con-

viction that the Learning Assistance Center should be the catalyst for change on college and university campuses (Hultgren, 1970; Kerstiens, 1972) led to the center accepting the function of watch dog (Roueche, 1971; Burk-Dietrich, 1974) and nipping the heels of the establishment now and then. On the other hand, the Learning Assistance Center also maintains a wise neutrality on campus: "The resource center does not define the goals of the learning it supports; it accepts the goals of the faculty and the students" (Henderson & others, 1971, p. 5). The development of mini-courses or individual instructional units to supplement regular course content and the insistence on real results from programs that treat personality factors reflect both the Learning Assistance Center's academic ties and the Learning Assistance Center's relation to counseling centers in its growth pattern.

The nineteen seventies, the Age of Systematization, would be marked by the coming together of isolated components derived from varying factors into an organic, responsive and accountable support organization operating out of a facility offering a relaxed ecology — the Learning Assistance Center.

Conclusion

When the Learning Assistance Center's origins and development, beginning with the yen to be scientific and continuing to the rewards of combining technology with humanism, are considered in retrospect, they show the evolution and the revolutionary realignment of many very basic educational concepts. The historical irony of the Learning Assistance Center is that, while it embodies most of the educational philosophies theorized since 1900, it works actively for futuristic education. Its present status reflects the diverse range of its origins and the snowball sequence of its development. The next stage in the history of the Learning Assistance Center may well be its systematic integration into the campus as a whole — taking its rightful place as the support service for the academic community.

References

Andrews, G. A. (1932, April). Study Training in the Junior College. *Junior College Journal*, 2, 385-389.

Balanoff, N., James, A. Wood (1963, April). Learning Center: A Saturation Experience at Stephens College. *Audiovisual Instruction*, 8.

Bamman, H. A. Study Skills Programs, Stanford University. *California Journal of Educational Research*, 5, 57-58.

Barbe, W. (1951). Reading Improvement Services in Colleges and Universities. *School and Society*, 74, 6-7.

Behrens, H. D. (1935). Effects of a "How to Study" Course. *Journal of Higher Education*, 6, 195-202.

Blake, W. S., Jr. (1955, November). A Basic Study Skills Program for Colleges and Universities. *Junior College Journal*, 26, 164-167.

Book, W. F. (1927, October). Results Obtained in a Special "How to Study" Course Given to College Students. *School and Society*, 24, 529-534.

Brown, E. T. (1965, September). A Community College's Learning Laboratory. *Wilson Library Bulletin*, 40, 80-83.

Burk-Dietrich, M. (1974, November). It's Time for Colleges to Practice What They Preach. *About Tutoring, Newsletter of the National Association of Tutorial Services*.

Carmen, R. A. (1970). *Systems analysis of a learning resource center*. Los Angeles: ERIC/CJCI, ED 035411.

Christ, F. L. (1969). The SR/SE Laboratory: A Systems Approach to Reading/Study Skills Counseling. In B. G. Schick and M. M. May (Eds.) *Psychology of Reading Behavior*. *18th NRC Yearbook*, Milwaukee: National Reading Conference, 212-215.

Christ, F. L. (1971, April). Systems for Learning Assistance: Learners, Learning Facilitators, and Learning Centers. In F. L. Christ (Ed.), *Interdisciplinary Aspects of Reading Instruction. WCRA proceedings*, 4, 32-41.

Delong, G. H. (1948, May). Reading and Study for the Average Student. *Educational Research Bulletin*, 27, 121-124.

Devirian, M., Enright, G., and Smith, G. (1974). *Learning Assistance: The State of the Center*. Paper presented at the Twenty-Fourth Annual National Reading Conference, Kansas City.

Ellison, J. (1970, Spring). Lane Community College Study Skills Center. *WCRA Newsletter*, 3, 2.

Entwisle, D. R. (1960, March). Evaluations of Study Skills Courses: A Review. *Journal of Educational Research*, 53, 243-251.

Henderson, D. D., Melloni, B. J., and Sherman, J. G. (1971, October). *What a Learning Resource Center (LRC) Could Mean for Georgetown University*. ED 055 417.

Hultgren, D. D. (1970). The Role of the Individual Learning Center in Effecting Educational Change. In G. B. Schick, and M. M. May (Eds.), *Reading: Process and Pedagogy*. *19th NRC Yearbook*, Milwaukee: National Reading Conference, 2, 89-94.

Jones, E. S., and Eckert, R. E. (1935). Value of a "How to Study Course" for College Students. *University of Buffalo Studies*, 10. Buffalo.

Jones, R. C. (1966, March). Multicampus Instructional Resources Services. *Junior College Journal*, 36, 11-13.

Kerstiens, G. (1972). The Ombudsman Function of the College Learning Center. In F. Greene (Ed.) *College Reading: Problems and Programs of Junior and Senior Colleges. 21st NRC Yearbook*. Milwaukee: National Reading Conference, 2, 221-227.

Kingston, A. J., Jr. (1959). Problems of Initiating a New College Reading Program. In O. S. Causey and W. Eller (Eds.) *Starting and Improving College Reading Programs. 8th NRC Yearbook*. Fort Worth: National Reading Conference, 15-24.

Leedy, P. A. (1959, May). History of the Origin and Development of Instruction in Reading Improvement at the College Level. *Dissertation Abstracts International*, 19, 2841. Ann Arbor: University Microfilms, No. 59-1016.

Lewis, J. (1964, Fall). A Study of the Effectiveness of Three Methods of Teaching One Segment of Elementary Political Science. *Journal of Experimental Education*, 33, 73-79.

Maxwell, M. J. (1966, May). The College Reading Laboratory. *Journal of Reading*, 9, 402-405.

Miklas, M. (1954). *An Analysis of Remedial Reading Programs in California Junior College, Four Year Colleges, and Universities*. (Ed.D., UCLA).

Newman, L. (1966). Remedial Reading in the Junior College. In M. P. Douglass, (Ed.) *Beyond Literacy, 13th Yearbook of the Claremont Reading Conference*, 206-214.

Parr, F. W. (1930, April). The Extent of Remedial Reading Work in State Universities in the United States. *School and Society*, 31, 547-548.

Raygor, A. L. (1966). Individualizing a College Reading Program. In Figueral, J. A. (Ed.) *Reading and Inquiry. Proceedings of the International Reading Association Conference*, 10, 168-170.

Robinson, F. P. (1945). Two Quarries With a Single Stone. *Journal of Higher Education*, 16, 201-206.

Roueche, J. (1971, January). Accountability for Student Learning in the Community College. *Educational Technology*, 11, 46-47.

Shaw, P. (1950). The Brooklyn College "Study Program." *School and Society*, 71, 151-153.

Simpson, R. G. (1942, May). The Reading Laboratory as a Service Unit in College. *School and Society*, 55, 621-623.

Spache, G. D., McDonald, A.S., Gallacher, D., Smith, D. E. P., and May, M. M. (1959, Summer). College Reading Programs. *Journal of Developmental Reading*, 2, 35-46.

Tresselt, M. E., and Richlin, M. (1951). Differential Prognosis in a College Study Methods Course, *Journal of Psychology*, 31, 81-89.

Triggs, F. O. (1942, December). Remedial Reading Programs: Evidence of Their Development. *Journal of Educational Fsychology*, 33, 678-685.

Triggs, F. O. (1941, October). Remedial Reading. *Journal of Higher Education*, 12, 371-377.

T. V. Retention and Learning. *School and Society*. September 1958, 86, 323-324.

Von Kleinsmid, R. B., and Touton, F. C. (1929). Effective Study Procedures in Junior College and Lower Division Courses. University of Southern California.

Walker, G. H., Jr. (1964, January). Remedial Reading Programs in Negro Colleges and Universities. *Journal of Negro Education*, 15, 119-121.

Weber, C. B. (1954, January). An Experimental Course in Remedial Writing. *Junior College Journal*, 24, 285-291.

Whipple, G. M. (1916, 1928). *How to Study Effectively*. Illinois: Public School Publishing Co.

Williams, G. (1967). Use of the Computer for Testing and Programming in a Reading Program. In G. B. Schick and M. M. May (Eds.) *Junior College and Adult Reading Programs/Expanding Fields. 16th NRC Yearbook*, Milwaukee: National Reading Conference.

Wittenborn, J. R. (1944). Classes in Remedial Reading and Study Habits. *Journal of Educational Research*, 37, 571, 578.

Zerga, J. E. (1940, December). Remedial Reading Programs. *Junior College Journal*, 11, 194-195.

(Editor's note: This article had a 75 item bibliography that we were unable to include due to space limitations. Readers who want to see the documentation for each statement should read the original article.)

Gwyn Enright is Professor of English at San Diego City College, San Diego, CA 92101.

Learning Centers shared the same titles but were based on quite different philosophies, depending on the nature of institution they served. Two contrasting programs are described: California State University at Long Beach's Learning Assistance Center was based on a business management model, provided individualized services to students including diagnosis and prescriptive materials, and offered outreach services to faculty by staff attending classes and providing inservice training. On the other hand, the U.C. Berkeley model was based on personalized one-to-one service through individual and small group tutoring, workshops and non-credit classes, and served faculty by cooperating on teaching-learning research and through offering tutoring for credit courses.

Employing a systems approach and corporate management techniques, the Learning Assistance Support System at California State University, Long Beach uses feedback from many sources to design, implement, and modify learning assistance programs and services for students, faculty, and staff.

Learning Assistance at a State University: A Cybernetic Model

By Frank L. Christ

In 1972, when the California State Legislature voted special funds to promote educational innovation within the nineteen state colleges and universities, California State University, Long Beach, proposed a learning assistance support system "to mobilize existing campus and community resources in order to make them readily accessible to students as aids to learning" (Challenge of Creative Change, 1975, p. 115).

Although the concept of assisting students to succeed academically is not new (Enright, 1975), the proposed learning assistance support system was significantly different from any previously existing learning skills service. In his article, entitled "Systems for Learning Assistance: Learners, Learning Facilitators, and Learning Centers," the author described a learning assistance center as "a facility where students (learners) come to effect change in their learning assistance skills and attitudes" (Christ, 1971, p. 35) and "any place where learners, learner data, and learning facilitators are interwoven into a sequential, cybernetic, individualized, people-oriented system to service all students (learners) and faculty (learning facilitators) of any institution for whom learning by its students is important" (Christ, 1971, p. 35).

This concept of a learning assistance center differed from most learning skills centers in postsecondary institutions where they were viewed as campus facilities for the inadequately prepared, the provisionally admitted, and the probationary student. Such centers also were limited, serving students in reading, or in writing, or in math, generally stigmatized as remedial services. Some campuses supported separate reading clinics, writing labs, and math tutorials with little if any cooperation or communication among them. These services were frequently located in basements and trailers far from the center of student activity. In addition, most centers were administered by faculty or counselors who had little if any background or training in management. Concepts like Management by Objectives, Organizational Development, and On-the-Job-Training were foreign to most directors of learning skills centers.

The proposed learning assistance support system for CSU–Long Beach specified an operational facility, centrally located, to house a reading lab, writing center, math lab, programmed instruction laboratory, study skills center, standardized test preparation service, independent self-paced learning center, staff training center, foreign students conversation service, and tutorial clearinghouse. This center, in the interest of cost effectiveness and to minimize the stigma of remediation, would serve not only students, but the total university community including its faculty, staff, and administration. The learning assistance system would use a systems approach with a strong emphasis on a cybernetic subsystem to elicit and use feedback from its users so that its programs and services would constantly reflect the needs, expectations, and concerns of the institution.

The Learning Assistance System was funded in 1972-73 and serviced over 3000 students its first year. The following year, the Learning Assistance Support System was awarded a continuation grant by the Chancellor's Office which enabled it to provide leadership and training in learning assistance for the other eighteen institutions in the California State University and College system. As a result of these awards and with strong support by central administration and faculty, the Learning Assistance Support System grew in usage, programs, space, staffing, materials, and equipment. In addition, the Learning Assistance Support System has fulfilled a leadership role not only for its sister institutions in the CSUC system but for many postsecondary institutions outside the California system.

Learning Assistance Programs and Services

Over the years, the Learning Assistance Support System developed and implemented the following programs and services:

1. Individual programs in personal learning skills for all students, faculty, and staff,
2. Course support programs for students as agreed to by faculty and departments,
3. Counselor intern training and fieldwork experience in learning assistance,
4. Program and facility support for staff development,
5. Facility support for the following: Academic Information Services, Upward Bound, Educational Opportunity Program, Project Chance (ex-felon program), English department writing services, Math department tutorial service, Veterans Academic Services and the Conversation Lab for international students,
6. Tutorial clearinghouse for students,
7. Individual programs for students, faculty, and staff to prepare for standardized tests,
8. Consultative service to faculty in the development of independent self-paced learning packages and courses as well as contract programs in learning assistance,
9. Personal learning skills workshops in the Learning Assistance Center,

10. Behavior modification including biofeedback, and desensitization services for students in cooperation with the educational psychology department and the counseling center,
11. Personal learning skills workshops in lecture halls and classrooms,
12. Facility support for alumni self-development skills program,
13. Program development, personnel, and facility support for special programs such as the nursing department's program for disadvantaged students,
14. Independent study, particularly at the graduate level, in the areas of instructional media, educational psychology, and secondary reading,
15. Facility support, as available, to the Center for Faculty Development, learning resources division, and individual departments.

The Learning Assistance Center also functions as a model for the CSUC system to train learning assistance personnel and as an innovation diffusion center for equipment, materials, research, managerial, and operational procedures. As resources permit, training opportunities have been extended to over fifty non-CSUC institutions.

All Learning Assistance Support System programs and services are based on a number of primary assumptions: (1) learning assistance begins where learners perceive themselves to be; (2) learning "how to learn" is a process that can and must be learned; (3) each learner is a unique person with different learning styles, background experiences, and motivations; (4) learning skills development must be meaningful and goal-oriented; (5) educational technology offers unlimited learning alternatives; (6) diagnosis, prescription, and follow-up are inseparable from learning skills development; and (7) independent, self-paced learning is successful whenever the following conditions are present: learners

are receptive before a program or activity begins, the skill to be learned is modeled, and reinforcement occurs immediately after an activity or exercise.

In addition, the Learning Assistance Support System uses a systems approach and follows a management philosophy known as Management by Objectives (MBO) to get the most out of its resources, to achieve program results, and to maintain quality of its services.

The Systems Approach to Learning Assistance

The development of the original systems approach at CSU–Long Beach and its subsequent evolution into an ongoing learning assistance support system were the results of incorporating concepts and strategies from educational technology, human development (counseling), psychology of learning, and corporate management into an operational rationale suitable for postsecondary education. From educational technology, the Learning Assistance Support System adapted Banathy's instructional systems design with its insistence on self-adjusting characteristics that "prescribe change as a perpetual process in the development, operation, and maintenance of systems" (Banathy, 1968, p. 83). This self-adjustment to effect change is the dominant characteristic of the Learning Assistance Support System and, as such, is dependent on documentation and data from its clients, its practitioners, its administrators, and from external evaluators. This capacity to solicit and be dependent upon such feedback is the cybernetic aspect of a learning assistance support system. It ensures that the system maintains integrity, relevancy, efficiency, and effectiveness through an evaluation process that provides ongoing feedback.

The Learning Assistance Support System adapted techniques and strategies from corporate management to ensure operational efficiency as well as visibility, credibility, and accountability. Practicing an adaptation of "Management by Objectives" (Deegan and Fritz, 1975), the Learning Assistance Support System fulfills its university mission — a mission whose goals and objectives are developed each year by its staff, based on feedback data from the previous year's evaluations. In addition, the Learning Assistance Support System uses organizational development and renewal strategies to provide opportunities for its staff to develop esprit de corps and a sense of community.

Management by Objectives (MBO)

Because the management approach and its reliance on feedback is seen as indispensable to a cybernetic model of learning assistance, selections from the MBO document for 1978-1979 are reproduced below along with some explanation of its development and implementation. Such a document is developed annually by the Learning Assistance Support System staff, distributed to interested administrators, revised and posted.

The MBO document begins with the following statement of its primary mission and concomitant goals: To mobilize for effective and efficient utilization by, students, staff, faculty, and administration all existing campus, community, and CSUC resources — including people, facilities, equipment, materials, programs, research, and information to support individuals, departments, or other campus groups who desire to learn more in less time with greater ease and confidence.

Specifically, the primary mission has six goals:

1. To assist learners to learn by providing accessible environments for a dynamic interface with equipment, materials, and learning facilities,

2. To prevent learning failures and to increase learning sophistication in personal learning skills by providing programs and services for learners to "learn to learn,"

3. To recruit and train personnel for Learning Assistance Support System programs and services,

4. To publicize programs and services of the Learning Assistance Support System to CSULB students, faculty, staff, and administration,

5. To continue to adapt the Learning Assistance Support System to the needs and expectations of CSULB consistent with the articulated goals and available resources of the institution,

6. To demonstrate the viability of the Learning Assistance Support System as a campus agent in developing and implementing approaches to learning and instruction that are individualized, personalized, cybernetic, mathemagenic, and accountable.

Next, the document states the secondary and tertiary missions of the Learning Assistance Support Systems — to become recognized as a management model of a Learning Assistance Support System that can be adapted by other CSU institutions and as a learning information center about learning assistance management for other institutions.

Frank Christ was formerly Director of the Learning Assistance Center at California State University, Long Beach. Currently he directs the Winter Institute for Learning Assistance Professionals of the University of Arizona-Tucson.

Marie-Elaine Burns explains how the LAC program at California State University
at Long Beach helps both faculty and students.

Management Strategies to Assist Students
in Improving Learning Skills

By Marie-Elaine Burns

(Condensed from the *Journal of Developmental Education*,
9(3), 2-4, (1985). Reprinted by permission of Marie-Elaine
Burns and the *Journal of Developmental Education*, Appalachian State University, Boone, NC 28608.)

A comprehensive strategy, carefully carried out, benefits faculty, students, and learning assistance personnel in helping students develop learning skills.

Abstract. In order to assist large numbers of students to develop learning skills, faculty of the Learning Assistance Center have developed a variety of
ways of providing learning skills workshops in the
LAC, university classrooms, dormitories and other
places where students gather. Following a comprehensive plan based on cooperation with content-
area faculty, hands-on experience, and evaluation,
LAC staff have developed procedures which are
applicable to many learning centers.

Many learning assistance centers, because of limited staffing, have problems reaching the large numbers of students needing learning skills development, improvement, and maintenance on a one-to-
one basis. Too often faculty are ignorant of services provided by the center or unconvinced that
these services are worthwhile. To overcome these
problems, the Learning Assistance Center (LAC) at
California State University, Long Beach, has added
the following programs:

1. Regularly scheduled skills workshops in the
   LAC,
2. Skills workshops in the classroom upon invita-
   tion of faculty,
3. Skills workshops through the Office of School-
   Based Programs, which markets support programs and services/or the eight schools of the
   university,
4. Skills workshops in dormitories, student associations, clubs, and Greek houses.

Workshops are not given for academic credit, and
students are taught to integrate skills into their
courses. All workshops, conducted either in the
LAC or elsewhere, are presented by learning assistance center staff or by interns assigned to the center. The workshops emphasize skills by demonstration rather than by lecture or exhorting students
to improve.

Program Design for Classroom
Learning Skills Workshops

Learning skills workshops conducted in the classroom make the LAC more visible and credible to
faculty and assist a greater number of students in
acquiring important learning skills. The design of
each workshop follows these guidelines:

1. Workshops require active student participation.
2. Workshop planning includes faculty input.

3. Each skill is modeled whenever possible by the LAC facilitator.
4. Emphasis is placed on application of skill.
5. Encouragement of drill and practice with self-paced materials available at the LAC is an integral part of the presentation.
6. Workshop success is related to user satisfaction and faculty feedback.

Classroom Learning Skills Workshops

The LAC offers faculty six learning skills workshops: time management, study/reading, listening/notetaking, term paper writing, preparing for and taking exams, and improving memory skills. Each classroom workshop begins with the distribution of LAC program worksheets. Students use these in lieu of taking notes. The worksheet requires students to respond to three items: (1) As a result of this workshop, what will you put into practice? (2) What will you no longer do? and (3) What questions and/or reactions would you like to share with others in the workshop?

During the workshop, students are asked to discuss what they have recorded. This dialogue allows students to examine their present learning habits and, more importantly, what they could do to improve. Students can also use the worksheets to develop personal objectives for improving their proficiency in a particular skill.

Before the end of the workshop, a handout specific to the skill is distributed to students. It lists additional individualized activities offered at the LAC, with reference to specific programs such as *You Can Learn to Learn* (Christ & Adams, 1979), *Seven Steps to Better Management of Your Study Time* (Christ, 1981) and *How to Survive in College* (Casabeer, 1969).

At the end of the workshop, instructors ask students to write a brief evaluation. These are later shared with LAC staff members.

The workshop in time management is described below to show an example of the active student participation and modeling that are hallmarks of the program design.

Time Management Workshop

Seven Steps to Better Management of Your Study Time (Christ, 1981) is the program used to teach time-management skills. Students take each of the following steps during the workshop:

Step 1: Deciding that managing time is important.

Step 2: Evaluating study needs for the present term.

Step 3: Discovering how much time is now devoted to study.

Step 4: Making a schedule based on needs and desires.

Step 5: Revising the schedule when necessary.

Step 6: Setting up a pre-exam review schedule.

Step 7: Incorporating the PLRS (preview, lecture, review, study) Learning Cycle into the schedule.

At Step 4, students are given blank college schedules and fill in their courses, labs, and personal commitments such as work, athletics, meetings, and worship. Further, the PLRS Learning Cycle in Step 7 is not merely explained; instead, students are shown how to incorporate the cycle into their schedules. Every student, at this point, will have scheduled a preview before each lecture, a review directly after each lecture, and a weekly review of course work. Thus students learn not only principles of time management but also to apply some of those principles.

Gaining the support and input of content-area faculty is critical to the success of learning assistance in the classroom.

Management Strategies for Eliciting and Maintaining Faculty Support

Faculty support of the classroom workshop program gives LAC staff access to larger groups of students and extends the LAC's capabilities to assist them. The LAC has used the following approaches to gain this support:

Be where faculty are.
Twice per week at least one staff member eats lunch in the faculty dining room, creating the opportunity to network with faculty. The purpose is to build a general relationship, both personal and professional, as well as to promote the center and its offerings.

Participate in faculty orientation.
The LAC is a regular agenda item on the faculty orientation program, conducted through the Faculty Development Office.

New faculty are introduced to LAC staff by the Faculty Development Officer and given a formal tour of the center. Instructors also receive a LAC "Faculty Fact Sheet," which describes learning assistance services at CSU–Long Beach (Griffin, 1978). The sheet also contains suggestions for interaction among faculty and LAC staff.

Be present at department meetings.
Upon request, presentations on LAC services are made at specific department meetings, particularly those meetings concerning campus resources available to students, student referral, and retention.

Show faculty the need for classroom learning skills.
A survey of learning skills asks students to rate their learning skills. These ratings are based on students' perceptions of each skill's usefulness in a particular course. Instructors rate the same skills according to their perceptions, and the results are compared. Thus instructors become more aware of the skills students feel are needed to successfully pass their courses, and how confident students feel in the level of their skills. Instructors can use this information to adapt lecture techniques to meet students' needs, refer students to the LAC for specific assistance, or request learning skills workshops to be presented in their classes.

Maintain records on faculty interrelationships.
The LAC operates on the management system of Management by Objectives (MBO), reviewing goals and objectives and establishing new ones every summer. This system keeps the LAC accountable for reaching goals, and it also demands that the organization documents its work both in terms of quantity and quality. LAC documentation includes identification of faculty who need to be reminded of LAC services; a record sheet is used at the LAC to document dates and times of workshops, workshop names, and the courses in which they were presented, by whom, and so on. Such documentation is also used to show new faculty how the LAC relates to their departments.

Persist both in publicizing and offering programs.
Program promotion must be an ongoing responsibility. Faculty, as well as staff and students, must be reminded regularly what the LAC is and what it

offers. Services must be offered on a consistent basis so that faculty and students can depend on the stability of the programs. Persistence and consistency among staff is also very important in eliciting cooperation. Staff members must stay with the center long enough to build the types of relationships on campus which assure the LAC's success. Further, it is in the best interest of the LAC that administrative staff know each other's jobs and are seen as equally important and competent in performing LAC services.

Conclusion

The program-design guidelines, workshop descriptions, and management strategies detailed in this article have been successful in assisting LAC staff to reach large numbers of students in the classroom. In 1983-84, for example, the LAC reached 1,000 students in 23 different classrooms representing eleven academic departments. In addition, faculty now use LAC program materials and activities as requirements in their courses.

These workshops, which combine the learning of steps and principles with the application of the method, give students intensive experiences with learning skills required for success in college. In addition, the overall workshop program helps reinforce the position of the LAC as an integral part of the academic community and offers LAC staff the opportunity for increased contact with students, faculty, and staff. The approaches to learning skills workshops can be adapted for use in any learning center which desires to strengthen its position as an essential part of the teaching community and to bring learning skills to students when and where they need them.

References

Adler, M. T. (1966). *How to read a book*. York: Simon & Schuster.

Casebeer, E. (1969). *How to survive in college*. Minneapolis: Education Marketing Corporation.

Christ, F. L. (1981). *Seven steps to better management of your study time*. Seal Beach, CA: Personal Efficiency Programs.

Christ, F. L., & Adams, W. R. (1979). *You can learn to learn*. Englewood Cliffs, NJ: Prentice-Hall.

Griffin, R. (1978). *The university yellow pages*. Long Beach: California State University.

Hanf, M. B. (1970). Mapping: A technique for translating reading into thinking. *Journal of Reading*, 14(4); 225-30, 270.

Johnson, H. W. (1964, Summer). Another study method. *Journal of Developmental Reading*, 269-282.

Robinson, E. P. (1970). *Effective study* (4th ed.), New York: Harper & Row.

Marie-Elaine Burns is Coordinator of The Learning Center and Director of the Special Services Program at Skyline College, San Bruno, CA 94066.

Establishing a learning center in a prestigious research university in the 70s posed many challenges. Although UC Berkeley's Student Learning Center survived its early difficulties, many learning centers today face some of the same problems.

Developing a Learning Center:
Plans, Problems and Progress

By Martha Maxwell

(Based on Maxwell, M. (March 1975). Developing a learning center: Plans, problems and progress. *Journal of Reading*, 18, 462-469 and *Improving Student Learning Skills*, San Francisco: Jossey-Bass, 1979. Reprinted by permission of Martha Maxwell and the publishers.)

Faced with declining enrollments, "steady state" budgets, and inflation, many colleges and universities in the 70s were reassessing student services just as they are doing today. Reading and study skills programs and separate minority tutoring programs were being replaced by "learning centers" that took many forms — from highly mechanized auto-tutorial programs to those that offered only reading and skills classes. This paper describes a learning center that reflected the 70s zeitgeist — that is, a person-centered program where educational technology is supplementary and where students receive help in any basic course from physics to Swahili, from architecture to organic chemistry. Perhaps these observations will aid those who are planning new learning centers or revising their present ones in the 90s.

During a major reorganization of all University of California at Berkeley (UCB) student services in 1973, the Vice-Chancellor of Student Affairs accepted a proposal by the author to develop a new department merging two existing services: a large minority tutoring program (part of the Educational Opportunity Program) and a small, counseling-oriented Reading and Study Skills Service which operated as a division of the Counseling Center. A new Learning Library Laboratory was included in the plan. The Student Learning Center was organized during the summer of 1973 and officially opened at the beginning of the fall term. We were allocated twenty-four full time positions and an annual budget of $233,000 to serve a student body of 30,000.

The Student Learning Center had three functions: (1) service to students; (2) training; and (3) research and program development. The primary mission of the Center was to help students become more independent, self-confident and efficient learners so that they were better able to meet the University's academic standards and successfully attain their own educational goals. To accomplish this mission, the Center offered a variety of individual and group programs and services to meet the diverse needs of Berkeley students. Services ranged from intensive individual help for the special-admit, educationally disadvantaged students whose grammar or math deficiencies might doom them to failure in freshman courses, to group programs for seniors who were competing with thousands of others for admission to law school or medical school, to doctoral students with problems organizing their ideas in writing their dissertations.

The philosophy of the Center which underlies all of its services was to help students improve their academic skills, to "learn how to learn" different subjects, as opposed to "reteaching" them their courses or the paternalistic practices of some compensatory education tutoring programs where tutors summarize the students' reading assignments, work their math problems, or correct their grammatical and spelling errors on themes. In our Center, each staff member was expected to function as a diagnostician of the student's learning difficulties, to prescribe appropriate remediation and to support the student's goal of developing effective skills.

To implement our goals and philosophy, staff members were encouraged to develop and test their own strategies and approaches to teaching their subject. For example, the chemistry staff offered large review sessions, small group tutoring and individual tutoring for those who needed intensive help. Some of the other tutoring strategies that were tried and shared included self-contained study groups where the tutor acts as a consultant, meeting with the group only one and one-half hours per six study hours (accounting); team learning (math and chemistry); nondirective tutoring using a Socratic questioning method (organic chemistry) and many others. To expedite the interchange of ideas and techniques, staff from different disciplines were housed in the same office (physics tutor with a reading specialist, chemist with writing specialist, and so on). Despite some initial staff resistance, this arrangement began to break down the barriers between disciplines and people.

To prepare future high school and college teachers the center provided undergraduate and graduate students with practical experience as tutors, and by giving inservice training helped them better understand the specific learning difficulties of students. In addition, the Center offered tutoring for credit courses for undergraduates through the Education Department (peer tutoring in reading, writing, social studies, mathematics, and science) and a practicum in college reading and study skills for graduate students. Learning specialists in the Center supervised each undergraduate taking peer tutoring for credit. Fifty-three undergraduates tutored for credit in 1973-74.

Inservice training meetings were held weekly. Professors from other departments were invited to give lectures on their specialties — for example, Kenneth Johnson spoke on "Black English," Tim Allen on "Review of Research on Speed Reading," Louis Schell on "Peer Tutoring in Mathematics," among many others.

The tutors in chemistry, mathematics, computer science and statistics were highly receptive to the training in language and reading; likewise, the reading and language skills people appreciated the talks by scientists.

A counseling psychologist from the Counseling Center spent eight hours a week in the Center consulting with individual staff members on how to deal with problem students, how to improve interviewing and diagnostic skills, and conducting regular staff seminars on "Helping Students with Exam Panic," "How to Cope with Problem Students," "Helping Students Improve Concentration and Memory," and other requested topics. The demand for this service was so great that we could have used a full-time counseling consultant.

The Center was organized into four service components each headed by a coordinator: (1) writing skills and social sciences; (2) math and related subjects; (3) science and languages; and (4) the library-laboratory. The latter service provided self-help programs and back-up tutoring material for the other three components, but as a separate entity it had its own staff, space and equipment. Coordination among the components was achieved through weekly meetings and through specific joint work assignments (e.g., representatives from each component planned staff inservice training; special student programs such as the MCAT Review; tutors in statistics and computer science and reading and writing specialists developed the Center's yearly evaluation plan, etc.). With the exception of the administrative and clerical staff, all other Center positions were part time. Since student demands varied during the year, tutors were hired accordingly — for example, during 1973-74 the staff ranged from thirty to ninety persons. Applicants for tutoring positions were required to have a letter of recommendation from a faculty member who teaches courses in their tutoring field. They were screened by a committee of three experienced staff members who rated them on their knowledge of the subject, ability to explain concepts, and their sensitivity to student problems.

The Center maintained a Tutor Clearinghouse as a service to veterans and other students needing intensive help who could afford to pay for their own tutoring. Tutors whom we were not able to hire for budgetary reasons were listed in the Clearinghouse. Besides the faculty-certified tutors, the Tutor Clearinghouse also listed Honor Society Members who offered free tutoring.

Starting a new service with a minimal budget for equipment and materials encouraged us to adopt the methods suggested by Frank Christ, Director of the Learning Assistance Center at Long Beach State University, and ask for donations from departments and faculty. We approached this cautiously and on a very limited scale as we were fearful of being deluged with antiquated equipment and out-dated materials which we would have trouble disposing

of even at used bookstores. However, we received a donation of three hundred current lower-division mathematics textbooks which formed the nucleus of an undergraduate math library. The math specialists developed a synopsis of each so that students could locate information on specific math concepts in the different books. Also, we obtained an extensive library of reading and study skills materials donated by education faculty. Our computer science specialist arranged to get us computer time from other departments and managed to get us computer terminals from the Pacific stock exchange for $1 a month. These computer terminals enabled our students to use existing CAI programs and made it possible for the staff to write their own CAI programs.

Each of the Center's tutors and learning specialists maintained regular contact with individual faculty members so that their work with students was consistent with the professor's goals and requirements. The Center had a faculty Advisory Committee of twelve members from different departments and colleges which met regularly and offered advice on Center policies, procedures, and programs.

Other Services

In addition to tutoring, the Center offered a number of special noncredit mini-courses in reading and basic skills including:

Reading and Studying the Natural Sciences — This group filled each quarter.

Improving Reading Speed and Comprehension — For honors students and those who aspire to be. Demand for this course was heaviest in the fall quarter; groups of fifteen to twenty-five fill sessions if they are scheduled early in the quarter.

Math for Nonmath students — Algebra Review. Good demand but student requirements too variable for group; we found an individualized program more appropriate.

Exam Skills — Good student response if scheduled just before midterm exams.

Professional School Exam Review – LSAT, GRE, MCAT — Included test structure, academic preparation, time usage, test-taking strategies. Three sections filled each quarter; enrollment ran as high as seventy students.

Math Review Sections for Professional School Exams — Practice tests given under exam conditions, explanations of solutions, test taking strategies. Three sections filled each quarter. (Note: We feel that these groups would fill even if they were scheduled on Christmas Eve.)

Mini-Courses That Had Variable Results

Reading and Studying the Social Sciences — Good response in fall quarter.

Reading and Studying the Humanities — Poor response so we dropped the group.

How to Like Reading — "An open ended group dedicated to the proposition that reading can be fun, interesting, worthwhile, meaningful, and that it need not be a bore, or just a task." Three students attended the first group and although they were enthusiastic, we did not offer it again.

Academic Survival Skills: Coping with Berkeley's Course Demands — Few students showed. They don't want to survive: they want to succeed. We changed the title to Study Skills but found similar results. Then we tried The Academic Game: How to Play and Win. Twenty students signed up, but many dropped out before the third meeting.

Writing Papers — Few students showed up for this two-session course though we offered it each quarter. Students seem to prefer individual help in writing, so we changed to offering a drop-in writing clinic every afternoon.

Incompletes — For students who have incompletes due to unwritten papers or uncompleted projects. The group dealt with procrastination, motivation, methods of research, structure and organization of writing papers. Only one student signed up for this program. It is clear that procrastinators are not likely to attend scheduled meetings to cure their procrastination.

Prechemistry — A review of basic chemistry concepts as preparation for college chemistry. Students are expected to learn from each other with no lecturing from the instructor. Students responded well to this format.

Advertising the Center

Students learned about the Center through brochures and bookmarks left at the library and given out by the bookstore. Also the Center was mentioned in the university catalogue and other information bulletins; orientation sessions for new students; through news releases to student newsletters — such as Black Thoughts, The Student Wives' Newsletter, Public Health Student Newsletter, and others; and through staff speakers for faculty and student groups. Close liaison was maintained with the other campus services for students such as counseling, advising, the student information service and housing.

Our most effective technique for informing students about services was through the student newspaper, *The Daily Californian*. To fill our mini-courses and special programs, we sent out announcements and posters; but we found that purchasing ads in the student newspaper was the best way to attract students.

The effectiveness of the ads varied with the topic and the time of year. For example, an ad stating, "Wanted: Slow Readers . . . to help us test and evaluate a new self-help program in speed reading . . ." drew 150 students in the winter quarter, but only five during the spring quarter. "Can you tune out the trivial, zero in on the important ideas in listening to lectures . . ." (an ad for the Xerox Listening Program) attracted fewer than five students each time it was placed. In short, we tried everything except skywriting to inform students about our service.

A follow-up survey of student users showed that more students stated that they had heard about the Center from their friends than from any other source. The next most frequent source was referral by counselors and advisors, and third was from reading our newspaper ads and stories.

Description of Student Clientele

The Center attracted a varied clientele. Twenty-five percent of the students using our programs were freshmen; 22 percent were sophomores; 35 percent were juniors; 13 percent were seniors; 4 percent were graduate students; and 1 percent came from other sources. Half the students using the Service were EOP (minority program) students. Over half the clientele were women. Students spent more hours in science groups and more hours in individual tutoring in mathematics than in English, social science, and reading activities.

Grants and Special Projects

The Center's applied research thrust had three objectives: (1) developing better ways of teaching and helping students learn college courses, (2) institutional research on student users' characteristics and needs for administrative decision making and planning; and (3) evaluation of the Center's services. The research activities were felt to enhance the staff's preparation for college teaching, for if they are to succeed in the competitive professorial system, they will be required to write grant proposals and conduct research. Also, with no prospect of increasing the Center's budget in the foreseeable future, outside funding would be necessary if new programs are to be developed.

The first year the staff developed six research project proposals; two of these were funded:

1. The math specialists received an $11,000 grant from the Regents' Fund for innovative instruction to develop and evaluate a new personalized precalculus course.

2. The Coordinator with Subject A (remedial writing course) received a Regents' grant of $1,000 to develop a new group-centered approach to teaching his classes.

Later, we received a small grant from the Women's Alumni Association to fund a speech therapist to work in the center one day a week.

And we also received grant funding for an apprenticeship tutoring program to motivate freshmen women and minority students to achieve in math and science courses — new students were apprenticed to an experienced tutor and learned to tutor as they learned the concepts in their courses. In addition, we developed computer-generated instructional films in mathematics, and proposed a training program for teaching assistants in other departments — a grant that was not funded. Two of the reading specialists conducted an experiment to determine the extent to which training in speed reading transferred to textbook reading.

Program Evaluation

During the first year, the center's programs were evaluated by telephone calls to student users, tutor evaluation forms written by students, and a postcard survey to a random sample of users. Results of the postcard survey were consistent with the results of the phone survey and tutor evaluation as follows:

1. Most students reported that the service had helped them.

2. Of the 195 students returning postcards, 54 percent rated the service "excellent," 34 percent "good," 7 percent "fair," and 1 percent "poor" and 4 percent said they received no service.

3. The most frequent student complaints about the Learning Center were problems in scheduling tutors such as, "You don't have enough tutors." "I had a problem in scheduling a tutor — they should have more hours." "The tutor has too many other students when I am in there."

4. From 10-25 percent of the students who sought help did not follow through and keep appointments. Results of a phone survey showed that most of these students either dropped the course or decided they did not need help.

5. Minority students did not volunteer for skills groups even when the instructors were minority members. During the spring quarter when over twenty skills groups were offered, only two Asian-American students and no black or Chicano students enrolled. However, white students did volunteer for groups. We tried a number of different ways to motivate minority students to attend small group sessions. (Note: The most successful turned out to be scheduling students for skills groups at the beginning of the semester when they registered for courses — these eventually became adjunct skills groups.)

6. Minority students preferred individual tutoring on specific courses — they wanted help in Math 16A or English 1A not individual skills help nor course review seminars (they want help in the assignment due tomorrow or the test scheduled this week). Although our studies show that students who attended course seminars as well as individual tutoring in the sciences got higher grades than students who only attended individual tutoring sessions, less than one-third of the students attending science seminars were minority students.

7. Fewer minority students used the self-help materials and audiovisual aids in the library/laboratory than did white students (for example, fewer than 30 percent of the library/lab users were EOP students and half of these used it simply as a place to study). White males were the predominant users of learning programs.

8. The demand for different skills mini-courses and course seminars varied during the quarter, but few students enrolled if mini-courses were scheduled in the middle or the end of the quarter. Chemistry seminars, on the other hand, typically had light enrollments at the beginning of the quarter but increased to as many as

fifty students in the two weeks before final exams.

9. We found that most published, prepackaged self-help materials, cassettes, and autotutorial programs were not suitable for our students without extensive revisions and altered instructions. Selected pieces of such programs were useful, but a careful monitoring of students' responses, reactions and evaluations was necessary to determine which sections were appropriate.

10. Another finding was that most students did not complete the self-help programs they started. For example, only one-third of the highly motivated students who signed up for the Xerox reading program finished it, although many had spent two months waiting to get into the program. We shortened and modified the canned program to provide more flexibility for students with different skills levels, and as a result more stayed in the program.

Facing the Problems

As is often the case with new departments, we faced staffing, space and budget problems our first year. Some of the personnel difficulties were a natural concomitant of setting up a new department with veteran staff members and trying to merge a small (four part-time persons) professionally trained and experienced white staff with a large, predominantly minority tutoring staff of varied backgrounds and competencies. Each tutor was completely convinced that he or she had perfected the best, if not the only way, to help students, and they resisted every change. A personnel freeze which lasted all year prevented us from recruiting new staff. We had to identify potential administrators and thrust them into supervisory roles.

A budget crunch, partially caused by an unexpectedly heavy student demand during winter quarter and partially by insufficient budget allocations for furnishing and staffing a new department, necessitated rigorous cutbacks in the number of tutors hired for spring. As it turned out, fewer students sought help in spring quarter, so we were able to maintain our service by requiring that staff conduct more groups and by referring sixty-nine students to the free Honor Society tutors.

Also, our limited finances required that we return furniture and equipment orders to the manufacturers and furnish our offices and group rooms with "period pieces" culled from the university storehouse. During Christmas break, a group of science tutors who enjoyed carpentry work, designed and built carrels for the library lab.

Space problems plagued us all year. Housed in "temporary" World War II barracks centrally located on the Berkeley campus, the new Center faced problems at the beginning of the fall quarter when two group rooms and the reception area were assigned to another department. The day classes began, the remodeling of the reception area and the library laboratory also started. Students tolerated the confusion created by carpenters, electricians and painters and came in for help anyway. Tutoring rooms were shared by four to six tutors, but the staff remained amicable.

Although half of the Center staff were minority group members, there continued to be allegations from militant pressure groups that "the Center is becoming more non-minority in hiring" and that "SLC discriminates against blacks" (charges made by black student groups); "the tutoring services have been cut" (according to the Committee Against Racism) even though we saw more students than the former EOP tutoring service; and "there are too many blacks on the staff" (complaint from Chicano, Asian, Native American and white individuals and groups). We were even accused of "reverse discrimination" for having no white males in administrative positions.

As long as minority programs and the question of whether the University should provide remedial services remain highly-charged political issues, we can anticipate continued problems and pressures from both student and faculty groups.

Post Script. Although there have been many changes since the 70s, the Student Learning Center has persisted over the years. In 1991 the center moved to new quarters outfitted with modern furnishing and equipment. Meanwhile the center's programs and staff have grown immensely, supported by the university's increased affirmative action efforts. For example, in 1992, center staff held an orientation program for over 400 tutors. Tutoring for credit courses continues to be popular with undergraduates, and some of the course-related minicourses became adjunct skills classes attached to freshman courses (e.g., psychology, political science, and sociology) and offered partial credit. The non-credit reading courses which train students in mapping, critical reading, and other techniques for coping with lengthy reading assignments still draw large numbers of students. Furthermore the Student Learning Center has been credited with being a major factor in improving the retention of minority students at the university.

Martha Maxwell founded the Student Learning Center at the University of California, Berkeley. Since retiring in 1980, she occasionally writes and consults.

Despite the present diversity of learning center goals and functions, Enright and Kerstiens suggest ways that centers in the future can more successfully serve their institutions.

The Learning Center: Toward an Expanded Role

By Gwyn Enright and Gene Kerstiens

(Excerpted from "The Learning Center: Toward an Expanded Role" by Gwyn Enright and Gene Kerstiens in Lenning, O.T. & Nayman, R. L. (Eds). New Roles for Learning Assistance, *New Directions for Learning Assistance*, Number 2. San Francisco: Jossey-Bass, 1980, pp. 1-22. Reprinted by permission of Gwyn Enright, Gene Kerstiens, and Jossey-Bass Publishing Company.)

The variety of titles by which learning centers have been called mirrors the diversity of learning center missions, services, audiences, locations and affiliations and (this) terminological inconsistency has made it possible for the learning center to assume different meanings. It has been described as an answer to the needs and demands of new students (Clymer, 1978; Park, 1976; Sullivan, 1978), as an activity to provide materials and expertise for university instructors (Merrill and Drob, 1977), as a merger of reading and study skills programs with tutorial services (Maxwell, 1979), and as a marriage of instruction and technology (Kerstiens, 1971). It has also been described as a place for nontraditional learning (Peterson, 1975) for instruction not usually included in the college classroom (McPherson and others, 1976), or for course-related support, where one might find the "combined atmosphere of a medical clinic, a mechanics shop, and a coffee house" (Roueche & Snow 1977, p. 124). This terminology reflects the evolution of the learning center and the snowball sequence of its development (Enright, 1975). * (See pg. 62)

The rapid growth of the learning center movement was due in part to the dismal failure of remedial and compensatory programs based on special classes (Kendrick & Thomas, 1970; Maxwell, 1979; Roueche, 1968). It seems likely that many of these remedial programs were token efforts — initiated hurriedly, somewhat desperately, with modest commitment, and only to enable institutions to point to an agency that lent credibility to an open-enrollment policy that was voiced though barely tolerated by faculty and administration (Kerstiens, 1971). By the end of the sixties, dissatisfaction with institutional efforts aimed at salvaging students essentially by having them major in remediation (Maxwell, 1979) — 80 percent of those students chose not to enroll in other college credit classes (Roueche and Snow, 1977) — led to hopes for approaches that did not isolate students from the regular curriculum, that attended to student affect, and that also worked to achieve more efficient and effective learning in the college classroom and lecture hall. **

(In the 70s), learning center theorists and practitioners directed their attention to promising avenues for helping students remain in school and succeed. Addressing affect and personality, they have used applications of motivation theory (Roueche & Mink, 1976), behavior modification, and cognitive-style mapping. Viewing scheduling and course outlines from the student's perspective, they developed minicourses and adjunct courses which served to connect skills development to content-area classes more clearly (Kazmierski, 1971).

Understandably, the use of learning centers in higher education has generated controversy. Because learning centers have grown rapidly in number, served a largely nontraditional population, invaded disciplinary boundaries, and because they are eclectically innovative, their propriety has often been questioned by the academic establishment. Within the movement itself, opinions differ on the legitimacy or feasibility of certain concepts, designs, approaches, and strategies that have been employed by learning centers. Consequently, an unapologetic exploration of the debate on some issues that has been inspired or catalyzed by the learning center movement will allow us to explain the nature and direction of its expanding role.

Assistance Versus Resources

When learning center staff and directors search for an academic mission, they have one of two options for the emphasis or comprehensiveness of the services that they will provide. One option (pro-learning assistance) is based on the following rationale: Since the curriculum and the typical lecture-classroom-textbook presentation that prevails in higher education today will continue into the indefinite future, and since increasing numbers of students need basic and/or academic skills in order to be successful with this curriculum, these students should be helped to obtain the necessary skills for classroom learning. The other option (pro-learning resources) may be stated thusly: Since a growing number of students possess talent for learning and achieving, although not in the traditional sense, and since these students can learn effectively through new modes of delivery, it is necessary to use advances in instructional media and technology to redesign and/or enrich conventional offerings. One option emphasizes the need for learning skills and prepares the student to accommodate himself to the instructional status quo, while the other views curriculum and instruction as in need of reform and sets out to change learning conditions to accommodate learners (Clark, 1980; Cross, 1979).

Indeed, the two approaches are hardly incompatible, and a comprehensive learning center will fulfill both expectations. Rather, the emphasis exerted by a given center more often reflects the expertise or enthusiasm of the center director and staff, the intramural environment for instructional change, the political temperament and the architectural flexibility of the campus itself. Indeed, the significant question is not whether to renovate instruction or remediate students, but where and when to employ limited energies and budget to best improve the learning environment. ***

Target Population

While most learning center directors and practitioners view their services as being designed to assist the entire campus community (Guskin and Greenbaum, 1979), there are those who see its function as chiefly remedial, in the most pejorative sense (Cross, 1976). Therefore certain student ability groups can become the target for de facto inclusion or exclusion. Some administrations and faculties have established such goals that the learning center at their institution can be seen as a protective device separating traditional faculty from inept students by keeping low achievers in a holding pattern until they reach an acceptable level of academic behavior (Guskin and Greenbaum, 1979; McPherson and others, 1976). However, other learning centers have been found to be effective and popular even at academically prestigious colleges and universities ("Help for the Brightest," 1976; Roueche and Snow, 1977; Walker and others, 1974) and most centers view their clientele as naturally and interestingly heterogeneous.

The Learning Disabled Student

Another problem involving the population to be served is the question of whether learning-disabled students should be diagnosed and given assistance. The fact that students with learning disorders have chosen to pursue higher education is hardly news (McAllister, 1972). Incalculable numbers of these students have lived up to their own expectations of failure, which are shared by the institutions. However, the political climate is changing, and strict interpretation of Section 504 of the Rehabilitation Act of 1973 mandates appropriate auxiliary services for such students. They are now guaranteed accessibility to higher education.

Although the concept of learning disabilities can be interpreted in many ways that can cause confusion, Sullivan's (1975) definition seems to place the term in reasonable perspective:

> Operationally, the concept of learning disabilities includes the educational factors within a student's learning style that impair rapid learning practices. This approach implies that such factors are not related to mental retardation, emotional disturbance, physical handicaps, visual or aural impairment, and that appropriate curricular and instructional responses can assist the learner in overcoming the disability (p. 6).

Critics point out, however, that instructional accommodation for the learning disabled is patently expensive, although failure to provide it could also, in the long run, prove an unwise economy. Critics argue that it is impractical to spend time and energy developing experimental learning strategies on behalf of students whose academic prospects are limited at best. Since learning-disabled students tend to gravitate to learning centers (Pflug, 1973) and learning disabilities specialists tend to be housed in them, learning centers find themselves at the center of this controversy and again are accused of misaligning their priorities.

Staffing

The unorthodox evolution and function of learning centers has occasioned atypical job specifications and duty assignments as well as questionable intraorganizational models. For instance, there is no consistency in the qualifications or credentials of the academic preparation, training, and disciplinary residence for the director of a learning center. Those chosen, recruited, or assigned to that position have come from a variety of backgrounds; sometimes, they assume directorship by default (McPherson and others, 1976; Roueche and Snow, 1977). Given the wide-ranging multidisciplinary mission of the learning center, which is without precedent, the assignment has been viewed as anything from a refuge for a marginal employee (Moore, 1976) to a residence for an academic renaissance man (Kerstiens, 1972; Maxwell, 1979). Learning center facilitators and instructors have been depicted both as plodding practitioners engaged in salvage work (Roueche and Snow, 1977) and as conspiratorial innovators threatening to change the academic environment (Kerstiens, 1972B). Perhaps heretically, Christ views degree and "professional" requirements for these facilitators as essentially inconsequential (Spann, 1979). Learning center professional personnel (tutors, peer counselors, student technicians, classified personnel) are viewed by some as inferiors carrying out the unchallenging routine work prescribed and monitored by a certificated person (McPherson and others, 1976), and by others as adventuresome zealots who accept the responsibility for providing services that previously had been the province of professionals (Matthew, 1971; McPherson and others, 1976). Finally, the team spirit that prevails among learning center personnel who share an advocacy role naturally established new working relationship and perceptions of duty that call for organizational and administrative lines of command and parameters of commitment that seem eccentric when compared with traditional models. In the 1970s, typically both learning assistance and learning resource programs were physically and emotionally isolated from the mainstream of the academic community (Kerstiens, 1971) and were often considered extra rather than essential components operating on the fringes of academic respectability. However, as learning centers themselves and their functions are both proliferating, the movement is achieving both exposure and recognition. First, since learning centers are commonly considered an integral part of developmental studies, they have benefited from the remarkable growth of developmental programs. New journals, conferences, and associations reflect their growth as does an increasing emphasis on research and evaluation. Finally, learning center personnel are becoming more successful in enlisting the cooperation and participation of departments and other campus agencies (Enright, 1976; Mayfield, 1979; K. Smith and others, 1976) which expands their sphere of influence and increases its diversity.

Future Directions and Emphases

To hazard a prediction for the future of the learning center movement, we will speculate on some programs, services, and strategies that are still in their early stages.

Leadership in Staff Development

As schools look for ways of accommodating today's learners, whether for egalitarian reasons or for the purpose of survival, they recognize that a change in faculty attitudes and behaviors is fundamental. Therefore, we can expect that learning centers will become more involved in encouraging content in-

structors to incorporate an increased number of learning alternatives into their methodologies, sponsor microteaching sessions or other behavior modification strategies that allow instructors to analyze, and hopefully improve their own teaching; organize and lead information sessions which the latest educational research and innovations can be shared with faculty; coordinate the design and development of instructional programs and modules at special workshop sessions; provide special and expert technical advice to curriculum committees aimed at reshaping the curriculum and its delivery system; lobby for administration sanction and support of responsible experimentation by enthusiastic faculty while monitoring the project's development and effects; and report the problems and progress of all these endeavors to faculty and other staff in a non-threatening way that encourages feedback and participation. In each of these roles, learning center directors and facilitators are equipped to be the leaders of change, for they are accustomed to respond to the changing and disparate needs of students upon whom the institution must refocus its attention.

Instructional Innovation and Implementation

We can anticipate that learning centers will multiply their involvement in procuring, producing, and managing individualized learning modules and packages, and that the sophistication, effectiveness, and integration of these materials into a highly accessible, interactive, and interrelated system will increase. To meet the challenge of managing all these resources, the computer will be exploited inventively, and its software will be redesigned so that computer-managed instruction (CMI) can attain the level of accessibility and individualization required for learners who bear the burden of specialness. Centers will successfully reverse the misapplications and abuses of instructional television and its relatives, the videotape recorder and videodisc, serving mass audiences and individual learners in an interactive system.

Above all, learning centers will learn to manage, adjust, and readjust all these components by effecting a marriage of humanism and technology and by developing an evaluation design that will render them accountable.

Institutionalization

Ideally, learning centers will accomplish all of these changes while fulfilling the routine aspects of their mission. If they continue to develop as we have predicted, and if the strategies, methodologies, and programs they espouse are assimilated by their institutions, learning centers will have so transformed their campuses that there will no longer be a need for centers. Learning centers will have succeeded when they have put themselves out of business. Less ideally, learning centers will continue to serve and to protect students as a group and to prod and push faculty as individuals, making slow headway toward renovation of the college. Under this construction, the learning center will be integrated into the educational system as a constructive critic. Least desirable, if learning centers prove indispensable and are institutionalized for that reason, their existence will no longer be questioned, and they will enjoy the serenity of those academic agencies whose primary goal is proprietary self-perpetuation. ****

References

Clark, R. E. (1980). What do we know for sure? *Instructional Innovation* , 25(1), 28-29.

Clymer, C. (1978). A national study of learning assistance evaluation: Rationale, techniques, problems. In G. Enright (Ed.), *Learning Assistance – Charting Our Course: Proceedings of the Eleventh Annual Conference of the Western College Reading Association*. Long Beach, CA: The Western College Reading Association.

Cross, K. P. (1976). *Accent on Learning: Improving Instruction and Reshaping the Curriculum.* San Francisco: Jossey-Bass.

Cross, K. P. (1979). Education as a superhighway. *Journal of Developmental & Remedial Education*, 3(2), 2-3, 32.

Enright, G. (1975). College learning skills: Frontierland origins of the Learning Assistance Center. In R. Sugimoto (Ed.), *College Learning Skills: Today and Tomorrowland, Proceedings of the Eighth Annual Conference of the Western College Reading Association*. Annaheim, CA: The Western College Reading Association.

Enright, G. (1976). The study table and panic clinic. In R. Sugimoto (Ed.) *Revolutionizing College Learning Skills: Proceedings of the Ninth Annual Conference of the Western College Reading Association*. Tucson, AZ: The Western College Reading Association.

Guskin, A. E., and Greenbaum, B. (1979). Quality and equality: Basic skill requirements at the university level. *Educational Record*, 60(3), 312-318.

"Help for the Brightest." *Time Magazine*, February 2, 1976, p. 44.

Kazmierski, P. R. (1971). Affecting change in college instruction and instructors. In D. M. Wark (Ed.) *College and Adult Reading, Sixth Yearbook of the North Central Reading Association*. St. Paul, MN: North Central Reading Association.

Kendrick, S. A., and Thomas, C. L. (1970). Transition from high school to college. *Review of Educational Research*, 40(10), 151-157.

Kerstiens, G. (1971). *Directions for Research and Innovation in Junior College Reading Programs.* Topical Paper No. 18. Los Angeles: ERIC Clearinghouse for Junior Colleges.

Kerstiens, G. (1972a). The ombudsman function of the college learning center. In F. Greene (Ed.), *College Reading – Problems and Programs of Junior and Senior colleges: Twenty-first Yearbook of the National Reading Conference.* Boone, NC: The National Reading Conference.

Kerstiens, G. (1972b). The reading-study skills practitioner as conspiratorial innovator. *Reading Instruction Journal,* 15(3), 49-50.

McAllister, J. M., Cowgill, S., and Stephenson, J. V. (1972). Why aren't your students learning? *Junior College Journal,* 42(6), 24-26.

Matthews, T. (1971). Twenty days in August: An intensive program. In F. L. Christ (Ed.), *Interdisciplinary Aspects of Reading Instruction: Proceedings of the Fourth Annual Conference of the Western College Reading Association.* Los Angeles: The Western College Reading Association.

Maxwell, M. (1979). *Improving Student Learning Skills: A Comprehensive Guide to Successful Practices and Programs for Increasing the Performance of Underprepared Students.* San Francisco: Jossey-Bass.

Mayfield, C. K. (1977). Establishing a reading and study skills course for law students. *Journal of Reading,* 20 (4), 285-287.

McPherson, E., and others. (1976). *Learning Skills Centers: A CCCC Report.* Urbana, IL: ERIC Clearinghouse on Reading and Communication Skills.

Merrill, I. R., and Drob, H. A. (1977). *A Criteria for Planning the College and University Resources Center.* Washington, D.C. Association for Educational Communication and Technology.

Moore, W., Jr. (1976). *Community College Responses to the High Risk Student: A Critical Reappraisal.* Washington, DC: American Association of Community and Junior Colleges.

Park, Y. (June, 1976). A conceptual basis for nontraditional study. *Community and Junior College Journal,* 46 (6), 29-31.

Peterson, G. T. (1975). *The Learning Center: A Place for Nontraditional Approaches to Education.* Hamden, CT: Lennet Books.

Pflug, R. J. (1973). The handicapped and disadvantaged students in the learning center. In G. Kerstiens (Ed.) *Technological Alternatives in Learning: Proceedings of the Sixth Annual Conference of the Western College Reading Association.* Albuquerque, NM: Western College Reading Association.

Roueche, J. E. (1968). *Salvage, Redirection or Custody? Remedial Education in the Community College.* San Francisco: Jossey-Bass.

Roueche, J. E., and Mink, O. G. (1976). Helping the "unmotivated student": Toward "personhood" development. *Community College Review,* 4(4), 40-50.

Roueche, J. E., and Snow, J. J. (1977). *Overcoming Learning Problems.* San Francisco: Jossey-Bass.

Smith, K. G., Clymer, C., and Brabham, R. D. (1976). Revolutionizing the attitudes of academia through a learning skills center. In R. Sugimoto (Ed.), *Revolutionizing College Learning Skills: Proceedings of the Ninth Annual Conference of the Western Reading Association.* Tucson, AZ: Western College Reading Association.

Spann, N. C. (1979). Interview with Frank Christ. *Journal of Developmental and Remedial Education,* (31), 8-11.

Sullivan, L. (1978). *A Guide to Higher Education Learning Centers in the United States and Canada.* Portsmouth, NH: Entelek.

Sullivan, R. J. (1975). Learning disabilities in college: The university role. *Journal of Reading,* 19(1), 6-7.

Walker, C., and others. (1974). A learning assistance center at Stanford. In G. Kerstiens (Ed.), *Reading Update-Ideals to Reality: Proceedings of the Seventh Annual Conference of the Western College Reading Association.* Oakland, CA: The Western College Reading Association.

Selections were taken from the following pages of the original article:
*pgs. 1-2, **pg. 8, ***pgs. 10-11, ****pgs. 14-17.

Gwyn Enright is Professor of English at San Diego City College and Gene Kerstiens is former Associate Dean of Learning Assistance at El Camino College, CA. and currently directs Andragogy Associates, College/Adult Learning Specialists, Rancho Palos Verdes, CA.

Beyond the philosophical and the personnel needs, learning center directors must carefully plan the center's physical space and furnishings.

College Learning Assistance Center Design Considerations

By William G. White, Jr., Barney Kyzar, and Kenneth E. Lane

(Condensed from *The Educational Facility Planner*, 28(4), 22-26, July-August 1990. Reprinted by permission of William G. White, Jr., Barney Kyzar, Kenneth E. Lane, and *The Educational Facility Planner*, Council of Educational Facility Planners, International, 8687 E. Via de Venture, Suite 311, Scottsdale, AZ 85258.)

Introduction

Learning assistance programs are a fairly recent phenomenon in American higher education, necessitated by a flood of new, more diverse and academically deficient student populations that began in the early 1970s. The past two decades have been characterized by efforts to address these students' learning needs and achievement levels, to seek means by which they could learn to cope with the traditional college curriculum and to reduce staggering student attrition rates (Baker & Painter, 1983; Sullivan, 1979).

Many institutions decided on special units, programs and/or facilities designed to assist students in developing and improving learning skills. From this, the learning center movement was born (Sullivan, 1979, 1980). "Today, the whole nation is involved in the effort to respond to learners who need to develop or refine the learning skills that are requisite for academic success" (Burnham, 1983, p. 33).

The learning assistance center is a support facility for the instructional program. Its design should spring from clearly determined purposes and from the nature of the instructional program the facility is intended to support (Currey, 1980; Karwin, 1973; White & Schnuth, 1989).

Individualized, prescription-based programs, which characterize learning assistance centers, require a facility with an open design (Garner, 1980) and interior flexibility, i.e., the capacity for convenient and routine rearrangement to meet user needs and changing instructional requirements for individuals and small and large groups (McPheeters, 1980; Peterson, 1975). The facility must be adaptable to people or it is destined to fail in its instructional purpose (College and Research Libraries, 1982).

With a team planning approach, the facility can be designed to provide appropriate space to meet institutional and instructional objectives and to accommodate present operation, anticipated future expansion and changes in educational mission, program and technologies (College and Research Libraries, 1982; McPheeters, 1980; Sharpe, 1978). An important consideration in estimating needed capacity is the types of students to be served. In most cases, students "drop-in" at their convenience; optimum availability is likely to prove most attractive to users (Karwin, 1973).

The facility should be attractive, comfortable and designed to encourage student use (Briley, 1976; Crettol, 1975; Garner, 1980; Henderson, 1972; Sharpe, 1978). Minkoff (1974, p. 17) claims that the physical appearance of the learning assistance center is an important tool to "hook them (students), to get them into the center." An attractive decor will enhance the design and create a better learning environment. As Robert Mager (Sharpe, 1978, p. 138) states, "Things that are surrounded by unpleasantness are seldom surrounded by people."

Specific Planning

Considerations

The specifications presented here are intended to provide parameters for planning a learning assistance center tailored to the needs of an institution in terms of its philosophy, objectives, instructional programs and students. These are only guidelines, not inflexible standards (White, Kyzar & Lane, 1989).

Location on Campus

Because learning assistance center activities are closely related, services are strengthened by proximity to others. Administrative time is reduced, staff are utilized more efficiently and learners benefit when programs are centralized rather than functioning in multiple sites on campus (Currey, 1980; Walker, 1980).

The name and location of the learning assistance center are important; more students, especially drop-ins, use the center when its name is "inclusive" and when they know where it is (Walker, 1980). For years, learning assistance programs were housed in basements and trailers far from the center of campus (Christ, 1980). A central, prominent location avoids any stigma associated with using the center (Briley, 1976).

Spaces

In determining space requirements and in other planning considerations, a basic guide is the standard for facilities established by the Council for the Advancement of Standards for Student Services/Development Programs which states that each functional area must be provided adequate facilities to fulfill its mission. Facilities must include, or the function must have access to: private offices/spaces for counseling, interviewing or other meetings of a confidential nature; office, reception and storage space sufficient to accommodate assigned staff, supplies, equipment, library resources and machinery; and conference room or meeting space. All facilities must be accessible to disabled persons and in compliance with relevant building codes (Council for the Advancement of Standards, 1986).

The learning assistance center should include adequate spaces and equipment for a wide range of teaching, learning and study situations pursuant to academic programs supported by the center (Karwin, 1973; Sharpe, 1978). A variety of spaces are required to bring students, learning facilitators and media together in varying configurations (McPheeters, 1980). The following discussion focuses on space allocation requirements, spatial relationships, technological concerns, furnishings, equipment and other design considerations for various areas of the center.

Learning/media Laboratory

35 asf (assignable square feet) per student station (Space planning guidelines, 1985; Dahnke, Jones, Mason & Romney, 1971). The open-space learning/media lab (Peterson, 1975) should be centrally located and constitute the largest single space in the center. It should be comfortable and quiet. Basic furnishing should include study carrels (Crettol, 1975; Karwin, 1973), tables and chairs (Briley, 1976). Dry cartels are for independent study; wet,

possibly networked, carrels are for the use of a variety of electronic media. Lounge chairs should be provided for reading (Henderson, 1972; Sharpe, 1978). Flexibility in this area is crucial (Sharpe, 1978; Whyte, 1980).

Resource/Learning Materials Center

The resource/learning materials center or library should be adjacent to the learning/media lab. It should have a library-style circulation center where students and staff check out instructional equipment and materials for use in or out of the learning assistance center (Henderson, 1972; Peterson, 1975). The area should accommodate the storage and retrieval of a variety of media and materials print, nonprint and electronic. Storage units should range from traditional library shelving to special units for audio and video cassettes to file cabinets. Open shelving is preferable for as many items as possible (Karwin, 1973). The collection will expand; therefore, it is essential to plan for years of growth (Hanson, 1972).

Technical Services/Support Space

The technical services/support area provides space for ordering, receiving and cataloging print and nonprint media. Print media will be mended, bound and laminated here. Electronic/instructional equipment will be maintained and serviced, and some items will be stored in this area. The space should facilitate the production of media, such as video and audio cassettes (Langhoff, 1980; McPheeters, 1980), and may house photocopying equipment services for the learning assistance center (Henderson, 1972; Peterson, 1975). The area may also be used to store supplies, as a mailroom, for shipping and receiving (Karwin, 1973) and as a general instructional work place (Whyte, 1980).

Seminar Rooms

[400 asf]. Seminar rooms should accommodate a maximum of 20 students in informal surroundings. The rooms will be used for seminars and other small group meetings (Karwin, 1973) and should provide opportunities for instruction with media (Langhoff, 1980; Sharpe, 1978; Whyte, 1980). Flexible walls would permit multiple use of these spaces (Henderson, 1972).

Tutorial Rooms

[240 asf]. Tutorial rooms should be adjacent to the learning media lab to be used for meetings of tutors with 1-5 students and for testing, individual assistance, and guidance of independent study (Karwin, 1973). They should be furnished with multi-person carrels, small tables and chairs (Henderson, 1972).

Classrooms

[16 asf per student (Space planning guidelines, 1985)]. Since many programs encompass developmental courses in English, reading, math, study skills, etc., the center may need classroom spaces (McPheeters, 1980). Classrooms should be designed with audiovisual media in mind, perhaps, including provision for rear screen projections and should be designed for easy control of lighting and equipment from the instructor's desk or lectern (Henderson, 1972; Sharpe, 1978).

Counseling Offices

[120 asf each]. Private offices permit counselors to work with students in personal and career counseling, in defining learning goals, and in academic advisement (Briley, 1976; Karwin, 1973; Whyte, 1980). The suite should have a career library; 200-300 asf is probably adequate (Peterson, 1975). A room (400 asf) furnished with tables and chairs for various types of individual and small group testing, diagnosis and assessment is desirable (Henry & Omvig, 1981; McPheeters, 1980).

Administrative and Staff Offices

Administrators' offices [140-160 asf] each (Space planning guidelines, 1985) must be large enough to allow for the direction of the learning center and to house administrative records, communications equipment, computer hardware, etc. (Karwin, 1973). Furnishings should be comfortable, attractive, and functional and set an appropriate "executive tone."

If there are multiple administrators or coordinators housed in the same suite, a shared conference room is desirable. Size will depend on the number of persons normally involved in meetings; 20 – 25 asf per person is usually adequate. If there is only one administrator, the office could be enlarged to accommodate a small conference area.

Faculty and staff offices should have 110-150 asf and be appropriately furnished. Administrative, faculty and staff offices should be clustered in groups of four or five around reception/clerical areas. Graduate assistant office space should have 40-70 asf (Space planning guidelines, 1985).

Reception/Clerical Station

[120 asf per person]. The receptionist/clerical station should be located near the main entrance of the center and should contain necessary office and communication equipment (Karwin, 1973). If serving the entire center, the station should be large enough to provide comfortable seating for individuals waiting to see staff members. Other stations should be located to serve suites of offices.

Typing/Word Processing Stations

[60 asf each]. Typing/word processing stations can be designed as part of receptionist/clerical stations or strategically located in the center for student use. In either case, stations should be acoustically treated to control noise. Student stations can also be used for individual study when not being used for typing or word processing (Karwin, 1973). Word processing could take place in the learning/media lab at carrels with printing taking place at a word processing station.

Storage Space

Many areas will need storage space for special materials and equipment. Adequate mechanical/custodial/utility spaces will also be required (Briley, 1976; Karwin, 1973).

Commons

[5-10 asf per person, maximum occupancy (Space planning guidelines, 1985)]. A commons area and/or lounge spaces should be provided for students and staff (Karwin, 1973). Such areas should be furnished with comfortable, durable tables and chairs. Food and drink vending machines could be located here (Henderson, 1972).

Child Care Center

Because increasing numbers of students have young children, a child care service may be desirable. The age and number of children to be served and the activities planned for them will determine space requirements. Kindergarten classrooms, for example, need 75 sf per child including storage and rest rooms (Castaldi, 1987; Karwin, 1973).

Other Considerations

There are other important considerations necessary to produce a functional, well designed learning assistance center. These include furnishings and equipment and environments for thermal comfort, acoustical integrity, electrical adequacy and lighting levels.

Furniture should be attractive and comfortable, yet durable, functional and easily maintained. A wide range of colors, fabrics and styles permit a decor that enhances the aesthetics and appeal of the center (Cobun, 1981). Flexible, movable furniture is essential for innovative and mediated instruction (Sharpe, 1978). Seating for individualized instruction requires comfort. "Research has shown that seated learners tend to generate discomfort with the passage of time. Expressed in broad humor, the activity of the cerebrum tends to vary inversely by the square of the compaction of the gluteus maximus" (Coburn, 1981, p. 182).

Facilities, to a large extent, determine the degree to which instructional media will be used effectively and innovatively. The wide array of instructional equipment used in the learning assistance center must be considered in its design. The selection of instructional equipment for the center should be guided by three principles: (1) flexibility to ensure maximum utilization, (2) compatibility, and (3) standardization (Lane & Lane, 1988; Langhoff, 1980; Materniak, 1980). Also, thermal and acoustical environments require careful planning (Briley, 1976; Crettol, 1975; Henderson, 1972; Henry & Omvig, 1981).

References

Baker, G. A. III, & Painter, P. L. (1983). The learning center: A study of effectiveness. In J. E. Roueche (Ed.), *A new look at successful programs* (pp. 73-78). San Francisco: Jossey-Bass.

Briley, P. (1976). *Planning and implementing learning skills centers in the state of Kansas.* Paper presented at the annual meeting of the International Reading Association. Anaheim, CA. (ERIC Document Reproduction Service No. ED 123 603).

Burnham, I. B. (1983). Profiles of success among Texas programs for low achieving students. In J. E. Roueche (Ed.) *A new look at successful programs.* (pp. 73-78). San Francisco: Jossey-Bass.

Castaldi, B. (1987). *Educational facilities: Planning, modernization, and management.* Boston: Allyn and Bacon.

Christ, F. I. (1980). Learning assistance at a state university: A cybernetic model. In K. V. Lauridsen (Ed.), *Examining the scope of learning centers* (pp. 45-56). San Francisco: Jossey-Bass.

Cobun, T. C. (1981). Facilities technology for individualized instruction. In P. J. Sleeman and D. M. Rockwell (Eds.), *Designing learning environments* (pp. 174-188). New York: Longman.

College and Research Libraries Board of Directors, (1982). Guidelines for two-year college learning resources programs, revised June 30, 1981. *C & RL News.* January/February, 1982.

Council for the Advancement of Standards for Student Services Development Programs. Consortium of Student Affairs Professional Organizations. (1986). *CAS standards and guidelines for student services/development programs.*

Crettol, M. (1975). *Libraries and instructional materials centers.* (ERIC Document Reproduction Service No. ED 109 802).

Currey, J. W. (1980). Creating functional learning resources centers. In K. Mikan (Ed.). *Learning resources center conference: Proceedings and evaluation,* (pp. 17-24). Birmingham, AL: (ERIC Document Reproduction Service No. ED 222 180).

Dahnke, H. I., Jones, D. P., Mason, T. R., & Romney, L. C. (1971). *Classroom and class laboratory facilities. (Higher Education Facilities Planning and Management Manual No. 2).* Boulder, CO: Western Interstate Commission for Higher Education.

Evans, N. D., & Neagley, R. L. (1973). *Planning and developing innovative community colleges.* Englewood Cliffs, NJ: Prentice Hall.

Garner, A. (1980). A comprehensive community college model for learning assistance centers. In K. V. Lauridsen (Ed.) *Examining the scope of learning centers*, (pp. 19-31). San Francisco: Jossey-Bass.

Guidelines for developing a program of requirements. (1985). Columbus, OH: Council of Educational Facility Planners, International.

Hanson, D. E. (1972, August). Systematic approach to learning resource center design. *Educational Technology*, 63-64.

Henderson, D. D. (1972). *Report on alternatives and considerations for the design of a learning resource center (LRC) at Georgetown University*. (ERIC Document Reproduction Service No. ED 124 121).

Henry, S., & Omvig, C. P. (1981). *Learning center handbook*. Kentucky University, Division of Vocational Education. (ERIC Document Reproduction Services No. ED 215 106).

Jenkins, J. (Ed.). (1985). *Guide for Planning Educational Facilities*. Columbus, OH: Council of Educational Facility Planners, International.

Karwin, T. J. (1973). *Flying a learning center: Design and costs of an off-campus space for learning*. Berkeley, CA: The Carnegie Commission on Higher Education.

Lane, M., & Lane, K. (1988). Design consideration for microcomputer laboratories. *CEFP Journal*. 26 (1) pp. 10-11.

Langhoff, H. F. (1980). Learning resource centers: Organizational components and structural models. In K. Mikan (Ed.), *Learning resources center conference: Proceedings and evaluation* (pp. 6-16). Birmingham, AL: (ERIC Document Reproduction Service No. ED 222 180).

Materniak, G. (1980). *Developing a learning center from A to Z: Guidelines for designing a comprehensive developmental education program in a postsecondary educational setting*. Unpublished paper. Pittsburgh: University of Pittsburgh.

McPheeters, V.W. (1980). Learning resources centers — past, present, and future. In K. Mikan (Ed.), *Learning resources center conference: Proceedings and evaluation* (pp. 1-5). Birmingham, AL. (ERIC Document Reproduction Service No. ED 222 180).

Minkoff, 11. (1974). A reading resource center: Why and how. *College Management*, 9(3), 17-18.

Peterson, G. T., (1975). *The learning center: A sphere for nontraditional approaches to education*. Hamden, CT: The Shoe String Press.

Sharpe, A. D. (1978). Essentials for an effective Learning environment. In J. D. Terry and R. W. Hotes (Eds.). *The administration of learning resources centers* (pp. 128-139). Washington, DC: University Press of America.

Space planning guidelines for institutions of higher education. (1985). Columbus, OH: Council of Educational Facility Planners, International.

Sullivan, L. L. (1979). *Sullivan's guide to learning centers in higher education*. Portsmouth, NH: Entelek/Ward-Whidden House.

Sullivan, L. L. (1980). Growth and influence of the learning center movement. In K. V. Lauridsen (Ed.), *Examining the scope of learning centers*. San Francisco: Jossey-Bass.

Walker, C. (1980). The learning assistance center in a selective institution. In K. V. Lauridsen (Ed.), *Examining the scope of learning centers*. (pp. 57-68). San Francisco: Jossey-Bass.

White, W. G., Jr., Kyzar, B., & Lane, K. E. (1989). College learning assistance centers: Spaces for learning. In R. M. Hashway (Ed.), *Handbook of Developmental Education* (pp. 244-267), New York: Praeger.

White, W. G., Jr., & Schnuth, M. (1989). College learning assistance centers: Places for learning. In R. M. Hashway (Ed.). *Handbook of Developmental Education* (pp. 212-243). New York: Praeger.

Whyte, C. S. (1980). An integrated counseling and learning center for a liberal arts college. In K. V. Lauridsen (Ed.). *Examining the scope of learning centers* (pp. 33-43). San Francisco: Jossey-Bass.

William G. White, Jr. is Associate Professor of Educational Leadership at Grambling State University, Grambling, LA 71245; Barney Kyzer is Director of Curriculum and Facilities at Mid-South Community College in West Memphis, AR 72301; and Kenneth E. Lane is Professor of Educational Administration at California State University at San Bernadino, CA 92407.

College Learning Assistance Programs: Ingredients for Success

By Brinda Van

(Condensed from the *Journal of College Reading and Learning* 1992, 24(2), 27-39. Reprinted by permission of the publisher and Brinda Van.)

Successful college learning assistance programs appear to exhibit nine essential variables which enable them to meet effectively the varying cognitive and affective needs of their diverse student populations. This article identifies those variables and provides a rationale for their inclusion in the academic milieu.

A comprehensive review of literature was conducted in the areas of developmental education, student development, and college retention. Based upon these data, nine variables were identified which are associated with effective practices in learning assistance programs:

1. systematic planning and design of the program based on level of student needs,

2. written policies, procedures, and goal statements indicating the university's commitment to the education of underprepared students,

3. administrative support for the program demonstrated by budgetary, staffing and facility allocations,

4. divisional or departmental status of the program,

5. program administered by a director and staffed by committed, well-qualified, and experienced educators who have chosen to work with underprepared students,

6. individualized instruction, programmed learning, and flexible programming structures which allow students to progress at their own pace,

7. support services to assist students in developing a positive self-concept and an internal locus of control,

8. assessment and placement strategies to insure that students are enrolled in correct course levels,

9. program evaluations which are based on program goals and include both formative and summative data.

Planning and Design of the Program

"The lack of planning and clear goals have contributed more to program failure than any lack of merit on the part of the educationally disadvantaged student" (Gordon, 1975, p. 15).

The first step in building a strong learning assistance program is to design a systematic planning component that assesses the needs of the institution and the learner. The more effective programs (1) identity student needs, (2) formulate policies and procedures, (3) set goals and objectives, (4) design programs to meet the identified needs, and (5) evaluate programs on an ongoing basis.

Institutional Policies and Procedures

The developmental concept that students should be given the opportunity to acquire the skills that are necessary for their academic success needs to be perceived as an institutional mission. "Student institutional departure is as much a rejection of the attributes of the institution as it is of the attributes of the student" (Tinto, 1987, p. 127). Roueche and Snow (1977) believe that institutions should be described as high- or low-risk environments, and that low-risk colleges should be noted as those which are able to help underprepared students graduate. Those institutions which have clear policies and objectives are cited as having impact on student success rates.

The extent to which institutions have developed written policies and procedures relating to academic performance, attendance of students, evaluation of professional staff, retention studies, and follow-up studies at various levels of the organizational hierarchy from the chief executive officer to the academic or unit were found to be important factors in the success of the program, as were a strong statement of the institution's high commitment to controlling behavior and affecting outcomes (Roueche, 1984, p.11).

Effective policies and procedures which have helped underprepared students to graduate are:

1. provision of early intervention strategies for high-risk students;
2. mentor programs or other student interactions with faculty and staff to help integrate students into the college environment;

3. an early warning system to identify potential drop-outs;
4. mandatory attendance in basic skill courses/programs for students with below-average placement and diagnostic test scores;
5. transcript credit for basic skill courses to increase motivation and to enable students to qualify for financial aid funding;
6. limiting the number of basic skill courses a student can take for removing deficiencies, and limiting the length of time required to complete course objectives;
7. restricting the course load during the first semester that the underprepared student is enrolled in regular college courses if the student carries outside responsibilities of family or employment.

Such policies indicate an institution's intent to assist students. "Successful programs occur where the college assumes responsibility for the progress of their students" (Roueche, et al., 1984, p. 88).

Amount of Administrative Support

"Programs thrive on the students' sense that the faculty and administration are committed to their learning and developing" (Spann, 1977, p. 30). Factors cited as evidence of administrative support of academic assistance programs are adequate funding, placement of the program director in the hierarchy of the institutional structure, ample facilities in a centralized location, length of time the program has been in existence, and a student-centered campus.

Integration of the Program into the Structure of the Institution

The more successful learning assistance programs are those that have a departmental or divisional structure. This organizational structure has several advantages:

1. administrative control over the program curriculum, funding, and support services;
2. effective promotion of program and services;
3. equitable allocation of funds;
4. systematic needs assessments;
5. on-going communication between faculty and staff of the academic support department and other departments on campus, particularly in the design of pre-college and follow-up regular college courses;
6. comprehensive coordination and delivery of instructional and support services;
7. on-going evaluations;
8. highly visible facility for innovation and change.

Qualifications and Number of Staff Members

A full time program coordinator who has good management skills, knowledge of and commitment to the underprepared student, support of the administration, a strong working relationship with academic departments, and autonomy in hiring, firing, and budgetary matters is essential to successful learning assistance programs.

Such programs should also include experienced full-time instructional staff members who possess a clear understanding of the underprepared learner, have elected to teach this population, and hold high expectations of the student.

In successful programs, support services are provided by counselors, mentors, and tutors who are responsive to student needs, encourage purposeful behaviors, and endeavor to enhance student self-esteem.

Types of Instructional Methodologies

According to Gordon, if schools are going to be responsible for providing equal opportunity for all learners, then they must compensate for the unequal learning achievements and patterns (that students) bring to the classroom, . . . emphasis needs to be placed on . . . individual learning experiences based on each student's unique learning characteristics (Gordon, 1974).

Such compensation can be achieved through individualized instruction which involves students in their own learning and increases their competence. Effective instruction is associated with (1) small units of instruction having specific objectives, (2) pre- and post-criterion reference tests for diagnosis and evaluation purposes, (3) the use of proctors in classroom settings to permit frequent testing, immediate feedback with increased personal and social interactions, and (4) paired learning among students and flexible time frames. The evaluation of student progress is ongoing in effective programs, as "one test score is (considered) a relevant measure for only a specific moment in time" (Walvekar, p. 92). If the evaluation of student performance is concentrated only at the end of the semester, there is little opportunity for feedback from the instructor or peers. In collaborative learning situations with peers, "students come to think of themselves as capable of engaging in independent thinking and of exercising control over their learning process" (Resnick, 1987, p. 33).

Unequal learning achievements among students can be compensated for by the mastery of basic skills and the use of competent study skills. Mastery of skills can enhance students' self concept and develop a sense of control over their academic futures. The ability to use competent study skills for reading, understanding, and remembering content has been found to be a reliable predictor of academic attainment.

Unequal learning achievements can also be minimized through variable entry and exit time frames that allow students to work at their own rate. Chickering has labeled the fixed time unit as "education's Procrustean bed, . . . and its most illogical flexibility" (Chickering, 1978, p. 328). Cross (1976) points out that if such scholars as Bloom and Bruner are correct in advocating that anyone can learn a subject if given ample assistance and time, then varying time and holding attainment constant is the key in providing for individual differences among learners.

Types of Support Services

The academic instruction provided to students through learning assistance programs is necessary, but by itself is insufficient. Underprepared students with few academic successes hold negative attitudes about their capabilities and individual worth. Holistic programs that address such affective needs through counseling and tutoring have positive impact on student retention. Successful programs place emphasis on helping students to (1) strengthen their self concepts, (2) overcome negative feelings about prior educational experiences, (3) increase their sense of control over their environment, (4) increase their understanding of institutional policies and procedures which affect their scores, (5) set realistic goals, and, (6) accept responsibility for their own learning.

Counselors and tutors need to be selected on the basis of their empathic abilities and represent the cultural diversity that exist on campus. Successful programs train tutors in teaching strategies, interpersonal skills, and self-esteem development.

Strategies for the Assessment and Placement of Students

If programs are to successfully meet the cognitive and affective needs of the underprepared student, efforts must begin with an accurate assessment of those needs. Underprepared students are usually identified by their SAT or ACT scores, high school rank, and high school grades. These measures have proven over time, however, to be poor predictors of college success among returning adults, minorities, and underprepared students. Neither do they provide data for course level placement. Research suggests the use of criterion reference diagnostic tests to more effectively evaluate the diversity that exists within the developmental education population.

Assessment of student abilities not only facilitates proper course placement, it also guides the design of courses and shows a commitment to effecting behavioral changes in students. The assessment provides information on the student's achievement levels, identifies those areas in which further study is required, and gives data for the improvement of instructional services.

Methods for Evaluating Programs

As one of the basic conditions for program success, program evaluation builds awareness of and support for learning assistance services. "A well designed and manageable evaluation program is one of the major building blocks, if not the cornerstone, in the design of effective developmental education programs" (Spann, 1977, p. 37).

Roueche & others (1984), however, found that few of the programs they studied had viable evaluation components. Optimally, the evaluation should be included in the program planning phase and be systematic and continuous. On-going evaluations of both a formative and summative nature are needed to provide feedback for planned change in modifying, deleting, or adding program services.

Research recommends that program evaluations be conducted by a team comprised of personnel from the learning assistance program and the regular college faculty. This cooperative approach facilitates acceptance of the program and enables both staffs to gain greater insight into each other's work. By utilizing a cooperative evaluation design, the processes of the learning assistance program and the regular college courses can be evaluated in a non-threatening manner. This can foster evolutionary curricular and instructional changes in both programs. "The objective of planned change is to produce an improved learning program for developing specific competencies or outcomes" (Spann, 1977, p. 37).

Due to a lack of consistency in evaluation designs, measures, and reporting of data in current learning assistance programs, there is little way to compare one program with another. Reported evaluations of programs have had two main limitations, e.g., insufficient data on relevant institutional factors and lack of evaluation criteria. The measures used to evaluate student learning also have limitations due to a lack of controls for (1) interaction between variables, (2) pre- and post-testing effects, and (3) intervention treatment. Thus, effects are often attributed solely to the learning assistance program.

More sophisticated and sensitive research designs that encompass both institutional and individual goals are recommended for use in learning assistance programs. These designs include:

1. policies and procedures for the regular college program and those of the learning assistance program;

2. number of students enrolled in the learning assistance program and the number on the waiting list;

3. criteria for measuring success in the mainstream college program and the learning assistance program;

4. instructional methodologies;

5. number and kinds of student-staff interactions, or learning center lab utilizations;

6. student evaluations of the program and staff;

7. number of students that faculty members refer;

8. student demographic data;

9. student retention and attrition rates;

10. qualitative data gathered from interviews, observations, case studies, and questionnaires.

Such context information provides the basis for an ongoing evaluation component that can fuel program change.

The ultimate validation of the success of learning assistance programs is the academic performance of students. Appropriate measures to determine student outcomes are:

1. successful completion rates in the academic assistance program;

2. rates of continuation in regular college courses;

3. grades in the basic skill courses and in regular college courses;

4. grade point averages;

5. rates of completion of a degree program;

6. drop-out rates;

7. credit hours earned in relation to hours attempted;

8. class and tutoring attendance figures, and number of hours of lab usage;

9. attainment of specific cognitive skills;

10. changes in attitudes or self-concept.

This article has provided a framework of essential theoretical principles or variables which college learning assistance educators can put into practice in accordance with the needs of their academic constituencies. Learning assistance programs offer comprehensive academic assistance and support services to underprepared college students who represent a wide range of ages, ethnicities, socioeconomic groups, and levels of academic preparedness. While the focus of the programs is on helping students become better prepared academically, there will be, by necessity, significant differences in how the essential variables are operationalized. The differences are due in large part to the academic distinctions among students, as well as the colleges and universities they attend.

References

Boylan, H. R. (1981). Program evaluation: Issues needs, and realities. In C. Walvekar (Ed.) *Assessment of Learning Assistance Services*. San Francisco: Jossey-Bass.

Chickering, A. W. (1978). *Education and identity*. San Francisco: Jossey-Bass.

Cross, K. P. (1976). *Accent on learning*. San Francisco: Jossey-Bass.

Gordon, E. W. (1974) Toward defining equality of educational opportunity. In L. P. Miller and E. W. Gordon (Eds.), *Equality of educational opportunity*. New York: AMS Press.

Keimig, R. T. (1983). *Raising academic standards: A guide to learning improvement*. (AAHE/ERIC Education Research Report, No. 4). Washington, DC: American Association for Higher Education.

Maxwell, M. (1981). *Improving student learning skills*. San Francisco: Jossey-Bass.

Resnick, J. L. (1981). *Minority access to higher education*. (AAHE: ERIC: Higher Education Research Report No. 1). (ERIC Document Reproduction Service No. ED 207474).

Roueche, J. E., Baker, G. A., & Roueche, S. D.(1984). *Colleges' responses to low achieving students: A national study*. Orlando, FL: HBJ Media Systems Corporation.

Roueche, J. E., & Snow, J. J. (1977). *Overcoming learning problems*. San Francisco: Jossey-Bass.

Tinto, V. (1987). *Leaving college: Rethinking the causes and cures of student attrition*. Chicago: The University of Chicago Press.

Spann, M. G. (1977). Building a developmental educational program. In J. Roueche, (Ed.) *Increasing basic skills by developmental studies*. San Francisco: Jossey-Bass.

Walvekar, C. C. (1981). Evaluating learning: The buck stops here. In C. C. Walvekar (Ed.), *New directions for college learning assistance*, No. 5, San Francisco: Jossey-Bass.

(Editor's note: This article had an extensive bibliography that we were unable to include due to space limitations. Readers who want to see the documentation for each statement should read the original article. Additional criteria for judging learning assistance programs can be found in the CAS Standards and Guidelines (see Materniack & Williams (1987) in the LAC Bibliography below.)

Brinda Van is Director of Learning Assistance at the University of Texas at Brownsville.

Further Readings on Learning Assistance Centers

Christ, F. L. (1978, November). Management is evaluation. *Audiovisual Instructor*, 26-62.

Christ, F. L. (1972). Preparing practitioners, counselors, and directors of college learning assistance centers: An intensive graduate workshop. In Greene, F. P. (Ed.) *College Reading: Problems and Programs of Junior and Senior Colleges, Twenty-first year book of the National Reading Conference* Vol. II, 179-188.

Christ, F. L. (1984). Learning assistance at California State University-Long Beach, 1972-1984. *Journal of Developmental Education*, 8(2), 2-5.

DeVerien, M. (1973). Data Collection: A cybernetic aspect of a learning assistance center. In G. Kerstiens (Ed.) *Technological alternatives in learning*. Sixth Annual Proceedings of the Western College Reading Association, vi, 51-58.

Hashway, R. M. (1989, Spring). Developmental learning center designs. *Research & Teaching in Developmental Education*, 5(2), 25-38.

Enright, G., & Kerstiens, G. (1980). The learning center: Toward an expanded role. In O. Lenning and R. Nayman (Eds.). *New roles for learning assistance*, San Francisco: Jossey-Bass, 1-24.

Materniak, G., & Williams, A. (1987, September). Standards and guidelines for learning assistance programs. *Journal of Developmental Education*, 11(1), 12-18.

White, W. G., Jr., & Schnuth, M. L. (1990). College learning assistance centers: Places for learning. In R. M. Hashway (Ed.), *Handbook of Developmental Education*. New York: Praeger Press, 157-177.

White, W. G., Jr., Kyzar, B., & Lane, K. E. (1990). College learning assistance centers: Spaces for learning. In R. M. Hashway (Ed.), *Handbook of Developmental Education*. New York: Praeger Press, 179-195.

Part 3

Peer Tutoring

Most institutions of higher learning have peer tutoring programs, the method of learning assistance that is offered most frequently.

Research indicates that tutor training is a major factor in successful programs for high risk students and the next four articles describe some of the different approaches used to train tutors.

Jace Condravy describes how much can be accomplished in an informal, 8 1/2-hour, non-credit tutor training program.

Learning Together: An Interactive Approach To Tutor Training

By J. C. Condravy

(From P. A. Malinowski (Ed.) *Perspectives on Practice in Developmental Education*, A 1992 Monograph of the New York College Learning Skills Association, 68-71. ERIC ED 341 323. Reprinted by permission of the New York Learning Skills Association and J. C. Condravy.)

Introduction

Peer tutoring programs now pervade our educational systems, their proliferation attesting in some part to their success. Elements that contribute to the success of such programs include institutional commitment; a skilled, knowledgeable, and respected program director; adequate funding; attractive facilities that can accommodate most students who use the program; and a well-developed training program for the student staff. It is the latter that is the focus of this article.

Most professionals in higher education who are responsible for developing and administering peer tutoring programs recognize that simply placing two students together, one of whom has demonstrated better academic achievement, does not guarantee that effective tutoring will occur (Niedermeyer, 1970; Reed, 1974; Whitman, 1988). In particular, potential tutors need to be relieved of the assumption that peer tutoring is the same as classroom teaching and guided to understand and fulfill their role as a collaborator in a learning context whose value lies in its distinction from the traditional classroom setting. Tutor training programs, aimed at

developing informed and sensitive paraprofessionals, take on a variety of forms that may be classified as either formal academic, credit-bearing courses or less formal, non-credit bearing seminars. Whitman (1988) briefly describes several models in each format, most of which include components that explore tutors' roles and responsibilities, interpersonal communication skills, and study skills. The tutor training program at Slippery Rock University, "Learning Together: An Interactive Approach to Tutor Training," falls into the category of less formal, non-credit bearing programs. The description that follows will focus on the components of the eight and a-half-hour training program which includes an orientation and workshops on communication skills, study skills, and tutoring problems, the latter centered on a director/tutor generated video tape. Grounded in small group interaction and the principles of collaborative learning, "Learning Together: An Interactive Approach to Tutor Training" is mandatory for all new tutors, invitational to experienced tutors and conducted once at the beginning of each semester.

Description

Directed at students newly hired to work as tutors, the program focuses on assisting them to develop a paraprofessional identity, including a familiarity with and a sensitivity to diversity in communication styles, study skills strategies, and students' varied learning needs. Four components comprise the tutor training program, attended by approximately 25 to 30 students each semester: a five-hour orientation, a one and one-quarter hours session on communication skills, a one hour session on study skills, and a one and one-quarter hour session on how to respond to tutoring problems. Conducted by the tutorial coordinator, each of the workshops deliberately requires the participants to draw on personal experiences, brainstorm and share ideas and feelings with each other, and solve problems together. Peer tutors are paid minimum wage to participate in the training program.

Orientation

It is appropriate to begin any group activity with a low-anxiety, non-threatening opportunity for participants to introduce and share relevant information about themselves. Pfeiffer and Jones (1974) offer a plethora of icebreaking activities. One such activity that works well to begin an orientation session directs members of self-selected dyads to interview each other using group-generated questions as the basis for the interview. Dyad members then introduce each other to the large group when reassembled (Jones & Pfeiffer, 1973).

> Members of self-selected dyads interview each other using group generated questions as the basis of the interview.

For new tutors, an orientation is a prime opportunity to clarify the policies and procedures that they will be expected to follow as paraprofessionals. Placing a review of these items early in the agenda for the orientation highlights their importance. Although the form may vary from institution to institution, at Slippery Rock University a folder of information regarding policies and procedures, is provided to each trainee. The folder includes an orga-

nizational chart; statements of goals, policies, and procedures; sample tutor request forms, progress reports, student evaluations, and payroll forms; and guides on study skills and tutoring strategies. A didactic review of the materials is the most efficient method of familiarizing the new staff with them.

The chair of the Academic Support Service Department is invited to the training program to discuss with the new tutors the special population of academically underprepared students that they may encounter and for whom they will need to complete progress reports. This contact solidifies the staff's understanding of their connection to an academic department as well as acquaints them with one member of the audience for the progress reports. This presentation followed by a short question and answer period, concludes the three hour morning segment of the orientation.

The activities comprising the remaining two hours of the orientation are more representative of the interactive nature of "Learning Together." The first activity aims at helping the trainees build a sense of their responsibilities and role as well as their limitations. The large group is split into five or six smaller groups of five and asked to identify a recorder and a spokesperson. Each group is given a large sheet of newsprint and a magic marker and the following directions:

Saving some room at the top of the sheet, split the remaining space into two columns, one designated "Tutor's Responsibilities," the other, "Tutee's Responsibilities." Given what you know about helping yourself and others to learn, and expectations stated so far regarding your performance as a tutor in the Tutoring Center, compile a list of what you imagine that you will have to do in order to be an effective, helpful tutor. Then, compile a similar list of what tutees will need to do to allow you to be an effective tutor. Also, before or after completing these two lists, at the top of the sheet, complete the fragment, "A tutor is . . ." as a metaphor.

Trainees are allowed fifteen to twenty minutes to complete this task. During this time, new tutors discuss their learning experiences and their experiences helping others and begin to abstract these other more general responsibilities. The importance of the interpersonal relationship to nurturing academic growth becomes a focus as they discuss self-esteem, motivation, and patience. Experienced tutors in the group facilitate the discussion by adding insights developed on the job. Looking at responsibilities from the tutee's perspective leads new tutors to appreciate the collaborative dimension essential to a successful tutoring relationship. Also, their conception of the tutor's role becomes more sharply defined as they recognize that tutees have responsibilities that they must fulfill to allow tutoring to be helpful.

Each group is then asked to post its lists and metaphors, and the spokesperson discusses the group's conclusions. The lists overlap to a large degree, the written and oral repetition effectively emphasizing important concepts. As each group presents its list, the tutorial coordinator may correct, modify, or expand the group's ideas.

Some of the metaphors produced by this activity include, "A Tutor is a Crutch, Not a Wheelchair," "A Tutor is a Blank Check Waiting to be Endorsed," "A Tutor is a Cheerleader on the Sideline of Education," and, dubiously, "A Tutor is Fertilizer on the Garden of Knowledge." The most creative metaphor becomes featured on a button provided to the

tutoring staff and other university personnel, serving as excellent public relations for the tutoring program. The newsprint texts are displayed on the Tutoring Center walls throughout the semester, easily readable reminders to tutors and tutees of the roles each must play for peer tutoring to be an effective support strategy.

> **The most creative metaphor becomes featured on a button provided to the tutoring staff and serves as excellent public relations for the tutoring program.**

The final activity for the orientation asks the small groups constructed for the previous activity to consider and brainstorm answers to two questions: First, what information do tutors need to obtain from students during the first tutoring session, and second, what information does the tutor need to share with tutees to lay the groundwork for a successful tutoring relationship. When the groups have finished, each reports their results to the Tutorial Coordinator, who lists the responses on a black board, supplementing the final lists if necessary. Trainees are then invited to role-play the first ten minutes of an initial tutoring session, sharing and requesting the kinds of information identified as important by the small groups. The role-play participants discuss the experience, and the large group offers positive and critical feedback. The role-play may be repeated as often as the coordinator feels is necessary for the new tutors to feel comfortable with this format; the coordinator also may participate as tutor or tutee in a demonstration role-play.

Communication Skills

The second tutor training workshop, an hour and one-quarter long session, focuses on communication skills. The goals of the workshop include sensitizing new tutors to their own, as well as their students, nonverbal communication, helping them identify their communication style and its implication for effective tutoring, and introducing them to an empathic communication style that reflects active listening.

To accomplish the first goal, the trainees participate in a fishbowl activity on non-verbal communication proposed by Pfeiffer and Jones (1975). The tutorial coordinator may preface this activity with a brief explication of non-verbal behavior, drawing examples from the group and emphasizing both the ambiguity and power of non-verbal communication. The activity requires two volunteers, one playing the role of the tutor, the other the role of the tutee, to take seats in front of or in the middle of the large group so that they can be easily observed. For the first scenario, the tutor and tutee sit back-to-back, without speaking, for thirty seconds, then directly facing one another for another thirty seconds, and finally side-by-side, chairs turned slightly towards one another, for thirty seconds. The role-players first are asked to speculate about the impact that each of their positions might have on their ability to participate productively in a tutoring session. Then members of the large groups are asked to comment on what they observed about the non-verbal behavior of the two role-players as well as the implications for effective tutoring that each of the seating arrangements had. In the next role-play, again conducted without speaking, the tutee deliberately avoids making eye contact with the tutor for thirty seconds; then the tutor deliberately avoids making eye contact with the tutee. Finally, tutor and tutee sustain normal eye contact for thirty seconds. Again, first the role-players, then the group at-large are asked to comment on the implications that eye contact has for the tutoring relationship. The third scenario features the tutor and tutee si-

multaneously slouching in their seats for thirty seconds, sitting rigidly upright in their seats for thirty seconds, and leaning in towards one another slightly for thirty seconds. Feedback on body posture and its impact on the progression of a tutoring session is again solicited from the role-players and members of the large group. The tutorial coordinator concludes the activity by summarizing the non-verbal behaviors of both the tutors and tutees. Tutors must be sensitive because of the impact these behaviors may have on the effectiveness of the tutoring session.

> **Trainees participate in a fish-bowl activity to sensitize them to non-verbal communication.**

To explore communication styles and their impact on the tutoring relationship, new tutors next are asked to complete a questionnaire on response styles adapted from an instrument appearing in Johnson's (1972) *Reaching Out: Interpersonal Effectiveness and Self-Actualization*. The questionnaire consists of ten items, each a statement that a tutee potentially could make in a tutoring session, followed by five responses that a tutor potentially could make in return. Each of the choices available to the tutor reflect one of five response styles — **evaluative, interpretive, supportive, probing, and understanding.** Trainees are asked to select the response that they would most likely make. Upon completion, they tally their results and, using a key, determine their predominant communication style. Trainees are also given a definition of each of the response modes. At this time, the tutorial coordinator may split the large group into five or six small groups and assign one response mode to each group, asking the members to discuss both the advantages and disadvantages of their assigned response style in the context of a tutoring session. Each group summarizes its discussion for the other groups. The tutorial coordinator may note that all response styles have strengths and weaknesses in promoting effective communication within the tutoring session; however, according to psychologist Carl Rogers, the response style that is most effective in establishing an open, trusting relationship is the one least characteristic of most communicators — the understanding response, which requires active listening.

The tutorial coordinator discusses the merits of the empathic understanding response and the difficulties in exercising active listening. To demonstrate the latter, she asks a group to volunteer to discuss a controversial subject of their choice, the rule being that before any member can respond to another's statement, the member must first offer an understanding response, which, in essence, accurately paraphrases the preceding speaker's statement. The discussion that emerges is halting and humorous as participants mis-paraphrase one another, forget what the preceding speaker said, or try to slough off the requirement of responding emphatically by saying, "I know what you mean, but . . ." The tutorial coordinator also may participate in the discussion to role-model how to give appropriate understanding responses.

The participants are asked to discuss the difficulties of responding emphatically as well as the experience of receiving empathic responses. For the former, most admit that they were too focused on formulating their own opinion rather than listening to the speaker's idea, and for the latter, they find themselves either surprised and gratified at having been accurately heard or prepared to clarify further if the responder inaccurately paraphrased their remarks. The tutorial coordinator concludes the activity by emphasizing the value of active listening, despite its difficulty, in communication in general, but particularly in initial tutoring sessions to lay the foundation for open, non-judgmental, and accurate communication.

Study Skills

This hour long workshop gives new tutors an opportunity to diagnose the study skills difficulties that tutees may be experiencing, to identify learning strategies that have worked successfully for them, and to familiarize themselves with study skills materials available in the Tutoring Center. Once again, the tutorial coordinator splits the large group into five or six smaller groups and distributes a hand-out that contains five short case studies, each describing a tutee who is attending class and the tutoring sessions regularly but is still experiencing a particular study skills problem that is impeding academic progress. The case studies for this workshop, which focus on time management, reading comprehension, preparation for exams, note-taking, and test anxiety, were developed by the tutorial coordinator; however, an excellent selection of already prepared cases is available in Moore and Poppino (1983) and Maxwell (1990). An example of one such scenario, which reflects a time management problem follows.

Case Study One

John, a sophomore, is experiencing difficulty with his Elements of Physics course. He attends this large lecture class regularly, but seems to have trouble keeping pace with the information presented. His math background is mediocre, which probably accounts for some of his difficulty. In the few tutoring sessions that you've had with him, you've noticed that he seems to be behind in his reading. John says he spends several hours on the weekend catching up on his reading and problems for the week, frequently getting stuck and abandoning the problems. He has been earning D's and F's on his tests for which he seems ill-prepared. As his tutor, what would you recommend?

The tutorial coordinator assigns one scenario to each group. Given the number of small groups and the number of scenarios, there may be more than one group working on any one case study. Trainees are asked to determine what the predominant study skills problem is for their particular case and then prepare a list of suggestions that they would offer to the tutee experiencing the difficulty. Their lists should be drawn from two sources: their personal experience and appropriate literature selected from a Study Skills Information Center, a multi-tiered stand located in the Tutoring Center, featuring booklets and hand-outs on time-management, effective reading, test-taking, and general study skills strategies which have been produced in-house or purchased commercially.

The perusal of material, brain-storming and compiling of lists takes approximately fifteen to twenty minutes after which the tutorial coordinator asks that one individual from each group discuss the members' conclusions, including the diagnosis of the learning problem and suggestions for strategies selected from personal experience as well as from materials selected from the Study Skills Information Center. Additional suggestions are sought from any other group assigned the same scenario and then from anyone else in the group at-large who has developed an especially effective strategy to overcome the problem.

The tutorial coordinator can guide the discussion through her questions and also supplement the presentations with her own knowledge of successful study skills strategies. New tutors leave this workshop having identified effective personal learning strategies, having discovered a valuable resource

center for their work with students, and having developed an alertness to weaknesses in students' learning processes that may be interfering with their ability to make academic progress.

Difficult Tutoring Sessions

The last workshop comprising the training program "Learning Together: An Interactive Approach to Tutor Training" is built around a video tape, featuring seven tutor-tutee scenarios in which the tutoring session is not proceeding satisfactorily. The video tape, produced in-house by the tutorial coordinator and several tutors (a staff professional development activity in itself), reflects tutoring session difficulties that might be characterized as the following: (1) BLOCKING in which the tutee feels the ability to learn is hopeless; (2) CONFUSION in which the tutee is disorganized, baffled, and feeling helpless about the class; (3) MIRACLE SEEKING in which the tutee is enthusiastic about being with the tutor, has high expectations for the outcome, but is passive in the actual tutoring process; (4) OVER ENTHUSIASM in which the tutee has high expectations but limited time to accomplish goals; (5) RESISTING in which the tutee may seem sullen, bored, hostile, disinterested or defensive about the class and his ability; (6) PASSIVITY in which the tutee is inattentive and uninvolved; and (7) EVASION in which the tutee attempts to manipulate the tutor away from the subject matter at hand. In each scenario, the tutor deliberately plays an ineffective role to allow the audience to develop strategies to respond effectively to the situation.

To organize this activity, the tutorial coordinator splits the group into five or six small groups, and, after playing each five to six minute segment, stops the tape and asks each group to respond to two questions: first, how would they characterize the tutee's behavior, and second, how would they intervene to transform the session into a more productive one. The tutorial coordinator allows the groups several minutes to formulate their thoughts and then asks that a spokesperson from each group report on the group's deliberations. The first group that responds has the opportunity to present the most complete analysis though each of the other groups is also asked to supplement from their perspective. For each new scenario, therefore, a different group is asked to take the responsibility for the initial response. The tutorial coordinator also, of course, may suggest strategies that tutors might want to consider to respond effectively to the problem.

This activity gives new tutors an opportunity to rehearse their role as a tutor before having actually met with a tutee as well as an opportunity to synthesize and apply the tutoring skills learned in earlier workshops. They are able to speculate freely about what they see and how they might respond in a context that is supportive of risk-taking and discovery. And they continue the process of learning from each other, recognizing and respecting their peers as viable resources for the valuable process in which they are about to engage.

Results

Each semester, the Tutoring Center solicits two kinds of evaluations of its services — one from the peer tutoring staff, another from the students who have used the program. The first evaluation is a 19 item questionnaire. For items 1 through 17, tutors are asked to assign a rating of unsatisfactory, satisfactory, good, or not applicable. The last two items are open-ended questions regarding the effectiveness of the tutoring program. Items one through five specifically ask tutors to evaluate the effectiveness of the components of the training program. Looking at the results of the evaluations by tutors who attended the training sessions from the 1989-90 academic year, we find the following: 80% ranked the tutor orientation overall as good, 20% as satisfactory; 79% ranked the small group definition of tutor/tutee roles and responsibilities as good, 21% as satisfactory; 71% ranked the communications skills workshop as good, 29% as satisfactory, and 75% ranked the video-tape "Difficult Tutoring Situations" as good, 25% as satisfactory. These results are representative of each year's evaluation.

In addition to the numerical ratings, tutors are also given space to record comments on each item. A sample of their comments regarding components of the tutor training program include:

"I learned some interesting speaking skills."

"It really helped me (learn to) encounter properly some of the situations I'll meet during tutoring."

"It was an excellent way of getting the new tutors prepared."

"It was a good way to get acquainted with fellow tutors,"

"Excellent opportunity to open up and share ideas."

"Gave good tips to establish communication with tutee."

"All the skills sessions help prepare for what to expect and do."

The peer tutoring staff clearly finds the training program relevant to their needs and effective in preparing them to take on their new roles as paraprofessionals.

Although the students who use the Tutoring Center do not participate in the tutor training program, their use of the services and their responses on an annual semester evaluation also reflect, in some measure, the effectiveness of the tutor training program. Over a ten year period, Tutoring Center use, which currently averages 1000 requests for help each semester, has increased by 127%. The percentage of students who return from having requested peer tutoring help in the fall semester to request help in the spring semester ranges from 46 to 49 percent. And student evaluations of the Center are invariably high.

The student evaluation consists of eleven items to be rated on a Likert-type scale from one as low to six as high. The items are statements about the effectiveness of the tutoring program such as, "Tutoring helped me better understand the course content," "Tutoring helped me become more confident in my ability to succeed in the course," and "The tutor was patient." Consistently, all items on the evaluation receive averages between five and six, the top of the scale. Item twelve simply asks "Would you use the Tutoring Center again if you needed academic help?" Out of the 150 to 200 evaluations that are returned each semester, 100 percent respond yes to this question.

References

Johnson, D.W. (1972). *Reaching out: Interpersonal effectiveness and self-actualization.* Englewood, NJ: Prentice Hall, Inc.

Maxwell, M. (1990). *When tutor meets student: Experiences in collaborative learning.* Kensington, MD: MM Associates.

Moore, D. P., & Poppino, M. A. (1983). *Successful tutoring: A practical guide to adult learning processes.* Springfield, IL: Charles C. Thomas, Publisher.

Niedermeyer, F. C. (1970). Effects of training on the instructional behaviors of student tutors. *The Journal of Educational Research,* 64(3), 119-123.

Pfeiffer, J. W., & Jones, J. E. (Eds.). (1973). *A handbook of structured experiences for human relations training* (2nd ed.) (Vol. 4, p. 3). San Diego, CA: University Associates.

Pfeiffer, J. W., & Jones, J. E. (Eds.). (1975). *A handbook of structured experiences for human relations training* (2nd ed.) (Vol. 5, p. 13). San Diego, CA: University Associates.

Pfeiffer, J. W., & Jones, J. E. (Eds.). (1977). *Reference guide to handbooks and annuals.* (2nd ed.). La Jolla, CA: University Associates.

Reed, R. (1974). *Peer-tutoring programs for academically deficient student in higher education.* Berkeley, CA: Center for Research and Development in Higher Education, University of California.

Whitman, N. A. (1988). *Peer teaching: To teach is to learn twice.* College Station, TX: Association for the Study of Higher Education.

J. C. Condravy is Coordinator of Tutoring at Slippery Rock University, Slippery Rock, PA.

Annette F. Gourgey addresses the role of the tutor in promoting the development of effective metacognitive strategies as well as strengthening students' confidence that they can learn. The model can be used to guide the tutoring process as well as to provide a framework for tutor training.

Tutoring Practices That Promote Cognitive And Affective Development

By Annette F. Gourgey

(From P. A. Malinowski (Ed.) *Perspectives on Practice in Developmental Education.* A 1992 Monograph of the New York College Learning Skills Association, 66-67. ERIC ED 341-323. Reprinted by permission of the New York Learning Skills Association and Annette F. Gourgey.)

Tutoring is an essential component of developmental education. While the most obvious purpose of tutoring is to help students learn material, a more subtle but equally important purpose is to enable students to become self-directed learners (Hartman, 1990). By this definition, tutoring must be a collaborative process in which tutors guide students toward ownership of their own learning.

Students seek tutoring in order to supplement their experience in the classroom. Consequently, the tutor's role is significantly different from the classroom teacher's; rather than deliver the curriculum, the tutor oversees the student's process of understanding and reasoning (Barrows, 1988). The tutor is in a unique position to do this because of his or her special access to students' individual thoughts and feelings in a non-judgmental situation.

The purpose of this article is to present a model for the tutorial process that helps promote cognitive and affective development. The model consists of the following elements: dialogue, development of

metacognitive response to affective needs, and re-education about the learning process. This model can be used both to guide the tutoring process and as a framework for tutor training.

Dialogue

Dialogue in tutoring is not a technique so much as an orientation toward the tutoring process, seeing it as a joint participation in learning. Studies of the tutoring process have shown it to be more effective when students take an active role than when they merely listen to the tutor (Maxwell, 1991). A fundamental element of this dialogue is active listening; research has demonstrated that instructors who listen with genuine interest, asking questions about students' underlying thought processes, discover a great deal about students' conceptions as well as their misconceptions and are better able to address their learning needs (Easley & Zwoyer, 1975).

Active listening has many benefits. It encourages students to participate actively rather than to depend on the tutor; it helps the tutor to differentiate what the student really understands from what is merely being repeated; it enables the tutor to detect difficulties the student is afraid to express directly, including beliefs, attitudes, and feelings about learning; it allows the tutor to understand the reasoning behind students' errors; and it communicates a respect for students' intelligence that they too rarely experience (Brown & Burton, 1978; Easley & Zwoyer, 1975; UCLA Office of Instructional Development, 1986).

The key to effective dialogue is, as noted, a genuine interest in understanding students' thinking. This interest will suggest questions that tutors can ask that will draw students out to explain their understanding in their own words, to identify what they do not understand, and to express their attitudes and expectations about learning. With this information, tutors can tailor instruction to meet individual needs in ways that classroom teachers may be unable to do.

Development of Metacognitive Skills

Metacognition refers to the executive-level thinking processes that students use to be aware of, to monitor, and to control their own learning (Baker & Brown, 1984). This includes being aware of what one already knows; reflecting on the learning task and what knowledge and skills it requires; formulating and testing hypotheses; realizing when one is confused and taking steps to clarify that confusion; strategic knowledge — knowing not only what information is relevant, but when and why, and how to use it; and drawing conclusions (Barrows, 1988; Hartman, 1990; Paris & Myers, 1981; Schoenfeld, 1987). These are the skills that enable a student to be an active rather than a passive learner.

> A metacognitive learner engages in constant self-questioning but unfortunately, developmental students often lack the knowledge of how to engage in this internal dialogue.

A metacognitive learner engages in constant self-questioning, such as: What is the point of this task? What do I already know? What additional information do I need? How do these ideas fit together? Did I leave anything out? Are there other ways to look at this? Have I accomplished what I set out to do? (Barrows, 1988). Unfortunately, developmental students often lack the knowledge of how to engage in this internal dialogue. The tutor's role, then, is to be the students' "metacognitive conscience" (Barrows, 1988) asking these questions for the student in order to develop his or her awareness and analytic processes. With enough practice in hearing and answering the tutor's questions, students eventually begin to ask themselves the same questions and to monitor their own learning (Barrows, 1988; Schuette, 1990). Tutoring for metacognitive development relies not only on factual questions but also on inferential questions that encourage students to think about the implications of the material, chosen according to the student's level of understanding and readiness for independent work (Schoenfeld, 1987; Swanson, 1990).

Response to Affective Needs

Learning is not just a cognitive process, but an affective one as well. Students bring to tutoring not only their prior knowledge and intellectual skills but also their attitudes and expectations about the subject, about themselves in relation to it, and about the learning process (Gourgey, 1992; Hartman, 1990; Schoenfeld, 1987). Hence, tutors must learn to listen not only to students' thinking but to the emotional processes — often only indirectly expressed — that may coexist with and influence students' thinking. Such emotions may include anxiety, humiliation, fear of failure or fear of being judged as stupid. Tutors must realize that the appearance of dumbness or refusal to cooperate may mask fear, both of the subject and of the tutoring situation.

> **Tutors must learn to listen not only to students' thinking, but to the emotional processes that may coexist with and influence students' thinking.**

Helping students with affective difficulties is more a matter of how the tutor sees students and what the tutor communicates than a matter of technique. The tutor must always see students as capable of learning, even when they do not see themselves that way and would like to convince the tutor not to expect too much from them (Gourgey, 1992). Accordingly, the tutor must balance sympathetic listening to students' feelings with a refusal to share students' negative views of themselves and an expectation that students can successfully take responsibility for their own learning. For many students, learning is an emotionally risky process — one must admit ignorance, risk failure, and be willing to be changed in unpredictable ways. Tutors can help students feel safer by their friendliness and willingness to listen and by their belief in the students' capability. Tutors can then gradually increase the level of difficulty and of students' active participation, while pointing out students' successes.

> **For many students, learning is an emotionally risky process – one must admit ignorance, risk failure, and be willing to change in unpredictable ways.**

The techniques for metacognitive, self-directed learning can help not only to develop students' thinking but also to enable them to see that they are capable of taking charge of their own learning; for many students, this discovery is quite startling. Ultimately, the experience of their own success in the face of anxiety and low self-esteem is the only antidote to affective difficulties (McCombs & Whistler, 1989). The tutor's goal, then, should be to help students not only to master the material but to experience personal success as learners.

Re-education About the Learning Process

Many developmental students hold unrealistic expectations about the learning process that erode their confidence and impede their progress. Three common beliefs are that learning is simply a function of how smart one is and how quickly one finds the correct answer; that learning means doing rather than understanding; and that making errors is a sign of stupidity (Brown & Burton, 1978; Gourgey, 1992; Shoenfeld, 1987). Students fail to appreciate the importance of intellectual struggle, including incubation, and understanding ideas rather than just following procedures. They may hold unrealistic expectations about specific subjects as well, often assuming that mathematics consists of rote procedures rather than of ideas for solving problems (Schoenfeld, 1987) or that writing is about grammatically correct text rather than communication (Williamson & Davis, 1987) or that sociology is about social work rather than about theories of social organization (Rose, 1989). These faulty expectations may masquerade as difficulties with basic skills.

When students fail to live up to unrealistic expectations, they blame themselves rather than their mistaken beliefs. Giving up prematurely to avoid humiliation, they deprive themselves of the opportunity to learn how to reason out their own difficulties, and consequently of the discovery of their own capability.

Tutors can encourage students to examine their misconceptions about learning and how these affect their self-esteem and behavior as learners. To do this, tutors need to create a learning environment in which students are forced to confront the material from a different perspective. For example, tutors can stress the clarification of written ideas rather than just grammar, or the logic of problem solving rather than just the use of formulas to calculate mathematical results (Schoenfeld, 1987; Williamson & Davis, 1987).

Equally important, tutors must help students to see errors not as signs of stupidity but as a normal and necessary part of the exploration involved in learning, and as a source of information about their own thinking (Brown & Burton, 1978). Tutors need to communicate that learning is not about knowing the right answers immediately, but about confronting confusion and lack of knowledge and struggling with these until they are clarified (Barrows, 1988). With this orientation, tutors can redefine intelligence as involving reflection, thoughtful analysis, perseverance, and an openness to considering an issue from many angles. Thus, the most profound education that students can receive in tutoring is not about a specific subject but about understanding how to learn, and about their personal role in that process.

Tutoring is at its best when it focuses not only on a subject but on cognitive and affective issues in learning. Good tutoring can help students to do more than master material: it can help them to discover what the learning process is about so that they can become lifelong learners.

References

Baker, L., & Brown, A. L. (1984). Metacognitive skills and reading. In P. D. Pearson, R. Barr, J. L. Kamil, & P. Rosenthal (Eds.). *Handbook of reading research.* New York: Longman Press.

Barrows, H. S. (1988). *The tutorial process.* Springfield, IL: Southern Illinois University School of Medicine.

Brown, J. S., & Burton, R. R. (1978). Diagnostic models for procedural bugs in basic mathematical skills. *Cognitive Science*, 2, 155-192.

Easley, J. A., & Zwoyer, R. E. (1975). Teaching by listening — Toward a new day in math classes. *Contemporary Education*, 47(1), 19-25.

Gourgey, A. F. (1992). Tutoring developmental mathematics: Overcoming anxiety and fostering independent learning. *Journal of Developmental Education*, 15(3), 10-14.

Hartman, H. J. (1990). Factors affecting the tutoring process. *Journal of Developmental Education*, 14(2), 2-6.

Maxwell, M. (1991). The effects of expectations, sex, and ethnicity on peer tutoring. *Journal of Developmental Education*, 15(1), 14-18.

McCombs, B. L., & Whistler, J. S. (1989). The role of affective variables in autonomous learning. *Educational Psychologist*, 24(3), 277-306.

Paris, S. G., & Myers, M. (1981). Comprehension monitoring, memory, and study strategies of good and poor readers. *Journal of Reading Behavior*, 13(1), 5-22.

Rose, M. (1989). *Lives on the boundary: The struggles and achievements of America's underprepared.* New York: The Free Press.

Schoenfeld, A. H. (1987). What's all the fuss about metacognition? In A. H. Schoenfeld (Ed.), *Cognitive science and mathematics education*, Hillsdale, NJ: Lawrence Erlbaum Associates.

Schuette, L. M. (1990). Tutoring? Why should I? In M. Maxwell (Ed.), *When tutor meets student: Experiences in Collaborative Learning*, Kensington, MD: MM Associates.

Annette F. Gourgey is Assistant Professor of General Education at Upsala College in East Orange, NJ.

In this article Karan Hancock and Tom Gier stress the similarities between tutoring and counseling and urge that tutor training also include counseling skills.

Counseling Skills: An Important Part of Tutor Training

By Karan Hancock and Tom Gier

(Condensed from "Counseling skills: An Important Part of Tutor Training." *Journal of College Reading and Learning*, XXIII(2), 1991, 55-59. Reprinted by permission of the College Reading and Learning Association and Karan Hancock and Tom Gier.)

Students desiring to be college/university academic peer tutors come to the tutoring situation with specific content area expertise. A review of eight college and university tutoring programs from across the country indicates that there are certain minimum requirements that tutoring programs have in common for students desiring to be tutors.

All of the tutoring programs reviewed have two basic requirements for prospective tutors: a 3.0 overall grade point average and faculty recommendation, although there are variations within these limits.

It is obvious that tutoring programs seek out and secure tutors who have specific content area knowledge and expertise. Most tutoring programs seek out tutors with good grades in the subject and what may not be so obvious is that tutors are providing more than content area supplementation — tutors are providing a form of counseling; and because of this, it is important that students providing tutoring be aware of this "double duty" and responsibility.

At this point it is useful to compare definitions of tutors/tutoring and counselors/counseling in order to ascertain similarity and compatibility. Addressing the definition of tutors/tutoring, definitions range from the simple to the complex. Martha Maxwell offered this definition of tutoring: " . . . tutoring is individualized instruction" (1979). Tutors are " . . . students who have been selected and trained to offer educational services to their peers" (Ender, 1984; Maxwell, 1979). These are traditional and simple definitions harking back to the original concept of tutoring from the Middle Ages: a tutor was a knowledgeable person hired to provide one-to-one instruction/tutelage.

As time evolved so did the definition of tutoring. Tutoring is now defined with such expanded terms as: " . . . an interpersonal experience, the interrelationship of two individuals working together toward the same goal" (Rose, date unknown).

Tutors continue to provide individual instruction but they also provide much more. Modern tutors assist their clients in adjusting to the academic environment and in setting and reaching their educational goals (Ender, McCaffey, & Miller, 1979). Tutors are also asked to be sensitive to students and work with their clients to help them become sophisticated learners who are able to work and learn independently.

How then are counselors and counseling defined and described? As with definitions and descriptions of tutors and tutoring, definitions of counselors and counseling are broad-based. To a Freudian, counseling might be described as a process that would " . . . enable the person to expend the energy heretofore wasted on internal conflicts on developing his/her highest potential" (Poppen & Thompson, 1974). As applied to a tutor/tutee relationship — the tutor/counselor would be helping the tutee learn more effective ways of coping with such things as test anxiety (internal conflict) so that high potential in a specific content area could be achieved with lessened internal conflict.

An Adlerian counselor looking for behavior patterns helps the counselee examine purposes and consequences of current behavior and seeks to help the individual decrease feelings of inferiority (Poppen & Thompson, 1974). Tutors are asked to do the same thing when they help tutees examine purposes and consequences of specific behavior and decrease feelings of inferiority. For example: A tutee who does not grasp specific content area concepts fails to complete and submit assignments; as failing grades in the course mount up, the tutee's feelings of inferiority increase as well. An effective tutor could help the tutee examine not only the content area deficits but the counterproductive behavior of not completing assignments as well.

A counselor of the Glasserian school would direct counselors and counselees away from focusing on past behavior (failures) and focus on current behavior (Glasser, 1965; Poppen & Thompson, 1974). Tutors should be versed in helping tutees realize that poor past content area performance or failure does not have to be a portent of present or future performance in the subject.

The Rogerian counselor respects the counselee as an individual who is cooperative, constructive, and forward-moving, while seeking to enable the individual to become a "fully functioning person" (Patterson, 1973). A tutor must also respect the individuality of the tutee and view the tutee as a forward-moving individual wishing to get from point A to point B. The tutor should realize that as long as the tutee experiences some content area difficulty the tutee is impeded in his/her progress toward becoming a "fully functioning person" in that content area; and because of the content area difficulty the individual may be less than "fully functioning" in toto.

These well-known counseling schools of thought can be supplemented by the following definitions and descriptions of counselors and counseling. English and English (1958) describe counseling as " . . . a relationship in which one person endeavors to help another to understand and solve . . . problems." A tutor's job is to endeavor to help the tutee understand difficult content area concepts and thus become more able to solve problems.

Counseling is an activity in which one individual helps another focus on personal growth, realize and explore alternatives, and make commitments. Tutoring is an activity in which one individual helps another focus on personal growth within a specific content area, realize and explore academic alternatives, and understand the importance of commitment in the academic arena.

Counselors are people who " . . . help a person cope effectively with an important problem or concern, to develop plans and make important decisions . . . to acquire information . . . and . . . to explore and consider options available" (Eisenberg & Delaney, 1977). Gustad (1953) maintained that counselors endeavor to help clients in a learning-oriented process that will enable the clients to learn more about themselves and set realistic goals. This is still a counseling endeavor today and it is a tutoring endeavor as well. Many tutees, especially those who are novice college/university students or academically underprepared, lack effective decision making skills, do not know how to acquire information useful for personal or academic needs, and subsequently are not able or comfortable in exploring options; nor are they proficient in recognizing or setting realistic personal or academic goals. In addition, tutees may not realize the importance of commitment in academics, especially in those difficult or boring, but required, degree or preparatory courses.

Counselors and counseling situations seek " . . . to assist the student (client) in becoming an independent person capable of resolving conflict situations" (Poppen & Thompson, 1974) and/or " . . . help individuals toward overcoming obstacles to their personal growth whenever these may be encountered, and toward achieving optimum development of their personal resources" (American Psychological Association, 1956). Tutors and tutoring situations also seek to help the tutee so that the tutee will no longer need a tutor — in essence to help the tutee become a confident, independent learner.

The operative words and thoughts throughout all the descriptions and definitions of tutors and counselors tutoring and counseling, are helping and assisting. Combs, Avila, and Purky (1978) sum up the idea best when they write that teachers (tutors) and counselors ". . . each hope to assist the student to learn new and better ways of dealing with him/herself and the world about him/her."

Counseling and tutoring can then be thought of as being very closely related, albeit not strictly synonymous endeavors. Both tutors and counselors are concerned with helping another individual work through problems. Both counseling and tutoring are situations in which a trained and learned individual seeks to provide " . . . purposeful assistance to other people which makes their lives more pleasant, easier, less frustrating, or in some other way, more satisfying" (Loughary & Ripley, 1979).

Therefore, it is only logical that tutors be equipped with basic counseling skills and expertise to enhance their already present content area acumen so that the tutors can best help each individual tutee on the way to a "pleasant, easier, less frustrating" academic life.

References

American Psychological Association (1956). Division of Counseling Psychology, Committee on Definition. Counseling psychology as a speciality. *American Psychologist*, 11, 282-285.

Combs, A. W., Avila, D. L., and Putkey, W. W. (1978). *Helping relationships: Basic concepts for the helping professions*. Boston: Allyn and Bacon, Inc., Eastern New Mexico University, (1989).

Eisenberg, S., & Delaney, D. J. (1977). *The counseling process*. Rand McNally College Publishing Company.

Ender, S. C., McCaffrey, S. S., and Miller, T. K. (1979). *Students helping students. A training manual for peer helpers on the college campus*. Athens, GA: Student Development Associates.

Ender, S. C., & Winston, R., (Eds.) (1984). Student paraprofessionals within student affairs: the state of the art. *New directions for student services*, 27. San Francisco: Jossey-Bass.

Endicott College. (1988). *Tutor goals and philosophy*. Beverly, MA.

English, H. B., & English, A. C. (1958). *A comprehensive dictionary of psychological and psychiatric terms*. New York: McKay.

Glasser, W. (1965). *Reality therapy: a new approach to psychiatry*. New York: Harper and Row.

Gier, T. (1989). Application for certification of tutor programs. Anchorage, AK: University of Alaska Anchorage.

Gier T. and Hancock, K. (1985). *Helping others learn: A guide to peer tutoring*. Anchorage, AK: University of Alaska.

Gustad, J. W. (1953). *Roles and relationships in counseling*. Minneapolis, MN: University of Minnesota.

Hampton, S. (1989). *Tutoring*. Missoula, MT: University of Montana.

Loughary, J., & Ripley, T. M. (1979). *Helping others help themselves: A guide to counseling skills*. New York: McGraw-Hill.

Maxwell, M. (1979). *Improving student learning skills*. San Francisco: Jossey-Bass.

Patterson, C. J. (1973). *Theories of counseling and psychotherapy*. New York: Harper and Row.

Poppen, W. A., & Thompson, C. L. (1974). *School counseling theories and concepts*. Lincoln, NE: Professional Educators Publications.

Rose, M. C. (date unknown). *Tutoring training handbook*. Fairmont, WY: Fairmont State College.

Karan Hancock is Affiliate Professor in the Psychology Department and Tom Gier is Professor of English at the University of Alaska, Anchorage.

Winnard describes one of the most common interpersonal problems that traps beginning tutors, working with a dependent student, and suggests some effective ways to train tutors to avoid becoming codependents.

Codependency: Teaching Tutors Not To Rescue

By Karin E. Winnard

(From the *Journal of College Reading & Learning*, 24(1) (1991) 32-39. Reprinted by permission of the College Reading and Learning Association and Karin E. Winnard.)

Codependency refers to an addiction to people and their problems or to a relationship between two people (Schaef, 1987). Addiction is "any process over which we are powerless. It takes control of us, causing us to do and think things that are inconsistent with our personal values and leads us to become progressively more compulsive and obsessive" (p. 18). An addiction consumes energy that one would prefer to put some place else, and can involve a substance, a process, or a person.

Wegscheider-Cruse (1989) described codependency in terms of volitional potential, the ability to make a healthy choice.

Rewards are for performance, thinking, and external accomplishments that help reinforce the family's denial and help the family look good on the outside. Members of a dysfunctional family learn to interpret experience through someone else. If Mom continually says, "Everything is okay," children learn they must believe it is okay, even though their own perceptions and feelings tell them it is not. They learn to override their own senses with someone else's information. As they continue to do so, they neglect or even become unable to recognize their own feelings and needs (p. 245).

As an adult, this learned behavior can manifest itself in feelings of inadequacy, boredom, perfectionism, and/or low self-esteem. Stress evolves because of the incongruency of one's feelings versus others' perceptions of a situation. The anxiety continues as the codependent adult tries to rationalize away or deny his or her feelings and accept a reality prescribed by someone else that may not fit (Woititz, 1987).

A Definition

For the purposes of this article, codependency is the need to rescue, take care of, fix, or control another person or situation. It can occur when one values the needs and goals of another person or persons more than one's own. Codependency happens when identity and self-worth are largely dependent on a need to be needed. It occurs when the helping behavior being offered becomes a pattern and continues despite negative consequences (Beattie, 1987; Wegscheider-Cruse, 1989).

Very little qualitative and quantitative research has been conducted regarding codependency and its manifestations in higher education with respect to learning assistance programs. Although Woititz (1985, 1989) recounted stories of a codependent administrator, an athlete, a medical student, and a teacher, Robinson (1989) wrote a similar testimonial of a program coordinator, and Landfried (1989) discussed teachers enabling students in the secondary school classroom, nothing substantial has focused on the dilemmas, needs, and/or processes of students in the learning assistance field.

Learning Assistance Centers lend themselves well to the application of dysfunctional behavior. The very notion of providing assistance or help is something that an effective tutor and an actively practicing codependent do to elicit positive reinforcement from others, feel needed, and feel indispensable (Landfried, 1989). These tutors want to do whatever is necessary to get the job done, fix whatever is broken, placate whoever is upset. They may also want to enable others by avoiding conflict (Landfried, 1989) rather than addressing the situation in question and working with the tutee to correct it. For example, students who exhibit codependent traits while tutoring were exposed for years to these behaviors while growing up in their family. Both Black (1981) and Wegscheider-Cruse (1989) discussed roles assigned to children in dysfunctional families. In healthy, functioning families, children learn to develop the ability to "adopt a variety of roles, dependent on the situation" (Black, 1981, p. 6). Children growing up in dysfunctional families seldom learn the combinations of roles which mold healthy personalities. Instead they become locked into roles based on their perception of what they need to do to survive and to bring some stability to their lives" (Black, 1981, p. 6).

Wegscheider-Cruse (1989) articulated five roles that occur in the dysfunctional family: the Enabler, the Hero, the Scapegoat, the Lost Child, and the Mascot. Although a switching of roles may occur within the family, it is usually the child who is assigned a particular role by the parent(s) or siblings according to family position (e.g., birth order) and/or because of family situations. Two roles which are found most frequently in tutors working in higher education learning assistance programs are the Hero and the Enabler. The other three roles also are found in students who tutor, but do not occur as frequently.

The Enabling and Heroic Tutors

The Enabler protects the dependent, in this case the tutee, from adverse or overwhelming consequences. The Enabler works hard to make things not look or feel as bad to the dependent as they might really be (Black, 1981; Wegscheider-Cruse, 1989). In other words, the Enabler protects the dependent tutee from his/her own feelings of frustration and disappointment by offering a more positive perception that will take the tutee away from uncomfortable feelings. Although this type of approach might work in the short run as a "quick fix," it will not empower the tutee with healthy perceptions and/or coping strategies to perform independently as well academically.

For example, a male tutee comes in requesting help. He is anxious and crying because he doesn't understand the last two homework assignments, and the upcoming exam is on the previous five homework assignments. As the tutor listens, the tutee explains that he does not understand parts of the homework because he was sick. The tutee continues to go on and blames the teacher for being unclear in her lectures and not offering office hours which are convenient for the tutee to attend. Although the codependent tutor believes that the tutee is responsible for getting the notes from another student and/or asking the instructor about the missed course material, the tutor feels that the student is anxious and uncomfortable and decides that "rescuing" this student is the only way to make both of their uncomfortable feelings go away.

The tutor sees no choice but to teach the tutee the information he did not understand and learn in class. The exam is in three days, and the tutor believes that the tutee's performance on the exam will be a direct reflection on tutoring effectiveness. If possible, the Enabling Tutor would take the exam for the tutee. In other words, instead of letting the tutee run the race and do the best he can given the circumstances, the tutor would much rather run the race for him and take responsibility for not finishing in the top three (Winnard, 1990). The tutor who plays the Hero role will differ little from the Enabler, except to go one step further (Wegscheider-Cruse, 1989). It is important to the Hero that the tutee pulls him/herself up and does well on the exam. The tutor will go to the faculty member to obtain advice on strategies to help the tutee in the future, and get solutions to unsolvable problems to bring back to the next session. Unlike the Enabler, the Hero doesn't want to run the race for the tutee. This tutor wants the tutee to run the race and will do everything possible to ensure that s/he wins, no matter what the personal cost might be. This tutor might spend time tutoring the student after program hours for free, cancel other commitments to assist the tutee, or give a home phone number to the tutee with the encouragement to call any time.

Six Characteristics of Codependent Tutors

Woititz (1987), Beattie (1987), and Wegscheider-Cruse (1989) identified traits shared by codependents. The following discussion highlights six codependent characteristics which are common in tutors.

1. Codependents are extremely loyal, even in the face of evidence that the loyalty is undeserved. Although the tutor may understand and respect the limits set by the Tutorial Program, loyalty to the tutee is unwavering and clearly stronger at that moment than to the program. For example, if a program director has implemented a policy limiting the number of hours a tutee can request assistance (except in cases where the tutee has a learning disability or is underprepared), the tutor may state that the tutee has been coming to tutoring for five weeks, has used the maximum number of hours per week allowed, and just needs one more hour that week because there is an exam on Friday. One more hour will not necessarily make the difference, but it appears to make all the difference to the tutor.

2. Codependents are either super-responsible or super-irresponsible. There are always several tutors who would help other tutors and the director. They try to be the best and most indispensable tutors in the program, working overtime and without pay in the center doing what needs to be done, even if it is outside their tutor job responsibilities. If asked to answer the phones for an hour, they would, even if they needed to finish studying for an exam the next day. The hero description is a perfect fit.

3. Codependents judge themselves without mercy. The codependent tutor relies on tutee performance to determine whether tutoring efforts have been effective, rather than trusting self-perceptions and opinions. After working with a tutee twice a week for three weeks, the codependent tutor will believe that the grade on an exam is as much a reflection on the tutee's knowledge as it is on the tutor's effectiveness. The tutor bases self-assessment on something which is out of his/her control.

4. Codependents consistently seek approval and affirmation. Although many tutors understand, accept, and adopt program guidelines and policies, it is the tutee and not these two dimen-

sional concepts who sits before the tutor asking for the answer or to "just show me this once how to solve this problem." When a tutee comes into the session and sets goals of solving ten word problems in one hour and does not understand the reading, the tutor often feels obliged to set the pace of the session to ensure that the needs of the tutee will be met. The need for acceptance is so great that the tutor capitulates to the tutee's request, even knowing that if this codependent activity is discovered by the Program Director, a supervisory meeting with the tutor will take place.

5. Codependents believe that they are different from other people. The tutor feels justified in bending the rules for a tutee because this case is different from the hundreds of other tutees who walk through the door. Tutors who believe that they are different or special usually exhibit attention-seeking behavior such as asking for exceptions to program policy. The tutor may also take responsibility for knowing all the answers to every question the tutee has. If this is impossible then the codependent tutor believes that he or she is responsible for approaching the instructor to obtain the correct information and informing the tutee during the next session.

6. Codependents feel terribly threatened by the loss of any thing or person they think provides their happiness. Depending on the nature of the relationship, sometimes it is the codependent tutor who needs the tutee more than the tutee needs the tutor. This happens when the tutor relies on the performance and evaluation of the tutee for validation rather than relying on feelings and perceptions to resolve whether or not the tutoring efforts were effective. The tutor may try to meet each tutor's goals and expectations rather than assisting the tutee to meet

his/her own goals. To paraphrase the proverb, the tutor will catch the fish for the tutee each day rather than assist the tutee to learn how to catch fish for a lifetime.

The common thread between these examples is that the tutor wants to be the hero, wants the tutee to do well so that the tutor will be liked, wants to look good and be in control of the process and the outcome. This parallels the family system profile of the hero in a dysfunctional or alcoholic family (Wegscheider-Cruse, 1989) where the key "rules" are:

1. Keep negative feelings to yourself. Deny that they are important and/or exist.
2. Express an overabundance of positive feelings even if they are not what you feel.
3. Give people what they want even if it is not what you want to give.
4. Do not talk to anyone about what you feel is not right within the program.

Discussion

After briefly reviewing the literature in the codependency field, the task of re-educating ourselves and our students to meet the standards of a healthy functioning family may seem overwhelming. To examine one's own philosophies and pedagogy concerning uncaring assistance in general seems unthinkable. Yet the decision to take the first step, actively deciding to re-examine one's goals and values, knowing full well that one's frame of reference on learning and life may change, is the hardest step of all (Winnard, 1990). Each step after that gets easier because it involves practicing putting one foot in front of the other.

The retraining starts within each individual. Clearly defined parameters (Beattie, 1987; Black, 1981; Wegscheider-Cruse, 1989; Woititz, 1987) in a learning assistance program will help to empower directors and tutors and subsequently empower the tutees to find and trust their own ideas and feelings. Several suggestions can be provided to assist directors in defining these parameters for themselves and their tutors:

1. **Trust and listen to yourself.** You were hired to direct a program the best way YOU know how. Trust your feelings and thoughts. Listen to yourself with as much compassion as you do when interacting with others.

2. **Re-evaluate and restate your program's goals and objectives so that they reflect empowerment rather than enabling.** Are your students helped to become independent learners or are they empowered to become independent learners? Are your students helped to build self-confidence or are they assisted in learning how to develop self-confidence? What are your goals for the program?

3. **Set limits: Implement guidelines and parameters to correct identified inconsistencies and clarify uncertainties within the program.** The development of a tutor information packet which clearly identifies the goals of the program, the operational aspects (e.g., program availability and opportunities, organizational chart, administrative instructions) and the Director's expectations is recommended. Although the inclusion of consequences for not following through or completing tasks on time and as agreed (e.g., timesheets in on a specified day/date, missing or being late to a scheduled session, etc.) can be uncomfortable, it is advisable to clearly establish parameters and identify consequences. It is recommended that guidelines for promotion, dismissal, and rehire are clearly articulated by the Director and that these are followed through when necessary.

4. **Articulate the responsibilities and parameters of each tutor's roles and show how each role and policy functions to support the goals and objectives of your program.** This component is key to any program because it ensures consistency in the quality of service being provided. Defining the roles of the tutor, and setting limits within those roles and the program is recommended to let both tutors and their tutees know what can be expected and what cannot. Encouraging tutors to maximize their network of resources to include more than just the Director or their supervisor will assist everyone in being more effective. Both these methods assist tutors in establishing boundaries consistent with pre-established program policies and guidelines. When appropriate, monthly staff meetings are advisable for all tutors to minimize isolation and re-energize team spirit.

5. **Take the time to develop and implement quality training programs for tutors.** Weekly staff or class meetings are recommended to provide new tutors with information, feedback, and support. Topics included in training need to be skills development oriented rather than prescription based. Sample content areas for this training may include: tutoring techniques, learning strategies, communication skills, conflict resolution, assertiveness training, empowerment, codependency, diversity, and tutor stress syndrome.

The most common role model that tutors have for their profession is the instructor as lecturer. Clearly, tutors are not lecturers because (a) they do not lecture, they tutor; (b) they do not present new information, they review information; (c) they do not replace the lecture, they supplement it; and (d) they encourage and expect active learning and thinking from each tutee rather than passive learning (Nyland,

1987; University of California, San Diego, 1979). Therefore, a recommended style of teaching is one that encourages tutors to change their frame of reference by introducing them to the world of tutoring through experimental learning. Although this takes more creativity and preparation on the part of the training instructor, the benefits to the tutor, the tutees and the program are significant and long-lasting. The tutor will have learned, applied, and retained the information experienced in class and practiced using the skills and information in situations outside the tutoring environment (Arkin & Shollar, 1982; Pauk, 1982). This repeated application inevitably changes the tutor's frame of reference with regard to learning and results in increased effectiveness as a tutor (Maxwell, 1979; Winnard, 1990).

Conclusion

As the need for learning assistance programs in secondary and higher education continues to outgrow their availability (Winnard, 1990), it is clear that the "quick fix" or bandaid approach is not the long-lasting solution (Maki, 1979). Learning assistance program administrators need to take a step forward individually and as a group, to make it clear to the education community that the goal of tutoring is not to provide the solutions for the tutees but to empower each tutee with the necessary skills to experience the process and arrive at a solution. Clearly articulated program parameters, goals, boundaries, and policies which support the development and attainment of independent learning and thinking will provide a healthy framework for tutors and tutees to work within and change their individual frame of reference.

References

Arkin, M., & Shollar, B. (1982). *The tutor book*. New York: Longman.

Beattie, M.(1987). *Codependent no more*. New York: Harper/Hazeldon.

Black, C. (1981). *It will never happen to me!* New York: Ballantine Books.

Landfried, S. E. (1989). "Enabling" Undermines Responsibility in Students. *Educational Leadership*, 47(3), 79-83.

Maki, J. (1979). Beyond the bandaid. *Journal of Developmental and Remedial Education*, 3 (1), 3-4.

Maxwell, M. (1979). *Improving student learning skills*, San Francisco: Jossey-Bass.

Nyland, B. (1987). Cone of learning. *Teaching and Professional Development Newsletter*, 1(4).

Pauk, W. (1989). *How to study in college*. Boston: Houghton Mifflin Company.

Robinson, B. (1989). *Work addiction: Hidden legacies of adult children*. Deerfield Beach, FL: Health Communications, Inc.

Schaef, A. W. (1987). *When society becomes an addict*. San Francisco: Harper and Row.

University of California, San Diego (1979). *Probing skills videotape*. San Diego, CA: University of California.

Wegscheider-Cruse, S. (1989). *Another chance: Hope and health for the alcoholic family*. Palo Alto, CA: Science and Behavior.

Winnard, K. (1990). Codependency: Training our tutors and ourselves not to rescue. Paper presented at the annual conference of the College Reading and Learning Association, Irvine, CA.

Woititz, J. G. (1987). Home away from home. Pompano Beach, FL: *Health Communications* (1989).

Woititz, J. G. (1989). The self sabotage syndrome, Deerfield Beach, FL: *Health Communications* (1985).

Woititz, J. G. (1985). Struggle for intimacy. Pompano Beach, FL: *Health Communications* (1985).

Karin Winnard is Director of Tutoring at Sonoma State University, Rohnert Park, CA.

Tutor trainers often wonder how to get tutors to incorporate study skills in their tutoring so that students can learn the tutored subject more effectively and apply their skills to other courses. This describes one way.

Using A Learning Model To Integrate Study Skills Into A Peer Tutoring Program

By Ronald V. Schmelzer, William G. Brozo, and Norman A. Stahl

(Condensed from *Journal of Developmental Reading*, (1985). 8(3), 2-5. Reprinted by permission of Ronald V. Schmeltzer, William G. Brozo, and Norman A. Stahl and the *Journal of Developmental Reading*, Appalachian State University, Boone, NC.)

A responsibility of the peer tutor is to offer instructional services to the individual college student who has an academic problem. Service is typically provided in the form of tutorial sessions focusing specifically on the student's immediate needs. Although the tutorial function of peer tutoring is a necessity and often a priority, the goal of our peer tutoring is to equip the student with the necessary tools to become an independent learner and troubleshooter and ultimately dissolve any dependency on tutorial instruction. Our peer tutors, therefore, provide another form of academic assistance that may improve the student's chances for long-range achievement: study skills.

> **Peer tutors, in order to be successful, must have a basic understanding of the learning process.**

When a peer tutor comes into contact with a student, it is generally to identify the immediate problem. The student claims to be failing a history class or is unable to write a term paper or cannot understand algebra. What is not easy to detect however, is **why** the student is having the problem. Although it is often much more difficult to determine the answer to this question, it may often be a key factor in eliminating the need for tutorial assistance.

In order for the peer tutor to more effectively detect the cause of a learning problem, it is necessary that he or she have a basic understanding of the learning process. One way to foster this understanding is through a model. A paradigm we have developed for training peer tutors to comprehend the rudiments of learning theory is the Integrated Learning Model (ILM). This model is based on a computer model of information processing (HIP) which postulates thought patterns during learning. In reviewing these HIP models, we were attracted by their simplicity, logic, and face validity, all useful for promoting retention and application. In the development of the ILM, we borrowed the main phase of these HIP models and then grouped learning elements around each (see Figure 1). It is important here to note that our model is only similar in design to, and not representational of, the models developed by HIP theorists.

The ILM consists of five phases: preparation, input, processing, storage, and output. The first phase in the learning process, **preparation**, includes those learning elements which are prerequisite to the actual input of information. In general, it concerns the uniqueness of the individual, who has certain needs that must be met before the higher level skills of gaining information can be utilized. The second phase, **input**, affects the quality of reading and studying. How well a person takes in information is to a high degree dependent upon how well prepared that person is to learn. **Processing**, the third phase, includes taking into consideration the depth to which the student wants or needs to comprehend the material to be learned. It involves effectively organizing the learning material, understanding the different reading requirements of specific subject areas, applying techniques that can be used to help one become actively involved in learning, and also increasing one's ability to read efficiently. The next phase, **storage**, involves remembering this processed information. It deals with techniques for improving memory and retention. The last phase, **output**, deals with the skills necessary for demonstrating that learning has taken place.

The purpose of this model is to help the peer tutor discover in what phase the learning process is breaking down. To illustrate how the model can be used for this purpose, let us consider this example: A student seeks help from a peer tutor because she is failing history. The student's complaint may be based entirely on failing test grades, but is likely that test failure is symptomatic of a more basic problem. After diagnostic questioning, the peer tutor might find that the student appears strong in all phases of the learning process but output. Perhaps the student's inordinate test anxiety or lack of test-taking skills is contributing to her poor performance. On the other hand, the peer tutor may find that the student's failure is tied to problems she is having with learning elements at phases of the learning process: studying in a noisy, busy environment; taking poor lecture notes; possessing limited vocabulary; reading textbooks without a study method; and cramming for tests. The tutor's sensitivity to the integrated nature of learning can translate into treatments that are more effective than tutorial patchwork. Endowed with an arsenal of good study skills, the student may go on to improve in and pass not only history but all of her courses.

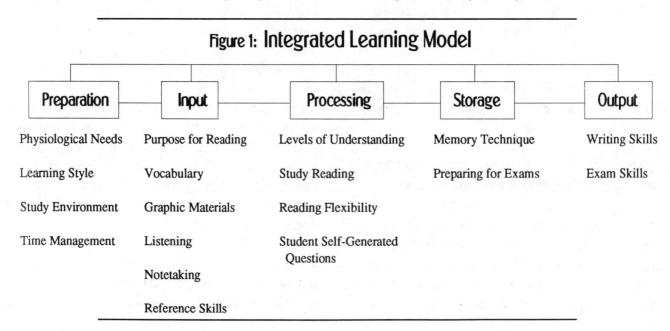

Figure 1: Integrated Learning Model

Preparation	Input	Processing	Storage	Output
Physiological Needs	Purpose for Reading	Levels of Understanding	Memory Technique	Writing Skills
Learning Style	Vocabulary	Study Reading	Preparing for Exams	Exam Skills
Study Environment	Graphic Materials	Reading Flexibility		
Time Management	Listening	Student Self-Generated Questions		
	Notetaking			
	Reference Skills			

Training Tutors to Use the Model

In order to show our peer tutors how to use the ILM, we conduct an initial formal training session of about 45 minutes in which peer tutors are asked to name activities related to the learning process. Emphasis is placed on observable activities which aid learning. Once this list is written on the board — and often supplemented by ideas from the trainer — the activities are grouped according to the five main phases of the ILM. Ensuing discussions bring out the integrated nature of learning as represented in the model.

In subsequent training sessions, peer tutors are given sample case studies which include diagnostic information of students' strengths and weaknesses. The tutor's task is to determine the possible contributing factors to problem areas. One case often used in this exercise centers around a student who is skillful in the learning elements of the first three phases of the ILM but for whom learning is breaking down in the storage and output phases. With help from the trainer, peer tutors inevitably discover that although this "sample" student is highly knowledgeable of good time-management techniques, she is unable to apply this knowledge when it comes to preparing for examinations, resulting in her poor test performance. The goal of these exercises is to lead the peer tutor to see that although each phase of the model is to be viewed on a continuum (with the preceding phase promoting the following phase), mastery of the previous phase does not guarantee success in the later phases but, typically and logically, contributes to final success. In this way, it can be seen how the different phases of the model are integrated but at the same time are independent of each other.

Two subsequent 45-minute training sessions are spent on developing the peer tutors interviewing strategies. The interview is an essential tool used by the peer tutor for determining the phase in which learning breaks down for a given individual. One way for the peer tutor to uncover this information is by asking the student key diagnostic questions based on the learning elements of the ILM. The answers to the questions indicate where the primary problem might be located. The peer tutor is then able to focus instruction on the deficient phase(s).

In the first session, peer tutors brainstorm all the possible questions that could be asked of a student relative to the learning elements of the ILM. Below are some key questions our peer tutors incorporated into their interviews as a result of this training. It should be recognized that the list is not exhaustive but serves as an example of the kinds of questions that could be asked relative to each learning phase:

Preparation
1. Are you getting enough sleep?
2. Do you have good eating habits?
3. Do you get enough physical exercise?
4. Do you have any physical impairments (poor vision, hearing, etc.)?
5. Do you know how you learn best (learning style)?
6. What kind of study environment do you have?
7. Do you find that you do not have enough time to complete assignments?

Input
1. Do you determine your purpose before reading?
2. Do you come across words that you do not understand or cannot pronounce?

3. Do you have a difficult time understanding graphs or charts?
4. Do you have difficulty with reference materials in the library?
5. Does your mind tend to wander while listening to a lecture?
6. What kind of notetaking system do you have?

Processing
1. Can you detect main points in a lecture and main ideas in textbook reading?
2. Can you put things into your own words after reading or after hearing a lecture?
3. Do you use a study reading technique (PREP, SQ3R) when reading textbooks?
4. Do you adjust your reading style to match your purpose?

Storage
1. Do you review regularly rather than just before tests?
2. Do you have trouble remembering important dates, names, or concepts? Do you have a system for preparing for exams?
3. Do you use mnemonics and other memory devices when appropriate?

Output
1. Are you familiar with basic test-wiseness clues?
2. Do you get extremely nervous and tense during exams?
3. Do you make a point beforehand of finding out what type of exam you will be taking?
4. Do you pace yourself when taking an exam?
5. Do you have trouble with written expression?

The second training session on interviewing techniques is concentrated on helping the peer tutor to ask appropriate, open-ended questions. The above questions are basically closed-ended and, therefore, restrict the amount of quality of information to be obtained from a student. Peer tutors are shown how to connect them to open-ended queries. For example, the question, "Are you getting enough sleep?" could be restated as, "Tell me about your sleeping habits." Or, "What kind of notetaking system do you have?" could become, "How do you take notes?"

In this way, as much information as possible about the student is gained in the diagnostic interview.

Simulations of prototypical peer-tutoring interviews are provided with the pre-planned student problems. Peer tutors are given the opportunity to be both interviewer and interviewee.

Follow-up staff sessions take place in which actual clients are discussed. Suggestions are given for interventions which further the model. Finally, to help our peer tutors appreciate more fully how the ILM can be used with students, we require them to become thoroughly familiar with the application of the model in their own reading and study.

> **This approach provides students with the skills to solve their academic problems independently.**

Strengths and Weaknesses of the ILM

We have found that the ILM is especially useful because of its inherent simplicity and because many of our tutors are already familiar with the linear computer paradigm; many have course work or experience with microcomputers. The ILM delineates the process of learning in an observable manner. This helps the peer tutor define more clearly his or her own limitations and range of expertise, thereby avoiding to some extent the peer tutor's dealing with issues he or she can not handle. These more complex problems are more quickly referred to professionals.

One of the weaknesses of the model lies in its simplicity. Some of our peer tutors tend to think that the model includes everything there is to know about learning; therefore, it is important to reinforce the idea that learning is complex. Even if the model is valid for a student's problems, the interaction between various aspects of it are complex and sometimes difficult, if not impossible, for the nonprofessional to discern. For example, it is not unusual for a peer tutor to assume that he has uncovered the reason for a student's failure to learn when he discovers that the student takes poor notes, yet the tutor may totally miss the fact that the student is a very poor reader or is failing because of emotional problems. The model is deceptive in its simplicity, and peer tutors are often reminded of this.

In monthly reviews of our peer tutors' own student-case notes, we have found that although tutoring sessions now last longer, they are more interactive. It appears that more learning does take place. We have noted that before using this model, a student would meet with a tutor only once or twice regarding a particular problem. Since we began using the model, average sessions last for approximately 30 to 50 minutes. In our discussions with the tutors, we have learned that both tutors and students are able to see a problem far more holistically. For example, the student and tutor both come to recognize that there is more to success in algebra than learning how to do a particular problem; rather, success in a course requires the application of good reading and study skills.

With the ILM as a guide and the ability to ask appropriate questions, the peer tutor is able to look beyond the symptom and address the student's primary problem. This approach has proven helpful to students because it provides them with methods for solving their own problems outside of the tutorial environment. Although we cannot provide empirical evidence at this time, it appears from our subjective analysis that as proper instruction is given, the student becomes less dependent on the peer tutor and more dependent on his or her own ability to learn. We say this because of the nature of the changed tutorial environment. It has moved from one of explanation (how to solve a problem or "This is what the concept is . . ."), to teaching students to uncover solutions independently. This, we feel, has been one of the more significant developments.

(Editor's note: This article had an extensive bibliography that we were unable to include due to space limitations. Readers who want to see the documentation for the ILM should read the original article.)

Ronald V. Schmelzer is Professor of Education at Eastern Kentucky University, Richmond, KY; William G. Brozo is Professor of Education, Texas A & M University, Corpus Christi, TX; and Norman A. Stahl is Director, College Reading and Learning Program, University of Northern Illinois, De Kalb, IL.

The program developed by the College Learning Association to certify peer tutors is one example of the trend toward professionalizing tutor services.

College Reading & Learning Association's Tutor Certification Program

by Tom Gier

(Reprinted by permission from the *Journal of Developmental Education*, Appalachian State University, Boone, NC.)

In 1988 the College Reading and Learning Association (CRLA) established a National Tutor Certification Program. Since then over 100 community college, college, and university tutoring programs in the United States and Canada have been certified by the CRLA. In 1992 the National Association for Developmental Education and the American College Personnel Association endorsed this certification program. Following are the purpose, procedures, and guidelines of this certification program.

1. Purpose
    The purpose of establishing a series of tutoring certificates is twofold. First, it allows tutors to receive recognition and positive reinforcement for their successful work from a national/international organization: CRLA. Second, the certificates help set up a standard for the minimum skills and training a tutor needs to be successful.

2. Procedures for Having a Program Certified
    (1) An institution that wishes to have a tutor program certified should designate one individual per tutor program or group of tutor programs who will act as liaison between the CRLA Tutor Certification Committee (TCC) and that institution's program or programs; (2) the designated individual will then complete and submit the originals and three copies of: (a) "CRLA Application For Certification Of Tutor Programs" (b) the necessary "Verification of Tutor Program" forms, plus (c) the necessary documentation concerning how the institution's tutor programs meets the criteria outlined in *CRLA's Requirements for Certification of Tutor Programs*. The originals of the application and documentation concerning an institution's tutor training program will remain on file with the CRLA TCC Coordinator; and once CRLA's TCC has certified an institution's programs and designated an individual who will act as liaison, then the appropriate masters and type of tutoring certificates will be issued to that institution.

3. General Information
    (1) Once an institution's tutor program is certified, that program will receive a certificate and be authorized to issue individual CRLA tutoring certificates. (2) There are three levels of individual certification: Regular/Level 1, Advanced/ Level 2, and Master/Level 3. (3) The initial institutional certification will be for a one-year period. (4) There will be one re-

newal certification which will be for three years. (5) After the three-year renewal certification, there will be recertifications for five years. (6) During the initial certification period, certification of tutors will be retroactive for one year from date of application.

4. Important Note
CRLA certifies programs, not individual tutors. In other words, CRLA certifies that a particular tutor training program is qualified to issue CRLA certificates to individual tutors at a certain level or levels. The responsibility lies with the institution's tutoring program(s) to keep track of individual tutor's training, tutoring hours, etc., and to issue certificates when an individual completes the necessary requirements for a certain level. Each institution is required to keep a record for each of its tutors who receives a CRLA certificate. These records, however, will be reviewed by the CRLA Tutor Certification Committee only when a need arises.

Anyone who has any questions concerning CRLA Tutor Certification or who would like to receive a Tutor Certification packet should write to: Dr. Tom Gier; Coordinator, CRLA Tutor Certification Committee; English Department; University of Alaska – Anchorage; 3211 Providence Drive; Anchorage, AK 99508.

Despite the popularity of peer-tutoring as a way to help high risk college students, there has been surprisingly little research showing its effectiveness. Generally, studies show that students who are tutored remain in college longer, but improvement in grades is much harder to demonstrate. This article discusses some of the reasons why.

Does Tutoring Help?
A Look at the Literature

By Martha Maxwell

(Adapted from an article that appeared in the *Review of Research in Developmental Education*, 7(4), 1990. Reprinted by permission of Martha Maxwell and *Review of Research in Developmental Education*, Appalachian State University, Boone, NC 28608.)

Although peer tutoring is a traditional method of helping students who are having academic difficulty and is extensively used today, it has attracted little attention from researchers. Its benefits tend to be taken for granted without the backing of formal studies. In fact, most papers published about college tutoring are narratives — descriptions of programs, techniques for tutoring, methods for training tutors and/or case studies. This paper reviews the research on tutoring that is currently available and examines the problems of doing research in this area.

In American colleges tutoring has endured ambiguous connotations. On the one hand, it is often considered as negative, associated with failing and needing a tutor. On the other hand, having one's own private tutor implies that one is wealthy and special. Although tutoring is a popular service on many college campuses, its stigma keeps some students who need help from using it.

Historically, tutoring has issued from and flourished in various academic arenas. Colleges have traditionally supported tutoring services for special groups like athletes, and the deaf. (For a history of peer tutoring, see Stahl & others, 1986). Student honor societies often provide free tutoring services and those who need more, and can afford it, hire their own tutors. Programs for veterans who returned to college under the G.I. Bill provided free tutoring services as have the federal and state funded programs for educationally and economically disadvantaged students since the 1960s. Almost all colleges in the United States today offer individual content tutoring and more than half offer group tutoring according to recent surveys. Many colleges provide tutoring to any student who needs it while others restrict free tutoring to students admitted under special programs and charge fees to others.

The literature on college tutoring suggests that programs are quite diverse. Tutoring programs vary in purpose and structure and tutor training programs are based on different philosophies.

Editor's note: See articles in this book for examples – e.g., Hancock & Gier on training tutors in counseling skills, Gourgey on metacognitive and affective training, and Condravy on an eclectic approach to tutor training. Schmelzer & others discuss training tutors to use study skills and learning theory.

Not only do tutoring philosophies differ, but tutor trainers use varied techniques as well. Some programs have developed their own videotaped training sessions while others use commercial tapes; some use campus residence and campus resources in training; turn evaluation into a developmental learning experience or employ interaction place maps as training devices. However, these examples may represent ideal programs since many tutoring programs lack the funds to offer tutors more than a brief orientation program and a set of guidelines. Unfortunately few research articles on tutoring specify the amount and kind of training or the experience of the tutors studied.

Experts do agree about what constitutes a successful tutoring program. At a minimum, tutors are recommended by a faculty member, carefully screened and selected on the basis of performance criteria and knowledge of the subject, given training before they start tutoring on how to work with underprepared students, given supportive supervision and evaluated regularly by their coordinators, instructors and their students (Maxwell, 1979). Of these factors, the most important seems to be tutoring training for it was the one programmatic factor found to differentiate between successful and unsuccessful developmental education programs in the EXXON Grant (Boylan and Bonham, 1992). That is, programs where more than 75% of their developmental students graduated had tutor training programs; those where fewer (less than 15%) developmental students graduated did not.

Editor's note: There are recent indications that tutor trainers are becoming professionalized. In 1989 a NADE committee developed standards and guidelines for college tutoring programs along the lines of the CAS Standards for Learning Assistance Centers (Materniak & Williams, 1987). Also the College Reading and Learning Association (CRLA) has set standards for certifying college tutor training programs to enable programs to award certificates to their tutors, and in 1993 a National Tutoring Association was organized based at East Stroudsburg University. Undoubtedly, these efforts will improve the quality of college tutoring.

The Unique Aspect of Peer Tutoring

Directors of developmental education programs seem to agree that a well-trained tutor can serve a vital role in helping fellow students attain their academic goals. Beginning students, particularly those who are educationally and economically disadvantaged, feel more relaxed with peers and relate to them in a different way than they do with professional helpers (Grant & Hoeber, 1978). Often programs encourage tutees to become tutors themselves in subsequent years and find them valuable assets.

"The technique that the basic skills 'student turned tutor' used to master the material may represent a mode of learning unknown to the basic skills faculty member but extremely valuable to the basic skills student in need of tutoring" (Snow as quoted in Grant & Hoeber, 1978, p. 29).

Additional support for the use of college peer tutors over more professional tutors comes from a study by W. C. Brown (1987) who found a significant relation between the degree of problem-solving tutees displayed in a college tutoring session and the college class standing of the tutors and tutees. The important variable was proximal class standing, not age. The closer the tutor and tutee were in college class, the more problem-solving the tutee engaged in during the tutoring session. Furthermore this study lends support to those who believe that tutor training is needed, for it found that tutors and tutees used different criteria to judge the success of a tutoring session. Tutors rated sessions that did not contain high problem solving behavior as better while tutees gave higher ratings to sessions with high problem solving behavior.

Again, in high problem-solving sessions, tutees demonstrate and structure more while tutors demonstrate and lecture less. Tutors seemed to be emulating the behavior of professors, expecting that lecturing and dominating was the appropriate way to tutor. Tutees disagreed.

There is a much larger research base in peer-tutoring in elementary schools than in college programs and the findings can be summarized as: (a) both tutor and student can improve in academic achievement and in attitudes toward class work; (b) the most effective tutoring programs are well planned and highly structured, where tutors are given instruction in basic skills and content; and (c) tutoring contacts are relatively short — a few weeks or months (U.S. Department of Education, 1986, p. 36). Older studies suggest that successful college peer tutoring programs share these same characteristics (see Maxwell, 1979, p. 101).

Does Tutoring Improve Grades?

Investigators often report that tutoring is an essential ingredient of a successful developmental skills course (Wepner, 1987; S. Roueche, 1983; Adams, 1971). However, because tutoring is only one part of the services for underprepared students, and because it can take many forms (individual, group, drop-in, class, as an adjunct to programmed material, etc.), it is often impossible to show that one-to-one tutoring, by itself, leads to higher grades for developmental students (Carman, 1975; Koehler, 1987; Vincent, 1983).

Some studies have found that students with rela-

tively high ability or those with more experience in college show grade gains as a result of tutoring. For example, Irwin (1980) studied 150 students who requested tutoring in statistics, and divided them into three groups based on their academic records. One-half of each group were randomly assigned to tutoring and the other half got no tutoring. Students at all levels of achievement who received tutoring earned significantly higher final grades in statistics than those receiving no tutoring. She replicated the study the following year and again found significant grade differences between students receiving tutoring and those who did not (Irwin, 1981).

It is also difficult to prove that students who use the most tutoring earn higher grades because the weakest students usually need more intensive tutoring. But at least one study suggests that if underprepared students receive enough tutoring, attend tutoring sessions regularly and begin tutoring early enough in the term, they will earn higher grades than students with equivalent ability who are not tutored. Watanabe and Maxwell, 1975 (as quoted in Maxwell, 1979, p. 99) reported that educationally disadvantaged students who attended tutoring sessions regularly at least once a week throughout the term, earned significantly higher grades in chemistry than those who received the same number of tutoring hours but whose attendance was irregular.

Typical of research showing that the amount of tutoring does not relate to grades is that reported by Irwin (1981) in an experiment where students were randomly assigned to tutoring and non-tutoring conditions. Irwin found no difference in achievement between tutored subjects who received different amounts of tutoring per week. In other words, those who had one to three tutoring sessions a week did as well as those who received four to six hours of tutoring per week. One can only speculate on the reasons for this. Perhaps those who came for tutoring more frequently were weaker students and/or became more dependent on the tutor.

Other studies suggest that the relation between tutoring and grades may be more complex and involve other variables. For instance, House and Wohlt (1989, 1990) in several studies with educationally disadvantaged freshmen found that there was a significant interaction effect between grades in a tutored course and the sex of the tutor and tutee. In other words, students who were tutored by a tutor of the same sex earned significantly higher grades than those tutored by a tutor of the opposite sex.

On the other hand, another type of program using peer leaders, Supplemental Instruction (SI) was designed to be an alternative for tutoring, and has consistently demonstrated that SI students improve their grades. In Supplementary Instruction a professional SI leader works with a course professor to identify the skills necessary to succeed in a course and trains student leaders to run SI sections where students develop new skills that they can directly apply to their course work. In a sense, this is a highly structured type of group tutoring. The SI model stresses voluntary attendance and the importance of choosing a high risk course — one in which many students make low grades. Studies have shown that students who attend SI sessions average grades about a half-grade higher in the parent course than matched comparison groups who do not attend SI groups (Blanc et al., 1983; Kenney, 1988; Martin & others, 1982).

Tutoring and GPA Improvement

Tabulating changes in GPA before and after tutoring and checking on retention rates for students who are tutored versus those who did not receive it are the most time-consuming, difficult and expensive measures to collect. Further, these measures may not be valid for the program if tutoring is given only to the weakest students. But because GPAs comprise hard data, "They provide more clout for the program if they are for it, but against it if they show no difference or are negative. Consequently, few tutorial programs use these measures and those that do usually base resultant decisions on an accumulation of data over an extended period of time" (Liberty, 1981, p. 71).

For this and other reasons, it is rare for studies to show that tutored students improve their GPAs. McGinty (1989) reported that students making marginal scores on the SAT who were tutored earned significantly higher GPAs than students not receiving tutoring. But for students with low SAT-Verbal scores, tutoring did not make a significant difference in earned GPAs. However, McGinty reported small but significant gains in the GPAs of students at all levels of ability who attended Supplemental Instruction sessions. This supports the findings of other studies of the effects of SI participation on students' GPAs (Blanc et al., 1983; Martin et al., 1982). That studies on differences in GPAs between tutored and untutored groups often do not reach significance (Carman, 1975; Koehler, 1987; Vincent, 1983) suggests that what the student learns in tutoring situations may not transfer to other courses, while the skills learned in Supplementary Instruction may indeed transfer.

Tutoring and College Persistence

Research does suggest that students who were tutored remained in college longer than those who were not tutored (Carman, 1975; Koehler, 1987; Vincent, 1983). Perhaps tutors encourage students to persist in their education by serving as mentors. Or it may be that students who seek tutoring are more highly motivated to stay in college than those who do not come in for tutoring.

Student Evaluations of Tutoring

Most programs administer questionnaires to tutees to evaluate their tutoring service. As mentioned above, researchers have difficulty demonstrating that tutoring improves grades, but when tutees are questioned, they often report that their course grade has improved. Woolley (1976) surveyed a random sample of students in California community colleges who had received more than ten hours of tutoring assistance, and found that 85% reported that their grades had improved. Also 57% said they would have dropped the course if they had not received tutoring.

How can one explain the discrepancy between the studies on the effects of tutoring on grades and the enthusiastic responses of grade improvement that students give on post-tutoring questionnaires? Certainly students appreciate the help they get from tutors and frequently give them high ratings. Results like those reported by Shaw (1989) where students gave tutors an overall average rating of 4.7 out of 5 are not uncommon.

Perhaps the unidirectional-rating scales that are used promote the "halo effect" or perhaps students who remain long enough to fill out questionnaires about their tutors are making more progress and are better satisfied than those who drop out of tutoring or perhaps students don't want to mark down a peer who is trying to help them. Whatever the reason, tutees generally report they are satisfied with the tutoring they received.

Or perhaps the problem lies in the questions we ask. I once analyzed questionnaires from twenty college tutoring programs and found a wide range of questions (Maxwell, 1991). Although the number of questions per questionnaire varied from 3 to 25, there were a total of 21 categories of questions. The spread must result from the differences between programs although most of the items from most of the surveys concerned tutor characteristics. The most frequently asked questions concerned the tutor's clarity of presentation, knowledge of the subject and rapport with the student and items like tutor's punctuality. Surprisingly few programs asked questions about how the tutee had changed as a result of tutoring or how much effort the tutee put into the tutoring sessions. Only 35% asked questions about whether the student's grade had improved and only 25% asked anything about improvement in study habits. Only 10 percent of the colleges asked any questions about the tutoring program itself (location, scheduling, noise level, receptionist, etc.). So there is room for improvement in the design of the measures used to evaluate tutoring, particularly in asking students about how they changed as a result of being tutored.

Why is there so little research on peer tutoring?

The dearth of research on college tutoring may result from the following constraints:

1. Tutor coordinators rarely have the research skills and almost never the incentive to undertake research projects with the exception of those individuals who are pursuing doctoral degrees.

2. Research and evaluation studies take money, time, and resources that are rarely available to the tutoring program.

3. Tutoring takes many forms — individual, group, in-class, etc., and is offered in many types of courses. This makes it difficult to find large enough numbers to find significant differences and to generalize about results. Furthermore, researchers rarely describe the amount of experience and training of the tutors.

4. Tutoring represents just one part of programs designed to help under-achieving students.

5. There is often staff resistance to attempting to measure the effects of complex, interpersonal interactions.

Perhaps this last factor explains why so many tutor directors are content to stop when they get good student evaluations and rest on their laurels. Mike Rose's (1989) description of his dilemma as a tutor coordinator echoes the feelings of many others in the field:

> *"Things that seemed sensible, and, in other contexts would never be challenged, now become questions to be solved by quantitative evaluation. The tutorial center was asked to demonstrate, with numbers, that getting individual guidance with material you don't understand is helpful, that having a chance to talk about what you're learning is beneficial. The drive to quantify became very strong, a reality unto itself, and what you couldn't represent with a ratio or a chart – what was messy and social and complex was simply harder to talk about and much harder to get acknowledged"* (Rose, 1989, p. 200).

Conclusion

Studies suggest that developmental students like peer-tutoring and feel that it helps their grades. However, the small number of studies on college tutoring provide no consistent evidence that high risk students who are tutored improve either their grades or their grade-point-averages. Students shown to earn higher grades after tutoring tend to be better prepared, have higher ability, and/or more experience in college. In other words, there is no evidence that tutoring helps the weakest students.

Research does suggest, however, that underprepared students who were tutored remained in college longer than comparable students who were not tutored.

As college tutoring programs adopt standards and develop better tutor training programs, there should be greater opportunities for researchers to reexamine the basic questions of whether, and under what conditions, and to what extent, individual tutoring can help underprepared students. A related question is whether some other method of using peers in course-related services, such as supplemental instruction, is more effective than tutoring in improving achievement. Current research suggests that methods other than tutoring might be more effective. Perhaps we have been focusing our efforts on the wrong group and should look instead at the effects of tutoring on the tutor. As W. McKeachie stated in his review of research in higher education in 1991, "If you want to succeed in college, pay to be a tutor, don't pay a tutor."

References

Adams, W. R. (1971). The use of tutors in the Santa Barbara City College reading laboratory. In F. Christ (Ed.), *Interdisciplinary aspects of reading instruction. Proceedings of the 4th annual conference of the Western College Reading Association.* Long Beach, CA: Western College Reading Association, 3.

Blanc, R. A., DeBuhr, L. E., & Martin, D. C. (1983). Breaking the attrition cycle: The effects of supplemental instruction on undergraduate performance and attrition. *Journal of Higher Education.* 54, 81-90.

Boylan, H., & Bonham, B. S. (1992). *Preliminary Results of the EXXON Grant.* Paper presented at the First National Research Conference in Developmental Education, Charlotte, NC.

Brown, B. E. (1981). A model university tutor training model. In F. L. Christ & M. Coda-Messerle (Eds.), *Staff Development for Learning Support Services New Directions for College Learning Assistance,* Number 4, San Francisco: Jossey-Bass, 75-85.

Brown, W. C. (1987). *Measuring tutoring effectiveness using interaction analysis research techniques.* Unpublished doctoral dissertation, University of California, Berkeley.

Carman, R. A. (1975). *A long-term study of developmental mathematics.* Santa Barbara, CA: Santa Barbara City College. (ERIC Document Reproduction Service. No ED 112 983).

Cohen, P. A., Kulik, J. A., & Kulik C. L. C. (1982, Summer). Educational outcomes of tutoring: A meta-analysis of findings. *American Educational Research Journal,* 19, 238-248.

Grant, M. K., & Hoeber, R. (1978). *Basic skills programs: Are they working?* AAHE-ERIC/Higher Education Research Report No. 1.

House, J. D., & Wohlt, V. (1989). The effect of student and tutor gender on achievement of academically underprepared students in mathematics and science. *Journal of Instructional Psychology,* 16(4), 192-198.

House, J. D., & Wohlt, V. (1991). Tutoring outcomes of academically underprepared adolescent minority students as a function of student and tutor characteristics. *Journal of Genetic Psychology,* 153(2), 225-227.

Irwin, D. E. (1980). Effects of peer tutoring on academic achievement and affective adjustment. In G. Enright (Ed.), *Proceedings of the Thirteenth Annual Conference of the Western College Reading Association,* XIII, 42-45.

Irwin, D. E. (1981). Final statistics grade as a function of the amount of tutoring received. In G. Enright (Ed.), *Proceedings of the Fourteenth Annual Conference of the Western College Reading and Learning Association,* (WCRLA), XIV, 55-62.

Kenney, P. A. (1988). *Effects of supplemental instruction on student performance in a college-level mathematics course.* Unpublished Doctoral Dissertation, University of Texas at Austin.

Koehler, L. (1987). *Helping students to succeed: A report on tutoring and attrition at the University of Cincinnati.* (ERIC Document Reproduction Service. No. ED 290 370).

Liberty, S. S. (1981). Learning by tutoring in two-year colleges. In F. L. Christ & M. Coda-Messerle (Eds.), *Staff Development for College Learning Support Systems, #4, New Directions for College Learning Assistance,* San Francisco: Jossey-Bass, 61-73.

Martin, D., Blanc R., & DeBuhr, L. (1982). Supplemental instruction: A model for increasing student performance and persistence. In L. Noel & R. Levitz (Eds.), *How to Succeed with Academically Underprepared Students.* Iowa City, Iowa: American College Testing Program National Center for Advancement of Educational Practices.

Maxwell, M. (1979). *Improving student learning skills: A comprehensive guide to successful practices and programs for increasing the performance of underprepared students.* San Francisco: Jossey Bass.

Maxwell, M. (1991). *Evaluating Academic Skill Programs: A Source Book.* Kensington, MD: MM Associated.

McGinty, D. (1989). *A path analysis of the effects of multiple programs on student retention.* Doctoral Dissertation, The University of Texas, Austin.

Rose, M. (1989). *Lives on the boundary: The struggles and achievements of America's underprepared.* New York: The Free Press.

Roueche, S. D. (1983). Elements of program success: Report of a national study. In J. E. Roueche (Ed.), *A new look at successful programs. New Directions for College Learning Assistance,* Jossey-Bass: San Francisco, 3-10.

Shaw, G. R. (1989). An experiential developmental training activity for tutors. *Journal of College Reading and Learning,* XII(1), 29-35.

Spann, M. G., Jr., & Vandett, N. M. (1982) Reality counseling: An approach to disciplined caring. *Journal of Developmental and Remedial Education,* 5 (3), 9.

Stahl, P. C., Stahl, N. A., & Hank, W. A. (1986). *Historical roots, rationales and applications of peer and cross-age tutoring: A basic primer for practitioners and researchers.* (ERIC Document Reproduction Service No. ED 256-244).

United States Department of Education (1986). *What works: Research about teaching and learning.* Washington, DC: U. S. Department of Education.

Vincent, V. C. (1983). *Impact of a college learning assistance center on the achievement and retention of disadvantaged students.* (ERIC Document Reproduction Service. No. ED 283 438).

Wepner, G. (1987). Evaluation of a postsecondary remedial mathematics program. *Journal of Developmental Education,* 11(1), 6-11.

Woolley, J. (1976, October). A summary of tutorial services offered by California community colleges. *About Tutoring,* 1-7.

(Editor's note: This article had a lengthy bibliography that we had to shorten due to space limitations. Readers who want to see the documentation for each statement should read the original article.)

Martha Maxwell founded the Student Learning Center at the University of California, Berkeley. Now retired, she writes and works occasionally as an educational consultant.

Further Readings On Tutoring

Beck, P., Hawkins, T., & Silver, M. (1978). Training and using peer tutors. *College English*, 40(4), 432-449.

Bruffee, K. A. (1993). *Collaborative Learning: Higher Education, Interdependence, and the Authority of Knowledge*. Baltimore, MD: Johns Hopkins University Press.

Gier, T., and Hancock, K. (Eds.) (1993). *Tutor Certification Registry and Resource Guide*. Chemeketa Community College, OR: College Reading & Learning Association.

Goldsby, J. *Peer tutoring in a basic writing: a tutor's journal*. (ERIC ED 250 717).

Goodsell, A., Maher, M., & Tinto, V. (1992). *Collaborative Learning: A Sourcebook for Higher Education*. University Park, PA: National Center on Postsecondary Teaching, Learning & Assessment (NCTLA), Pennsylvania State University.

Gourgey, A. F. (1992). Tutoring developmental mathematics: Overcoming anxiety and fostering independent learning. *Journal of Developmental Education*, 15(3), 10-14.

Frey, L., & Reigeluth, C. M. (1986). Instruction models for tutoring: A review. *Journal of Instructional Development*, 9(1), 2-7.

Hartman, H. (1990). Factors affecting the tutoring process. *Journal of Developmental Education*, 14(2), 2-7.

House, J. D., & Wohlt, V. (1990). The effect of tutoring program participation on the performance of academically underprepared college freshmen. *Journal of College Student Development*, 31, 365-370.

Hawkins, T. (1980). Intimacy and audience. *College English*. 42, 61-68. ERIC EJ 229 969.

Lichtenstein, G. (1983). Ethics of peer tutoring in writing. *Writing Center Journal*, 4(1), 29-34.

Maxwell, M. (1993). *Evaluating Academic Skills Programs: A Sourcebook*. (Chap. 4, Evaluating Tutoring Programs). Kensington, MD: MM Associates.

Maxwell, M. (Ed.) (1993). *When Tutor Meets Student, 2nd Edition*. Ann Arbor, MI: University of Michigan Press.

Maxwell, M. (1991, Fall). The effects of expectations, sex, and ethnicity on peer tutoring. *Journal of Developmental Education*, (15), 14-16. ERIC EJ 431 647.

MacDonald, R. B. (1991, Fall). An analysis of verbal interaction in college tutorials. *Journal of Developmental Education*, 15 (1), 2-12.

McDonald, R. B. (1993, Winter). Group tutoring techniques: From research to practice. *Journal of Developmental Education*. 17(2), 12-18.

Medway, F. J. (1991, Fall). A social psychological analysis of peer tutoring. *Journal of Developmental Education*, 15 (1), 20-26, 32.

Meyer, E., & Smith, L. (1987). *The Practical Tutor*. New York: Oxford University Press.

Rings, S., & Sheets, R. (1991). Student development and metacognition: Foundations for tutor training. *Journal of Developmental Education*, 15(1), 30-32. ERIC EJ 431 649.

Rizzolo, P. (1982). Peer tutors make good teachers. *Improving College and University Teaching*, 30, 115-119. ERIC ED 272 926.

Roueche, J. E., & Mink, O. G. (1982). Overcoming learned helplessness in community college students. *Journal of Developmental Education*, 5 (3), 2-5, 20.

Spann, M., & Vandett, N. (1982). Reality counseling: An approach to disciplined caring. *Journal of Developmental Education*, 5(3), 6-9, 32-33.

Part 4

Assessment

Morante argues for mandatory assessment and mandatory placement of students in basic skills courses.

Selecting Tests And Placing Students

By Edward A. Morante

(From the *Journal of Developmental Education*, (Winter 1989), 13(2), 1-6. Reprinted by permission of Edward A. Morante and the *Journal of Developmental Education*, Appalachian State University, Boone, NC 28608.)

Abstract: The need for testing and placement of incoming college students is argued and the premise that students need access to all information regarding their personal attributes and institutional options before they can exercise their "right to fail" is presented. Recommendations for offering students the "right to succeed" are discussed including specific factors for selecting appropriate placement tests and making placement decisions.

> Testing should be mandatory because too many students, especially those who most need assistance will avoid it wherever possible.

Thousands of students enter college in the United States every year underprepared to handle college-level coursework (Lederman, Ribaudo, & Ryzewic, 1985). Between a third and half of all entering students do not possess the basic skills proficiencies of reading, writing, or mathematics needed to perform successfully in college (Abraham, 1987; Grable, 1988; Plisko & Stern, 1985). While there has been much focus on the causes of this phenomenon, there has also been very little improvement, if any, in the depth and breadth of this national problem. Further, there is overwhelming evidence to support the conclusion that successful completion of high school courses or the reception of a

diploma does not necessarily mean proficiency in basic skills (New Jersey Basic Skills Council, 1989). While someday this may be reversed, there is currently no end in sight. Indeed, since colleges will always have entering students who did not complete or perform successfully in high school, there will always be a need for developmental education.

A comprehensive developmental education program must include mandatory assessment (placement testing is a part of this) and mandatory placement (Baker & Thompson, 1981; Rounds & Anderson, 1985). "Mandatory" is used deliberately in both aspects: testing and placement. Testing is needed because, frankly, other information is not adequate; other data can be helpful when used in conjunction with appropriate testing, but this information is frequently unreliable, insufficient, or nonexistent. The testing should be mandatory because too many students, especially those who most need assistance, will avoid assessment wherever possible (Maxwell, 1979; Friedlander, 1986).

> It borders on the unethical to know that a student lacks basic skills but is still allowed to enroll in college courses requiring that skill.

Placement must be mandatory since it borders on the unethical to know that a student lacks basic skills but is still allowed to enroll in college courses requiring that skill. Why shouldn't a college require a mandatory placement policy? Do we allow students to enroll in calculus without determining if the student has the prerequisite math skills? What about enrolling in an advanced foreign language course? Or any upper level course? The prerequisite system common to virtually every campus is designed to prevent this mismatch. Consequently why should we allow students who can't read to take an English course? Or a psychology course? Is reading not a requirement for most college courses? What college courses do not require reading?

Whether or not a college has a comprehensive developmental education program, or whether testing or placement is mandatory, frequently a decision needs to be made about selecting a placement test. This article will focus on the process and the factors involved both in selecting a placement test and in placing students. Before describing some concrete suggestions, however, it is important to realize that the attitudes of faculty and staff and the resulting messages sent to students, direct or implied, will likely play a significant role in the success of any developmental education program including its testing and placement components (Roueche & Snow, 1977).

Attitudes and Messages

The "right to fail" is a pernicious concept too often prevalent in higher education. Essentially, proponents of this philosophy argue that, as adults, students have the freedom to choose courses even if there is a low probability of succeeding in these courses. This philosophy of the right to fail is based on the concept of freedom and a process of decision-making. But freedom and decision-making are both based on knowledge of the self (strengths and weaknesses), as well as the options, the risks, and the consequences of making a decision. In making a good decision — a truly free decision — an entering student needs to know what

his/her strengths and weaknesses are as well as interests and goals, the courses available at the college, and the standards and requirements of the institution. Without an appropriate understanding of these factors, decision making is a guessing game and little true freedom is present. Very few students know these factors and they are rarely learned by students in a short time period.

Instead of encouraging failure, we need a philosophy that encourages a "right to succeed": this is defined as "a reasonable chance of achieving at a quality level." The right to succeed begins with an approach that emphasizes caring and helping since that is what assessment (placement testing) ought to be. A message like the following needs to be communicated to all entering students: "We care about you and we want to help you to succeed at our college. We will begin by assessing your strengths and weaknesses and then by designing a series of courses that best suits your needs. In that way we help to match you and the curriculum and increase your chances to learn and to succeed." This message can be stated in various ways and repeated at key times. The biggest obstacle to a successful program of mandatory placement testing is frequently the attitude of the faculty and staff involved in the program. Students, especially entering students, will follow the lead of the people they make contact with at the college.

A second major obstacle to developmental education, including testing and placement, is the fear that "students won't come to our college if we enact such policies." The evidence is quite apparent that quality attracts students. A college without a comprehensive developmental education program will lower standards by eliminating some topics and watering down other topics and by marking on the curve so that grades are awarded on the basis of the norm of the group (to a greater or lesser extent determined by the proficiency of the entering students) rather than standards set by the faculty and the institution. Mandatory testing and placement helps institutions to maintain (and even raise) standards by identifying and placing students in courses designed to teach them the skills they need so that the standards of college courses do not need to be lowered. This type of policy will tend to attract students, not turn them away; it will also help in retaining students.

A corollary to the "no one will come" theory is that testing, placement, and developmental education are burdensome to the students in terms of time and money. So is teaching the students! Why don't we eliminate the burdens by simply awarding the degree? Testing, placement, and developmental education do take extra time and cost extra money, but the students need them for a quality education. What are the alternatives? Failing? Achieving a meaningless degree? Forcing faculty members to teach underprepared students in college-level courses? What happens to prepared students in that course as the instructor is forced to devote time to underprepared students of lower quality? What about the reputation of the institution which passes these students on or becomes a revolving door? Or the community or society when these students either don't graduate or the fraud is found out by a degree that, like the high school diploma, is not dependable in claiming proficiency and knowledge?

> What happens to prepared students in a course where the instructor is forced to devote time to underprepared students or to lower quality?

Obviously, these arguments support developmental education, not merely testing and placement. But a developmental education program cannot be either comprehensive or successful without beginning with

an assessment of all students and mandatory placement for those who need it into appropriate basic skills courses.

Factors in Selecting a Placement Test

Figure 1 (pg. 125-126) provides an overview of the principal factors in selecting a placement test. No attempt is made here to discuss other areas that may be assessed beyond reading, writing, and mathematics such as study skills, interests, or values. It may be quite appropriate to assess these areas, but they are not considered part of a placement test.

While the order of factors in Figure 1 should not be construed as indicating an order of priority, the first factor, "Content," must be considered the most important. If a test does not include an appropriate sampling of reading, writing, and math at an appropriate level of difficulty, the remaining factors are insufficient to justify the purchase or use of the test.

Making Placement Decisions

A comprehensive developmental education program should have multi-level basic skills courses. Most colleges have entering students who will need more than one quarter or semester to become prepared for college-level proficiency (Keimig, 1983). After the students have been tested with a placement test (Reminder: messages and attitudes are crucial) but before enrolling them in courses, decisions must be made about which courses and which levels of courses are best suited to meet the needs of each student within the available resources of the college.

Here a counseling/advising system is most helpful with information collected and assembled for each entering student (Roueche & Snow, 1977). Ideally, given sufficient time and resources, students would meet with a counselor/advisor on an individual basis, review appropriate facts, and make decisions about which courses and levels of courses to take. The placement process can also be carried out in small groups or completely by use of a computer. One scenario of this latter method would be to test the students, make decisions about their placement, and then notify them while suggesting or even encouraging each student to call in or visit a counselor/advisor to discuss the placement decisions. This procedure would significantly decrease the workload while focusing on those students who most need assistance. The number of possible models of placement is considerable. Options range from including testing and placement on the same day to a completely separate operation. In addition, individual counseling/advising can be offered to each student or these services can be provided on a voluntary basis to those who feel the need. Each college must make these decisions on the basis of philosophy and resources.

Whatever is decided, however, all colleges will need to: (1) test all entering students; (2) collect and complete information on each student; (3) analyze these multiple variables; and (4) make a decision about the placement of each student.

Before reviewing the multiple student factors that should be used in making placement decisions, a series of "cut ranges" should be set up. The term "cut ranges" is used instead of "cut scores" because "ranges" implies a confidence interval of scores which is much more realistic than a dichotomous yes-or-no decision implied by a single score. In other words, neither the information about students nor test scores are perfect. What is needed is a system that systematically takes into account multiple variables and increases the probability of making accurate decisions. Thus, two warnings must be strongly stated:

1. Never use one score on one test as the sole factor in making placement decisions (see Fig. 2); and
2. Never set up dichotomous cut-scores in making placement decisions.

The following model would be appropriate using any test (including a locally-developed test) with a two-tiered developmental education course system. Writing is used as an example; any area would be appropriate. The scores used are also illustrative only; real scores can be substituted accordingly.

In this model, the placement test scores (preferably both an essay and a multiple-choice writing component of a placement test) are used most heavily in those areas outside the grey areas. The "other information" becomes especially important in making placement decisions when the test scores fall in the grey areas.

Model

Test Score	Course
0-10	English 90: Remedial Writing
11-15	Grey area
16-25	English 95: Developmental Writing
26-30	Grey area
31+	English 101: College Composition

Figure 1
Criteria for Selecting a Placement Test

Variable	Explanation
1. Content	Most critical variable, test or test battery should include reading, writing, and mathematics (with other areas possible according to the needs of individual programs or institutions).
a. Reading	Reading should be realistic and holistic, topics or passages should cover broad range of subject areas, comprehension, understanding, and inferential reasoning are essential, not literal translations; vocabulary should be in context, standards should be set no lower than equivalent of eleventh grade.
b. Writing	Use of both an essay and a multiple-choice section are strongly recommended; essay should be expository requiring assessment of logic and organization (taking a position and defending it with examples) as well as mechanics of English (syntax, grammar, punctuation, capitalization, and spelling); multiple choice section should assess students' understanding of English, preferably in context, rather than merely identification of mechanics in isolation; standards should be set no lower than equivalent of eleventh grade).
c. Mathematics	Arithmetic (computation) and elementary algebra are essential; higher levels are appropriate; arithmetic should include both problem solving and word problems using fractions, decimals, and percents; estimation problems are essential for measuring understanding of concepts; algebra should include both problems and word problems including at least linear equations involving number, fractional, and literal components, assessment of vocabulary is not important; scores should be separate for arithmetic, algebra, and other math areas.
2. Criterion-Referenced	Levels of difficulty and proficiency should be established by faculty judgments of what students should know, not by norm-reference procedures based on what skills students bring at entry.
3. Discrimination	Defined as the ability to accurately differentiate students along a continuum of proficiency, essential in making decisions on need for remediation/developmental education and within levels of basic skills courses; a placement test should discriminate best among students with low or poor proficiencies.
4. "Speededness"	A good placement test is a power test where speed should not be an important factor (time limits are appropriate for administrative purposes); general rules of thumb: 100% of the students complete at least 75% of the items and 90% of the students attempt all of the items.
5. Reliability	Defined as the consistency of a score or the likelihood that a student will achieve the same score if retested (assuming no treatment intervention). Test-retest and split-half reliability are most commonly used methods; reliability coefficients should be at least .90; Kuder-Richardson -20 (KR-20); reliability coefficients are inflated by length of test and speededness.

6. Validity	Defined as measuring what a test is supposed to measure. Includes: content validity (the test includes the material agreed to by faculty); concurrent validity (relationship to other similar tests); and predictive validity (how well a test predicts or is correlated with some criterion, e.g., course grades). Content validity is by far the most important validity of the appropriateness of a placement test. The predictive validity of placement tests are especially difficult to judge because, if a developmental or remedial course is functioning well, correlations between placement test scores and grades should approach zero.
7. Guessing	In all multiple choice tests and most other tests, guessing is an error factor that throws off the accuracy of the placement decision. Guessing only inflates scores and some tests contain a factor that lowers scores accordingly. Efforts should be made to decrease random guessing as much as possible by increasing choice options (four or five are considerably better than two; true-false choice tests, for example, have a 50% error factor) and by directing students accordingly.
8. Alternate Forms	All placement tests should have an alternate, equivalent form both for retesting when necessary and for post-testing.
9. Cost	The cost of a test, including materials, administration, and scoring must be considered. Placement tests should be able to be scored both by machine and by hand.

Factors Important in Making Placement Decisions

Figure 2 (pages 127-128) provides a listing, in order of decreasing importance, of the factors that are important in making placement decisions about each student. Lower order factors add to the decision making process; they do not override the higher order factors. For example, if a student clearly needs a basic skills course on the basis of a placement test, achieving a "B" in a high school course would not overrule the test score. But if the same student fell into the "grey" on the test, the high school grade could help in determining where the student should be placed: above or below the grey area.

Retesting should rarely be used and is usually implemented only when the other information is not sufficient or is too conflicting to make a decision. When retesting is used, the additional data should become part of the cumulative information already existing for this student. In no case shall the new test be used as the sole criterion for making a decision. There is no guarantee that the retest results are more accurate than the initial placement test results. Indeed, the retest may be less accurate, especially in those circumstances where either in-class homemade tests are administered or when most of the retesting occurs with those students most likely to need developmental education (a phenomenon called "regression toward the mean"), where the least proficient students will have a tendency to improve simply by being retested.

Administrative Decisions

Much of this article has focused on decisions relating directly to students. Decisions from a programmatic or institutional perspective are also needed. In this regard, the following steps are suggested in creating a systematic placement process for entering students:

1. Estimate the number of sections needed for each level of each basic skill area based on prior experience (including any changes in curriculum requirements, standards, or cut ranges).

2. Set up course schedules so that different levels of developmental courses and college courses are offered at the same time to allow flexibility in students' schedule changes.

3. Allow flexibility with faculty and with scheduling to allow for changes in original estimates of the number of sections for each level based on actual student placements.

4. Develop a "bear-proof" registration system that "flags" or prevents students from dropping or shifting developmental courses without signed approval of developmental education coordinator or equivalent.

5. Review each student's test performance and background individually for each basic skill area and make placement decisions using the factors in Figure 2 without regard to the numbers of sections available. Do not let schedules dominate educational decisions.

6. Make placement decisions for all or nearly all entering students; then adjust the number and kinds of courses offered on the basis of these placement decisions. Leave a significant number of seats open when possible for late registrants. Assign only those students with inconclusive or contradictory placement data according to available seats.

Figure 2
Factors Important in Making Placement Decisions

1. Placement test scores — Consider both actual scores and consistency of scores. Scores falling well above or well below the cut-score range have higher probability of accuracy and should be weighed more heavily than scores falling in the "grey area." Similarly, scores which demonstrate a consistent pattern (e.g., low essay score and low multiple-choice writing score) are probably more accurate than conflicting patterns.

2. Other available tests — These include ACT or SAT scores and any other tests, including in-class information, tests and diagnostic tests, which have been administered. Look for consistency in patterns of test scores and include these scores in the decision-making process.

3. High school background — School attended, number and kinds of courses taken, grades, and high school rank can all be helpful factors. Caution must be emphasized, however, as there is little consistency in data across different schools and even courses within the same school. Important: Successful completion of high school courses (good grades) does not necessarily mean proficiency in basic skills.

4. Other background data — Consider such factors as years since high school, jobs and work activities, financial aid situation, extracurricular activities, and so on. In general, the more personal life difficulties and responsibilities the greater the probability that a lightened course load and/or developmental education is needed.

5. Age	Older students tend to be more fearful, more cautious, and more motivated. Everything else being equal, older students probably have a better chance for success in college courses.
6. Student opinion	Students' self choice can help in making a placement decision only when other factors are confusing, contradictory, or inconclusive. Many students, especially recent high school graduates, tend to overestimate their proficiencies.
7. Additional testing	This can occasionally help to clarify conflicting criteria. Care must be taken to use retest results within the context of the other data. Diagnostic testing should be used only to identify specific skills area, not to contradict placement decisions.

Conclusion

Developmental education is an essential ingredient in higher education. Developmental education links the presenting proficiencies of many entering students with the need for high standards of quality. At the same time, it offers individual attention and a focus on the teaching/learning process. Developmental education is a proven success factor in retention (New Jersey Basic Skills Council, 1989).

Placement testing and decision making are critical components of developmental education. When carried out appropriately, it is a counseling/advising model that reflects the tone of the institution. With careful planning and attention to the needs of both students and the institution, placement testing and decision making set the stage for increasing the likelihood of success for students, for faculty, and for the institution.

References

Abraham, A. A., Jr. (1987). *A report on college level remedial/developmental programs in SREB states*. Atlanta, GA: Southern Regional Education Board.

Baker, G. A. III, & Thompson, T.T. (1981). Coping with complexity: A challenge for open-door colleges. *Community College Frontiers*, 9, 29-33.

Friedlander, J. (1986). Why students drop courses. *ERIC Junior College Resource Review*. Los Angeles, CA:UCLA.

Grable, J. R. (1988). Remedial education in Texas two-year colleges. *Journal of Developmental Education*, 12(2), 2-5.

Keimig, R. T. (1983). *Raising academic standards: A guide to learning improvement*. (ASHE-ERIC/Higher Education Research Rep. 4). Washington, DC: Association for the Study of Higher Education.

Lederman, M. J., Ribaudo, M., & Ryzewic, S. R. (1985). Basic skills of entering freshmen: A national survey of policies and perceptions. *Journal of Developmental Education*, 9(1), 10-13.

Maxwell, M. (1979). *Improving student learning skills*. San Francisco: Jossey-Bass.

New Jersey Basic Skills Council. (1989). *Results of the New Jersey college basic skills placement testing*, Fall, 1988. Trenton, NJ: New Jersey Department of Higher Education.

Plisko, V. W., & Stern, J. (1985). *The condition of education: A statistical report*. Washington, DC: National Center for Education Statistics.

Roueche, J. E., & Snow, J. J. (1977). *Overcoming learning problems*. San Francisco: Jossey-Bass.

Rounds, J. C., & Anderson, D. (1985). *Placement in remedial college classes: Required vs recommended*. Community College Review, 13(1), 20-27.

Simpson and Nist describe how a comprehansive testing program is integrated into their developmental reading courses.

Toward Defining A Comprehensive Assessment Model For College Reading

By Michele L. Simpson and Sherrie L. Nist

(From the *Journal of Reading* (1992), 35, 452-458. Reprinted by permission of the *Journal of Reading* and Michelle L. Simpson and Sherrie L. Nist.)

Although literacy assessment is currently under scrutiny and reconceptualization in U.S. public schools, college programs have been slow or reluctant to examine traditional assessment methods. Many developmental programs rely exclusively on one standardized reading test not only to place and diagnose incoming students but also to evaluate program effectiveness (Wood, 1989). In fact, assessment at the postsecondary level is often viewed only as an accountability issue — a means to an end — with the end being an improved score on a standardized test. Whether it is a percentile rank, a Degrees of Reading Power unit, or a cut-off score on a state test, these scores all too often determine how many students will be in the program, in what materials they will be placed, and how long they will remain. Scores also can indicate the success or failure of college reading programs and thus affect funding.

To remedy the situation, some reading professionals search for a "better" standardized test, but unfortunately the solution is not that simple. Rather than simply changing tests or viewing assessment merely as an accountability issue, college reading programs need to conceptualize a comprehensive model of assessment that reflects current reading research and theory, is appropriate to the philosophy and goals of their program, and is unique to the characteristics of their students. Obviously, this task is not easy.

The purpose of this article, then, is to share our perspectives on college reading assessment through an examination of characteristics of a comprehensive assessment model and then to discuss how we have designed an assessment program unique to our university and students.

An Operational Definition

First, however, it is important to operationalize what we mean by the assessment. Cross and Paris (1987) discuss three major purposes for reading assessment, sorting, diagnosing, and evaluating.

1. Reading tests that **sort students** do so by arranging them on a continuum from highest to lowest scores. Such tests are usually formal. Sorting is used to predict academic success or to indicate mastery of an instructional program and is usually part of a large-scale educational assessment. An example of sorting at the postsecondary level would be using a combination of Scholastic Achievement Test (SAT) or American College Test (ACT) scores and high school level grade point averages to determine which students should be screened for a college reading program.

2. The second purpose of assessment, **diagnosing individuals' reading problems**, calls for

gathering information about a particular student's strategies and processes. The diagnostic findings should be used to make informed decisions about individuals, not decisions about group changes. These diagnostic tests generally focus on a narrow range of reading skills or strategies, and may be informal. Self-report measures, such as the Learning and Study Strategies Inventory (LASSI), are common as are tests like the Self Concept of Academic Ability that target affective characteristics.

3. The final purpose of assessment, **evaluating**, calls for determining whether a particular experimental treatment or program has had an effect on dependent variables such as persistence in college or improved reading performance. Program evaluations typically use standardized or formal tests that are specifically designed to measure the effects of institutional intervention on groups of students. Student improvement is often determined by formal tests such as the Nelson-Denny, the Degrees of Reading Power, or the Descriptive Test of Language Skills and by institutionally designed tests, any of which might be given at the beginning of the term and again at the end. Programmatic, instructional, or textbook changes are often made as a result of evaluations.

> A comprehensive model of assessment, then, includes a variety of formal and informal instruments that sort, diagnose and evaluate.

Characteristics of a Comprehensive Model of Assessment

It is obvious that assessment is multidimensional. The information gleaned should be viewed as an integral part of the instructional process that informs and empowers students and instructors.

Campione and Brown (1985) refer to this type of assessment as dynamic, and others label it interactive. As instructors interact with students and texts and model strategic reading processes, they look for patterns in how students construct meaning. This procedure, in turn, informs and shapes decisions about materials, tasks, pacing, and feedback for future lessons.

Such a recursive model of instruction and assessment can also empower students so that they become informed about and are responsible for their own learning. When all pieces of the assessment puzzle are in place and operating effectively, students learn how to capitalize on their strengths and improve their weaknesses, instructors are well informed about students' progress and institutions can make informed decisions about programmatic issues.

More specifically, we believe from our own experiences and a review of the literature that a comprehensive model of assessment has the following characteristics:

1. A match exists between the philosophical base, the short- and long-term goals of the reading program, and the assessment instruments used. Without this match, program vitality is seriously compromised.

2. Sorting, diagnosing, and evaluating occur across tasks and texts since mastery of a strategy is a relative condition. Texts especially those used for diagnosis are lengthy, varied (theoretical versus factual, low prior knowledge versus high prior knowledge), and representative of the college texts students encounter (considerate as well as inconsiderate).

3. Multiple cutting scores and multiple variables are used for sorting and diagnosis, rather than a singular test or score (Morante, 1989).

4. Assessment instruments measure various types of processing. Wixson and Peters (1987) suggest assessing students' processing at the intersentence, text, and beyond text levels. At the college level, assessing students' processing across texts is also important — knowing if students can modify their processing strategies according to content area and task is critical.

5. Diagnosis and evaluation are ongoing and inextricably involved with the recursive instructional phase. The information gained from diagnosis and evaluation informs instructors about strengths and needs as students move toward strategy mastery.

6. Students are involved in their own diagnosis as well as in the evaluation of whether they accomplished short- and long-term programmatic goals.

7. Testing for testing's sake is avoided. Assessment measures provide pertinent and practical information that is used to improve instruction and inform students.

It is difficult, perhaps impossible, for one reading program to possess all of these characteristics. However, the difficulty of achieving perfection should not deter college reading professionals from incorporating as many of these characteristics as possible into their assessment program. What follows is a description of our still evolving assessment model. As you will note, it is neither perfect nor complete. It does, however, incorporate many of the characteristics mentioned above.

Toward a Comprehensive Assessment Model

The assessment program described here sorts all university freshmen and diagnoses and evaluates those identified as at risk using a variety of formal and informal measures. These measures were selected to reflect the short- and long-term goals of the program. Because this assessment model is goal-driven, it is important first to discuss the nature of our college reading course.

The course could best be described as process-based in that we assume that reading is a constructive process and that meaning emerges from interactions among tests, tasks, and students (Jenkins, 1979). As instructors, our short-term goal is to help students become strategic readers and active independent learners. The long-term goal is to help students succeed in college.

Rather than isolating discrete reading skills or objectives to be mastered, we describe the characteristics of strategic readers and directly teach strategies that lead to the development of these characteristics.

We generally use longer pieces of text (e.g., an entire text chapter) and teach strategies that focus on cognitive and metacognitive processes such as encoding, organizing, monitoring, planning, and evaluating. Hence, our assessment procedures not only measure these processes, but also determine whether or not students have mastered them. To make this determination, we diagnose, and evaluate students using a variety of measures.

Sorting

When students apply to our university, their SAT scores and high school grade point averages identify whether they need a college reading class. These two pieces of information together are used in a regression equation that predicts grade point average at the end of their first year. Those identified as not needing a reading course enroll in regular courses; those needing intervention are further sorted to determine which level of reading course is most appropriate.

To make this determination we first administer a state-mandated test similar to traditional reading tests. Students read a series of short passages and answer multiple choice questions over vocabulary, main ideas, details, tone, and mood. Because this particular test supplies little information about process, except at the sentence and intersentence levels, and because we believe in the importance of using multiple measures, students are further sorted with two informal measures developed specifically for our purposes and population.

Second, students take a more informal sorting measure, an excerpt taken from a college level psychology textbook, to simulate a task that they will encounter frequently during their first two years of college. They read and study the 2,500-word excerpt in preparation for an objective test. Following reading and studying, they hand in the excerpt and any study materials (e.g., notes) and answer 15 text explicit and implicit multiple choice questions.

Scores on the extended reading yield information about students' abilities to process college level material. With additions beyond our format, instructors can gather even more information about individuals. For example, students could answer essay questions as well as objective items. These essays could be scored holistically or by using a template with assigned points.

Because of time constraints and the number of students involved at this stage of our sorting process (over 400), we eliminated the essay portion. However, programs might seriously consider including essay writing as it provides considerable insights into students' constructive processes that objective tests cannot.

Thus, in order to place students as accurately as possible we use the multiple pieces of data that we have gathered. Using SAT scores, state-mandated test scores, and raw scores on the extended psychology excerpt, we sort the new students into three groups. Those who score at or above a predetermined cutting score on all three measures are exempted from taking any reading course. Those who score at or above the cutting score on two of the three measures are placed in the developmental level reading course. Those scoring below cutting scores on two of the three measures are placed in the lower level course.

All students have been sorted prior to the first day of class. As they progress through the term, they enter the second phase of assessment, diagnosis.

Diagnosing

As mentioned earlier, many college reading programs use formal, standardized measures for student diagnosis. But some of these tests have not been designed for diagnostic purposes, so they provide only a limited sample of student outcomes (Wood, 1989). Diagnosis should be an ongoing process directly related to instruction. Moreover, we believe that diagnosis should evolve into a responsibility between students and instructor.

Over time we have depended on a wide variety of informal diagnostic measures, all of which are tied to the goals of the reading courses. Some of these measures rely on student self-report. Although self-report has some limitations (i.e., Alexander & Judy, 1988; Baker, 1982; Garner & Alexander, 1982), we find the information gained extremely useful.

One measure used at the beginning of the course is the Learning and Study Strategies Inventory (LASSI) by Weinstein, Palmer, & Schulte. The LASSI provides both students and instructors with valuable information about perceived strengths and weaknesses in both affective and cognitive domains and in skills such as time management, information processing, and self-testing.

Once students have completed the LASSI profile, they write a brief journal entry answering the following questions:

1. According to the LASSI, what are your areas of strength? Do the results make sense with what you know about yourself. Explain. Any surprises? Explain.
2. According to the LASSI, on what areas do you need to focus this quarter (the low scores)? Do the results make sense with what you know about yourself? Explain. Any surprises? Explain.
3. Using the information from the LASSI and what you know yourself as a reader and learner, what are your goals for this quarter?

Students hand in the LASSI profile and journal entry, which are saved for discussion in later conferences. In addition to providing meaningful discussion points for student conferences, these profiles and entries serve several other vital instructional purposes.

First, we compile a list of students who score low on test anxiety (indicating high anxiety) and refer them for special assistance. Second, we use the profiles as each strategy is introduced during the term. For example, when textbook marking is introduced, we ask students who score low on the information processing scale to pay particular attention to and practice this strategy since it will improve their ability to read and process textbook information elaboratively.

Finally, at the end of the term, we return these journal entries to students so they can write their final self-evaluation entry, an evaluation measure we will describe later.

Perhaps, the greatest amount of diagnostic information gathered about students, however, comes from their practice endeavors. After we introduce a strategy and provide modeling and examples, students practice the strategy on a full length content area chapter. For example, as students learn to mark text by noting key points in the margin, they complete a part of the chapter and receive extensive feedback before finishing the remainder of their chapter annotations.

This feedback takes two forms. First, we mark any key information missed and reword any misstatements of ideas. Second, we provide more global feedback in the form of a checklist. (For a detailed explanation of both notation procedure and the checklist see Simpson & Nist, 1990.) From the checklist students learn what they did correctly and what needs revising before they prepare for the exam over the chapter. More importantly, the checklist informs instructors about the problems students are having as they construct meaning from the text and represent that meaning in their annotations. The checklist reveals which students are attempting to memorize the text as opposed to paraphrasing, or which students are focusing on details to the exclusion of superordinate ideas.

Using diagnostic information such as this, we design the next day's lesson. This cycle is repeated for each strategy taught and for each text chapter read and studied.

Gradually, we encourage students to take the responsibility of diagnosis on themselves. During class they meet with partners or in small groups to examine one another's strategies. In addition, they learn to diagnose errors on using PLAE, a test evaluation strategy (Nist & Simpson, 1989).

As part of the PLAE diagnosis, students answer the following questions:

1. Was the test what I expected? Why or why not?

2. Did I follow my plan for studying? If not, what events or situations interfered with carrying out the plan? Explain.

3. How many hours did I study? Were those hours distributed or massed?

4. Did I miss questions because I didn't know or recognize information? If so, where did the information come from? Lectures? Textbooks?

5. Was there a pattern to my errors? What was the pattern?

6. Did I select the most appropriate study strategies for this test? If not, which strategies would be more appropriate next time? List.

By the end of the term, many students become proficient in determining the strategies that work best for them in a particular learning situation. Those who struggle with self-diagnosis may find conferences helpful for examining the strategies they have created and going over the test. Not only is the conference useful in helping students diagnose their efforts objectively, but it also provides instructors with additional diagnostic information to help those still having difficulty.

The process of ongoing diagnosis, consisting almost totally of informal measures, is perhaps the most important aspect of our assessment model. Because we continuously monitor student change and adaptation to strategies, we can modify instruction to meet student needs. But our model is still incomplete. The final step is to determine how well the diagnosing worked by once again examining the group as a whole to see how successful they have been in applying the strategies in actual college learning situations.

Figure 1

Questions for the final self-evaluation journal entry:

1. What areas on the LASSI do you feel you have improved upon? Why do you feel this way? What strategies or ideas have helped you see this improvement?

2. What areas on the LASSI do you feel you have remained the same? Why? What could you do to improve them?

3. What have you learned since September about college level tasks?

4. How have your textbook reading and exam preparation methods changed since September? Compare your high school experiences to these past ten weeks.

5. How have your reading fluency, flexibility, and rate changed since September? (Check your text for the meanings of these words if you have forgotten them.)

6. How has your reading, writing, listening, and speaking vocabulary changed since September?

7. How have your time management skills improved since September? If no change has occurred, why?

8. Imagine that a younger brother/sister or friend has asked you about college. What would you tell them that you have learned in these past ten weeks that you wished you had learned in high school?

Note: **The Learning and Study Skills Inventory** (LASSI) is a self-report measure revealing perceived strengths and weaknesses in both affective and cognitive domains and in skills such as time management, information processing and self-testing.

Evaluating

Data are collected in the evaluating stage to examine both short- and long-term program goals. Every student enrolled in our program must retake the mandated reading test again at the end of the term. We administer this test merely to comply with the rules since it does not provide us with much evaluative information about whether students have become strategic learners. Consequently, we have developed several evaluation measures that are more reflective of our programmatic goals.

Perhaps the most useful short-term evaluative information comes from students' performance on the final exam given in the reading course. In some ways the kind of processing required to do well on the final exam is similar to but more complex than that which is needed on the extended text excerpt used in the sorting stage.

For example, the final exam in the upper level course focuses on information about the U.S. in the 1960s. Students read a history chapter that covers Kennedy's and Johnson's presidential administrations as well as a *Newsweek* article about Vietnam. In addition, they listen to a lecture on the Vietnam War and see a film about civil rights. Hence, students have to process a variety of texts, a more demanding task than the extended reading that covers only one piece of text.

Over time we have developed a final exam that we believe is a fair representation of tasks students will face once they enroll in regular classes. Students scoring a C or above appear to be strategic learners ready for those challenges in core college courses such as psychology, history, and sociology.

Students themselves are involved in the evaluation process in two different ways. At the end of the course, they are required to complete a final self-evaluation journal entry. They answer eight questions focusing on strategies and processes taught in the course (see Figure 1 for the questions). They refer to their LASSI profiles from the beginning of the term and to their practice endeavors to determine possible personal changes.

Marty's answers to four of the eight questions can be seen in Figure 2. His initial scores indicated that he needed work on almost all of the LASSI subscales, but, in particular, he needed to concentrate on Attitude, Motivation, Test Anxiety, and Self-Testing. Note that he evaluated himself as improving in most areas except for test anxiety.

The second way students become involved in the evaluation process is through responding to a questionnaire. After students have completed two quarters of the university's regular core courses, we often send them a questionnaire asking them to describe the strategies they are using, the difficulties they are having, and the strategies from the reading course that they find most and least useful. The return rate is never high, but we still receive some insightful data.

Figure 2

Marty's answers to four questions from final self-evaluation journal entry:

1. What areas on the LASSI do you feel you have improved upon? Why do you feel this way? What strategies or ideas have helped you see this improvement?

Marty's reply: *The last ten weeks have just seemed to speed by. I just reviewed my first journal entry and it seems like I wrote it a couple of weeks ago. I think I have improved in many areas that were covered by the LASSI. My attitude, motivation and time management have all improved. I believe that I now select main ideas better thanks to the repeated annotation of chapters. And my use of support techniques and test strategies have improved due to the annotations and the recitation strategies that we learned.*

2. What areas on the LASSI do you feel remained the same? Why? What could you do to improve them?

Marty's reply: *I think my test anxiety has remained the same. It will improve with better preparation for exams. It remained the same because I did not think of it as a big problem and did not pay too much attention to it. I guess that is good, in a way, not thinking about test anxiety.*

3. What have you learned since September about college level tasks?

Marty's reply: *The college level assignments, lectures, and exams are a great deal larger than anything I had previously had in high school. Specifically, the lectures and reading assignments are filled with much more material than those in high school courses. In the last 10 weeks I have spent a greater percentage of my time studying than I ever had in high school.*

4. Imagine that a younger brother/sister or friend has asked you about college. What would you tell them that you have learned in these past 10 weeks that you wished you had learned in high school?

Marty's reply: *Finally, my advice to my younger sister. In the last 10 weeks I have learned many study skills and habits that make my studying more efficient. This is a big help because lately there just has not been a lot of my time in which I had absolutely nothing to work on. And if you fall behind it is not as easy to catch up in college as it was in high school. I just wish I knew some of these study methods in high school. I could have done so much better.*

To evaluate our long-term goal of improving student performance at the university, we examine how students perform in regular college courses. Their grades are collected for one year following matriculation into the regular curriculum. Not only do we learn their grades for each course, but we also collect data concerning how they compare with students who were not enrolled in our courses.

> **Overall our students are quite competitive with regularly admitted students. Approximately 70% of those who satisfactorily complete reading courses make a C or better in introductory social science courses.**

This information is especially useful in determining how well we are preparing students for tasks required in a variety of content areas. If our students are experiencing problems in specific courses with specific task demands, we alter the curriculum to meet these needs. For example, two years ago we modified our curriculum to include more practice in writing essay examinations when we discovered that students were performing poorly in introductory history courses that used essay examinations.

Overall, our students are quite competitive with regularly admitted students. Approximately, 70% of those who satisfactorily complete reading courses make a C or better in introductory courses such as psychology, history, sociology and political science. About 85% of regularly admitted students' averages are also in the C range, but it is important to keep in mind that our students were predicted to make D's in those courses without intervention.

While we cannot draw any causal links between reading course performance and performance in introductory content courses, we believe that continued collection of data such as these assists us in our program evaluation.

Additional Considerations

Our assessment program is evolving, is in no way perfect, and continues to change. We are still developing and refining ways in which we sort, diagnose, and evaluate in an attempt to make our assessment procedures valid, reliable, and useful to instruction and students. Some other assessment measures that deserve consideration include the following:

1. *The Sentence Verification Task* (SVT). (Royer, Greene, & Sinatra, 1987; Royer, Marchant, Sinatra & Lovejoy, 1990) — This instrument appears to have potential for both sorting and diagnosing. We are currently piloting this test as part of the initial sorting package, but the early data indicate that the SVT may be equally valuable as a diagnostic tool.

2. Student interviews — Although we feel that interviewing students would be a valuable way to gather important information for evaluation, we also realize that it is time consuming. One type of interview that we find particularly intriguing would focus on task specific and domain specific strategies. Finding out what particular strategies students find useful in specific courses would provide information that would help determine the reading curriculum.

3. Posttesting on instruments given during sorting — Although most programs give some sort of pre- and post-test standardized test to measure cognitive growth, few give any kind of measure that looks at affective growth. Instruments such as the LASSI, while expensive to use as both a pre- and post-test, would provide evidence in knowledge of study strategies, for example. In addition, programs might consider more informal measures, such as beginning and ending journal entries, as a means of affective evaluation. We feel strongly that more evaluation procedures like these should be piloted.

College reading professionals who are grappling with assessment issues might start by asking the questions we did when we began examining our assessment model: What is it that we want to accomplish? Do we want more from our program than student improvement on a standardized test? If so, what do want students to learn on a short- and long-term basis?

Once the questions of program goals and philosophy have been defined, the issue of outlining a comprehensive model of assessment designed for a unique and specific program can be addressed.

References

Alexander, P. A., & Jody, J. E. (1988). The interaction of domain specific and strategic knowledge in academic performance. *Review of Educational Research*, 58, 375-404.

Baker, L. (1982) An evaluation of the role of metacognitive deficits in learning disabilities. *Topics in Learning and Listening Disabilities*, 2, 27-35.

Campione, J. C., & Brown, A. L. (1985). *Dynamic assessment: One approach and some initial data.* (Technical report No. 361). Urbana, IL: Center for the Study of Reading.

Cross, D. R., & Paris, S. G. (1987). Assessment of reading comprehension: Matching test purposes and test properties. *Educational Psychologist*, 22, 313-322.

Garner, R., & Alexander, P. A. (1982). Strategic processing of text: An investigation of the effect of adults' question/answering performance. *Journal of Educational Research*, 75, 144-148.

Jenkins, J. J., (1979). Four points to remember: A tetrahedral model and memory experiments. In L. S. Cermack & F. I. M. Craik (Eds.), *Levels and processing in human memory* (pp 429-445). Hillsdale, NJ: Erlbaum.

Morante, E. A. (1989). Selecting tests and placing students. *Journal of Developmental Education*, 13, 2-6.

Nist, S. L., & Simpson, M. L. (1989). PLAE, a validated study strategy. *Journal of Reading*, 33, 182-186.

Reynolds, W., Ramirez, M., Magrina, A., & Allen, J. (1990). Initial development and validation of the Academic Self-Concept Scale. *Educational and Psychological Measurement*, 40, 1013-1016.

Royer, J. M., Greene, B. A., & Sinatra, G. M. (1987). The Sentence Verification Technique: A practical procedure teachers can use to develop their own reading and listening comprehension tests. *Journal of Reading*, 30, 414-423.

Royer, J. M., Marchant, H. G. III, Sinatra, G. M., & Lovejoy, D. A. (1990). The prediction of college course performance from reading comprehension performance: Evidence for general and specific prediction factors. *American Educational Research Journal*, 27, 158-169.

Simpson, M. L., & Nist, S. L. (1990). Comprehension assessment: An effective and efficient study strategy for college students. *Journal of Reading*, 34, 122-131.

Weinstein, C. E., Palmer, D. R., & Schulte, A. (1987). *Learning and Study Strategies Inventory (LASSI)*. Clearwater, FL: H&H Publishing (800)366-4079.

Wixson, K. K., & Peters, C. W. (1987). Comprehension assessment: Implementing an interactive view of reading. *Educational Psychologist*, 22, 332-356.

Wood, N. V. (1989). Reading tests and reading assessment. *Journal of Developmental Education*, 13, 14-18.

Michelle L. Simpson is Associate Professor in the Division of Developmental Studies and Sherrie L. Nist is Professor in the Division of Academic Assistance at the University of Georgia, Athens, GA 30602.

Computerized testing can reduce testing time for both students and staff and increase the time spent on instruction and learning.

Computerized Adaptive Testing in Reading

By Pat Smittle

(From the *Journal of Developmental Education*, Volume 15, Issue 2, Winter 1991, pages 2-5. Reprinted by permission of the *Journal of Developmental Education*, Appalachian State University, Boone, NC 28608 and Pat Smittle.)

Abstract: Some students who are placed in developmental reading courses by entry test scores only need a short review of reading skills before they are ready for college-level reading. Reading competency that distinguishes between the two levels is usually measured by some form of tests. Most testing procedures are time consuming and reduce instructional time. The Computerized Placement Tests (CPTs) proved to be an effective and efficient assessment tool for this purpose. This efficiency allows the Santa Fe Community College faculty to remove the time barriers of a semester and facilitates the acceleration of the students' academic programs.

Computers are rapidly earning an indispensable position in the role of test administration. Their inherent capabilities allow them to perform some mundane, time-consuming tasks as well as some sophisticated functions that exceed our expectations with traditional paper and pencil tests. According to William Ward (1988), "The potential benefits of administering conventional tests using microcom-

puters range from opportunities to individualize assessment to increase in the efficiency and economy with which information can be manipulated" (p.3). With the combination of a measurement theory called item response theory (Lord, 1980), these benefits are expanded to provide for a new delivery system of an old concept in test administration. This theory allows for the selection of appropriate questions based on the response to previous questions and calculations of scores according to item difficulty.

> "Paradoxically, the testing is, in a sense, a return to old-fashioned individualized examinations."

Computer adaptive testing is a new concept that uses microcomputers to adapt examination to individual students. In reference to computer adaptive testing, Howard Wainer (1983) reported that:

We are now on the verge of a technological revolution in testing as a result of the availability of extensive inexpensive computing and some recent developments in statistical theory. Paradoxically, the new testing is, in a sense, a return to old-fashioned individualized examinations (p 83).

The College Board and Educational Testing Service moved this technological revolution into education with the development of the Computerized Placement Tests (CPTs). The CPTs are basic skills assessment programs designed primarily for the purpose of placing students in appropriate entry-level courses at the beginning of their college careers. The complete battery consists of four untimed subtests: reading comprehension, sentence skills, arithmetic, and algebra. According to the College Board Computerized Placement Tests (CPTs) Coordinator's Notebook (1986), this computer adaptive test offers these advantages.

For students, adaptive testing:
    reduces testing time, frustration, and boredom;
    provides immediate score results;
    challenges students without discouraging them;
    lets students work at their own pace; and
    gives a more accurate estimate of their ability.

For test administrators and guidance staff, adaptive testing:
    individualizes the test questions and testing time;
    provides immediate scoring;
    reduces problems of test security; and
    moderates problems of paper handling that are associated with conventional tests.

It is this revolutionary testing process that has allowed Santa Fe Community College to implement a program that breaks the time barrier of a traditional semester for developmental reading students. This project indicates that although the CPTs were primarily designed for placement into appropriate courses, they are also effective and efficient tools for exit criteria and feedback to students regarding their progress.

Background

The Reading Program at Santa Fe Community College reflects the long standing commitment the college has to underprepared students. Studies reveal that during the last four years approximately 33% of the incoming freshmen have been enrolled in developmental reading classes. The placement of these students was in accordance with State Rule 6A-10.0315, College Preparatory Testing Placement and Instruction (1986). This rule states, in part:

> First-time-in-college applicants for admission to community colleges and universities who intend to enter degree programs shall be tested prior to the completion of registration, using one (1) or more of the tests listed herein, and effective the 1985 Fall term, shall enroll in college preparatory communication and computation instruction if the test scores are below those listed herein (p. 441).

The approved tests are: ACT Assessment, American College Testing Program; ASSET, American College Testing Program; MAPS, College Entrance Examination Board, and SAT, College Entrance Examination Board.

Description of College Preparatory Reading Class

The ACT, one of the state approved tests, has been used as the on-site assessment instrument for several years; however, after a lengthy experimental study, this instrument was replaced with the Computerized Placement Tests (CPTs) which were recently added to the list of state approved tests. Based upon the establishment of local norms at Santa Fe Community College, a scale score of 80 or lower on the Reading Computerized Placement Test places students in the College Preparatory Reading class (REA0010).

Structure

The College Preparatory Reading class is designed to accommodate various skill levels and learning styles within a structured curriculum. The weekly schedule consists of the following components:

1. **Classroom instruction – 3 hours per week.** During this time, the reading instructor introduces specific skills and directs related reading activities.

2. **Scheduled Reading Lab – 2 hours per week.** Students work in the computer lab using Computer Assisted Instruction (CAI) one hour each week, and they work in the traditional reading lab using individually prescribed paper/pencil reading materials one hour.

3. **Open Lab – approximately 1 hour per week.** Students work independently in either lab if they need additional work.

Curriculum

To assist students in the development of reading skills that are required for college work and to comply with the state rule, the following reading skills are taught:

Literal Comprehension
>   Main Ideas
>   Supporting Details
>   Meanings of Words in Context

Critical Comprehension
>   Author's purpose
>   Tone
>   Valid Arguments
>   Explicit and Implicit Relationships
>   Bias Detection
>   Fact from Opinion Distinctions
>   Logical Inferences and Conclusions

Many students do not need a full semester to develop the minimum competence required in College Preparatory Reading.

Exit Criteria

To pass the reading course, students are required to meet two of the three following criteria: attain a score of 81 or higher on the Reading CPT, attain a score of 75 or higher on the Santa Fe Community College Reading Competency Test (this is an in-house reading test in which the prescribed reading skills are applied to reading passages taken from textbooks required in the general education courses), and attain both of the following scores on the Nelson Denny Reading Test:
>   10.5 Grade Level in Vocabulary,
>   10.5 Grade Level in Comprehension.

After students have demonstrated minimum competency by passing two of the three tests, they are awarded a grade of A, B, or C. Students who do not meet minimum competency receive a grade of D or F. Those students who receive a D or F are required to register for the course again the following semester.

Early Exit Reading Project

After several years of observation, the reading staff acknowledged that many students do not need a full semester to develop the minimum competencies required in the College Preparatory Reading Course (REA0010). This is especially true of students who are repeating the course as well as students who had marginal entry test scores. This observation led to the exploration of several alternative strategies that would accelerate the students' progress and still maintain high standards.

The purpose of this project was to accelerate the academic progress of students who demonstrate minimum competency in College Preparatory Reading early in the semester by moving them into a college-level reading course in which the curriculum is designed to meet the demands of general education course work, to motivate students to perform to their maximum potential, to prepare students for the reading portion of the College Level Academic Skills Test (a state mandated skills test designed to assess mastery of skills by the end of the sophomore year) and to allow the students to earn 3-semester hours of academic credit toward the Association of Arts Degree.

Procedure

After four weeks of intensive instruction, students were scheduled to take the Reading CPT during their scheduled computer lab time. This test served as a screening test for further testing. Students who scored below 70 were advised to consult with their instructor concerning their reading deficiencies and develop a plan of action for the remainder of the semester. Students who attained a score of 70 or higher were considered eligible to proceed with the exit testing process. They were given appointments to take the Competency Test and the Nelson Denny Reading Test as needed to meet the exit criteria. A CPT score of 70 was not a passing score but was selected as a "safety net" so students who might pass the other tests would not be screened out. Since this was the initial project, we did not want to place too much emphasis on any one test, however, students who had scored between 70-80 on the CPT were required to pass both of the other exit tests. To accommodate students' schedules, the following week was devoted to the additional paper/pencil testing. At the end of the testing week, students who had demonstrated competency on two of the three tests were given the opportunity to drop College Preparatory Reading (REA0010) and register for Advanced College Reading (REA2205) for an intensive 10-week semester of study. Since no ad-

ditional matriculation fees were required, the only expense to the students was the purchase of the textbooks for the new course. Because the reading staff was shifted to accommodate the student shift, there was no additional expense to the college.

Results

The first day of testing revealed that the project was going to be far more successful than we had expected. Students appeared motivated and expressed excitement about taking the Reading CPT. By the end of the week, 515 of the 621 students registered for the daytime REA0010 classes had completed the CPT and were advised to proceed according to their scores. Of those students, 277 attained a score of 70 or higher and were scheduled for the other two tests. When testing was completed, 129 students (25% of those who were originally tested) met the exit requirements for REA0010 and were eligible to move into REA2205. Of those students who were eligible, most completed the registration process and moved to the higher level course; however, a few elected to stay in the preparatory course because they felt they still needed that level of instruction.

> When testing was completed, 129 (25%) of those who were originally tested met the exit requirements and were eligible to move into Advanced College Reading.

Obviously the project proved to be highly successful and produced the following advantages:

1. Capable students were given the opportunity to accelerate their academic program after remediating their reading skill deficiencies.

2. Students were motivated.

3. Benchmarks of progress were provided for all reading students whether they passed the tests or not.

4. Test results provided opportunities for teacher/student conferences and goal setting, especially for those students who failed to meet minimum competencies.

5. Student/teacher advocate relationships were developed as opposed to the adverse relationships that often follow failure of teacher-made tests.

6. Instructors were given the opportunity to focus on specific skills for a more homogeneous population of students remaining in REA0010.

The enormous success of the project produced one major disadvantage: the paper/pencil testing that followed the initial CPT testing proved to be an insurmountable task. A total of 136 working hours was required to administer the tests, score them, and report the results. It became obvious that additional staff had to be employed to handle the paper/pencil testing. Due to budget constraints, this was not a viable option, so other solutions were explored.

Examination of the logistics of the testing procedures revealed that while 136-working hours were required to administer the paper/pencil tests to 277 students who had earned eligibility by scoring 70 or better on the CPT, only 25 hours were required to administer the CPT to all 515 students. This observation led to a more thorough analysis of the data and revealed that of all the 129 students who met the exit criteria of passing two out of three designated tests, 108 (40%) of them had achieved passing scores on the CPT while only 21 (16%) had failed the CPT and achieved passing scores on the Nelson Denny Reading and the Santa Fe Community College Reading Competency Test. Therefore, the safety net of the CPT had allowed a few more students to meet the exit criteria, but the tremendous workload of scoring paper/pencil testing was placing the entire project in jeopardy.

The data were analyzed to determine the average gain during the 4-week instructional period. The average gain for the entire class was 8 points. Further analysis indicated that students with lower pre-CPT scores made greater gains than those with higher scores.

Editor' Note: That weaker students made greater gains may reflect regression toward that mean.

Table 1
Average Reading CPT Gain at Various Intervals

Pre-CPT Score	# Students	Average Gain
0-10	0	0
11-20	0	0
21-30	4	15
31-40	19	15
41-50	19	9
51-60	31	7
61-70	46	7
71-80	78	7

Information of this nature will serve as a valuable counseling tool in the future. Although it would be ideal to continue the extensive testing program, it was not practical in terms of budget or time.

Recommendations

Based on this information the reading staff decided that the CPT alone is sufficient to determine minimum competency that will allow students to exit REA0010 after 4 weeks of instruction and accelerate their academic program. This solution will attain the effectiveness reported in this study through a system that is highly efficient in terms of time, money, and space (not to mention the frustration to staff and students).

Conclusion

Obviously underprepared students in the College Preparatory Reading Program are at various levels of preparedness. Given the demands of time on students and staff, the expense, and the need to excel, it behooves educators to be creative in seeking ways to help students develop the academic skills necessary to move into college level course work as efficiently as possible. However, we must carefully protect our existing standards as we seek avenues for acceleration. Extensive testing is the method used at Santa Fe Community College, but testing requires a great deal of time and manpower which are precious commodities at most colleges. Based on the results of this project, computer adaptive testing will replace the laborious, time consuming task while maintaining predetermined standards for college-level reading at Santa Fe Community College.

References

College Preparatory Testing, Placement, and Instruction, Florida Administrative Code Ann. 6A-10.0315 (1986).

Educational Testing Service & the College Entrance Examination Board. (1986). *College Board Computerized Placement Tests* (CPTs) *Computerized Adaptive Testing Program for College Placement, Coordinator's Notebook*. Princeton, NJ: Author.

Lord, F. M. (1980). *Applications of item response theory to practical testing problems*. Hillsdale, NJ: Erlbaum.

Wainer, H. (1983). On item response theory and computerized adaptive tests: The coming technological revolution in testing. *The Journal of College Admissions*, 28(4), 83-90.

Ward, W. (1988). Using microcomputers for adaptive testing. In *Computerized adaptive testing: The state of the art in assessment at three community colleges* (pp.3-8). Laguna Hills, CA: League for innovations in the community college.

Pat Smittle is Chairperson, Learning Labs/Developmental Education at Santa Fe Community College, Gainesville, FL 32602

Part 5

Reading
&
Study Skills

Although the ten recommendations in this article are addressed to reading and study skills courses,
they are equally applicable to math and writing classes.

Ten Recommendations from Research for Teaching High Risk College Students

By Norman A. Stahl, Michele L. Simpson, and Christopher G. Hayes

(From the *Journal of Developmental Education*, 16 (1), 2-10. Reprinted by permission of the *Journal of Developmental Education*, Appalachian State University, Boone, NC 28608 and Norman A. Stahl, Michele L. Simpson, and Christopher G. Hayes.)

Abstract. Finding practical ideas about college reading that have been drawn from theory and research is difficult for most veteran instructors, but it is even more difficult for the beginner unaware of professional organizations and journals. This problem of dissemination is exacerbated by the fact that there are very few formal university programs that focus on the training of college reading specialists. Consequently, the authors of this article decided to generate a list of their own "best ideas" that they have culled from their years of teaching college reading. These ten ideas, though not comprehensive, represent a synthesis of research and theory. More importantly, they are ones that have made a difference in the performance of the authors' students. In addition, the authors have purposely cited many scholarly sources in order to provide an extensive bibliography for colleagues new to the field.

> The college reading and learning profession has yet to develop the same rigorous training requirements and credentialing generally expected of our peers in elementary and secondary education.

Formal college reading and study programs have been with us since the early days of the 20th century when schools such as Harvard (Moore, 1915), the University of Chicago (National Society for the Study of Education [NSSE], 1920), and the University of Illinois (Stone & Colvin, 1920) observed the need to promote students' advanced reading and learning skills. Furthermore, over the past century more than 600 texts and workbooks have been published for use by instructors and students in college reading programs (Stahl, Hynd, & Brozo, 1990). Of equal importance, reports of research with college readers dating back to the Victorian Era (Abell, 1894) can be found in the literature. Hence, the profession has a time-honored history of program development, curriculum innovation, and published research of which we can be proud.

On the other hand, the primary vehicles for disseminating pertinent theory, research, and practical teaching ideas have been rather diffuse and have changed routinely over the years. Moreover, the profession has yet to develop the same rigorous training requirements and credentialing generally expected of our peers in elementary or secondary education. Although recently several "generalist-oriented" degree programs focusing on developmental education have evolved, formal training programs at the level of the terminal degree are all but nonexistent for the college reading and learning professional.

Indeed, many of us serving in the college reading and learning field entered through a side door and developed expertise through a self-help program based on personal reading, conference attendance, peer interaction, etc., (see Mealey, 1991; Simpson, 1983; Stahl, Brozo, & Gordon, 1984 for discussion). While we each may have a background in reading pedagogy, in most cases the focus of our initial training was at the elementary or secondary levels, since credentialing programs typically ignore the special needs of the college learner.

As an example of this assertion, recently one of the authors was talking with a colleague new to teaching high-risk college students. She had never heard of this journal, nor the other journals sponsored by organizations such as the International Reading Association, the College Reading Association, or the College Reading and Learning Association. Her experience reminded us again that the first few years of teaching in a college reading and learning program can be overwhelming. Practiced ideas enmeshed with theory and research are difficult to find for most veterans, but even more difficult for the beginner who is unaware of professional organizations and journals. So we decided to create our own "best ideas" for our new colleagues and for other interested novices. Though not comprehensive, these ten ideas have made a difference in our teaching of college students. We present these ideas in an order that moves from broader conceptualizations of pedagogy to the more practical concerns of the educational program.

Adopt a Cognitive-Based Philosophy

Many college programs either explicitly or implicitly emphasize a deficit model of reading instruction drawn from the diagnostic-compensatory movement. In this case, the short-term goal becomes teaching students specific skills that they have not yet mastered (i.e., recognizing the main idea or the author's tone of a selection). The long-term goal becomes student improvement on a standardized reading test such as the ubiquitous Nelson-Denny Reading Test or a state mandated reading exam as used in Texas, Georgia, New Jersey, etc. Unfortunately, many students learn to excel on reading tests to the degree necessary to exit a developmental program but still do not fully function as independent learners in the academic milieu of higher education. That is, the teaching of discrete reading skills rarely transfers to students' immediate and real tasks (i.e., the mastery of concepts and complex principles in their college courses!). More importantly, the deficit model can stigmatize and demoralize college freshmen who are eager to leave the trappings of high school and begin college-level work. The cognitive model has proven to be an effective alternative to the deficit model.

Most cognitive psychologists maintain that effective learning is more the result of internal structures and processes than of external influences such as materials, teachers, and instructional sequences (Resnick, 1981). The cognitive model posits that college students are, or should be, active participants in control of their learning, they are self-regulated, autonomous, and good strategy users (Harri-Augstein, Smith, & Thomas, 1982; Pressley, 1986; Thomas & Rohwer, 1986; Zimmerman, 1986). Common to all these labels is the operational definition of effective independent learners as those who plan, implement, and control the study strategies that enhance learning. Since most college students are not efficient and effective independent learners (Weinstein and Rogers, 1984), the most logical goal for college reading and learning programs would be to teach students a repertoire of strategies and tactics that will prepare them for the tasks and texts they encounter in college.

Students need to learn more than how to develop and when to employ the strategies, however. They also need to learn how to transfer specific strategies to the particular academic literacy demands of each course. Indeed, without effective training for transfer, college reading and learning courses face the very real danger of standing in isolation from the academic disciplines and of remaining mired in the deficit model.

Use a Course Model That Stresses Transfer

Strategy transfer occurs more naturally when students have a chance to practice the newly learned strategies on their own texts and with tasks perceived to be "real." In many mandated reading courses, such as developmental studies programs or bridge programs, typically students are not enrolled concurrently in a credit bearing, content-area course that allows for this transfer. Hence, instructors should consider teaching strategies through a simulations model (King, Stahl, and Brozo, 1984; Nist & Hynd, 1985).

> Consider the use of assessment procedures that reflect the reading/learning tasks students will be required to undertake in lower division classes.

The goal of such a model is to replicate the tasks and texts of a typical required, lower division course (e.g., history, psychology). Because the transfer mandates close simulation of the chosen course, students must purchase the course's textbook and supplemental materials. Then throughout the simulation experience, they must read and study the chapters as the instructor teaches the domain-specific study strategies. Students can also receive practice in taking lecture notes with appropriate videotaped lectures or guest lectures from professors who regularly teach the targeted course. During the lecture presentations, the instructor should model good note-taking strategies on an overhead projector. The end point of the simulation experience is passing an examination like that encountered in a regular course. When students exit the simulation course, they take with them a physical product (annotated text, lecture notes), a cognitive product (greater prior knowledge and experience), and several domain-specific and general study strategies.

For students enrolled concurrently in credit-bearing, content-area courses, the learning specialist should implement an instructional model that permits each student to become a strategic learner with the content and the materials encountered in a course of his or her own selection. Throughout the term as each learner is introduced to and practices with various strategies and tactics, he or she develops a portfolio of materials (e.g., course notes, concept cards, graphic organizers, process guides, course exams) demonstrating the mastery of the content course's goals and also the development of the individual's successful repertoire of learning strategies.

While at first glance it may appear that the number of possible student choices for a target course might make this model unwieldy, the realities of the undergraduate curriculum for the lower division student greatly limit the breadth of courses in which one may enroll. Hence, our experience suggests most students will elect to employ the strategies and tactics you introduce to a handful of introductory, survey courses such as Psychology 100, Sociology 100, Anthropology 100, U.S. History 100, etc. In fact, we have discovered that the range of options is so limited that the instructor may easily introduce forms of cooperative learning through the constitution of content-specific cluster groups and learning triads or dyads.

A second model for promoting transfer of learning strategies for students enrolled in content classes involves the development of more formal ties between the academic program and reading/learning strategy course. Over the past decade this model has been labeled either supplemental instruction (Martin, 1980), adjunct or paired courses (Mallery & Bullock, 1985), the language study model (Sartain et al., 1981), or the learning counseling model (Garfield & McHugh, 1978). Basic to all of these models is the premise that the content of the reading or learning strategy instruction or mentoring is tied to a credit-bearing course that freshmen or sophomores typically take (e.g., biology, geography, or history). The instructor of the reading and learning strategies does not teach the content of the content course nor supplant the role of the professor in presenting the content. Rather, the reading/learning specialist teaches processes and strategies necessary to succeed in the targeted course in seminars or sessions held outside of class. These specially arranged sessions may be voluntary or required, depending upon the institution and the professor involved with the program.

While the new member of our profession may not be in a position to implement such a program initially, there is value in being cognizant of the "paired course" program (Bullock & Madden, 1986) that limits enrollment in a rather traditional yet theme-oriented (e.g., psychology, sociology) study strategies course to those students enrolled in the respective academic speciality. Since all the students in a particular section are going through similar academic experiences, study strategy training can be focused on specific tasks and thus can improve the possibility of transfer. Regardless of which models of course delivery are employed, the measures of success must focus on the transfer of learning strategy training. Hence, we present our next idea or recommendation.

Use Reliable, Process Oriented Assessment Procedures

Many college reading programs rely on standardized reading tests to place students in programs and to assess their strengths and weaknesses after placement (Simpson & Nist, 1992). In addition, these tests are often used to evaluate the success of a program by determining whether the students significantly improve their reading level or their comprehension and vocabulary scores. In some situations, the standardized test may even determine whether students can exit the mandated program. Rather than an over-reliance upon standardized measures that are typically product orientated, instructors should consider the use of assessment procedures that reflect the reading/learning tasks students will be required to undertake in lower division courses. One way such process-oriented assessments can be accomplished is through simulation of a typical learning process.

In undertaking this simulation, the instructor might distribute to students an introductory chapter from a sociology text on a Monday with the assignment to prepare for an objective and essay examination over the material on Friday. Then on exam day, the instructor would collect the chapter and materials the student used for study, ask the students to summarize briefly how they studied and for how long, and then administer the examination under normal exam conditions. Before handing in the examination, students could report what grade or percentage they think they will receive on the exam (Sartain et al., 1982). Thus, the instructor has collected a variety of process information from the students: (a) copies of their chapters which may reveal any markings; (b) tangible products of their self-selected strategies such as maps, outlines, jot lists, etc.; (c) self-reports on their methods of study;

and, d) measures of their metacognitive awareness of performance.

To evaluate the students' processes of study, instructors can use checklists enumerating the attributes of effective text marking and study strategies (i.e., mapping, charting). For instance, Simpson and Nist (1990a) have developed one checklist for text annotation that allows the instructor to determine whether the students use text structure to identify and organize superordinate and subordinate ideas and whether they translate information into their own words. Similarly, Stahl, King, and Henk (1991) have developed a checklist for evaluating lecture notes. These checklists, based on cognitive theory and research, allow the instructor to quickly evaluate student-generated materials and thus to see strengths, needs, and patterns in an organized manner.

To evaluate the products of study, instructors can score the objective and essay questions noting differences in scores between the two measures. In addition, a holistic evaluation of the essay could provide an additional measure of students' abilities to articulate a clear understanding of content and relationships among superordinate and subordinate ideas. The results of these process and product assessments can then be shared with students in small groups or in individual conferences.

However, if after mastering successful studying processes the students still earn low test scores, the problem may not be ability to implement strategic learning or to draw upon metacognitive awareness, but rather weak background knowledge of the subject being tested. Such is not an unusual situation with developmental learners who underwent a secondary school experience that left them underprepared or misprepared for the academic literacy demands of postsecondary learning. Naturally, then, the learning specialist must think of ways to help students develop a broadened world view supportive of college success.

Broaden Conceptual Background Knowledge

Most students required to take a college reading course can read but are not efficient and effective independent learners. Because these students are often illiterate and suffer wide gaps in their prior knowledge, they are not generally prepared to read regularly, widely, or critically. Furthermore, many of these students have not been required to undertake higher level reading/learning tasks while in the secondary school (Alvermann & Moore, 1991). Hence, the instructor must meet the needs of students who have both deficiencies in content knowledge and misconceptions about the learning process. Moreover, as recent research has demonstrated in a college freshman-level history course (Simpson & Nist, 1990b), students may even have misconceptions about specific content areas.

Obviously, such problems cannot be overcome in one course, but instructors can intervene by promoting the habit of reading extensively through the creative use of periodicals such as *Newsweek*, *U.S. News and World Report*, or *Time* during the weekly classroom routine. In addition to discussing selected articles, instructors or students could select general vocabulary words such as **ameliorate** and **exacerbate** or any of the regularly used idioms, allusions, and foreign terms identified and presented by Boese (1986) for study.

As another alternative, instructors can provide higher level background experiences while teaching students to learn about a specific theme (e.g., "coming of age," "the American experience," "personal courage") or concept by using or adapting Bartholomae and Petrosky's (1986) "basic reading/basic writing" model. In such a model, basic readers undertake extensive reading of five to six texts with a similar unifying issue. Furthermore, since each text builds upon the previously read book, the student's conceptual understanding of the theme and his or her relationship to it grows in progressive degrees of sophistication. In addition, greater facility with various forms of discourse is promoted as the student moves from the more comfortable narrative forms of text to the expository forms generally encountered in lower division courses. Along with the extensive readings, the learner is expected to undertake carefully integrated writing assignments, in both formal and expressive modes.

Such a program is indeed time consuming for all involved — both student and instructor. Still, the age-old adage is true: one becomes a better reader by reading extensively. Unfortunately, many of the students enrolling in developmental course work report to us that they simply were not required to read in high school. Hence, it is not surprising that the reading load encountered in college or the level of vocabulary required is troubling to our students. The basic reading/basic writing model clearly helps to prepare the students for the former. Now let us turn to the latter issue.

Reconceptualize Vocabulary Development

Students entering postsecondary education need to understand from the outset that the fundamental avenue for academic success is the ability to quickly expand their vocabulary (Simpson & Dwyer, 1991; Stahl, Brozo, & Simpson, 1987). Instructors must provide experiences that immerse students in (a) the language of the academy or the terminology that allows the institution to function (e.g., terms such as provost, bursar, financial aid); (b) the "language of the educated" or the advanced general vocabulary used by scholars as they communicate; and (c) the specialized "languages of the disciplines" (Sartain, 1981) or those unique technical terms, symbols, etc., that permit scholars within a field to communicate effectively. Students also must understand that learning these words means more than the rote memorization of a brief definition; it implies conceptual understanding of words. With conceptual understanding, students know multiple definitions, examples, characteristics, synonyms and antonyms, and are able to apply the word and its variant forms (e.g., zealous versus zealot) in a variety of situations (Simpson & Dwyer, 1991).

> Students need to understand from the outset that the fundamental avenue for academic success is the ability to quickly expand their vocabulary.

To help students master the vocabulary in the first category, instructors can draw heavily upon the institution's printed materials, particularly the college catalogue and student handbook. Effective strategies for developing greater vocabulary fluency in the second category include generative vocabulary activities such as Haggard's (1982) word of the "week," Beck's (personal communication, 1979) "self-collection strategy" and Pauk's (1984) "frontier system." Finally, instructors can teach students how to learn technical vocabulary by using activities such as Sartain et al., (1982) "technical vocabulary log for study triads" or Simpson, Nist, and Kirby's (1987) "concept cards."

Vocabulary development, like other instruction, calls for innovative teaching. But instructors may spend unnecessary time (and disappointment) reinventing strategies that have already been tested

Without relinquishing their own creative expertise, instructors need to be aware of, and use, research-validated strategies.

Use Research-Validated Learning Strategies

Instruction with textbook study systems (e.g., SQ3R, PQRST) has been a staple of the college reading/learning program for over 50 years (Caverly & Orlando, 1991; Stahl & Henk, 1986). Still, many of the methods and strategies presented to college students have yet to be validated credibly by research or have been researched with students atypical of the population served in mandated developmental courses. More research needs to be conducted with high-risk college students, especially research concerned with student processes rather than research comparing one strategy to another.

While the research base is not as large as with younger students, a few strategies have been validated with high-risk college students. For example, after training students to use textbook annotation, Simpson and Nist (1990a) reported developmental students performed significantly better than an equivalent control group on three different content area exams. More importantly, the annotation group reported spending less time studying for those three exams. Another promising strategy, PORPE (Simpson, 1986), was developed to help students prepare for essay examinations. With PORPE, students learn to predict potential essay questions to guide their studying; organize key ideas that answer those predicted questions using their own words, structure, and methods; rehearse key ideas; practice the recall of those key ideas in self-assigned writing; and evaluate the completeness, accuracy, and appropriateness of the essays by means of a checklist. These five steps are synergistic as they build upon each other and lead learners through the cognitive and metacognitive processes essential to successful independent learning. PORPE has been validated in three investigations (Simpson, Stahl, & Hayes, 1988; Simpson, Hayes, & Stahl, 1989; Simpson, Hayes, Stahl, Connor, & Weaver, 1988) involving high-risk college students trained to employ the strategy while studying *Introduction to Psychology* textbook chapter excerpts. For additional descriptions of validated learning strategies pertinent to high-risk college students, see the recent International Reading Association Monograph, entitled *Teaching Reading and Study Strategies at the College Level*, edited by Flippo and Caverly (1991).

It is not enough simply to introduce students to proven strategies. As instructors, we must also be sure that we train students how to use them and how to choose among them. This is an onus that has often been overlooked as college reading specialists have attempted to provide great breadth of content coverage but often not enough depth with instruction. Let us then turn to the training issue.

Systematically Train Students to Employ Strategies

One of the primary goals of the college reading instructor should be to train students to be able to select, modify, and transfer a variety of strategies to their own learning tasks. To accomplish this goal, self-control training (Brown, Campione, & Day, 1981) is essential. Students who have received self-control training not only "know" a strategy, but they also have knowledge of the conditions under which the strategy is appropriate and why it is appropriate. Paris, Lipson, and Wixson (1983) refer to this type of knowledge as conditional knowledge. In contrast to this systematic type of training is the most prevalent form of training, labeled blind training by Brown, et al., (1981).

Students receiving blind training in a strategy are not as likely to learn why, how, or when to use a strategy but instead tend to blindly imitate the instructor. With blind training students will not be as likely to transfer the strategies they learned to their own learning tasks.

Validated training approaches and models (Garner, 1988; King & Stahl, 1985; Nist & Kirby, 1986; Pressley, 1986; Stahl, King & Henk, 1991) are numerous, but they do agree that instruction should be direct, informed, and explanatory. In other words, students can be trained to employ a strategy if they receive intensive instruction over a reasonable period of time that is characterized by (a) strategy explanations and rationales (i.e., steps/tactics, advantages, performance enhancement issues, appropriate time and use considerations); (b) strategy modeling and talk throughs by the instructor; (c) examples from real tasks and texts that students will encounter; (d) guided practice with real texts, followed by immediate and specific feedback and correction; (e) debriefing sessions that deal with questions, student doubts, and fix-up strategies for difficult concepts; (f) frequent independent practice opportunities across appropriate texts; and (g) guidelines on how to evaluate a strategy's success or failure.

Training sequences such as these can help students with the declarative and procedural knowledge about strategy use. That is, such instruction will help students learn the what, how, and why of strategy employment. Once students master the declarative and procedural knowledge of a strategy, instructors must then consider the issues of strategy control and self-regulation. With our next idea we will address this important concern.

Promote Strategy Control and Regulation

To be effective independent learners, college students need to be able to control and regulate the strategies they employ. Such control is a critical aspect of metacognition that involves learners in planning, monitoring, and evaluating a plan of action across a variety of tasks and texts (Kluwe, 1987). Unfortunately, research has demonstrated consistently that most college students, and particularly those at risk, lack the abilities to plan, monitor, and evaluate their own learning (Weinstein & Rogers, 1984). Practically speaking, this means that college instructors should teach their students to (a) define tasks, establish goals, and allocate resources; (b) make a plan of action that incorporates the appropriate strategies and distributes time; (c) activate and monitor the plan of action and make appropriate changes, when necessary; and, (d) evaluate their plan's success or failure in terms of goals and the task in order to plan for future situations. In addition, to have strategic control, students must have a repertoire of strategies to choose from so they may select and adapt the most appropriate one to the specified task and text.

Though difficult to obtain, strategic control and regulation can be facilitated when instructors use cognitive-based course models that emphasize systematic training and realistic transfer opportunities. In addition, strategies such as PLAE (Simpson & Nist, 1984) can help students and instructors operationalize these metacognitive processes. PLAE is a research driven, recursive model that involves students in four stages of mastering strategy control and regulation. In Stage 1, **Preplanning**, students define the task and set performance goals by answering a set of guiding questions. In Stage 2, **Listing**, students list the most appropriate strategies and construct a task-specific study plan that outlines their specific goal for each study session, the amount of time they predict it will take to reach their goal, and where they will study. In Stage 3, **Activating**, students implement and monitor the plan, making adjustments if their plans are not working. Stage 4, **Evaluation,** occurs after students have received their test scores. Students evaluate their performance by diagnosing errors and looking for patterns of strengths and weaknesses. Students then use this information as they plan for subsequent tasks (e.g., exams). PLAE has been successful with high-risk college students in improving their metacognitions and test performance across a variety of content areas (Nist & Simpson, 1989).

Strategies such as PLAE are among the most valuable students can learn. But learning how to use them effectively also requires time and practice. Unfortunately many developmental level students may not be motivated to expend such effort until they encounter immediate success with and benefits from the strategies they are learning in the reading and learning class. A number of other strategies offer more direct benefits to college learners in shorter instructional time.

Use High Utility Strategies for Immediate Acceptance

Experienced instructors realize that many students enter required reading/study strategies courses with negative attitudes about having been assigned to a "remedial" class. Consequently, rather than starting the term with processes that may take several weeks or all term for students to reap benefits from, begin by teaching a high-utility strategy that promotes immediate transfer to other course work. Instruction on how to take notes from lectures (Stahl, King, & Henk, 1991) or how to read and remember information from text through annotation (Simpson & Nist, 1990a) provides such an avenue to imme-

diate use and probable course success. Once students realize that there is value in these strategies and develop a degree of trust in the instructor as a mentor, they are more apt to accept with equal value those techniques such as scheduling and planning activities which might seem a bit "preachie," or methods such as multistep textbook study systems that require both time and effort to master.

Indeed, being careful not to overlook the student's vantage point is of importance in designing a postsecondary reading/learning program. Yet we must be careful not to be so myopic in our desire to produce better readers and learners that we forget that there is power in integrating reading with writing activities in the developmental learning program. Many instructors, however, overlook the value of writing to teach reading, either as a step in a strategy or by itself.

Incorporate Writing into the Curriculum

Writing aids students in becoming co-creators of the texts they read, in creating their own articulated understanding of content material, and in providing a means of monitoring and revising that understanding (Hayes, Stahl, & Simpson, 1991). For instance, to elicit background knowledge before a reading assignment, the instructor could ask students to freewrite on the general subject of the assignment, to write down all the questions the reading passage's title brings to mind, skim the passage and then freewrite on what they predict the passage will say, or formulate questions or objections to what they think will appear in the passage. The instructor could also ask that, as students read, they pause for three minutes before going on to the next main heading (or if no headings appear), after every couple of pages to summarize what they have just read, to write down questions about what remains unclear, or to respond personally to what they have read. An instructor could have students reflect on an assignment during a 10-minute writing before class discussion of key concepts. Not only do such writing activities engage students in the reading material, but they afford students an opportunity to monitor their understanding and to contribute more actively and knowledgeably to discussions (Hayes, 1990). In a sense, writing about reading assignments turns the reading process inside out, exposing readers to the inescapable constructivist activity of creating meaning in and from words.

A growing body of research supports the benefits of incorporating writing within the reading curriculum. Best known perhaps, are studies showing that having students write summaries of reading selections can improve their reading comprehension and recall abilities (Brown, Day, & Jones, 1983; Johnson, 1982; Taylor & Berkowitz, 1980). Analytic writing has proven to engage students with reading material in even more cognitively complex ways (Langer & Applebee, 1987; Marshall, 1987). Such written analysis, and its concomitant thinking, leads students to forge connections among the various levels of generality in a reading passage as it also engages them in recreating coherent text structures. Daily reading logs and directed writing activities have been shown to increase remedial college students' reading comprehension and writing abilities (Hayes, 1987). The process of writing, then, can be an effective means of making sense of the written product.

Conclusion

These ten recommendations certainly do not begin to touch on all that a beginning instructor of reading and learning strategies should know. They do provide a beginning point for the novice. At the least, they offer some practical ideas for the classroom and provide some direction for further exploration. We also hope that they reinforce a commitment to teaching reading and learning as holistic, complex processes, not as discrete, simplistic skills.

> Writing about reading assignments turns the reading process inside out.

Professional growth is a continuing process that comes with the deliberate decision to be part of the professional community of post-secondary reading and learning specialists. This is the professionalism that has been required of all of the nation's developmental educators whether they be serving in community colleges, liberal arts colleges, or universities or whether they be employed in developmental programs, learning assistance centers, or Educational Opportunity Programs. This is the professionalism that comes with the ongoing reading of our professional journals and literature, and with the regular attendance at and participation in the local, state, regional, and national conferences offered throughout the year. This is the professionalism that is fully formed when one understands and appreciates Manzo's (1983) conception that college reading and learning is both a generator of new ideas and a repository of considerable wisdom. Yet, most of all, it is a level of professionalism that comes shining through the first time you share your own pedagogical knowledge of our field with a new member of the field who also wishes to be known as a college reading and learning specialist.

References

Abell, A. M. (1894). Rapid reading: Advantages and methods. *Educational Review*, 8, 283-286.

Alvermann, D. E., & Moore, D. W. (1991). Secondary school reading. In R. Barr, M. L. Kamil, P. B. Mosenthl, & P. D. Pearson (Eds.), *Handbook of reading research: Volume II* (pp. 951-983). New York: Longman.

Bartholomae, D., Petrosky, A. (1986). *Facts, artifacts and counterfacts: Theory and method for a reading and writing course*. Upper Montclair, NJ: Boynton/Cook.

Boese, H. (1986). *Common allusions and foreign terms*. Redlands, CA: Simplicity Press.

Brown, A. L., Campione, J. C., & Day, J. D. (1981). Learning to learn: On training students to learn from texts. *Educational Researcher*, 10, 14-21.

Brown, A. L., Day, J. D., & Jones, R. S. (1983). The development of plans for summarizing texts. *Child Development*, 54, 968-979.

Bullock, T., & Madden, D. R. (1986). Developmental reading program innovations and practices. In D. Lumpkin, M. Harshberger, & P. Ransom (Eds.), *Evaluation in Reading: Learning, Teaching, Administering — Sixth Yearbook of the American Reading Forum* (pp. 126-131). Muncie, IN: American Reading Forum.

Caverly, D. C., & Orlando, V. P. (1991). Textbook study strategies. In R. A. Flippo & D. C. Caverly (Eds.) *Teaching reading & study strategies at the college level* (pp. 86-165). Newark, DE: International Reading Association.

Flippo, R. A., & Caverly, D. C. (1991). *Teaching reading and study strategies at the college level*. Newark, DE: International Reading Association.

Garfield, L., & McHugh, E. A. (1978). Learning counseling: A higher education student support service. *Journal of Higher Education*, 19, 382-392.

Gamer, R. (1988). *Metacognition and reading comprehension*. Norwood, NJ: Ablex.

Haggard, M. R. (1982). The vocabulary self collection strategy: An active approach to word learning. *Journal of Reading*, 26, 203-207.

Harri-Augstein, S., Smith, M., & Thomas, L. (1982). *Reading to learn*. London: Methuen.

Hayes, C. G. (1987). Teaching basic reading to basic writers. *Journal of Reading*, 31, 100-108.

Hayes, C. G. (1990, May 1). Using writing to promote reading to learn in college. Paper presented at the Annual Convention of the International Reading Association, Atlanta, GA: ERIC Document Reproduction Service No. ED 322 499).

Hayes, C. G., Stahl, N. A., & Simpson, M. L. (1991). Language, understanding, knowledge: Theories and strategies for empowering developmental students to participate in the academy. *Reading Research and Instruction*, 30, 89-100.

Johnson, N. S. (1982). What do you do if you can't tell the whole story? The development of summarization skills. In K. E. Nelson (Ed.), *Children's language Vol. 5*. New York: Gardner.

King, J. R., & Stahl, N. A. (1985). Training and evaluating notetaking. In L. M. Gentile (Ed.), *Reading Education in Texas: A Yearbook of the Texas State Council of the International Reading Association* (pp. 115-119). Irving, Texas: State Council of the International Reading Association.

King, J. R., Stahl, N. A., & Brozo, W. G. (1984). Integrating study skills and orientation courses. *Forum for Reading*, 16, 6-13.

Kluwe, R. H. (1987). Executive decisions and regulation of problem solving behavior. In F. E. Weinert & R. H. Kluwe (Eds.), *Metacognition, motivation, and understanding* (pp. 31-64). Hillsdale, NJ: Earlbaum.

Langer, I. A., & Applebee, A. N. (1987). *How writing shapes thinking: A study of teaching and learning*. (NCTE Research Report No. 22). Urbana, IL: National Council of Teachers of English.

Mallary, A. L., & Bullock, T. L. (1985). Two models of developmental reading instruction: Fused or paired. In G.H. McNinch (Ed.), *Reading Research in 1984: Comprehension, Computers, Communication-Fifth Yearbook of the American Reading Forum*. Athens, GA: American Reading Forum, 87-91.

Manzo, A. V. (1983). College reading: Past and present. *Forum for Reading*, 14, 5-16.

Marshall, J. D. (1987). The effects of writing on students' understanding of literary texts. *Research in the Teaching of English*, 21, 30-63.

Martin, D. C. (1980). Learning centers in professional schools. In K.V. Lauridsen (Ed.) *New directions for college learning assistance: Examining the scope of learning centers*. San Francisco: Jossey-Bass.

Mealey, D. L. (1991). Doctoral program guidelines for college reading instructors. *Journal of College Reading and Learning*, 23(2), 47-54.

Moore, E. C. (1915). An experiment in teaching college students how to study. *School & Society*, 2, 100-107.

National Society for the Study of Education (1920). Reading instruction for college students. In *New Materials for Instruction-19th Yearbook of the National Society for the Study of Education* (Part 1). Bloomington, IL: Public School Publishing Company, 52-57.

Nist, S. L., & Hynd, C. R. (1985). The college reading lab: An old story with a new twist. *Journal of Reading*, 28, 305-309.

Nist, S. L., & Kirby, K. (1986). Teaching comprehension and study strategies through modeling and thinking aloud. *Reading Research and Instruction*, 25, 254-264.

Nist, S. L., & Simpson, M. L. (1989). PLAE, a validated study strategy. *Journal of Reading*, 33, 182-186.

Paris, S. G., Lipson, M. Y., & Wixson, K. K. (1983). Becoming a strategic reader. *Contemporary Educational Psychology*, 8, 283-316.

Pauk, W. (1984). *How to study in college* (3rd ed.). Boston: Houghton Mifflin.

Pressley, M. (1986). The relevance of the good strategy used model to the teaching of mathematics. *Educational Psychologist*, 21, 139-161.

Resnick, L. B. (1981). Instructional psychology, *Annual Review of Psychology*, 32, 659-754.

Sartain, H. W. (1981). *The language of the disciplines*. Pittsburgh: University of Pittsburgh and the Fund for the Improvement of Postsecondary Education.

Sartain, H. W., Stahl, N. A., Ani, U. A., Bohn, S., Holly, B., Smolenski, C. S., & Stein, D. W. (1982). *Teaching techniques for the languages of the disciplines*. Pittsburgh, PA: University of Pittsburgh and the Fund for the Improvement of Postsecondary Education.

Simpson, M. L. (1983). The preparation of a college reading specialist: Some philosophical perspectives. *Reading World*, 22, 213-222.

Simpson, M. L. (1986). PORPE: A writing strategy for studying and learning in the content areas. *Journal of Reading*, 29, 407-414.

Simpson, M. L., & Dwyer, E. J. (1991). Vocabulary acquisition and the college student. In R. A. Flippo & D. C. Caverly (Eds.), *Teaching reading & study strategies at the college level* (pp. 1-41). Newark, DE: International Reading Association.

Simpson, M. L., Hayes, C. G., & Stahl, N. A. (1989). PORPE: A validation study. *Journal of Reading*, 33, 22-29.

Simpson, M. L., Hayes, C. G., Stahl, N. A., Connor, R. T., & Weaver, D. (1988). An initial validation of a study strategy system. *Journal of Reading*, 28, 218-222.

Simpson, M. L., & Nist, S. L. (1984). PLAE: A model for planning successful independent learning. *Journal of Reading*, 28, 218-223.

Simpson, M. L., & Nist, S. L. (1990a). Textbook annotation an effective and efficient study strategy for college students. *Journal of Reading*, 34, 122-131.

Simpson, M. L., & Nist, S. L. (1990b, December). A situational analysis of academic tasks. Paper presented at the National Reading Conference, Miami, Florida.

Simpson, M. L., & Nist, S. L. (1992). Toward defining a comprehensive assessment model for college reading. *Journal of Reading*, 35, 452-458.

Simpson, M. L, Nist, S. L., & Kirby, K. (1987). Ideas in practice: Vocabulary strategies designed for college students. *Journal of Developmental Education*, 11(2), 20-24.

Simpson, M. L., Stahl, N. A., & Hayes, C. G. (1988). PORPE: A comprehensive study strategy utilizing self-assigned writing. *Journal of College Reading and Learning*, 22, 51-55.

Stahl, N. A., Brozo, W. G., & Gordon, B. (1984). The professional preparation of college reading and study skills specialists. In G. H. McNinch (Ed.), *Reading Teacher Education-Fourth yearbook of the American Reading Forum*, (p. 47-50), Athens, GA: American Reading Forum.

Stahl, N. A., Brozo, W. G., & Simpson, M. L. (1987). Developing college vocabulary: A content analysis of instructional materials. *Reading Research & Instruction*, 26, 203-221.

Stahl, N. A., & Henk, W. A. (1986). Tracing the roots of textbook-study systems: An extended historical perspective. In J. A. Niles (Ed.), *Solving Problems in Literacy: Learners, Teachers, Researchers – 35th Yearbook of the National Reading Conference*. Rochester, NY: The National Reading Conference, 366-373.

Stahl, N. A., Hynd, C. R., & Brozo, W. G. (1990). The development and validation of a comprehensive list of primary sources in college reading instruction. *Reading Horizons*, 31, 22-41.

Stahl, N. A., King, J. R., & Henk, W. A. (1991). Enhancing students' notetaking skills through systematic, self-directed training and evaluation procedures. *Journal of Reading*, 34, 614-622.

Stone, C. W., & Colvin, C. (1920). Study of a source of motive in educational psychology. *Journal of Educational Psychology*, 11, 348-354.

Taylor, B. M., & Berkowitz, S. (1980). Facilitating children's comprehension of content area material. In M. Kamil and I. Moe (Eds.) *Perspectives on reading and instruction*, pp. 64-68.

Thomas, J. W., & Rohwer, W. D. (1986). Academic studying: The role of learning strategies. *Educational Psychologist*, 21, 19-41.

Weinstein, C. E., & Rogers, B. T. (1984, April). Comprehension Monitoring: The neglected learning strategy. Paper presented at the American Educational Research Association, New Orleans, LA.

Zimmerman, B. J. (1986). Becoming a self-regulated learner: Which are the key subprocesses? *Contemporary Educational Psychology*, 11, 307-313.

Norman A. Stahl is Associate Professor, Faculty in Reading, Northern Illinois University, DeKalb, IL, 60115-2854. Michele L. Simpson and Christopher C. Hayes are both Associate Professors in the Division of Developmental Studies at the University of Georgia, Athens, GA 30602.

Current research suggests that some of the study skills we teach are more complex than previously thought and supports the vital importance of students' attitudes in skills improvement.

Are The Skills We Are Teaching Obsolete?
A Review Of Recent Research In Reading And Study Skills

By Martha Maxwell

(Reprinted from *Research in Developmental Education*, 10, (5), 1993. Reprinted by permission of Martha Maxwell and *Research in Developmental Education*, Appalachian State University, Boone, NC 28608.)

In the past decade there have been many changes in the way educators and psychologists view learning. Research studies based on new theories in cognitive psychology, information processing, linguistics, and neurophysiology have produced results that challenge old ideas about memory, intelligence, and learning skills. More sophisticated statistical designs and methods have made it possible to plan studies that tell us more about the interaction between methods, students characteristics, and learning outcomes, and experimenters are finding ways to control variables that are difficult to include like background knowledge and motivation.

Not only have there been changes in theory, research methods, and technology, but the demographics of those who attend college have changed. Diversity in culture, educational background, age, and ability characterize today's college student, and this diversity has had an impact on every phase of college life, even teaching. Faced with budgetary restrictions, many institutions have increased the size of classes. Modern technology, including computers and better teaching aids, is increasingly incorporated into classes, and today's students may participate in a broader range of learning experiences.

This paper addresses these challenges and asks: "Do the study skills we teach today reflect these recent changes? Are we preparing today's students for the real world of college study? Or are our methods locked in the assumptions and traditions of the past?" To answer these questions, we will examine a sampling of recent research studies in time scheduling and note-taking, as well as studies on the effects of affective factors such as locus of control on learning.

As you read through these summaries, remember that no one study is meaningful unless it is placed in context with other studies. In other words, there is no "final answer," for any conclusion we may reach will change as conditions change.

Recent Research On Time Management

Study skills programs routinely include skills in time management based on principles from business management training programs. Although many authors have written on this topic, most agree that students should identify needs and wants, rank them in regard to their importance or priority, and then allocate time and resources appropriately. Other time-honored tips include: delegate work, handle each piece of paper only once; and continually ask yourself, "What is the best use of my time right now?"

That management tips and schedules are the most popular handouts that students request from learning centers suggests that managing their time is a major adjustment problem of freshmen. For example, the Learning Skills Center at the University of Texas-Austin reports that it distributes an average of 5,000 time schedules each semester. Even at exclusive Harvard some freshmen have difficulty in planning time to study. Light (1992) in his assessment of Harvard students and faculty about teaching, learning, and student life, points out that for some students the inability to manage their time will spell failure. He encourages advisors to work with these students on time management and states that how they allocate their energies and plan their study time is crucial to success.

Despite the prevalence and pervasiveness of the problem for students, there has been surprisingly little research on time management until very recently. Academic counselors have been satisfied to suggest the same strategies that were developed for business managers without questioning their appropriateness for college students. When research has been done, it has mainly concerned how training in time management can change behavior and, although a number of studies have reported behavior changes, few studies have shown that time management training reduces stress or improves overall performance. Macan, Shahani, Dipboye, and Phillips (1990) point out that the research so far has dealt with time management training aimed at teaching what is assumed to be a unidimensional construct of good time management. Furthermore, there have been no systematic attempts to develop a test that assesses conventional time-management behaviors. Therefore, little is known about the correlation of naturally occurring time management with personality and indicators of stress and performance.

To consider some of these variables, Macan et al. (1990) developed a time-management questionnaire, administered it to college students, and checked it against time-management behaviors, attitudes, stress, and self-perceptions of performance and grade point average (GPA). They discovered that time management is multidimensional, and their test revealed four independent factors: Factor 1 – ability to set short-term goals and priorities; Factor 2 – use of mechanics (scheduling, planning, and checking off lists); Factor 3 – student's perception of control of time (feelings of being in control of time versus being overwhelmed by trivialities); and Factor 4 – student's preference for disorganization (feeling that a messy workplace is preferable, or that disorganization helps creativity).

Of the four factors revealed by the questionnaire, Macan et al. (1990) found that the one most predictive of GPA was *perceived control of time*. Students who felt they were able to control their own time reported significantly greater evaluations of their performance, greater satisfaction with work and life, less role ambiguity, less role overload, and fewer job induced and somatic tensions and also reported higher GPAs. Overall scores on the time management questionnaire were found to be positively correlated with age and sex. Older students were more likely to engage in traditional time management activities, and women made significantly higher overall scores on the time management questionnaire but were significantly lower on one factor: they did not feel that they were in control of their time. In other words, women were better time managers than men but rated themselves lower on perceived control of time.

In a more recent study on time management, Britton and Tesser (1991) gave 90 freshmen a time-management questionnaire and compared their responses with their cumulative grade-point averages four years later. Two time management components were found to be related to overall grades: a time attitudes factor and strong short-term planning skills. Both are consistent with the findings of the Macan et al. (1990) study. Students with positive time attitudes seem to be able to control their time, say "No" to people, and stop unprofitable activities or routines. The time attitudes factor is also consistent with these findings which showed that feelings of self-efficacy allow and support more efficient cognitive processing, more positive affective responses, and more persevering behavior.

Britton and Tesser (1991) report that long-term planning skills did not correlate with final GPA and postulate that, in a college environment, short-term planning may be more important than long term planning due to faculty changes in expectations and demands on students that are relatively rapid and frequent.

> Different parts of the course may unpredictably vary in difficulty; the overlapping of demand from different courses is often unpredictable; instructors may even change their mind about the due date on papers or the date an exam will be scheduled; on occasion, there is no syllabus and even in courses where there is a syllabus, there are often consequential deviations from it. Perhaps in this type of environment if the goal is to maximize grades, a short-term planning window is more optimal . . . long range planning may be more important in a less volatile, more stable environment (Britton & Tesser, 1991, p. 408).

These studies suggest that time management is a more complex activity than we had previously considered. It may be comprised of several independent factors, and, although more research is needed, time management is probably not a unitary trait. Both studies indicate that the most important factor in predicting achievement (whether it is current GPA or GPA at graduation) is whether students feel that they are in control of their own time, *not* the mechanics nor activities they engage in. Both studies agreed on a second independent time-management factor – short-term goals setting. The finding that people who are long-term planners are at a disadvantage in college and don't do as well as those who plan only for the short-term is intriguing. Perhaps we should avoid stressing that students need to have long-term goals and encourage them to be more responsive and adaptable to the inevitable changes they will face as they move through each college course.

Recent Research On Note-Taking

Recent research on using notes for review yields surprising results. Kiewra, Mayer, Christensen, Kim, and Risch (1991) investigated three note-taking functions: taking notes/no review, taking notes/review, and absent self from lecture/review somebody else's notes. (Note: This third condition is similar to what students do when they rent note-taking services.) The results indicated that taking notes and reviewing them was superior both to taking notes and not reviewing them and to reviewing borrowed notes on students' performance on a recall test and also superior to not reviewing notes on a test of synthesis. However, on a test of synthesis, borrowing someone else's notes was superior to taking notes and not reviewing them. The investigators also reported that taking notes in a matrix fashion (i.e., mapping) was superior to linear note-taking in preparing for examinations. However, Boyle and Peregoy (1991) studied the effects of mapping on learning from college texts and concluded that students trained in mapping improved their ability to write but not their reading comprehension. So whether mapping is superior to outlining seems to depend on what skills are involved and how students are tested.

In a study similar to the Kiewra et al. (1991) research, McIntyre, (1992) examined the relationships among information-processing, notetaking effectiveness, and academic performance indicators of students with above average verbal SAT scores. Subjects were given four different notetaking conditions: notes/no review, notes/review, no notes/no review, and no notes/review. The investigator found that information processing ability (as measured by two tests) accounted for about 5% of the variance of notetaking effectiveness. As was expected, students who reviewed their own notes outperformed students who did not review their notes on a lecture-specific quiz when verbal ability and information-processing ability were controlled. This result suggests that the act of taking notes improves students' information processing but reviewing one's notes is important.

Finally, McIntyre (1992) found that students recalled an average of less than 60% of the information in the lecture and were able to record only about half of the ideas that the lecturer presented. This suggests that students need to be taught and given practice if they are to develop effective notetaking skills.

Recent Research on Test Taking Skills

Typically we advise students to spend some time planning their answers before they begin writing an essay exam. Is there evidence that this is a good policy? Gillis and Olson (1991) studied the notes students made on exam papers after they had been given instructions to plan their answers by brainstorming or outlining before they wrote. The researchers found significant differences between the scores of students who did various amounts of planning with students who did extensive planning scoring the highest. The conclusion was that those students who plan before writing earn higher marks on essay tests, but the question remains as to whether students who are specifically required to plan will do as well as those who use these metacognitive strategies spontaneously, as did the students in this study.

Recent Research On The Importance Of Affect On Learning

Increasingly research results are supporting the idea that attitudinal and emotional factors play a crucial role in determining whether high risk students will respond to assistance efforts and will succeed in college. Among the affective factors that are currently viewed as most important are locus of control, self-efficacy, and self-esteem. Here are some recent studies on these attributes that should be of special interest to developmental educators.

The effects of locus of control on achievement. Educators have long believed that marginal, at-risk students should be exposed to the most effective teaching from the best teachers. But previous research on control theory suggests that unless students perceive that they have some control over and can influence their environment, their capacity to learn from good instruction is limited. The feeling that one has lost control can be induced by many factors in the typical college classroom such as unannounced tests, excessive content, and poor organization as well as such internal factors as believing one cannot learn the subject. However, research (Perry and Penner, 1990) suggests that giving students with low perceived control *feedback* on individual aptitude test items before a lecture temporarily altered their perceptions of control and improved their performance, a finding that has been replicated in three separate studies.

Arguing that if perceived control can be increased in at-risk students then their achievement should improve, Perry and Penner (1990) studied the effects of *attributional retraining*, a therapeutic method for reinstating psychological control, in groups of students with internal and external locus of control. Students with an internal locus of control tend to blame themselves when they don't do well, while those with an external locus of control place the blame on outside forces like the teacher or a lousy exam.

The attributional retraining involved in this study consisted of a short, 8-minute videotape that was given before a class experiment. On the tape, a male college professor described his freshman year at university, recounting an instance in which, despite repeated failure, he persisted only because a friend urged him and went on later to succeed in university and graduate school. He encouraged students to attribute poor performance to lack of effort and good performance to ability and proper effort. Following the training tape students were given an aptitude test consisting of analogies where they learned the correct answer after they had answered each item.

The investigators found that the experiment improved external, but not internal students' performance on a test following the lecture, a test given a week later and on homework performance. The results suggest that cognitive factors influencing students' perceived control (e.g., internal or external locus) must be taken in account when remedial interventions for academic achievement are developed and that brief training can influence the learning of students with low perceived locus of control.

The effects of affect on Supplemental Instruction. Visor, Johnson, and Cole (1992) studied the effects of locus of control, self-efficacy, and self-esteem on students' participation in Supplemental Instruction (SI). (In Supplemental Instruction students attend weekly sessions led by a trained student where they learn and practice the skills necessary for success in a specific course, usually a high risk course like chemistry, physics, etc.) Students were tested for affective variables and given the opportunity to voluntarily attend SI sessions in a psychology course in which they were enrolled. Afterward, they were divided into three groups: regular participants (attended four or more SI sessions), occasional participants (attended one to three SI sessions), and non-participants (attended no SI sessions). Results indicated that regular participants had the most internal orientation for locus of control, the highest mean on self-efficacy, and a higher level of self-esteem than the other groups (although they did not improve on these scores significantly as a result of their participation in SI).

The authors discuss the implications of these findings for the marketing of SI to at-risk students who are often the target of SI programs. They point out that the study suggests if we want students to attend regularly and actively participate in SI, the program must be marketed to appeal to students with different affective characteristics.

Furthermore, the SI sessions themselves must be designed to demonstrate to students with low self-esteem and external locus of control that they can succeed. Information must be carefully sequenced so as not to frustrate these students, and leaders must find new ways to encourage them to continue to attend. Perhaps the attributional retraining described by Perry and Penner (1990) is one approach that might also be helpful in SI classes.

Correlates of help seeking. Skills counselors and others who offer academic support services have long observed that students who need help the most are often reluctant to seek it, while students who are doing relatively well in their courses will volunteer. Karabenick and Knapp (1991) describe three studies in which they examined factors that correlate with a college student's seeking help when faced with the prospect of failing. In the first study seeking help was found to be related to whether the student viewed help as learning the process (instrumentally motivated) rather than gaining the minimum assistance to solve the problem (dependency-motivated); directly related to the student's global self-esteem, and inversely related to students' perceptions that seeking help is threatening. In all three studies, students who were willing to seek help in an academic context viewed it as an enhancement-related rather than a dependent behavior.

Summary

We have reviewed studies in a number of areas related to college study skills and the affective variables that influence learning. The results suggest that in many instances the behaviors we wish to change are more complex and less amenable to change through teaching than we previously believed. Tests of study skills, for example, reveal several factors that are related to college achievement, not a single factor. Since there is no one "best way" to manage ones time, take notes, etc., students should be helped to find the method that works best for them.

Some of the research results support our traditional study skills teaching strategies, others seems counter-intuitive to ideas we have long accepted. For example, the finding that students who are good at short-range planning are more successful than those who prefer long range planning suggests that we'd better examine our assumptions, conduct more research, and rethink intervention strategies. Affective factors such as locus of control, self-esteem, and self-efficacy appear to be vital factors in how well students learn. Certainly these studies can give us clues about how to work with the students who manage to fail despite our best efforts. Whether we are teaching courses or counseling students on skills, it is apparent that it's not what we teach but the way that we teach it and the way students feel about it that determines whether they will learn.

References

Boyle, O. F., & Peregoy, S. F. (1991, Spring). "The effects of cognitive mapping on students' learning from college texts." *Journal of College Reading and Learning*, xxiii: (2), 14-22.

Britton, B. K., and Tesser, A. (1991). Effects of time-management practices on college grades. *Journal of Educational Psychology*, 83:3, 405-410.

Gillis, M. K., and Olson, M. W. (1991). Do College Students Who Plan Before Writing Score Better on Essay Exams? In T. V. Rasinski, N. D. Padak, and J. Logan (Eds.), *Reading Is Knowledge, 13th Yearbook of the College Reading Association*. Pittsburg, KS: College Reading Association, Pittsburg State University, 7-9.

Karabenick, S. A., and Knapp, J. R. (1991). Relationship of academic help seeking to the use of learning strategies and other instrumental achievement behavior in college students. *Journal of Educational Psychology*, 83:2, 221-230.

Kiewra, K. A., Mayer, R. E., Christensen, M., Kim, S., and Risch, N. (1991). Effects of repetition on recall and note-taking strategies for learning from lectures. *Journal of Educational Psychology*, 83:1, 120-123.

Light, R. J. (1992). *The Harvard Assessment Seminars- Second Report, 1992*. Cambridge, Massachusetts: Harvard University.

Macan, T. H., Shahani, C., Dipboye, R. L., & Phillips, A. P. (1990). College Students' Time Management: Correlations with Academic Performance and Stress. *Journal of Educational Psychology*, 82:4, 760-768.

McIntyre, S. (Fall 1992). Lecture notetaking, information-processing, and academic achievement. *Journal of College Reading and Learning*, XXV:1, 7-17.

Perry, R. P., and Penner, K. S. (1990). Enhancing academic achievement in college students through attributional retraining and instruction. *Journal of Educational Psychology*, 92(2), 262-271.

Visor, J. N., Johnson, J. J., and Cole, L. N. (1992, Winter). The relationship of supplemental instruction to affect. *Journal of Developmental Education*, 16:12, 12-19.

Editor's Note: A shorter version of this article appeared in *Research in Developmental Education*, 10(5), 1993.

This lab is unique in that it combines individualized practice with direct individual instruction.

The College Reading Lab:
An Old Story With A New Twist

By Sherrie L. Nist and Cynthia R. Hynd

(Condensed from *Journal of Reading*, vol. 28, #4, January 1985, 305-309. Reprinted by permission of the International Reading Association and Sherrie L. Nist and Cynthia R. Hynd.)

In most college reading labs, students are tested and individual study plans are then prescribed. Students work through a series of materials to remediate their weaknesses; they check their own work, record their scores, and proceed to the next set of assignments.

Two problems are apparent in this approach. First, tests that are used to diagnose strengths and weaknesses are more likely than not survey tests rather than diagnostic instruments, e.g., a vast number of programs use the Nelson-Denny, a survey instrument, for diagnostic purposes. Second, this kind of program provides little individualized instruction as students are often left on their own to work through the exercises with little help from a trained, qualified instructor. What good does it do to tell students to complete Jamestown's *Finding the Main Idea* when they may not have any idea of how to find the main idea in the first place? While labs emphasize individualization, many omit the instruction so important to improving reading ability.

Another consistent finding is that most reading labs teach reading skills, not reading and study strategies. Students, practice reading brief, isolated passages, answer questions about main ideas, inferences, etc., and learn vocabulary in isolation. In no way do these activities prepare students for reading, analyzing and synthesizing college textbooks, nor does it teach the learning strategies needed in college core courses.

The New Twist

At the University of Georgia, our developmental reading program was established on the firm conviction that reading should be taught using a holistic, content based approach. Even the most deficient students are taught comprehension processes using a combination of novels, magazines, and textbook chapters from a variety of disciplines (Nist, Kirby, and Ritter, 1983). We believe that this approach prepares students better than a skills-drill approach.

Our lab was focused on two targeted groups – those who needed instruction specifically for passing a state mandated Basic Skills Exam (BSE) in reading and those whose SAT scores or grade point averages were significantly lower than other students.

The BSE groups were taught test-taking techniques and practiced taking sample BSE tests. Some students took the test on computers, others took regular paper-pencil tests. All received diagnostic feedback about the sample tests, instructors reviewed missed items, focusing on why specific answers were correct and how to go about selecting the right answer.

Students Were Taught How To Learn
From Their Mistakes

In the second targeted group, half showed severe difficulty with word recognition, all of them had difficulty with oral language and comprehension, and many also exhibited extremely poor planning and study strategies and had very poor reading habits. Less than half had ever read magazines, and several said they had never read a book.

Although this group required special assistance, we felt it important to maintain the content-based approach and involve these students in group discussion. Thus we used a strategies orientation, emphasizing text comprehension and word recognition mastery, often using material from their regular reading course. We also used *sustained silent reading* (students were given 20 minutes to read their regular reading course assignment in the lab); computer coursewear including critical reading exercises from the PLATO business and science curriculums and fiction; and *direct instructional strategies* using materials assigned in regular courses – e.g., in List/Group/Label, students brainstormed as many terms as they could relating to a particular topic from their exit assignment (e.g., political opinion). They then placed the words in categories based on group consensus of criteria and labeled them. This was used as both a pre-reading and post-reading activity. Prereading techniques such as the Directed Reading Lesson, the Directed Reading Thinking Approach, and REQUEST (Tierney, Readence, and Dishner, 1980) were taught in the regular reading course and reinforced in the Lab.

Success or Failure?

Despite the difficulty level of assignments and the pace of the work, students achieved considerable reading gains after the first quarter of work. An informal reading inventory given as both a pretest and post-test (using equivalent forms) revealed that all but one student gained at least one grade level in word recognition skills. In addition, 86% of the students had read a book they regarded as their all time favorite during the quarter and more students read a wider range of materials (79% now read magazines as compared with 43% previously).

In evaluating the reading lab, we found several drawbacks, the primary one being the difficulty level of the regular class material. Students experienced frustration and had difficulty completing and handing in work. During the next quarter, we grouped students homogeneously and modified the difficulty as well as the pace of assignments and required students to spend more time in the lab.

These modifications prompted student comments like, "I'm going to make it this quarter!" and students tended to view themselves as readers and students for the first time in their lives. Further adjustment in the curriculum should encourage even more gains.

This lab approach is successful not because of individualization but because of individualized direct instruction. We believe that in any lab, the materials are secondary in the success of students. The teacher and the approach are the primary elements in providing a comprehensive program to help deficient college students become readers. While other college reading labs focus their resources on materials and machines, we made our investment in staffing the lab with qualified instructors attuned to providing direct instruction. Our reading lab is an effective component in the total reading program, because it complements and reinforces what occurs in the reading class.

References

Nist, S. L., Kirby, K., & Ritter, A. (1983, December). Teaching comprehension processes using magazines, paper-back novels, and content area texts. *Journal of Reading*, 27, 252-61.

Tierney, R. J., Readence, J. E., & Dishner, E. K. (1980). *Reading Practices and Strategies: A guide for Improving Instruction.* Boston, MA: Allyn & Bacon.

Editor's note: It was necessary to condense the reference list in this article. We refer you to the original article for complete documentation.

Sherri L. Nist is Professor and Cynthia R. Hynd is Associate Professor in the Division of Academic Assistance, University of Georgia, Athens, GA.

Further Readings on Reading and Study Skills

Carver, J. B. (1988, November). Ideas in practice: Plan-making: Taking control of study habits. *Journal of Developmental Education*, 12(2), 26-29.

Hull, G., & Rose, M. (1990). This wooden shack place: The logic of an unconventional reading. *College Composition and Communication*, 41, 287-291.

Long, J. D., & Long, E. W. (1987, September). Enhancing student achievement through metacomprehension training. *Journal of Developmental Education*, 11(1), 2-5.

Maxwell, M. (1993). New insights about college reading: A review of recent research. *Journal of College Reading and Learning*, (In press).

McGlinn, J. E. (1988, Winter). Essential education in the reading class. *Journal of Developmental Education*, 12(2), 20-24.

Mikulecky, L., Clark, E. S., & Adams, S. M. (1989). Teaching concept mapping and university level study strategies using computers. *Journal of Reading*, 32(8), 694-702.

Napoli, A. R., & Hiltner, G. J., III. (1993, Fall). An evaluation of developmental reading instruction. *Journal of Developmental Education*, 17(1), 14-20.

Simpson, M. L. (1993, Fall). Cutting edge: Reality checks as a means of defining ourselves. *Journal of Developmental Education*, 17(1), 36-37.

Smittle, P. (1993, Fall). Computer adaptive testing: A new era. *Journal of Developmental Education*, 17(1), 8-12.

Sternberg, R. J. (1991). Are we reading too much into reading comprehension tests? *Journal of Reading*, 34 (7), 539-544.

Weinstein, C. E., & Rogers, B. T. (1965). Comprehension monitoring: The neglected learning strategy. *Journal of Developmental Education*, 9(1), 6-9, 28-29.

Editor's note: Also see the bibliography attached to the first article of Part 5, "Ten Recommendations from Research for Teaching High Risk College Students," for a list of many important articles on reading and study skills.

Part 6

Writing

In a truly developmental spirit, the writing center at the University of Wisconsin-Madison serves students at all levels and in all disciplines.

Reaching Across The Curriculum With A Writing Center

By Bradley Hughes

(Reprinted from *Illinois English Bulletin*, (Fall 1986), 74 (1), 24-31. Reprinted by permission of Bradley Hughes and the *Illinois English Bulletin*.)

On a recent Wednesday morning, I gathered the records of students conferences in the writing center where I teach at the University of Wisconsin-Madison to see who was coming for instruction. Here is what my quick survey revealed about the twelve students who had come for help already that morning:

Student	Subject of the Conference
1. Sophomore, Occupational Therapy major	Women's Studies Paper on Attitudes toward Childbirth
2. Sophomore, Pre-Journalism major	Introductory Sociology paper on Kinship Networks and Her Family
3. Sophomore, BA	Essay exams from a history course
4. Ph.D. Meteorology	Doctoral Dissertation
5. Senior, Secondary Ed. Major	Political Science Paper on the Cult of the Presidency
6. Freshman – Pre-Business Major	Introductory Literature Paper on Hemmingway and Owen
7. Freshman, BA	German Literature Paper and Introductory Philosophy Paper
8. Sophomore, BA	Psychology Lab Report
9. Freshman, BA	Philosophy paper on Hume
10. Junior, BS	Introductory Literature Paper on Wordsworth
11. Freshman, BA	No Show (a fact of life in writing centers)
12. MS Pharmacy Major	Pharmacy Thesis

Not every Wednesday morning in our writing center is like this one, but what is most striking about this list is its variety — in the levels of students coming for instruction and in the kinds of papers they were writing. Although some of this variety can be attributed to our writing center's being located on a large diverse campus, I choose to interpret it more as a confirmation of what those who teach in writing centers firmly believe: that providing writers with an opportunity to talk about a paper while it is still in progress is not something of value only to a particular group of student-writers. Its appeal should cut across disciplines and levels of ability. In this paper, I would like to suggest some ways a writing center, in either a high school or a college, can extend its reach across the curriculum so that there is frequent and rewarding contact with faculty in different departments, and so that students think of the writing center as a place to discuss their writing from all courses, not just English. The match between writing across the curriculum and writing is a natural one, in fact, an inevitable one. Even if a school does not have a formal or established writing-across-the-curriculum program, a great deal of writing is being done in many courses, and it is appropriate for writing centers to be a part of it.

Unfortunately, writing centers are often limited in all sorts of ways. They frequently have been and sometimes have allowed themselves to be cast in very narrow roles. Many serve primarily or even exclusively particular groups of student writers — often only those in writing courses and often only special students who are at the most basic level. Some serve only special subsets of those students — perhaps only those who are referred by instructors or only those who score below a certain level on a standardized test. Even if there are not such explicit limitations as these, there are often implicit ones, many of them having to do with the way writing centers are perceived. Too many faculty and students simply do not know what happens in writing centers, or do not know the extent of their services. Writing center directors need to make sure that they do know and they must subtly but firmly correct misconceptions, for it is in the definition and understanding of writing centers that limitations in perspective begin.

There are, of course, almost as many different models for writing centers, as there are writing centers. What distinguishes the best, however, is not how large they are, or whether their staff consists of peer tutors or professionals, but rather what their philosophy of writing instruction is and how well they convey it to faculty and students. Writing centers should not be viewed as safety nets for writing courses, or as fix-it shops, or as intensive care units where only maimed and diseased writing is treated, or worse yet, where only failed writers go. Good writing centers are not filled with students, injured in some way, dutifully completing workbook exercises which magically cure them of all writing ills and the air in these places is not thick with grammatical terms, but rather they are places for writers in all disciplines, regardless of their ability, to improve actual papers in process.

> Good writing centers are places for writers in all disciplines, regardless of their ability, to improve actual papers in process.

This kind of instruction takes the form of a conversation, one designed to help a student discover ways to get started, to make the assignments her own, to develop her ideas, and to revise a draft to make it square with her intentions. A writing center provides the kind of patient and experienced reader who is sympathetic but tough.

When writing centers are able to overcome the actual and the perceived limitations that are imposed on them, they can become a far more integral part of the curriculum. And more and more writing centers are doing exactly this. The fact that they are breaking free from curricular boundaries is not accidental, nor is it solely a consequence of the shrewd political instincts of writing center directors. Instead, this growth stems from the fact that many of the principles underlying writing center instruction are the same as those promoted by composition theorists and researchers and by writing-across-the-curriculum programs (WAC). A quick review of a few of the most basic principles of WAC reveals the obvious connections.

First, there is understood to be a crucial link between writing, thinking, and learning. Thus, writing is no longer considered (and taught as) simply a skill, something that can be learned once and for all at some early level (just as thinking cannot be), and that never needs to be used in any way again except as a means to test knowledge. If writing is connected to thinking, it then becomes the domain of all teachers, not just those in English departments. Second, writing is understood to be developmental: as students grow and mature intellectually, they take on new and more challenging writing tasks. A corollary of this is that writers sometimes regress when they move to new levels or begin to write in new disciplines. Thus, writing instruction needs to be ongoing and help with writing needs to be available outside composition courses. And a final point worth noting in this connection — writing is understood to be a process, something far more than simply a static product. Student-writers need to learn that writing is necessarily and profitably recursive, and they need to have opportunities to discuss their writing with an audience while it is still changeable.

> **If writing is connected to thinking, it then becomes the domain of all teachers, not just those in English Departments.**

Precisely because writing centers can be extremely flexible — able to help students whenever they are ready to learn, to tailor instruction to their individual needs, and to provide a convenient audience at any stage of the writing process — they are in an ideal position to complement course instruction across the curriculum. And because writing centers see so many different kinds of students and assignments, they can be an especially valuable resource to writing-across-the-curriculum programs, helping to discover and teach the generic principles which cut across disciplinary boundaries as well as the conventions of thought and form which characterize different disciplines.

> **A writing center director needs to reach out to faculty in various disciplines for insularity can be dangerous to a writing center's health.**

If we agree that writing centers should be working with students writing papers of all sorts, how then can they prepare themselves to do this effectively? I would like to suggest a range of approaches, some of which we have tried at Wisconsin, others which have worked at other schools and colleges. Above all, a writing center director needs to reach out to faculty in various disciplines, for insularity can be

dangerous to a writing center's health. A director must meet with colleagues in other departments, must talk with them in detail about the ways students write in their courses, and must offer to go into their classrooms. Following are some ideas for getting started.

First, survey the field. What kinds of writing are being done in your school? Who is assigning it? At what levels? Ask to see some sample assignments and some sample papers (be sure to explain to your colleagues that you are interested in learning from them, not in judging their assignments or responses to students' papers). Ask teachers what they are looking for in students' writing and what they hope students will learn from writing. Ask what their students are doing well and how they could improve.

Do some basic reading in a good writing-across-the-curriculum textbook to discover more about the ways writing can be used to promote learning in subject areas and to develop an appreciation for the conventions of writing in different disciplines.

> **Students profit from hearing a discussion of writing between a course instructor and a writing specialist, who, in turn, learn a great deal from each other.**

Offer to make a joint presentation on writing in a colleague's class. We have had good success doing this with courses of many sorts, including geography, political science, and sociology, usually in connection with a particular paper assignment. But we insist upon certain ground rules, designed to ensure that presentation is truly appropriate for the students and that we are supporting, not undermining, the principles of writing across the curriculum. Well before the class session, we meet with the course instructor to discuss how writing is being used in the course and the goals of the writing assignment, and we then plan the class jointly. As a result of these discussions, we are often asked to make suggestions for improving assignments or about alternative ways to use writing to promote learning in the course, and this collaboration often leads a faculty member to participate in a future writing-across-the-curriculum program. The writing center instructor and the course instructor then share responsibility for leading the actual class session, during which they discuss the writing assignment and provide students ample opportunity to talk about their writing and to raise questions. Students profit from hearing a discussion of writing between a course instructor and a writing specialist, who, in turn, learn a great deal from each other. We always close these sessions by explaining to students how best to use the writing center and encourage them to come in as they work on papers for this course.

> What we offer is an intelligent, experienced, general reader who understands something about how writers write and what constitutes good writing, and who has both the confidence and the good sense to refer students back to course instructors when it is appropriate.

The preceding suggestions are essentially external activities which help establish contact between the writing center and the various departments. Activities within the writing center itself are equally important to ensure that the staff is prepared to help students with all sorts of papers. First of all, the director and the tutors need to believe that they can be helpful even if they have not taken the particular course in which a paper was assigned. This is in fact a tenet of writing center instruction. We do not promise to provide an expert in the subject matter

of every course. Instead, what we offer is an intelligent, experienced, general reader who understands something about how writers write and what constitutes good writing, and who has both the confidence and the good sense to refer students back to course instructors when it is appropriate.

Some Other Ideas For Preparing A Center Staff

The staff itself should be chosen to represent a variety of academic interests. Consult with faculty in various departments for suggestions for new staff. Effective tutors are more than good writers themselves; they need to have broad interests, to be naturally curious about different subjects.

Staff members need to be exposed to all sorts of writing assignments, especially those which are most alien to their own academic experiences. Faculty members are usually glad to share some of their assignments and successful papers for the writing center to use in training.

Writing center handouts should include examples from across the disciplines, and they should cover the forms of writing used in different departments.

Faculty from other disciplines often make excellent guest speakers at staff meetings. With the last year, for example, we have had faculty from engineering, law, psychology, sociology, women's studies, and biology speak to our staff about the kind of writing done in their fields.

> Students listen to what their friends tell them about writing center instruction; if the word is good, students come.

In many ways, the preparation for reaching across the curriculum I have been describing helps persuade students and faculty from courses other than English to take advantage of the writing center. Every effort the writing center makes to reach out to faculty and to take their teaching of writing seriously helps lead to increased use of the writing center by students from their courses. But the most important promotion of all is good teaching — students listen to what their friends tell them about writing center instruction; if the word is good, students come. In most writing centers though, it is still necessary to do some special things to attract students writing papers in a wide range of courses. Here are a few suggestions for doing that, the first few aimed at students:

◊ Have a cross-disciplinary approach in publicity materials.

◊ To use a marketing term (yes, there is marketing involved in writing center instruction), segment the market: put posters up in certain parts of the school (by the chemistry or history classrooms, for example); design some flyers specifically addressed to the needs of particular groups of writers.

◊ Have tutors talk with students who come in for composition papers about the other kinds of writing they are doing, and specifically urge them to use the writing center for all kinds of papers. Despite a center's best efforts at publicizing the breadth of its program, some students are still surprised when they are told that the writing center offers help with all kinds of writing.

◊ Design some programs specifically for advanced students: hold a special session on writing an honors paper or create a special peer review group for an honors class. Associating the writing center with the best students and the most challenging classes almost inevitably attracts students writing in all sorts of disciplines.

◊ Offer some special sessions on non-academic writing, such as writing job letters and resumes or college applications; for graduating seniors, offer a short program on writing in the workplace.

Other Ideas For Broadening The Use Of A Writing Center Involve Faculty

◊ Ask faculty to mention the writing center on their syllabi or assignment sheets; help them by sending out reminders at appropriate times.

◊ Ask faculty to talk about the writing center in their classes (or invite the director to do so), urge them to describe instruction in the writing center not as something punitive or remedial but instead as a wonderful opportunity.

◊ Try to bring faculty themselves into the writing center by having a presentation on science or history writing or by scheduling a meeting there; hold a public tutorial; have a panel of tutors discuss their experiences in the writing center; arrange a faculty panel for students to interview about their writing and about writing in their disciplines; if the center has computers, hold a special session about ways computers can help faculty writers.

◊ Ask some faculty members from outside the English department to volunteer some time to tutor (be sure to have them participate in the center's training program).

◊ And, finally, do not be shy about sharing some success stories with faculty in other disciplines.

It is important to ask, since time and money are always scarce, whether the advice offered here is worth the effort. Obviously, I think the answer is yes. First of all, it is exciting and rewarding as a teacher to be doing new things; it keeps us vital. In addition, we should accept the reality that it is politically wise for writing centers to broaden the base of their support. Writing centers often find that many of their strongest supporters come from outside the English department, from faculty who see the center as providing essential instruction for their students.

> **Students writing papers for English courses should need us the least.**

But reaching across the curriculum does more than ensure our survival; it has genuine educational benefits. Students writing in all sorts of courses need what we can offer. In fact, and this may seem surprising, students writing papers for English courses should need us the least. Or, put a different way, in most non-composition courses, when writing itself is not the subject matter of the class, students need the kind of instruction offered by writing centers the most. We all agree that writing should be part of these courses as an aid to learning that discipline and as a way to ensure that writing is practiced frequently, but we must recognize that there will never be as much time in them to discuss writing as in a composition course.

Ultimately, writing centers should, like the concepts of writing across the curriculum itself, touch every department, at every level in our schools, for in both theory and practice, they are resources for the entire curriculum. By breaking free from narrow, prescriptive roles, writing centers benefit everyone in a school or college — students and faculty in all disciplines — and what is often overlooked, they reinvigorate themselves. Writing centers ought to be, then, as their name suggests, not on the periphery, but at the center of a lively, exciting, and fresh dialogue that is writing across the curriculum.

For a very persuasive statement of what writing centers are and how they suffer from being misperceived, see Stephen North (1983). "The Idea of a Writing Center." *College English*, 46, 433-446.

Bradley T. Hughes is Director of the Writing Center and Director of Writing Across the Curriculum at the University of Wisconsin-Madison.

Intimacy and Audience: The Relationship Between Revision and the Social Dimension of Peer Tutoring

By Thom Hawkins

(From Hawkins, T. (September 1980). Intimacy and audience: The relationship between revision and the social dimension of peer tutoring, *College English*, 42(1), 64-68. Copyright 1980 by the National Council of Teachers of English. Reprinted by permission of Thom Hawkins and *College English*.)

Since 1973 the peer writing tutors at the Student Learning Center of the University of California, Berkeley have handed me over one hundred journals that are part of the required work in a course I teach. The course gives juniors and seniors academic credit from the School of Education for tutoring freshmen and sophomores who voluntarily come to our Writing Center to do extra work, with no additional credit, on papers they are preparing for their courses. As a group, these tutors have written approximately one-and-a-half-million words describing and analyzing their tutoring sessions with inexperienced student writers.

It is evident to any careful readers of these journals that tutors are teaching something valuable about the nature of writing. In their entries, tutors often reflect on and assess how their involvement in the student's writing process contributes to the development of writing abilities. They feel that they are providing a vital link in the writing process, a link between writer and audience which is often missing when students write only for teachers. Tutors explain that the missing link is the opportunity to use oral language in discursive intellectual discourse and that discourse helps teach students the skills and judgment necessary to revise. It seems to me

that tutors are particularly successful at engaging students in this discourse because of the intensely personal characteristics of the social contract between them and their students.

For instance, tutors write about how they become concerned, even preoccupied, with the welfare of their students, especially with the students' struggle to master academic language. Students attempt to mimic the faculty with what Richard Lanham (*Revising Prose* [New York: Scribners, 1979]) has dubbed "The School Style," but they confuse it with the "Official Style" of university administrators. Evasion, obfuscation, and redundancy pervade both the classroom and the registration line. Thus, students come to perceive all academic language as inseparable from the bureaucracy itself. Tutors refer frequently to something they call "the system." To them the system is not just the academic establishment and its regulations, it is the set of intellectual standards used to measure student performance and, most important, it is the manipulation of language to enforce these standards. Knowledge is dispensed through the academy's language, and the academy protects its language from outsiders. A favorite word used to characterize this system is "impersonal." It is big, teachers are inaccessible, and the competition for grades is so fierce that students are atomized, cut off from each other, relating only to the center of power at the head of the classroom, just as they did in high school. The passivity they learned in high school is reinforced three and four times over in a large university such as Berkeley. I would conjecture that in such an environment language is not seen as a neutral tool, accessible to all. Rather, it becomes the instrument teachers sometimes use to intimidate students and to keep them at a distance; it is also the weapon students use against each other in the battle for grades.

Students want to have power over their environment, to be in control of what happens to them, and they sense that they must learn to manipulate language the way their teachers do before they will be able to play the academic game the way the insiders do. But the system is "impersonal," so where do they start? A beginning tutor wrote, "Given a campus the size of Berkeley's, you've got to be aggressive in order to get any personal attention." The trouble is that aggressiveness fosters distance rather than closeness. Thus, the language of a beginning writer can hardly be anything more than a thin, distorted echo of official style if she lacks the confidence in her personal voice that comes from close contact with a receptive audience. Can there be real communication when a writer feels that the distance between him and his audience is so great that he is powerless to fill the gap? The distance is present in the competitive social atmosphere of the classrooms, but it is also there in the very language of academe, a language that many students view as some sort of secret code decipherable only by the elite.

We all know that the combination of formal usage and standard English grammar is one of the hallmarks of the system's official communication code. To open up that code to inexperienced and insecure writers, a tutor must use the unofficial closeness of the peer relationship.

I'm trying to play it by the book while throwing out the book. Laying down the workings of gram-mar and trying to relax those workings at the same time. I want to stress the accessibility of these language skills, not grant them some kind of elitist status.

This tutor's technique is to break down the distance between persons, a distance students perceive as between language systems. Tutors step in and create a receptive audience sometimes overcoming years of misguided effort.

I'm trying to give my students some confidence with formal usage, yet I'm really working to play down the formal, because that seems to be where they've gotten stuck. It's the formality of academic English that hangs them up — when they try to approximate it on paper it comes out stilted.

> **Student writers try hard to control their language on paper, but they feel that the language, like the system, is controlling them.**

When peer writing tutors write in their journals about their students' sense of distance from the impersonal academic system and its language, they do not suggest that standards be softened or that teachers should abandon grades or start talking like blue-collar workers. They want standards for themselves and for their students; they find that fair, consistent grading provides an essential measure of progress, and they want a language that can deal with the complex abstractions of argumentation and exposition. At issue is how these standards are exacted. In the past the system has been one-sided in its emphasis on competition. It has traditionally ignored a rich resource close at hand — the students themselves and their capacity for cooperative intellectual work within a community of learners.

In contrast to what tutors have to say about the "system," they write about the relationship between themselves and their students as "personal" not "impersonal"; as intimate, not distant; as involved not detached. The tutoring contract is productive because there is a reciprocal relationship between equals, a sharing in the work of the system (for example, writing papers) between two friends who trust one another. Tutors write at length about this special association.

I learned that there is no such thing as learning in a vacuum, tutoring in a vacuum, and that tutees are human beings fully equipped with goals and fears, and not merely students with a particular academic problem.

Intellectually, the student may not respond to tutoring, but I think an emotional response is unavoidable. Everyone wants to know someone cares about them. At Berkeley it is particularly nice and unusual to find that someone is concerned about your academic results . . . If someone keeps after you enough, maybe, just maybe, a trusting relationship will emerge, and the tutee will not only develop an obligation to his tutor, but an obligation to himself as well.

These testimonials imply that the social dimension of peer tutoring is precisely what allows the work to get done, particularly the work on written language. Tutors are secure enough to insist that students produce their own papers: "I lose all sympathy when a student refuses to think for himself." Tasks are accomplished because there is a mutual effort between friends, a situation of closeness, not distance, that fosters a sense of community in which the language learner can take risks without fear of penalty, can let his language become personal, not impersonal. One tutor writes: "I pursue two roles, instructor and friend, although I believe it is essential that I be sympathetic and reassuring so that my student will gain confidence." A friendship goes

beyond the work, beyond the content of the paper, and lasts after "class" is out; hence peer tutors lean toward being a friend. Tutors concentrate on the writing task, but unless they put intimacy together with work there is not a real intellectual community. This subtle, sometimes precarious, juggling of a dual role is a pedagogical stance unique to tutors. They are, after all, the best equipped for such a role by merit of their student status and their accessibility.

A peer tutor, unlike a teacher, is still living the undergraduate experience. Thus, tutor and tutee are more likely to see each other as equals and to create an open communicative atmosphere, even though the peer tutor is a more advanced student who has already gained a foothold in the system. The tutor's credibility as an "instructor" stems from the fact that she has already learned to compete successfully, something the tutee would like to do. The tutor is further along than the tutee, but both know that the tutor is not so far along as to have forgotten what learning how to cope with the system is like. He is, from the tutee's point of view, both an insider and an outsider. When working together they comprise a social structure that enables both to rehearse being insiders.

Peer tutors can provide student writers with a generous amount of time to verbalize — to think out loud — and the trusting personal relationship allows the dialogue to be relatively unrestricted. Compare that situation to the conference with an overburdened teacher who can provide not regular, extended periods of one-to-one dialogue with students, and whose formal, critical dialogue must remain restricted because the writer knows he will be judged by the teacher who, if she is doing her job, is comparing the student to other members of the class. A tutor, in contrast, uses informal, congenial dialogue to guide students through the writing process, from pre-writing to revision to editing. Instructors rarely observe this entire process, let alone evaluate it. The nature of a classroom teacher's job is generally such that he can only examine and judge the product of a student's work, not the process the student uses to achieve that product. Good teachers give instruction about the process, but seldom can they monitor and evaluate it in the way a tutor can during regular weekly sessions of an hour or more with each student.

The trust and the relatively unhurried time together allow tutees to respond broadly to tutor's questions without fear of reprisal. No mistake, no blunder is irretrievable; they are not being graded. The truly discursive nature of the talk between tutor and tutee is, I would argue, at the heart of learning how to revise, how to refine thoughts from draft to draft. Students learn that revision involves much more than mechanically correcting errors, that it is a recursive process concerned primarily with shaping ideas into suitable form. Tutors often write in their journals about how important it is to build confidence in tutees so that they will have the courage and self-assurance it takes to make substantive revisions. They tell me that they build that confidence through talk, that it is the dialogue that teaches students how to argue, to analyze, to restate. Conversing with a peer tutor is, for many students, their only chance to thoroughly know the academic audience by talking at length to that audience in the language of that audience. They won't have the confidence to make changes, to revise, if they don't know what is expected of them.

I find that many students who come to our Writing Center do not know what the academic audience really wants. Kenneth Bruffee has observed this same problem at the Brooklyn College Writing Center.

Many of the students who walked through the doors of the Writing Center, however many discrete bits of information they may have been able to check off reliably on multiple-choice examinations, did not really seem to know the subjects they studied when they were asked about them. Yet given the opportunity to talk with sympathetic peers, these same students seemed to discover knowledge they did not know they had. They could identify and examine issues in these subjects, take positions on them and defend their positions in ways they (and some of their teachers) had not thought possible.[1]

Not until students have had sufficient experience talking with a sympathetic representative of their intended audience can they begin to develop the kind of intellectual judgment necessary to know how to benefit from criticism.

The students in our Writing Center are hungry for the information about what their audience is like and for the experience of being listened to and understood by that audience face to face. They need to observe the reactions and solicit the feedback of potential readers while they tentatively shape what they know into a form that will reach an academic audience. They must find out spontaneously if the receiver is getting the same message that is being sent. And, as they rephrase their thoughts into alternate spoken statements, so too will they learn to revise their writing in a sequence of drafts, checking each draft with a reader — either teacher or tutor — until they have demonstrated that they have something to say and someone to say it to.

[1] The Brooklyn Plan: Attaining Intellectual Growth Through Peer Tutoring. *Liberal Education*, 64(1978), 447-468.

Now retired, Thom Hawkins was Coordinator of the Writing Center at the University of California Berkeley, Berkeley, California 94720.

What teachers need to know about how and why poor writers ignore their written comments and what to do about it.

Developmental Students' Processing of Teacher Feedback in Composition Instruction

By Ross B. MacDonald

(Condensed from the *Review of Research in Developmental Education*, 8(5), 1991. Reprinted by permission of Ross B. MacDonald and the *Review of Research in Developmental Education*, Appalachian State University, Boone, NC 28608.)

Developmental writing courses comprise a significant portion of developmental education programs at many colleges, enrolling large numbers of students. Since a core component of any developmental writing course is the feedback (fb) teachers give students about their writing, the nature of that feedback and the use students make of it are critically important concerns for developmental educators and researchers.

This article reviews existing literature regarding feedback in two fields, English education and social psychology, in order to (a) develop a supportable set of suggestions for developmental English instructors and other instructional staff to use when providing feedback to composition students and (b) clarify useful directions for future research. This review and the inferences drawn from it are intended as a progress report on the state of our knowledge at this point. Suggestions for practice must be viewed as guidelines, not prescriptions, informing teachers to apply judgment, knowledge, and sensitivity to instructional encounters in developmental English.

Research on Written Feedback in English Education

Teachers' feedback (fb) on students' compositions is an important channel of teacher-student interaction which, if prevalence of practice is an indicator, is widely assumed to be a useful instructional procedure. For this article, the term feedback refers to the process of providing some commentary on student work in which a teacher reacts to the ideas in print, assesses a student's strengths and weaknesses, and suggests directions for improvement. This feedback is typically written on blank spaces on the students' essays for return to the student or spoken to the student in short conferences. Traditionally, written feedback (wfb) is episodic: students receive it on the formal occasion of the return of their graded essays. More recently, feedback, both written and oral, is integrated into the writing process: students receive it as they are working on their compositions. Regardless of when it is delivered, teachers presume that students attend to the feedback, learn about their writing in relation to some ideal goal or a next step, and incorporate this learning into their future writing efforts.

However, an examination of research in the area of teacher fb and student processing of that fb shows that the ideal of teacher-student shared understanding and the development of students' writing is at best imperfectly realized in practice. Teachers' fb often lacks thought or depth; students often misunderstand their teacher's fb; the writing skills of students receiving fb may actually regress; and many students do not attend to teachers' fb to begin with!

Research examining the qualities of teachers' written feedback on student essays has found that teachers write confusing or superficial comments. Some suggest that perhaps because they tend to read looking for errors, teachers tend to mark surface errors and to write "rubberstamped" comments which are neither text nor student specific, and tend to provide feedback which conflicts with other feedback or reflects paternalistic attitudes.

It is not surprising then that students misunderstand and therefore fail to benefit from their teachers' feedback. Researchers suggest written "squiggles" may be meaningful to the teacher but uninterpretable for the student and, even in classrooms in which current research is being applied to practice, teacher feedback is misunderstood. Often, teachers' feedback is associated with students' negative attitudes; students have trouble interpreting the teacher's comments and teachers' feedback to student writers may reflect teachers' misunderstandings of their students' writing.

On the positive side, some studies have found that teachers' feedback concerning essay content is associated with better essays than feedback concerning essay language, grammar, and usage; however, lengthier comments are less effective than shorter ones. In addition, as compared to positive comments, several researchers report that negative comments are related to less desirable student attitudes about aspects of the writing process.

Given that teachers' feedback to students' writing seems to be unclear, misunderstood and ineffective, it shouldn't surprise any of us to hear that researchers suggest that (a) feedback, especially in written form, does not make much of a difference in improving students' writing, and (b) students don't seem to pay attention to it anyway. Several studies have shown that many students do not read their teachers' wfb, and those who do read the comments seldom used them as guides in revising existing papers or writing new papers.

Why Don't Students Attend to Feedback?

It's important to understand *why* students don't pay attention to teacher feedback. Obviously, understanding the psychological and emotional mechanisms which underlie students' ignoring or rejecting teachers' feedback provides direction for instructional practice as well as future research.

The grade one receives may determine the attention one gives to the feedback. For example, one study reports that students' primary interest is their grade on a given composition, not the teacher's comments. A poor grade may discourage a student from reading the feedback while a good grade may encourage a student to read the feedback. Other research on students' reactions to positive and negative fb provides some evidence for the suggestion that students receiving poor grades on their compositions may be gaining less from teachers' comments than students receiving higher grades.

Gestalt theory of learning suggests the psychological processes of avoidance and disassociation may impede the development of poor writers while psychological processes of accommodation and assimilation propel the development of more skilled writers. When integrated with current writing research on teacher written feedback (wfb), Gestalt theory suggests that the composition student will attend to the grade first. If the grade is low, then the student will experience cognitive dissonance and will likely attempt to reduce this tension by discrediting the fb. It further suggests that composition students are likely to have one overall reaction, not a separate set of possibly conflicting reactions to a teacher's fb, and that this reaction will determine the degree to which students accept the teacher's fb.

Social Psychology Research on Feedback

Results of studies on feedback in social psychology further support the notion that poor writers, to preserve a positive view of self, will tend to discredit their teachers' wfb, ironically resulting in continued poor achievement. Social psychological research on feedback has tended to utilize oral feedback, not written, but taken as a whole, research suggests that students will react to oral feedback in the same ways they react to written feedback.

Social psychological research indicates the factor that most strongly influences one's acceptance of fb is whether it is positive or negative. Researchers have found that both the receiver and the giver prefer positive feedback over negative. Positive feedback is also rated by receivers as more accurate and more useful than negative.

> **The grade the student received and the grade he or she expected to receive appear to be most important in determining whether a student uses teacher feedback.**

Implications

Theory. There are four implications of this research for composition theory. First, students' reaction to their teachers' evaluations would seem to be a Gestalt process: students have an overall reaction to their performance, not a set of discrete reactions to discrete components of the teacher's wfb. In initial encounters between students in college composition classrooms, students' overall reaction to their performance as evaluated by a teacher determines the degree to which shared meaning about the fb can be constructed. This effect may be mitigated by a trusting relationship between teachers and students. It's also possible that, as time passes, students' initial negative reactions to fb are reduced. Researchers need to investigate each of these possibilities.

Second, when students are disappointed by their grades on writing assignments, they tend to behave like the ancient king who killed the messenger for reporting a disastrous loss in battle. The student "kills" the teacher's message because it is so displeasing. At least in the short term, our desire for a positive view of self leads to a discounting of the message, rather than a changing of our perception of self, and, unfortunately, rejecting the enriching message maintains the student's level of impoverishment in writing.

Third, the research supports a socio-cognitive theory of writing. Because feedback occurs as a part of teaching-learning interaction in which both the teacher and the student contribute to the accomplishment of meaning, it is both a social and a cognitive process centering on collaboration. The social component of socio-cognitive theory is concerned with how successfully we communicate with others and the cognitive component refers to a set of distinctive thinking processes which a writer applies in the act of composing.

Practice. Optimum instruction in developmental writing courses requires strengthening the communication between teachers and students first by reinforcing students' processing of written feedback in spite of the students' disappointment, second by examining the qualities of the teacher's comments, and third by questioning the simultaneous delivery of grades and comments.

Attending to and learning from feedback should be an ongoing process, not merely a series of discrete traumatic events. To increase students' processing of feedback teachers should provide activities which reinforce students' attention to it. For example, students might be asked to write summaries of the main points of their teacher's feedback. Perhaps the impact of a disappointing grade could be mitigated by having each student summarize the teacher's fb on another student's composition. Students might then articulate goals for their performance on the next assignment based on their understanding of the fb received to date. In addition, students might be asked to evaluate the strengths and weaknesses of their own and others' work while it is being written and as it is submitted. Students might benefit from the opportunity to discuss their self-assessments, the teacher's assessments, and the tension which may exist when these assessments are misaligned. Active involvement in evaluating, being evaluated, and discussing feelings may reduce the negative impact of the teacher's evaluation and help students understand the value of feedback.

Further, students may perceive teachers' positive comments as the sugar coating on a bitter pill that has no purpose other than to make the "true" message more palatable. If so, students may not attend to reinforcement of what they are doing well and so may not learn to keep doing it. Activities can be developed which require the student to focus on the positive aspects of the feedback. For example, students could list their strengths and identify particular passages where those strengths are evident. They could discuss ways to utilize their strengths to address their weaknesses. In small groups they can identify strengths in each other's papers. Students could be identified as in-class "consultants" according to their individual strengths on certain aspects of the writing process and be available to provide assistance to their peers. Every student could be a consultant on some aspect of the writing process. However, not all of the responsibility for improving students' understanding of teachers' feedback should rest with the student.

> The evaluation of a student's work should be separated from personalized instruction or feedback.

The final instructional implication of this research involves changing some fundamental patterns of instruction in developmental English classes. Despite research showing the futility of correcting essays after they are completed, the practice persists. We must shake loose from the assumption that grading students' work and commenting on it necessarily occur at the same time. Traditionally, each student paper receives a grade and written feedback, resulting in a system in which two very different kinds of teaching are forced together: formal evaluation, which produces a grade intended to let a student know how she or he is doing in relation to some standard, and personalized instruction, which provides feedback intended to help a student learn. The research reported here suggests that the student displeased with the formal evaluation will discredit the personalized instruction. It seems likely that the evaluation of a student's work should be separated from personalized instruction. Researchers and practitioners have developed instructional methods, appropriate for developmental college students, which separate formal evaluation from personalized instruction. These include conferencing, grading portfolios of accumulated work rather than singled finished essays, and peer or cross-aged tutoring.

Further research is needed to determine the answers to a number of questions raised about feedback. For example, are comments on deficiencies more specific and focused and more extensive than comments on student achievements? If so, perhaps teachers are training students to attend to the negative feedback at the expense of the positive. There are many other questions about the nature of feedback that remain to be explored further.

Conclusion

This review indicates that students' initial reactions to grades can obstruct their acceptance of accompanying information, that students have one overall reaction to the teacher's written feedback, and that these reactions are unaffected by students' gender or the positive-negative sequencing.

Compared to their more highly skilled peers, less skilled writers are more likely to write poorly and are consequently more likely to receive negative feedback from their teachers. Therefore, less skilled writers may suffer the harshest consequences of the confusion between teacher feedback and student understanding, in that those who need to learn the most from teachers may be learning the least. If we are aware of factors contributing to this result and if we can change traditional patterns of developmental instruction in writing, then we may give developmental students the power to clearly and thoughtfully express their ideas and feelings and to critically question and define their worlds.

Editor's Note: Due to lack of space we were not able to include the references cited by the author. For these and other details, we refer you to the original article.

Ross B. MacDonald is Director of the California Tutor Project and an English Instructor at Los Medanos College, Pittsburgh, CA 94565.

This article describes two carefully researched and proven methods for teaching basic writers and ESL students.

Two Powerful Methods For Teaching Writing Skills: Sentence Combining And Text Reconstruction

By Arthur Whimbey, Myra J. Linden, and Eugene Williams, Sr.

(From *Review of Research in Developmental Education*, (1992), 9(1). Reprinted by permission of Arthur Whimbey, Myra J. Linden, and Eugene Williams, Sr. and *Review of Research in Developmental Education*, Appalachian State University, Boone, NC 28608.)

"Caveat Emptor: The Writing Process Approach to College Writing" is the title of a major article on writing pedagogy published in the September 1990 issue of *The Journal of Developmental Education* (Devine, 1990). For those whose Latin has gotten rusty, caveat emptor means, "Let the buyer beware." The abstract of the article begins: "In the past decade an enormous amount of material has been published about writing instruction, almost all of it, unfortunately, from a single point of view: that of the writing process approach" (p. 2). The author, Devine, expands on this in the article: "Advocates of the process approach have been so persuasive and so vigorous in promotion that the bandwagon some of them started 30 years ago now appears to have almost everyone aboard" (p. 2). This is unfortunate, Devine explains, because, "No evidence yet supports the belief that the writing process approach leads to better writing" (p. 2).

Devine's conclusion is buttressed by research which he cites and by other major studies, such as *The Writing Report Card* (Applebee, Langer, & Mullis, 1986): "At all three grade levels assessed, students who said their teachers regularly encouraged process-related activities wrote about as well as students who said their teachers did not" (p. 12).

Weaknesses of the Process Approach

Devine lists several reasons which explain why the process approach fails to produce better writers. These reasons and others are discussed in detail in *Why Johnny Can't Write: How to Improve Writing Skills* (Linden & Whimbey, 1990). In order to better understand the advantages of two other writing-instruction procedures discussed later, these reasons will be summarized briefly in terms of the following four stages of the process approach.

1. Prewrite: pick a topic and think of ideas to write about.
2. Write a first draft.
3. Revise: look for ways to improve the first draft.
4. Write the final draft.

In the first stage of the process approach, students are supposed to find a topic to write about. However, finding a topic which is appropriate for a class paper -- a topic on which 300 to 500 words can be written — presents a problem for most students, and the sincere complaint, "I don't know what to write about," is familiar to all English teachers. The textbook, *Writing with a Purpose* (Trimmer & McCrimmon, 1988), admits to readers, "Many student writers complain that their biggest problem is finding a subject" (p. 9). The accompanying Instructor's Guide warns teachers, "The advice to write from what you know or what you care to learn is often difficult for students to follow"(p. 5).

And Bill McCleary (1991) observes in *Composition Chronicle*, "Composition's most intractable problem is finding topics for students to write about" (p. 7).

While students are looking for ideas to write about, they are not learning to write. Various strategies have been developed to help students find ideas, such as freewriting, and clustering. But a major study of methods used for teaching writing by the National Conference on Research in English (Hillocks, 1986) found that these strategies contribute little to the improvement of writing skills; they just take time away from learning to write. For example, regarding freewriting, Hillocks wrote, "It is less effective than any other focus of instruction examined" (p. 249).

In the second stage, students are told to write a first draft. However, as Devine (1990) points out, the process approach does not explicitly teach students to write: how to cast ideas into different sentence patterns or how to start, organize, and end papers. Nor are students given good writing to study and emulate. The result, according to Devine, is that skills remain relatively unimproved, particularly for the type of mature, formal writing required in most academic courses and business situations.

In the third stage, students are to revise their papers. But without skills, they have no basis for making revisions. It was hoped that peer review could be useful at this stage. However, in our classroom experience, peer review has worked best with advanced students who already possess strong skills. Unskilled peers cannot make useful suggestions. Moreover, students tend to limit their comments to superficial aspects of writing, such as the correction of spelling and grammatical errors.

According to *The Writing Report Card* (Applebee, 1986), quality of teacher feedback is a major variable in the effectiveness of writing instruction. But the amount of feedback needed by many students to improve their writing with the process approach is beyond the realm of feasibility for teachers with several full classes.

Effective Approaches

Sentence Combining

Fortunately, there are other methods for teaching writing which have proven to be highly effective. Dozens of studies over the past 20 years (reviewed by Hillocks, 1986) show that sentence combining (SC) is very powerful for improving writing skills. SC teaches students how to combine simple sentences into more complex ones. Here is an elementary example (Whimbey & Jenkins, 1987, p. 23):

Use the word "before" to combine these two sentences into one:
1. The pool was drained.
2. The bottom was repaired.

Possible answers:
1. The pool was drained before the bottom was repaired.
2. Before the bottom was repaired, the pool was drained.

Research reviewed later shows that SC not only improves a student's ability to write mature, informative sentences but also reduces grammatical errors. Furthermore, SC tends to enhance the overall quality of a student's paper. And as an extra bonus, several studies indicate that SC can build reading skill (Linden & Whimbey, 1990). In short, SC strengthens many aspects of a student's capacity to handle written material.

One major study on SC was conducted with 300 Miami University freshmen (Kerek, Daiker, & Morenburg, 1980). Half the students followed the traditional department syllabus which covered modes and elements using a standard college reader and composition text. The other students practiced SC exclusively. After 15 weeks, the SC students wrote original papers which were judged by a panel of experienced English teachers to be superior in overall quality to the compositions written by the traditionally trained students.

Numerous other studies, using a variety of students, have also obtained positive results. For example, in a study of 50 fifth graders, McAfee (1980) found that students who used SC scored higher than students in the regular curriculum on a standardized test of written language, on a reading test, and on papers they wrote. Stoddard (1982) found fifth and sixth graders who used SC wrote better than those who followed the regular gifted-education program. And Argall (1982) found that college freshmen in developmental writing classes who had five weeks of intensive SC showed a 100% decrease in garbled sentences, 21% decrease in comma splices, 31% decrease in sentence fragments, 67% decrease in fused sentences, and 14% decrease in comma errors.

Several formats for SC exercises have been developed. One of the first successful SC studies by O'Hare (1973) used "cued" exercises, such as those below, in which four sentences must be combined.
1. Weightlifting is a method.
2. It is a method of exercising.
3. Some athletes find it useful. (WHICH)
4. Others claim it leads to sluggishness. (BUT)

Answer:
   Weightlifting is an exercising method which some athletes find useful, but others claim leads to sluggishness.

This is called a cued format because cues are given to students on how the sentences should be combined. The cues follow rules such as these:
1. The main sentence is presented first.
2. Words to be inserted are underlined.
3. Connecting words, such as WHICH are written in parentheses after the sentence they connect.

An alternative to cued SC is "open" SC (Kerek et al., 1980). In open SC exercises, students are not given cues as to how to combine sentences. Instead, they are presented with examples of how sentences can be combined and then given several sentences which can be combined in a number of ways. Students are encouraged to try to write several different combinations. Then the sentences written by various students are compared and discussed so that students learn many options for expressing ideas.

Both open and cued SC exercises produce improvements in writing skills. For example, the successful Kerek et al. (1980) study described earlier used open exercises. O'Hare (1973), using cued exercises like that above, also obtained positive results. He found that after seventh graders went through an SC program, their writing was well above that of typical eighth graders in syntactic maturity — a measure of the richness or complexity of information within sentences. Also a team of experienced English teachers rated compositions written by the SC students higher than compositions of traditionally trained students.

While numerous SC studies have shown positive results, the Hillocks (1986) survey of writing instruction states: "The one clear negative report . . . was later rescinded as the researcher admitted that poor teaching was probably the cause of negative attitudes and results" (p. 144).

In light of all this positive research, why is SC not used more widely? A major reason is that it has been overshadowed by the enthusiasm of the process-approach advocates. Devine (1990) observes that, although the process approach lacks any research base, it ". . . was so stimulating to teachers (it seemed so 'right') that it now appears to have become the primary approach to writing instruction at all levels" (p. 2). However, with over ten years of disappointing results from the process approach, SC may finally take its rightful place as a major procedure for improving writing skills.

Text Reconstruction

A second procedure which is proving effective for strengthening students' writing skills is based on methods professional writers have used to improve their writing. For example, in his autobiography Benjamin Franklin (1909) describes an exercise he used as a teenager to become a more, effective writer. For essays he admired, he wrote, ". . . short hints of the sentiments in each sentence" (p. 17), which he then jumbled into random order and set aside. Several weeks later he tried arranging the hints into their original order to recreate the logical organization of the essay. Franklin says, "This was to teach me method in the arrangement of thoughts" (p. 17). Then he attempted to write the complete sentences from just the hints, checking back to the originals and noting deviations, trying to master the vocabulary and style of the writer.

Following is a related text reconstruction (TRC) from the workbook *Analyze, Organize, Write*, (Whimbey & Jenkins, 1987, pp. 119-120) which has been found useful with students in developmental writing courses.

The Company Needs A New Truck

When you recommend an expensive purchase like buying a new truck, you need convincing reasons with specific facts to win your case. The following sentences can be arranged to make a well-supported argument for a new truck.

Exercise 1. Number the sentences in each paragraph to form the best logical order.

I. _____ Nevertheless, we should buy a new truck because the old truck is unreliable, obtaining parts for it is difficult, and the greater economy of a new truck would help repay the purchase price.

_____ It is true that new trucks are expensive and the company's budget is tight.

II. _____ Worse yet, last Friday it quit running on the expressway and had to be towed to a garage.

_____ Three times last month deliveries to customers were late because the truck would not start.

_____ The company is sure to lose business if this continues.

_____ The old truck is constantly breaking down.

Exercise 2. Check your numbers with a neighbor. Where you disagree, explain to each other why you arranged the sentences as you did.

Exercise 3. Write the sentences in the order that you numbered them. But do not just copy them word-for-word. Write from memory as much as possible. For each sentence, follow these steps:

1. Read as many words as you believe you can write correctly from memory (usually five to ten).

2. Write those words from memory, including all capitals and punctuation marks.

3. Check back to the original sentence and correct any errors you made.

4. Read the next group of words and repeat the steps.

Arranging sentences in a paper such as the one above which presents supporting evidence for a main idea, is the type of work on logical organization needed by many students.

Teachers report that TRC has both instructional and diagnostic value and that students like the exercises (Vavra, 1990). In addition, TRC contributes to writing skills by asking students to copy the sentences partially from memory. Many outstanding writers copied models in developing their skills. Somerset Maugham (1978) recalls:

> *The prose of Swift enchanted me. I made up my mind that this was a perfect way to write, and I started to work on him in the same way I had done with Jeremy Taylor. As I had done before, I copied passages and tried to write them out again from memory (p. 24).*

Malcolm X (1977) reports that to improve his vocabulary and writing skills, he copied an entire dictionary, reading over his notes to commit words and definitions to memory and periodically checking his recall; and James Jones, author of *From*

Here to Eternity, said, according to his biographer McShane (1985), that ". . . one could read until his eyes are red, but only by copying word for word could one see how a writer builds up his effects" (p. 118).

Linden found that the combination of arranging and copying sentences greatly improved the skills of her developmental students (including a full range of ethnic and age groups) at Joliet Junior College. Examples of both TRC and SC avoid what McCleary (1991) calls "composition's most intractable problem, finding topics for students to write about" (p. 7). With both methods, students do not waste time trying to think of a composition subject. They spend all their time practicing and strengthening writing skills. Then, when they do have things that need to be written — content-oriented papers in social science classes, lab reports in physical science courses, and letters in business — they have writing skills to do the job.

Since many college students today come from homes in which standard English is not the primary language, educators now more than ever need effective methods for teaching standard written English to all students. In SC, students create combinations of correctly written sentences. In TRC they organize and recreate sentences from memory as much as possible, checking back to the originals and correcting any deviations. This immediate feedback counteracts tendencies of students from various backgrounds to use language habits and patterns which differ from standard written English. Both SC and TRC immerse students in models of the language which improve their vocabulary, spelling, grammar, and punctuation. As more teachers begin using SC and TRC, it will be easier for all students to learn to write in the way required for success in academic and business pursuits.

References

Applebee, A., Langer, J., & Mullis, I. (1986). *The writing report card: Writing achievement in American schools.* Princeton, NJ: Educational Testing Service.

Argall, R. (1982, March) Sentence combining: An incisive tool for proof reading. Paper presented at the annual meeting of the Conference on College Composition and Communication, San Francisco, CA.

Devine, T. G. (1990). Caveat emptor: The writing process approach to college writing. *Journal of Developmental Education,* 14(1), 2-4.

Franklin, B. (1909). *Autobiography of Benjamin Franklin.* In C. Eliot (Ed.), *Harvard Classics, Volume 1.* New York: P. F. Collier & Sons.

Hillocks, G. (1986). *Research in written composition.* Urbana, IL: National Conference of Research in English.

Kerek, A., Daiker, D., & Morenberg, M. (1980). Sentence combining and college composition. *Perceptual and Motor Skills,* 51, 1059-1157.

Linden, M. J., & Whimbey, A. (1990). *Why Johnny can't write: How to improve writing skills.* Hillsdale, NJ: Lawrence Erlbaum Associated.

Malcolm X (1977). *Autobiography of Malcolm X.* New York: Ballentine.

Maugham, S. (1978). *The summing up.* New York: Penguin.

McAfee, D. (1980). *Effect of sentence-combining instruction on the reading and writing achievement of fifth grade children in a suburban school district.* Unpublished dissertation, Texas Women's University, Benton, TX.

McCleary, B. (1991). Topics are always an issue, *Composition Chronicle,* 4(5), 7-8.

McShane, F. (1985). *Into Eternity: The life of James Jones: American writer.* Boston: Houghton Mifflin.

O'Hare, F. (1973). *Sentence combining.* Urbana, IL: National Council of Teachers of English.

Stoddard, E. (1982). *The combined effect of creative thinking and sentence combining activities on the writing skills of above average fifth and sixth grade students.* Unpublished doctoral dissertation, University of Connecticut, Storrs, CT.

Trimmer, J., & McCrimmon, J. (1988). *Writing with a purpose,* short edition. Boston: Houghton Mifflin.

Vavra, E. (1991, October). Theory and the composition instructor: Is ignorance bliss? Paper presented at the New Modern Language Association Conference, Cortland, NY.

Whimbey, A., & Jenkins, E. (1987). *Analyze, organize, write.* Hillsdale, NJ: Lawrence Erlbaum Associates.

Arthur Whimbey, former Coadministrator with Hunter Boylan of the Developmental Education Program at Bowling Green University, is a cognitive psychologist interested in the development of basic skills. 3920 Avalon Rd., NW, Albuquerque, NM 87105. Myra J. Linden is Professor Emeritus of English, Joliet Junior College, Joliet, IL 60436-9985. Eugene Williams, Sr. is the Director of Test Improvement for the Washington, DC Public Schools.

Further Readings On Writing

Ackerman, J. M. (1993, July). The promise of writing to learn. *Written Communication*, 10 (2), 334-370.

Bartholomae, D. (1985). Inventing the University. In Rose, M. (Ed.) *When a Writer Can't Write: Studies in Writer's Block and Other Composing Problems*. Guilford Press.

Bartholomae, D. (1980). The study of error. *College Composition and Communication*, 31, 253-269.

Behm, R. (1989). Ethical issues in peer tutoring: A defense of collaborative learning. *Writing Center Journal*, 10(1), 3-12 ERIC EJ 402-160.

Beck, P., Hawkins T., & Silver, M. (1978). Training and using peer tutors. *College English*, 433-449.

Brooks, P., & Hawkins T. (Eds.). (1981). *Improving Writing Skills*, New Directors for College Learning Assistance, No. 3, San Francisco: Jossey-Bass.

Bruffee, K. (1984). Collaborative learning and 'The Conversation of Mankind.' *College English*, 46, 635-52. ERIC EJ 306 541.

Clark, I. (1985). *Writing in the Center*. Dubuque, IA:Kendall/Hunt.

Clark, I. L. (1988). Collaboration and ethics in writing center pedagogy. *The Writing Center Journal*, 9(1), 3-13.

Devine, T. G. (1990, Fall). Caveat emptor: The writing process approach to college writing. *Journal of Developmental Education*, 14(1), 2-4.

DiPardo, A. (1993). *A kind of passport: A basic writing adjunct program and the challenge of student diversity* (NCTE Research Report # 24), Urbana, IL: National Congress of Teachers of English (NCTE).

Ede, L. (1990). Writing as a social process. *The Writing Center Journal*, 9:2, 3-15.

Flower, L. (1979). Writer based prose: A cognitive basis for problems in writing. *College English*, 41, 19-37.

Harris, M. (Ed.) (1982). *Tutoring Writing: A Sourcebook for Writing Labs*.

Harris, M. (1978). Individualized diagnosis: Searching for causes, not symptoms of writing deficiencies. *College English*, 40, 318-323.

Hawkins, T. (1980). Intimacy and audience: The relationship between revision and the social dimension of peer tutoring. *College English*, 42, 64-69.

Hull, G., & Rose, M. (1990). This wooden shack place: The logic of an unconventional reading. *College Composition & Communication*, 41, 287-298.

Jacobs, S. E., & Karliner, A. B. (1977). Helping writers to think: The effect of speech roles in individual conferences on the quality of thought in student writing. *College English*, 38, 489-505.

Lichtenstein, G. (1983). Ethics of peer tutoring in writing. *Writing Center Journal*, 4(1), 29-34.

McKoski, M. M., & Hahn, L. C. (1987, November). Basic forms, basic writers. *Journal of Developmental Education*, 11(2), 6-12.

North, S. M. (1984). The idea of a writing center. *College English*, 46(5), 433-446.

Seward, J. S., & Croft, M. K. (1982). *The Writing Laboratory*. Glenview, IL: Scott Foresman.

Snyder, W. C. (1987, September). Ideas in practice: A sentence-revising format for basic writers. *Journal of Developmental Education*. 11(1), 20-22.

Sommers, N. (1980). Revision strategies of student writers and experienced adult writers. *College Composition and Communication*, 31, 378-88.

Valeri-Gold, M., & Deming, M. P. (1991, Spring) Computers and basic writers: A research update. *Journal of Developmental Education*, 14(3), 10-14.

Pollard, R. H. (1991, Spring) Another look: The process approach to composition instruction. *Journal of Developmental Education*, 14(3), 30-32, 37.

Whimbey, A., Johnson, M. H., Williams, E., & Linden, M. J. *Blueprint for Educational Change: Improving Reasoning, Literacies, and Science Achievement with Cooperative Learning*, EBSCO Curriculum Materials, Box 486, Birmingham, AL 35201, 1-800-633-8623. (Note: Whimbey, et al. also have a workbook called *Keys to Quick Writing Skills: Sentence Combining and Text Reconstruction* also published by EBSCO).

Zelenak, B., Cockriel I., Crump, E., & Hocks, E. (1993, Fall). Ideas in practice: Preparing composition teachers in the writing center. *Journal of Developmental Education*, 17(2), 28-34.

Part 7

Course-Related Learning Services: Adjunct Skills and Supplemental Instruction (SI)

Mary G. Dimon discusses six reasons why adjunct courses work, not the least of which is that they really deliver what they promise, and explains the theoretical underpinnings of the approach.

Why Adjunct Courses Work

By Mary G. Dimon

(From the *Journal of College Reading and Learning* (1981) XXI, 33-40. Reprinted by permission of the *Journal of College Reading and Learning* and Mary G. Dimon.)

Briefly stated, adjunct courses work because they have a definable purpose, function as a support group, challenge students, promote participation, are flexible, and do what they say they do. These conclusions are the result of a six-year program at California State University at San Bernardino. Although some problems still remain in this fairly new form of supplemental instruction, it holds promise for today's college students because it helps them to succeed.

The first of the six reasons why adjuncts work is that they have a definable purpose. Students who are enrolled expect to receive help with a particular content course at the same time as they take the course. Loban (1985) believes that pupils learn best when they see an evident meaningful purpose in everything they do. This is not a new idea, but it has special implications not only for the overall objectives but for structuring day-to-day adjunct activities as well. Each day's agenda is directly related to an assignment required by the content course instructor. If a paper is due later, but a chapter or set of exercises must be completed in two days, both purposes are given some time in the adjunct course.

A look into the writing of Shuy (1981) helps to differentiate between this type of definable purpose and one associated with a general study skills course.

In Shuy's *Holistic View of Language*, he elaborates on the theory that function always precedes form. He defines a reductive learning theory (learners learn small things before large ones, and by taking language apart and cutting it into pieces, learners benefit), and a constructive learning theory (we come to know our world by actively constructing it). He divides language into surface and deep concepts, and explains how each relates to reading, writing, and speaking. The skills approach contains a surface-level content, e.g., decoding, vocabulary, and grammar mechanics, for example, but Shuy's holistic approach emphasizes deep-concept content, e.g., comprehension, cohesion, discourse, and, most importantly, function (for reading, writing, and speaking). He contends that it is more important to know how people use language to get things done (function) than to know language elements out of context (form). This emphasis on context and function is what insures an adjunct student that all of his or her learning will be in a specific, definable context, and that all the language modes will be exercised to get things done. In summary, students will analyze and construct meaning from a context, realizing that using language to learn the concepts of a discipline will inevitably improve their form, whether it be in reading a text, writing a paper, or giving a speech. Concentration on the job at hand is the surest road to growth at all levels. This is a clearly definable purpose.

The second reason adjuncts work is their ability to provide a support group. It is indeed rare for an individual to overcome significant problems over the long term solely through individual effort. The fact that man is a social animal is never more evident that in problem solving, where interaction in a group setting has enhanced the recovery rate of addicted individuals. One reason support groups succeed is their view of errors. Another is the shared conviction that they will gain self-knowledge through the group process. Finally, success is based on an awareness that expressions of feelings are welcome and appropriate. Poplin (1986), also a constructionist, addresses these same concerns, along with many others, in the principles advocated for those who teach. Poplin argues that, unlike an associationist, a constructionist perceives errors as critical to learning; mistakes should be free of penalties. She believes that by allowing students to think and reflect, to compare and contrast their thoughts with those of others, they will experience new meaning. Although her writing on self-knowledge is far more complex, it should be noted that self-knowledge is self-regulating and self-preserving. Thus any effort devoted to helping students understand what is happening mentally when they read, and how they can reduce their test anxiety, or why they are only able to remember what they understand, will improve the way they approach a textbook, approach a test, or cope with an information overload. Just as self-evaluation in group therapy enables the addict to deal with reality, so does self-knowledge enable the adjunct student to solve academic problems. Poplin, finally, believes that people learn best those things about which they feel passionately; without feeling there is no quest for meaning. Her criticism of many cognitive psychology experiments in memory and learning is that those performing the experiments deliberately strip themselves and their subjects of feeling in order to

observe learning in a "pure form." She concludes, however, this is why teachers find educational research meaningless when juxtaposed with their classroom needs. Adjunct class activities, on the other hand, are organized to provide group support in the same areas emphasized by Poplin. Discussion, study groups, and question periods are structured for students to have the opportunity to risk, and with risk comes error. Students are encouraged to express themselves openly as long as they don't hurt others. "I don't get that," is a common refrain, as is, "Why did I get so many wrong?" Answers to questions such as these promote the self-knowledge often attributed to support groups.

Bruner (1987), in his reflections on thought and emotion, also pursued the question of how condition and emotion interact. His theory about the structural interdependence of three elements, cognition, emotion, and action, instructs those who would design an adjunct (or any college course) to integrate these elements once considered only separately. At a practical level, our cultural system provides a setting to combine acting, thinking, and feeling, but a classroom can also provide the climate, activities, and guidance necessary.

The third reason why adjunct courses work is that they challenge both the students and the instructor. Students must not only be supplied with challenges, but must be provided with the means for meeting them.

In *Mind and Society* (1978), Vygotsky provided insight into good instruction, which he maintained must always be in advance of development. His writing has been an inspiration for structuring the adjunct at this institution. His experiments with concept formation established principles useful not only for adjuncts but in any learning situation.

Vygotsky's theory differs from the traditional one which holds that concepts are formed through the interplay of associations. Vygotsky sees the process as a movement of thought which constantly alternates from specific to general, and from general to specific, in a sequence which moves from thought to meanings to words, and one which is only able to evolve with the aid of strenuous mental activity on the part of the student. The implications for helping students learn dictate that instruction be both specific/concrete and general/abstract, that it is directed at aiding students to express what they think through analysis of meanings, and that a challenge is an opportunity for growth. In one English adjunct, students were studying the relationship of morphological rules to the structure of English grammar. A specific morphological rule was reviewed first, then it was compared to a family rule: "No bike riding allowed after twilight." This last rule was then integrated with how a family's use of rules operates; next, it was expedient to shift back to the specific morphological rule. This was followed by an explanation of the larger context of English grammar. Before students forgot the connections, an exercise from the text was presented in which the students could at once apply their grasp of the concept as they worked hard to solve it. Oral comparisons of answers stimulated corrections, motivated more questions, and moved the students toward a higher level of thought about morphological rules. This sequence exemplifies Vygotsky's teachings that good instruction precedes development, that a challenge is necessary for it to happen, and that we reach the speaking level of a concept only after we have mastered the meaning.

The fourth reason why adjuncts work is that they depend upon active student participation. Goodman (1976) proclaimed a revolutionary doctrine which has served the adjunct philosophy well. "Literacy has to be the natural extension of language-learning, not something new, not something different, but something that in fact grows out of and builds on the natural tendency to communicate" (p. 17). This doctrine is the essential difference between learning in the content course and learning in the adjunct. The number of students in an adjunct permits this natural tendency to communicate. Students ask questions about the textbook and lecture content; answers are forthcoming both from their peers and from the instructor. They feel no constraints when it comes to finding out if the answers they wrote to text exercises were the same as those of their friends or, if they had a paper topic, they asked questions to determine which was pleasing to the content instructor, which was manageable, or which one was in their interest area. An open, relaxed, trusting, yet controlled class atmosphere is necessary to facilitate this type of interaction.

Adelman and Taylor (1983) attempted to correct motivational problems by emphasizing the personalization of the environment in order to accommodate a wide range of individual differences. A major component of programs they designed was the enabling of students to select options. Adjunct classes also follow these principles. The choice of completing practice tests, writing essays, analyzing text, or participating in a partner study is left to the student, with no penalty for non-compliance and with no provision for "checking up," yet a variety of options offered. This also minimizes the feeling of being pressured and accentuates the purpose of an adjunct as that of a helping hand rather than a raised fist.

Bruner, Shuy, and Vygotsky are contributors to the rationale for building active participation into an adjunct course. Vygotsky (1962) is a growth theorist whose view of mind nurturing is suited to discussion methods and dependence upon a social support system because he believes that language is the agent for altering the powers of thought. In Shuy's *Dialogue As the Heart of Learning* (1987), both oral and written dialoguing techniques are described. Both of these have been used successfully in adjunct classes. Bruner (1987) is a developmental psychologist who believes that meaning and reality are created, not discovered. His devotion to narrative as a means of attaining the creation of meaning also has its place in specific adjunct classes, and is utilized whenever appropriate situations arise. Student participation assumes that classroom activities will encourage interaction, which, outside of class meetings, will enable students to understand the benefits of working with others.

The fifth reason adjuncts work is that they are flexible. This means that they are elastic enough to permit altering the "plan of the day" to suit any change of assignments in the content course; flexible enough to permit spending extra time with a student's question without making the rest of the class feel neglected; innovative enough to promote an awareness of the need to present concepts in a manner which is understandable by both freshmen and seniors in the same class, and open enough to respond to spontaneous student suggestions.

Perry (1970) presented a scheme of development in the form of nine positions through which college students progress over time. Freshmen, who believe right answers are to be memorized by hard work, must be directed differently from sophomores, who believe everyone has a right to his or her opinion, or from juniors, who state that knowledge depends on context. When students balk at forming small study groups (usually in the second year), other methods for interaction must be implemented. This requires constant flexibility.

Eisenberg (1986) reviewed issues which also have relevancy to flexibility. She recommends combining reading and writing in a science classroom. Science courses often have adjuncts, providing an ideal setting to test her theory. The relationship of her arguments to flexibility is concerned with the use of reading and writing (about any topic) as an alternate way of enhancing understanding of textbook material. In order for students to understand the difference between reading and remembering, it has proven useful to ask them to read two pages of text, then close the book while they write the meaning of what they have read. This is but one adjunct application of Eisenberg's reading/writing theory. Any situation in which students see the value in writing about reading, or while they are reading, encourages them to combine these language areas. Their past learning experiences have usually been directed toward performing one activity separate from the other, so these activities require retraining.

The final reason for stating that ". . . adjuncts work because . . ." is that they deliver what they promise in a quantifiable manner. This means that it is possible to tell students at the beginning of an academic period what they can expect from their adjunct course, and to show them statistics which support the expectations. It has not been difficult to compare the final grades of adjunct students with those of non-adjunct students in a given college course, and to show that in every quarter (twelve, at this writing) a significantly higher percentage of grades above "C" were earned by adjunct students, while a significantly higher percentage of grades below "C" were produced by non-adjunct students. It is further possible to show that the proportion of students with high G.P.A.'s who enroll in adjunct courses is far lower than in the non-adjunct control group. A show of hands at the start of a quarter will also reveal that while many students are enrolled in the adjunct as volunteers, others are present because of a combination of suggestion and curiosity, and still others were explicitly told to take the adjunct course. This mix, incidentally, has proven to be a healthy one.

After combining the reasons for success with their sources and some applications, it is helpful to connect these aspects of an adjunct course with some basic tenets which have guided the evolution of the adjunct course program on which this paper is focussed. As background for the five tenets (all related to why an adjunct works), it is instructive to consider the practical setting of the program in its current working environment. At the college, an adjunct course meets for two 50-minute sessions each week, where attendance is taken and both credit and letter grades are awarded for participation on a regular basis. Currently, six disciplines have adjuncts, and these six are taught by one faculty member. When graduate students do teach sections, they follow the procedures and utilize the materials and teaching techniques developed for the course by the adjunct faculty person. The program is partially funded by a Federal Grant which has imposed stringent evaluation procedures for the past four years.

Five basic tenets, derived from both the practical limitations of an adjunct and the theoretical base discussed earlier, provide guidelines for the number and the nature of ongoing course activities. Many of these have evolved from refining early attempts at establishing an adjunct curriculum or from filling a new need imposed by the novel requirement of a content course.

The first tenet is also the most important one: all adjunct instructors must understand the concepts related to the course which is being adjuncted. This is best accomplished through reading the textbooks, listening to the lectures, and being familiar with the literature in the discipline. If the adjunct class is primarily concerned with content in context (reason one), and provides students with a genuine challenge (reason three), is founded on flexibility (reason five), and really delivers, (reason six), then the person in charge cannot be bound solely to a text or a set of notes. The corollary to this tenet is to staff with seasoned faculty to the fullest extent possible, and provide extensive training and observation for those who teach.

The second tenet addresses the general structure of an adjunct. It should be stable, graded ABC/NC, structured, and accountable, but outside-of-class assignments are better received when they are voluntary and have a direct bearing on those of the content instructor. Structure relates to the definition of purpose, insuring student participation and optimizing the support group aspect. A strict structure for an adjunct can be defended on all six lines of reasoning because an adjunct, in which attendance is not a priority, in which students drop in occasionally, in which grades are not awarded, will have no definable purpose, will not fulfill the function of a support group nor offer a challenge, and will not accommodate either regular student participation nor flexibility. Evaluation with credibility is also impossible.

The third tenet addresses what some would consider major problems with adjunct courses: recruiting students, and getting permission to offer an adjunct for a given content course. These obstacles present the most serious problems, and they are the toughest to solve. Student recruitment must occur at several levels. Information concerning the success of an adjunct must be made available regularly to administrators, especially if they disburse funds, in order to prove that the program is effective. Counselors must be made aware of the success rate of students who take adjunct courses so that additional students will be advised to enroll. Finally, the instructor must address related content classes each term, making a personal appeal to enroll during the first class session.

General education requirements provide the most fertile ground for new adjuncts, and absolute cooperation with a department's chairperson and each content instructor is necessary. The cardinal rule is that adjuncts enable content instructors to award an improved ratio of higher to lower grades, provide help when students are unable to utilize the instructor's regular office hours, and provide instruction in those areas in which the content teacher assumes the students are backgrounded. It is vital for the adjunct instructor to drop in on lecture classes at least one hour weekly; this assures the content instructors that adjunct material will follow content. Regular, yet not burdensome, communication between adjunct and content instructors is of major importance. Never impose unnecessarily on the time of a content instructor.

The fourth tenet which has been followed ritualistically at the university is to follow the advice of the constructionist theorists by relegating study skills to a secondary position.

The final tenet pleads with anyone who is involved in the process to keep records. This means keeping meticulous attendance records so that those who do not attend regularly can be contacted. It means a statistical evaluation must be completed following each academic period, and it means that the post-course progress of adjunct students must be tracked in order to provide viable retention statistics. A primary reason that adjunct classes deliver is that record keeping is a top priority; data are recorded accurately and consistently; data are analyzed, and results are promulgated. Changes occur in adjuncts as a result of this analysis.

The ultimate success of any adjunct rests with the individual adjunct instructor. Those who are success-oriented will establish the adjunct as a standard form of supplemental instruction and provide learning assistance with additional reasons why the adjunct course works.

References

Adelman, L. S., and Taylor, L. (1983). Enhancing motivation for overcoming learning and behavioral problems. *Journal of Learning Disabilities,* (7), 384-391.

Bruner, J. E. (1986). *Actual minds, possible worlds.* Cambridge, MA: University Press.

Eisenberg, A . (1986). Combined reading-writing using technical and scientific texts. In P. T. Peterson (Ed.), *Convergencies: Transactions in reading and writing,* (pp. 159-161). Urbana, IL: National Council of Teachers of English.

Goodman, K. S. (1976). *Manifesto for reading revolution. 40th Annual Claremont Reading Conference Yearbook,* (pp. 16-20). Claremont, CA: Claremont Graduate School Publishing.

Loban, W. (1985). *A deepening understanding of reading and writing. 40th Annual Claremont Reading Conference Yearbook*, (pp. 16-20). Claremont, CA: Claremont Graduate School Publishing.

Perry, W. G. (1970). *Forms of intellectual and ethical development in the college years.* New York: Holt, Rinehart and Winston.

Poplin, M. (1986). *The quest for meaning. 50th Annual Claremont Reading Conference Yearbook*, (pp. 15-26). Claremont, CA: Claremont Graduate School Publishing.

Shuy, R. W. (1981). Holistic view of language. *Research in the Reading of English*, 18(2), 101-111.

Shuy, R. W. (1987). Dialogue as the heart of learning. *Language Arts*, 60(8), 890-897.

Vygotsky, L. S. (1978). *Mind in Society.* Cambridge, MA: Harvard University Press.

Vygotsky, L. S. (1962). *Thought and Language.* Cambridge, MA: M.I.T. Press. (Original work published 1934).

Mary G. Dimon, now retired, was formerly on the faculty in the California University System.

This article describes some of the ground rules for successful SI programs and cites the results of outcome studies on students who attend SI sessions.

The Challenge of Supplemental Instruction (SI): Improving Student Grades and Retention in High Risk Courses

By Sandra Burmeister

Supplemental Instruction (SI), a structured course-related skills program developed by Deanna Martin at the University of Missouri-Kansas City (UM-KC) in the mid-70's, is one of the best known academic support models in the country. Funded by a U. S. Department of Education grant for the dissemination of information on validated, exemplary programs, SI has been adapted by over 300 U. S. colleges and universities, and new professionals continue to be trained each year by the staff at UM-KC and by National Certified Trainers who conduct regional trainings throughout the country. In a 1990 competition, SI won the Noel/Levitz Award for Student Retention as the nation's finest retention program (Martin, 1991).

The initial article on SI describes how SI differs from traditional study skills programs:

"Typical learning center programs operate on a drop-in basis, offering services primarily designed to address the needs of high-risk students. Staff devote a high percentage of time to one-to-one tutorial instruction, with basic skills courses and workshops complementing individual services.

The SI program differs in two major respects. First, the emphasis has been shifted from identification of high-risk students to the identification of high-risk courses. High-risk courses, as they are defined here, are those traditionally difficult entry-level courses wherein student D and F rates and withdrawals exceed 30 percent of course registrants. Second, services are attached directly to each course. Learning Center skills specialists, whose content competency has been approved by the course instructors, integrate learning skills instruction with course content during specially scheduled review sessions.

Supplemental Instruction is designed to assist students in mastering course concepts and, at the same time, to increase student competency in reading, reasoning, and study skills. In order to do this, the specialists attend course lectures where they take notes and complete assigned reading (just as the enrolled students do). The specialists also schedule and conduct three or four, fifty-minute SI sessions each week at times convenient to the majority of the students in the course. Student attendance (at SI sessions) is voluntary" (Blanc, DeBuhr and Martin, 1983, page 81).

The original SI model has changed only slightly since 1982. Now instead of professional SI leaders, more often SI leaders are undergraduate or graduate students who have passed the course earning an A or B grade, and who have been recommended by the course instructor as content competent. This shift to student SI leaders from the traditional learning center professionals requires that student leaders receive extensive training, support, and supervision.

Early research on the effects of using professional SI leaders substantiated positive effects on students' course grades in the targeted high-risk courses and on their reenrollment at the institution. The achievement of students participating in SI were compared with that of non-participants including a group who expressed high motivation to attend SI sessions but were unable to attend them. Table 1 below shows the results of the comparison of parent course grades and reenrollment by entry scores.

Table 1
Course Grade and Reenrollment Statistics of Students Using and Not Using SI, by Entry-Test Score Quartile. (For UM-KC Students)

Percentage Group	Percentage of Group	Course Grades	Reenrollment during Subsequent Semester
Top Quartile (N = 149)			
SI	30	3.10*	86%
Non-SI	70	2.30*	78%
Bottom Quartile (N = 75)			
SI	31	1.72*	74%
Non SI	69	.88*	62%

Note: Top quartile students were those scoring in the 75-99th percentile range on entrance tests, and the bottom quartile students were those scoring in the 0-25 percentile range.*Statistical test and level of significance: .0.05 using t-test.**Statistical test and level of significance: 0.10 using chi-square test. (Blanc, DeBuhr, & Martin, 1983, page 86).

A more recent report of data from 180 institutions currently using the SI model shows that students attending SI earn significantly higher grades in targeted high-risk courses and persist at the institution longer than those who do not attend SI. Typically, SI students average about one-half a grade higher in the parent course than those not attending SI. A selected sample of SI in 49 institutions again confirms the grade differences earned by SI students and the reduced numbers of SI students receiving D, F, and withdrawals from the course (University of Missouri-Kansas City Center for Academic Development, April 1992).

In a study of SI in a community college, Wolfe (1987) also substantiated grade gains for SI participants and further showed that these gains occurred despite the fact that SI participants were at a disadvantage — their scores on the Scholastic Aptitude Test averaged 60 points lower than those who did not attend SI.

Aggregate data from a widely diverse group of institutions that use SI for an even more diverse selection of courses seems to support the effectiveness of SI in helping students succeed in difficult courses (University of Missouri-Kansas City Center for Academic Development, 1992). In order to investigate the results of SI support for courses that have similar curricular content, several colleagues and I investigated the effects of SI in assisting students in mathematics courses (College Algebra, Calculus, and Statistics). Our research included data from 45 institutions with a total of 11,252 students enrolled in 177 classes. Our results showed that SI students seemed to persist longer in the targeted courses and had higher course grades as indicated on the table below (Burmeister, Kenny, Nice 1994).

Table 2
Comparison of Average Final Course Grades for SI and Non-SI Groups

	College Algebra (Classes=60; Campuses=21)	Calculus (Classes=78; Campuses=21)	Statistics (Classes=39; Campuses=14)
Average course grades: SI	2.21	2.28	2.49
Average course grades: Non-SI	1.98	1.83	2.32
t-value	t = 2.514*	t = 3.263**	t = 2.394***

*significant at the .05 level, df = 2104; **significant at the .01 level, df = 5740; ***significant at the .05 level, df = 1548. (National Center for Supplemental Instruction, September, 1992).

There are still many unanswered questions that researchers should address about the academic, social and attitudinal effects of attending SI sessions. Particularly important are questions on how best to attract high risk students and others who need help but are reluctant to attend SI. For example, the article by Visor, Johnson, and Cole (1992) on the relationship of SI participation and affect that follows this paper presents some interesting but mixed results.

Perhaps the most impressive long-term results of SI to date are the grade changes and graduation data released from UM-KC based on follow-up studies through Winter 1990. These data show that students at every aptitude test level who attended SI sessions made higher course grades, higher term GPA's and higher cumulative GPA's than non-SI participants. Furthermore, 31% of the SI group graduated from college after six years compared with 18% of the non-SI group (Center for Academic Development, 1991).

Although studies on program effectiveness using grades and persistence show that SI programs seem to work well, it is always difficult to define what factors in a program contribute to these positive results. In her early research, Martin speculated that the following factors contributed substantially to the positive effects of SI:

1. The service is proactive rather than reactive.

2. The service is attached directly to specific courses.

3. The SI leader's attendance at each class meeting (of the targeted course) is considered essential to SI effectiveness.

4. SI is not viewed by students as a remedial program. (The goal of SI is to be viewed as an assistance program for students at all levels and that all students be assisted in the same groups to avoid the stigma usually associated with developmental/remedial services.)

5. SI sessions are designed to promote a high degree of student interaction and mutual support (Blanc, DeBuhr, & Martin 1983, page 87).

As an experienced SI supervisor and a National Certified Trainer for UM-KC's program for dissemination of the SI model, I have come (like many of my colleagues) to the conclusion that wisely planned and carefully monitored SI programs not only improve student learning of the content of high risk courses, but also create academic communities where small groups of students learn collaboratively. Consider this working definition of collaborative learning:

In an atmosphere which is cooperative and safe for risk-taking, students generate ideas, evaluate and categorize these ideas, and teach one another as they work on common tasks. This "cross-teaching" technique: (a phrase from Moffett, 1968) involves mu-

tual contributions and mutual decisions regarding what to do and how to proceed (Burmeister, 1992).

That kind of collaborative learning defines exactly what happens in well run SI sessions. The following observation of an SI session in mathematics illustrates this collaborative learning which is at the heart of SI's success.

Observation. Particularly as the semester progresses, the SI leader encourages the students who come to SI to take charge of the session. The SI leader steps back and takes the role of challenging students' thinking. The SI leader encourages students to attempt problems, take the next step, whether that next step is right or wrong. The peer relationship between the students and the SI leader makes it comfortable for students to take risks. Even though doing well in a mathematics course is serious business, SI leaders keep the sessions informal and collegial. During SI sessions, participants have a sense of working hard together, with a sense of humor at times, and this atmosphere breaks through barriers to risk-taking and to learning.

The SI leader introduces a game, "The name of the game is *Pass the Chalk*. We'll start with someone reading a problem. The first person to get the chalk will write the problem on the board and then she will pass the chalk to someone else. When you get the chalk you need to write the next step or, if you think the last step upon the board is wrong, you can correct the last step. Coaching from the audience is encouraged."

As the students work at the board, the students in their seats ask and answer questions about the correct method, allowable shortcuts, and different ways of doing the same step. The SI leader asks students why they did what they did or if they could think of another way to do a step.

One of the SI leader's roles is to be sure that students share more than the mechanics of getting the right answer. Doing the right next step is only half of the task; knowing why you do the next step is just as important. Another role for the SI leader is to be sure that the group is responsible for solving the problem — that is, that no single student becomes stranded at the board unable to do the next step and feeling threatened.

As students work together, they discover that there is more than one way to do some problems. The focus is on using alternate methods to understand concepts and on being confident about why you proceed in a particular way (Burmeister, Carter, Hockenberger, Kenney, McLaren, Nice, 1994).

Similar collaborative learning occurs when SI participants work together to create timelines for history classes, or draw a chart or graph to sort out terms for psychology classes, or prepare for tests in any class by categorizing information as major or secondary.

The collaborative learning which takes place in SI sessions allows students to use the language of the discipline of the high risk course, frequently test their knowledge of course materials, and keep pace with the course work. The SI leader serves as a model student, and because she is trained in the use of active learning strategies, the SI leader facilitates collaborative learning. The results is an academic community of students working together for mutual success — a combined academic and social community which links students together and therefore affects retention at the institution. Further clinical observation and other methods of testing are needed to verify these positive effects.

An additional comment regarding the SI model: it is a politically sound model for higher education because it does not compromise academic standards, but instead supports the fair, yet challenging teaching of professors in rigorous disciplines. Faculty support is integral to the success of the SI model. Methods of securing and acknowledging faculty support are emphasized throughout the three-day training workshop used to disseminate the UM-KC SI model to professionals who wish to implement the model. After all, a SI leader is hired only with the endorsement of the faculty member who teaches the targeted course, and the leader attends class sessions with the approval of that faculty member. Furthermore, the SI leader and the SI supervisor ask the faculty member to encourage students to attend SI sessions and ask for the faculty member's assistance in planning appropriate SI sessions. Interestingly, for cooperating faculty, the SI model both improves student learning and also raises the student's positive perception of the faculty member who helped offer the SI support (Blanc, DeBuhr, & Martin, 1983).

References

Blanc, R. A., DeBuhr, L. E., and Martin, D. C. (1983). Breaking the attrition cycle: The effects of Supplemental Instruction on undergraduate performance and attrition. *Journal of Higher Education*, 54,(1), 80-90.

Burmeister, S. B. (1993, March 19). *Collaborative learning in small groups*. Presentation at the National Association of Developmental Educators (NADE), Washington, DC.

Burmeister, S. B., Carter, J. M., Hockenberger, L. R., Kenney, P. A., McLaren, A., Nice, D. L. (In press). *SI sessions in college algebra and calculus. Supplemental Instruction: Increasing student achievement and persistence*. San Francisco: Jossey-Bass.

Burmeister, S. B., Kenney, P. A., and Nice, D. L. (In press). *Research in Collegiate Mathematics Education*, a publication of the American Mathematical Society.

Center for Academic Development. (1991). *Graduation rates for students who entered UM-KC, Fall 1983*. Kansas City, MO: University of Missouri-Kansas City.

Martin, D. C. (1991). *SI Report*. Kansas City, MO: Center for Academic Development, University of Missouri-Kansas City.

National Center for Supplemental Instruction. (1992, September). *Supplemental Instruction (SI): Review of research concerning the effectiveness of SI from the University of Missouri–Kansas City and other institutions from across the United States*. Kansas City, MO: Center for Academic Development, University of Missouri-Kansas City.

Visor, J. N., Jones, J. J., and Cole, L. N. (1992). The relationship of Supplemental Instruction and Affect. *Journal of Developmental Education*, 16(2), 12-18.

Wolfe, R. F. (1987). The Supplemental Instruction program: Developing thinking and learning skills. *Journal of Reading*, 51,(1), 228-232.

Sandra Burmeister is Director of Student Support Services (Title IV) at Cazenovia College, Cazenovia, NY and is a National Certified Trainer for Supplemental Instruction through the University of Missouri-Kansas City. She is also a former president of the Midwest College Learning Center Association.

This study sheds some light on why some students who need it don't attend SI and why others drop out of SI sessions.

The Relationship of Supplemental Instruction to Affect

By Julia N. Visor, James J. Johnson, and Lisa N. Cole

(Condensed from the *Journal of Developmental Education*, (Winter 1992) 16(2), 12-18. Reprinted by permission of Julia N. Visor, James J. Johnson, and Lisa N. Cole and the *Journal of Developmental Education*, Appalachian State University, Boone, NC 28608.)

Abstract: The positive effects of SI on student achievement and persistence to graduation have been well documented. To date, however, no study addressed the relationship of SI and affect. This study addressed the following questions: (a) Are students who elect to participate in SI affectively different from those who choose not to do so? (b) Does SI affect positive change in noncognitive factors for participants? The noncognitive factors examined were locus of control, self efficacy, and self esteem. Results showed that those who participated regularly in SI were affectively different from those who participated only occasionally or not at all. The study also suggests that the groups often targeted for SI are not being reached.

Developed during the mid-1970s to address rising attrition rates at the University of Missouri-Kansas City, Supplemental Instruction (SI) is an academic support model which has been achieving success for over a decade across this country and now in at least four foreign countries. It has been adopted by numerous institutions of higher education nationwide, and it has been validated by the U.S. Department of Education as an exemplary program in higher education. As part of its continuing vali-

dation, the SI program undergoes extensive impact studies assessing effectiveness. Time and time again it has been shown to have a positive impact on academic performance consistent across type of institution. As has been verified in research studies, academic success is a major predictor of persistence to graduation. It is clear from recent literature on retention, however, that academic performance is not the only, and perhaps not even the most important factor in student persistence. Several scholars indicate that noncognitive factors, factors in the affective domain, are extremely important reasons for student persistence. Yet, to date, no one has concentrated scholarly efforts on the relationship of SI to the affective domain to ascertain whether there is a relationship between SI and noncognitive factors related to academic achievement. This study begins to address that lack.

We have only to look at the work of such researchers as Tracey and Sedlacek (1985), Tinto (cited in Spann, 1990), and Lent, Brown, and Larkin (1986) to understand the relationship between affect itself and student achievement and persistence.

Tracey and Sedlacek (1985) tell us that the factors which predict grades for both African-American and European-American students at a statistically significant level are (a) positive self-concept and (b) realistic self-appraisal. Tinto (cited in Spann, 1990) indicates that there are eight or nine reasons that students leave college. Some are related to achievement, some are not. For instance, he discusses uncertainty/indecision with regard to academic major and/or career choice. He discusses commitment: ability to sustain a desire to stay in school, given experiences and external pressures. He discusses transition: ability to adjust to an alien environment, be it intellectual, social, academic, or personal. He discusses match or fit: students' feelings of ease in the college environment; they are more likely to leave if they don't feel at ease than if they do. Lent, Brown, and Larkin (1986) indicate that student expectations about self-efficacy are related to academic performance.

Considering the review of the literature, the researchers in this study specified affect to mean the personality variables of locus of control, self-efficacy, and self-esteem, three variables recognized as major — albeit not all-inclusive — psychological components of affect related to student achievement and persistence (Lent, Brawn, & Larkin, 1986; Phares, 1976; Tracey & Sedlacek, 1985).

The impact of SI on performance is clear; the impact of performance on persistence is clear; the impact of affect on persistence is clear. The questions left to ask are what impact does affect have on participation in SI, and, subsequently, what impact does SI participation have on affect? This study has been designed to determine what, if any, relationship exists between SI and locus of control, self-efficacy, and self-esteem.

Description of the Supplemental Instruction Model

Developed at the University of Missouri-Kansas City by Dr. Deanna C. Martin, Supplemental Instruction is a nonremedial academic support program which targets high-risk courses. Offered to all students enrolled in a particular course, SI provides assistance on an outreach basis and in regularly sched-

uled, out-of-class collaborative study sessions that begin during the very first part of the academic term.

The SI supervisor coordinates the program on campus and is responsible for managerial aspects. Prior to the first of class, the SI supervisor trains SI leaders in theory, strategies, and procedures. The supervisor provides constant close SI support for SI leaders during the first few weeks of the term and periodically monitors SI sessions throughout the remainder.

An SI leader is a student who is hired by the SI supervisor and approved by the instructor of the targeted course. SI leaders receive intensive training just prior to the academic term, attend all lectures, take notes, complete readings, and conduct at least three one-hour SI sessions each week. By modeling effective student behavior and facilitating interactive study sessions, SI leaders assist students with the language of the discipline, the organization and integration of lecture notes and readings, and the development of questioning techniques. Students become actively involved in the content material in a safe environment, free from concerns about evaluation.

Studies at the University of Missouri-Kansas City (UMKC) and data gathered from adopting institutions show that the group of students in a given class who participate in SI generally earn a higher mean course grade and semester GPA than the group of students in the same class who elect not to participate. In courses offering SI, rates of unsuccessful enrollments (D, F, or withdrawal) are lower than they were prior to the addition of SI. While postsecondary institutions adapting SI differ from UMKC and from each other in a variety of ways, their data show similar results.

By 1981, the SI model was validated as an exemplary program by the U. S. Department of Education. Since 1984, the UMKC Center for Academic Development has received funding from the National Diffusion Network to assist other institutions to implement the program. The program has now been disseminated to hundreds of postsecondary institutions across the nation (Center for Academic Development, 1992).

Review of the Literature
Supplemental Instruction and Student Achievement

The positive effect that participation in Supplemental Instruction (SI) has on student achievement has been well-documented. Blanc, DeBuhr, and Martin (1983) found that undergraduate students participating in Supplemental Instruction earned significantly higher final course grades than did students not participating in SI, even when they controlled for motivation. As a group, SI participants also demonstrated a significantly lower percentage of unsuccessful enrollments than did the SI participants. Wolfe (1987) replicated this study with similar results. However, the academic results achieved by Wolfe's SI group seem particularly impressive when considering the following: Blanc, et al., (1983) had reported the equivalence of the SI and the non-SI groups on the basis of previous academic achievement (high-school class rank and college entrance test scores). However, Wolfe's (1987) non-SI group had a distinct advantage as far as previous academic achievement: they scored 60 points higher on the Scholastic Aptitude Test (SAT). In spite of the seeming advantage of Wolfe's non-SI group, the SI group still received higher course grades.

Affective Characteristics and Student Persistence

Generally, the longer students stay in school, the greater their chances for persisting to graduation. Yet many do drop out along the way. Students may decide to terminate their education (voluntary withdrawal), or they may be asked to leave by their institutions (academic dismissal). Reasons offered for some students' decisions to leave are as diverse as the individual students themselves. Availability of finances, individual commitment, mismatches between the individual and institution, and individual affective variables are a few of the explanations students give for leaving (Tinto, 1987). While it is clear that affect does have an impact on overall student persistence, the extent of that influence in not so clear.

Affective Characteristics and Student Achievement

Various researchers have shown that a relationship also exists between certain affective variables and academic achievement (Astin, 1975; Bingaman, 1989; DeBoer, 1985; Tracey & Sedlacek, 1985), but, as it is with the relationship of affect to persistence, it is difficult to pinpoint just how the specific personality variable affects academic achievement. This difficulty arises from, among other things, a lack of consistency in the definitions of specific variables of personality among research studies. However, certain broadly defined variables are generally recognized as affecting achievement; locus of control (Phares, 1976), self-efficacy (Lent, Brown, & Larkin, 1986), and self-esteem (Tracey & Sedlacek, 1985) are among those.

Locus of control
Locus of control centers on individuals' feelings that they are "in charge" of their own destiny. Individuals may be described as having an internal lo-

cus of control, an external locus of control or any degree in between. "Internals" believe that the things that happen to them are largely due to their own actions, while "externals" attribute events that shape their lives to forces and factors outside of their own control. It is generally recognized that students who are more internal attain higher levels of achievement academically than do students with external control (cited in Liebert & Spiegler, 1990, p. 448).

Self-efficacy

Self-efficacy involves individuals' beliefs that they have the ability, or competence to succeed at a given task. It has been argued by some that self-efficacy is merely a task-specific form of locus of control. Persons who perceive themselves as being able to "undertake and perform assuredly" (Bandura, 1982 p. 123) a given task are described as self-efficacious. Additionally, Bandura states, "The stronger the perceived efficacy, the more likely are people to persist in their efforts until they succeed" (p. 128). It would seem, then, that those who feel they are academically efficacious would receive higher grades. This is, in fact, the case (Lent & others, 1986).

Self-esteem

Individuals' beliefs about their worth as a person is referred to as self-esteem. Students who have high self-esteem are more likely to achieve highly in many areas. One of those areas is academic achievement (Bingaman, 1989; Tracey & Sedlacek, 1985).

> Students who have a more internal locus of control attain higher levels of academic achievement.

Purpose of the Study

The current study addressed some of those issues by working to answer the following questions: (a) Are students who elect to participate in SI affectively different from those who choose not to do so? (b) Does SI affect a positive change in noncognitive factors for the participants?

This study utilized an auditorium section (300 students) of an introductory psychology class consisting mostly of students in their first two years of college. SI was made available to all class members. This study took place at a midsize 4-year university which had been using the SI model for five years.

> Research showed that the effects of participating in SI began to be most noticeable after four sessions.

Design of the Study

All students in an auditorium section of the introductory psychology course were pretested during the first week of the fall semester and posttested during the last week of regularly scheduled classes. Due to attrition within the class, and errors in completing one or more of the instruments, the sample sizes were smaller on the pre- post- comparisons than at the time of the initial testing. A comparison of the pretest scores of those who attended with those who did not revealed no significant differences within the nonparticipant group, supporting the belief that the sample for the pre- and posttesting continued to be representative of all of the nonparticipants.

Instrumentation

Three relatively brief measures were chosen that purport to measure the three affective variables studied: Roter's IE Scale (1976) to measure locus of control; the self-efficacy test developed by Sherer and others in 1987; and the Hudson Scale for Measuring Self-esteem (1987).

Procedure

The hypotheses were tested using an analysis of variance statistic of pretest scores in order to determine initial differences among the groups. Pairwise comparison follow-up tests were employed where indicated by having obtained significance. In order to determine the effects of participation in SI over the course, analyses of co-variance were performed on posttest scores using the pretest scores as the co-variate.

Results

We sought to describe subjects in terms of locus of control, self-efficacy, and self-esteem at the beginning of the academic term, before any of them had the opportunity to participate in SI.

Based on previous unpublished research which showed that the effects of participating in SI began to be most noticeable after four sessions (Webber-Davis, 1988), the subjects were divided into three groups: those who had attended four or more sessions of SI, termed Regular Participants; those who had attended one to three sessions, termed Occasional Participants; and those who had elected not to participate, termed Nonparticipants.

Consistent with the hypothesis, the Regular Participants were found to have the most internal orientation for locus of control (lowest mean), although an analysis of variance indicated that the observed differences were not statistically significant. Somewhat surprisingly however, the Nonparticipants fell between the Regular Participants and the Occasional Participants.

The results on the pretesting with respect to self-efficacy were also consistent with the hypotheses in that the Regular Participants had the highest mean (greatest self-efficacy). Although the analysis of variance failed to indicate statistical significance, it was extremely close ($p<.055$). As was the case with locus of control, the Occasional Participants fell at the opposite extreme, the Nonparticipants in the middle. Pairwise comparison follow-up tests showed a significant difference at the .50 level between the Regular Participants and the Occasional group, and the Nonparticipants approached significance as well ($p<.10$).

With respect to self-esteem, the hypothesis was disconfirmed, since those attending more than four session groups had the lowest mean (highest self-esteem), and in this case the observed differences were significant ($p<.01$). The Occasional Participants had the highest mean (lowest self-esteem) and follow-up tests revealed this group to be significantly different from both the Regular Participants and the Nonparticipants at the .05 level of confidence.

We hypothesized that participation in SI would have a positive impact on these personality variables. That is, by the end of the semester students who participated in SI should have had greater gains than those who did not participate. The analyses of covariance failed to reach statistical significance in each case, indicating that greater gains were not associated with any group.

In the absence of statistical significance, follow-up tests were not appropriate, and little can be said conclusively about the results. We want to note, however, that all groups moved toward greater internality in locus of control, even though the movement did not test at the significance level. Also, the Regular Participants moved toward less self-efficacy and lower self-esteem, which is counter to the predicted direction.

Interpretation of Results

The literature suggests that students with external locus of control, low self-efficacy, and low self-esteem are at the high risk level for persistence in college. That being the case, one goal of this study was to determine whether those students for whom SI would be most beneficial — that is, students with external locus of control, low self-efficacy, and low self-esteem — are choosing to participate in the program. This study also sought to determine whether SI actually produces positive changes in the portion of the affective domain related to personality.

> **In this study positive change associated with SI was not substantiated for any of the measured affective variables.**

Descriptive Findings

While the descriptive phase of the study yielded statistical significance only on the self-esteem variable, it does point some interesting directions for the other two variables.

Who Participates in SI?

One result of the study shows that students with internal locus of control were likely to participate in SI. This result should come as no surprise given the literature. As well, it should come as no surprise that students with the greatest feelings of self-efficacy would participate. What did appear surprising was that students who participated most in SI had the highest sense of self-esteem. On closer consideration, even that finding should not have been unexpected. Initially, we thought that students with a high sense of self-esteem see no need to attend SI sessions. They might just suppose that they had enough of what it takes to "go it alone." But in point of fact, the SI supervisor marketed the SI program in a way that could easily attract students who have done well in the past and want to continue to do well. In the introduction of SI in the targeted class, for instance, students were given statistics showing how much better those who went to SI last year fared in the course than the students who did not participate. No wonder students with a high sense of self-esteem participated. They can see the program as a way to help maintain their sense of self-esteem.

Students in the study who began with the most external locus of control, the lowest self-efficacy and the lowest sense of self-esteem did go to the SI sessions. They just did not stay long. These were Occasional Participants. Unquestionably, active participation in SI is challenging academic work. One possible explanation for the SI dropout rate of Occasional Participants is that students who are unsure about themselves and about being able to meet the demands of the class are frustrated (when they) encounter SI as yet another challenging academic experience for that class, no matter how non-threatening it is. Without specific and pointed individual support, these students may find it less painful to just stop participating. As pointed out earlier from the literature, these are not the students most likely to achieve at high academic levels. However, these are the students that many of us seek to serve through SI.

Implications for Practice

From this study we now know that students who attended SI regularly came with more internal locus of control, self-efficacy, and higher self-esteem than others in the class. We know that students who attended SI only occasionally came with more external locus of control, lower self-efficacy, and lower self-esteem than others in the class. How does this information affect the marketing of the program? How does it impact the way SI sessions are conducted?

Marketing SI to At-Risk Students

The people in the Occasional group are the ones many of us think we are targeting when we offer SI. This study suggests that if we want those in the Occasional group to attend regularly and actively participate in SI, we must market the program in order to appeal to all three affective features. Standing in front of the class from time to time during the academic term and saying, "Y'all come!" won't do.

An excellent strategy, in fact, part of the SI model, is to get the hosting faculty member — a strong authority figure for the course — to publicly support the SI program. Another good strategy is to get other academic authority figures, such as academic advisors and counselors, to support the program and personally encourage students to attend. Yet another strategy, as discussed earlier, is to have the SI leader or supervisor announce statistics showing how those who went to SI last year fared compared to those who did not go. These strategies may get students to attend initially, but the design of the SI session encourages them to stay and, indeed, begets word-of-mouth advertisement — among the strongest of marketing strategies — if it is a successful design.

Design of the SI Session

If the desire is to meet the needs of students at risk due to the noncognitive variables addressed in this study, new dimensions may need to be added to the current design of the SI session. When students with external locus of control, self efficacy, or low self-esteem do attend the sessions, we must find new and different ways to demonstrate to them their own ability to succeed. We must be careful in sequencing information and in pacing the sessions so as not to deepen their frustration. In addition, we have to find new ways to reinforce positive feelings of worth in each individual. Typically SI leaders encourage, in a non-threatening manner, every attendee's successful involvement. Apparently that is not enough. We must train leaders to be sensitive to these noncognitive variables and to be able to assess the needs of the students who hold them. While the leaders should continue to encourage student involvement, supervisors and shapers of the program need to look for concomitant means of empowering these students to be successful.

Making an Impact on Persistence

While the SI model targets high-risk courses and not students, many of us who use the conventional SI model do so in order to reach the students at high-risk levels for persistence in college. This study shows that if one high-risk level for students is characterized by external locus of control, low self-efficacy, and low self-esteem, as the literature suggests it is, we are not seeing the students who are at risk often enough to have a positive impact on their individual persistence. When we can see them more often and be more effective when we see them, we can have a greater impact on factors in the affective domain that influence their persistence.

References

Astin, A. W. (1975). *Preventing students from dropping out.* San Francisco: Jossey-Bass.

Bandura, A. (1982). Self-efficacy mechanism in human agency. *American Psychologist*, 37, 122-147.

Bingaman, D. E. (1989). *The relationship of cognitive and affective variables in college grade point averages among highly successful high school graduates.* Lewisburg, PA: Bucknell University (ERIC Document Reproduction Service No. ED 320-512).

Blanc, R., DeBuhr, L., & Martin D. (1983). Breaking the attrition cycle. The effects of Supplemental Instruction on undergraduate performance and attrition. *Journal of Higher Education*, 54, 80-90.

Center for Academic Development (1992). Supplemental Instruction: Review of research concerning the effectiveness of SI from the University of Missouri-Kansas City and other institutions from across the United States. Unpublished manuscript.

DeBoer, G. E. (1985). Success and failure in the first year of college: Effects on affect, and persistence. *Journal of College Student Personnel*, 26, 234-239.

Hudson, W. W. (1987). Index of self esteem (ISE). In K. Corcoran & J. Fisher (Eds.) *Measures for clinical practice: A sourcebook* (pp. 188-190). New York: The Free Press.

Kenney, P. (1989, March) Effects of Supplemental Instruction on student performance in a college-level mathematics course. Paper presented at the Annual Meeting of the American Educational Research Association. San Francisco, CA.

Lent, R. W., Brown, S. D., & Larkin, K. C. (1986). Self-efficacy in the prediction of academic performance and perceived career options. *Journal of Counseling Psychology*, 33, 265-269.

Liebert, R. M., & Spiegler, M. D. (1990). *Personality: Strategies and issues (6th ed.)*, Pacific Grove, CA: Brooks/Cole Publishing.

Phares, E. J. (Ed.). (1976). *Locus of control in personality.* Morristown, NJ: General Learning Press.

Pryor, S. A. (1989). The relationship of Supplemental Instruction and final grades of students enrolled in high-risk courses. (Doctoral dissertation, Western Michigan University, 1989). *Dissertation Abstracts for Social Sciences*, 50, 1963A.

The Rotter internal-external control scale (1976). In E. J. Phares (Ed.), *Locus of control in personality* (pp. 178-180). Morristown, NJ: General Learning Press.

Rotter, J. B. (1966). Generalized expectancies for internal versus external control of reinforcement. *Psychological Monographs,* 80, (1, Whole Number 609.)

Sherer, M., Maddux, J. E., Mercandante, B., Prentice-Dunn, S., Jacobs, B., & Rogers, R. W. Self-efficacy scale (SES). In K. Corcoran & J. Fisher (Eds.). *Measures for clinical practice: A sourcebook* (pp. 294-296). New York: The Free Press.

Spann, N. G. (1990). Student retention: An interview with Vincent Tinto. *Journal of Developmental Education*, 14, 2, 24.

Tinto, V. (1987). *Leaving college: Rethinking causes and cures of student attrition.* Chicago: University of Chicago Press.

Tracey, T. J., & Sedlacek, W. E. (1985). The relationship of noncognitive variables to academic success: A longitudinal comparison by race. *Journal of College Personnel*, 26, 405-410.

Webber-Davis, Y. (1988). [Efficiency of individual vs. Supplemental Instruction]. Unpublished data, Illinois State University, University Center for Learning Assistance, Normal, IL.

Wolfe, R. F. (1987). The Supplemental Instruction program. Developing thinking learning skills. *Journal of Reading*, 51, 228-232.

Further Readings on Adjunct Skills Programs and Supplemental Instruction

Ayub, V. (1980). Learning assistance approaches for study reading in the sciences. *Proceedings of the 13th Annual Conference of the Western College Reading Association*, 84-87.

Blanc, M., DeBuhr, L., & Martin, D. (1983). Breaking the attrition cycle: The effects of Supplemental Instruction on undergraduate performance and attrition. *Journal of Higher Education*, 54(1), 80-90.

Bullock, T., Madden, D., & Harter, J. (1987). Paired developmental reading and psychology courses. *Research and Teaching in Developmental Education*, 3(2), 22-31.

Center for Academic Development (ND). *Supplemental Instruction*. Kansas City, Missouri: National Supplemental Instruction NDN Project, University of Missouri-Kansas City.

Herlin, W. R. (1978). An attempt to teach reading and writing skills in conjunction with a beginning biology course for majors. *Proceedings of the Eleventh Annual Western College Reading Association Conference*, 134-136.

Katz, I. C. (1983). Adjunct classes: Teaching college students strategies for learning from texts. *Journal of Reading and Learning*, XVI, 75-80.

Martin, D. C., Arendale, D. R., & Associates (1992). *Supplemental Instruction: Improving First-Year Student Success in High-Risk Courses. Monograph Series #7*. National Resource Center for the Freshman Year Experience, University of South Carolina, Division of Continuing Education.

Martin, D. C., and Blanc, R. (Preprint). *Video-based Supplemental Instruction: A Pathway to Mastery and Persistence*. (Order from D.C. Martin, Center for Academic Development, SASS#210, University of Missouri-Kansas City, Kansas City, MO 64110-2499.)

Matthews, S. & Associates. (1993, Summer). Supplemental instruction and biology. *SI News*, 1, 3.

Maxwell, M. (1991). Cost effective alternatives to tutoring. *Journal of Learning Improvement*, 1(1), 1-4.

Mayfield, C. K. (1980). How to teach a reading and study skills course to law students. *Proceedings of the Thirteenth Annual Conference of the Western College Reading Association*, 13, 119-122.

NADE Self Study Questions for Adjunct Skills Programs. Order latest draft from: Dr. Susan Clark Thayer, Director, Gino A. Ballotti Learning Center, Suffolk University, 41 Temple Street, Boston, Massachusetts 02114-4280.

National Center for Supplemental Instruction (1992, September). *Supplemental Instruction (SI): Review of Research Concerning the Effectiveness of SI from the University of Missouri-Kansas City and Other Institutions from Across the United States*. Kansas City, Missouri: University of Missouri-Kansas City.

Quinn, K. B. (1990). Retaining undergraduates and training graduates: A variation of supplemental instruction in a college biology class. In R. H. Atkinson and D. G. Longman (Eds.) *Celebrating our past: Creating our future – Selected Conference Abstracts*, National Association of Developmental Education Conference. Boston, MA, March 1-4, 1990.

Schaefer, S., and Hopper, J. (1991). Successful funding and implementation of a biology adjunct. *Journal of College Reading and Learning*, XXIV:1, 1991, 55-62.

Sheets, R. A., & Rings, S. (1989, January). Ideas in practice: Tailor-made study strategies: A success story. *Journal of Developmental Education*, 12(3), 22-24.

Wilson, M. M. (1978). Report on an adjunct course of intergrade reading and study skills in a university academic class. *Proceedings of the Eleventh Annual Western College Reading Association Conference*, IX, 172.

Wolfe, R. (1987, Fall). Writing across the curriculum through Supplemental Instruction: An approach to writing essay exams. *Maryland English Journal*, 21(2), 43-48.

Wolfe, R., & Wells, E. (1988, October). Community mentors for SI. *National Association of Developmental Education Newsletter*, 13(3), 18-20.

SI Periodicals

Supplemental Instruction: A Publication of the National Supplement Instruction NDN Project. University of Missouri-Kansas City.

SI News – A Publication from the National Supplemental Instruction NDN Project, The Center for Academic Development, University of Missouri-Kansas City. (Note: This is a periodical that contains training workshop dates and information and short articles on SI from user institutions.)

Part 8

Technology

Perhaps nothing changes as rapidly in the field of developmental education as the technology available to help students learn.

Techtalk: Choosing and Purchasing Software

By Bill Broderick and David C. Caverly

(From the *Journal of Developmental Education* (Fall 1993), 17(1), 40-41. Reprinted by permission of Bill Broderick and David C. Caverly and the *Journal of Developmental Education*, Appalachian State University, Boone, NC 28608.)

Any computerized developmental program that wants to succeed must have quality software. But how can those of us in charge of selecting that software know that we are choosing the right product? And perhaps as important a question in these fiscally constrained times is this: How can we pay the lowest price for the software we choose? This column will look at these questions and make appropriate recommendations.

In previous columns (Broderick & Caverly, 1992b; Caverly & Broderick, 1993) we identified developmental software as interactive tutorial, simulation, drill-and-practice, or customizing courseware. To find the best programs in these categories, you should look at three sources: published courseware evaluations, periodicals, and catalogues. Published evaluations were discussed in a previous column (Broderick & Caverly, 1976). Let's look at the other two sources, beginning with periodicals. We recommend that you subscribe to the following publications: *T.H.E. Journal* (150 El Camino Real, Suite 112, Tustin, CA 92680-9883); *Campus Tech* (P.O. Box 52180, Pacific Grove, CA 93950-9935); *Higher Education Product Companion* (1307 S. Mary Ave., Suite 218, Sunnyvale, CA 94087); and *New Media* (P. O. Box 1771, Riverton, NJ 08077-7331).

Subscriptions to each of these magazines is free. Each periodical has articles that are written for postsecondary education. Each also contains descriptions and reviews of various software products appropriate for higher education. *Higher Education Product Companion* is especially useful in that it supplies manufacturer's addresses, prices, and the target audience.

A second source to consult is a catalog. It should be from an educational software distributor rather than from an individual company. Probably the most comprehensive is the E.I.S.I, (Educational-Interactive Software Institute) *Computer Courseware Catalog* (225 Grant Road, Los Altos, CA 94024). Courseware is organized according to subject matter with separate categories for Reading, Language Arts, Mathematics, ESL, and Study Skills. Within each subject, product titles are listed, and the following information provided:

    a. hardware requirements;

    b. name of publisher;

    c. suggested grade level, including identification of courseware appropriate for special populations such as adults and "at-risk" students;

    d. courseware descriptions in a clear, concise manner;

    e. special designations noting "Exemplary" or "Desirable" courseware that has been identified by the California Technology in Curriculum Project as high quality, and courseware that has received special awards from panels of educators throughout the country;

f. products that have been reviewed by an independent source are given a Review Grade (i.e., a letter grade of A, B, etc.); and,

g. cost, including a price for lab packs, and networked versions (E.I.S.I. provides a discount for orders over $500).

In another column (Broderick & Caverly, 1992a), we identified software designed to turn your computer into a tool. Several categories were specified, including management/organization, diagnostic/prescriptive tool, communication tool, and production tool. All of the above catalogs can be used to find software that falls into the first two categories. However, if you are looking for software that will enhance your computer's communication ability or productivity, you will need different sources. We recommend that you subscribe to one or more of the following weekly publications: *PC Week* (P. O. Box 1769, Riverton, NJ 08077-7369); *Mac Week* (Coastal Associates, Computer Publications Division, 1 Park Ave., New York, NY 10016); and *Infoworld* (P. O. Box 1164, Skokie, IL 60067-8164).

Subscriptions are free to qualified applicants, including educators. Designed mostly for the business community, these publications provide up-to-the-minute information on hardware and software. One of the best features is Infoworld's "Product Comparison," which provides a comprehensive evaluation of similar products. Assessments are made for hardware, such as color notebook computers or e-mail systems, and for software products, such as spreadsheets or Windows word processors. The reviews are exhaustive. Software evaluations consider attributes such as power, flexibility, ease of learning, documentation, and techni-

cal support. Each product is then rated on a scale of 1 to 10. This information should help you to decide which package is the best value for your use.

By using the above sources, you should be able to locate products that will fit your needs. The next step is to find the best possible price. This can best be done by cross-referencing your findings with catalogs from one or more of the following courseware distributors: Projected Learning Programs (P. O. Box 3008, Paradise, CA 95967-3008); Educational Resources (1550 Executive Dr., Elgin, IL 60123); Opportunities for Learning (941 Hickory Lane, P. O. Box 8103); Learning Lab Software (20301 Ventura Blvd., Suite 214, Woodland Hills, CA 91364); Learning Services (P. O. Box 10636, Eugene, OR 97440); and Educorp (7434 Trade St., San Diego, CA 92121-2410).

Each of these catalogs lists and describes software, though none approach the number of products listed or the level of detailed review that you will find in the E.I.S.I. catalog. However, you may find the product you are looking for at a lesser price.

There are other means of purchasing software at a significant discount. Companies that offer commercial software packages usually have one price for business and one for education. Call the manufacturer direct and ask for their educational sales department. The sources listed above often include the phone number of the manufacturer. Educational discounts are almost always available and are typically significant. For instance, in researching for a future column on multimedia presentations, we called a company to inquire about their multimedia authoring system. The business price was $4000. The educational price was $1399. This sort of discount is standard throughout the industry.

Another type of discount worth asking about is called a "competitive upgrade." This means that if you have purchased a competitor's product and want to purchase the product of the manufacturer you are talking with, you will likely be given a price that is even lower than the educational price. Here is an example. After reading the product comparison for Windows word processors, we became intrigued by AMI Pro 3.0 from Lotus. It was given the highest rating of any of the programs reviewed. We called the manufacturer and were given an educational price of $129 for this $495 product. However, we were informed that if we could verify that we had already purchased a competitor's product such as Microsoft Word for Windows or Word Perfect for Windows, the price of Ami Pro would drop to $99. Verification meant sending in the first page from the owner's manual. It did not require sending in identification numbers for the previously purchased product. We received similar offers when we called Microsoft, Word Perfect, and WordStar.

A second source to contact is an educational discount house such as Edutech (P.O. 51755, Pacific Grove, CA 93950) and Campus Technologies (P.O. Box 2909, Leesburg, VA 22075). They offer educational prices for the most popular communication and production software from all of the leading software companies. Their prices are comparable to and often equal to the manufacturer's educational prices.

Finally, you should reference *Computer Shopper*. This is a huge (over 800 pages) monthly magazine that contains hardware and software reviews, technology trends, listings of bulletin boards and user groups, and thousands of advertisements on hardware and software. If you have the time, this can be a useful source.

A systematic approach to choosing and purchasing courseware and software can ensure that you find the right product at the right price. We feel confident that our approach will help you get what you want and help you save money in the process.

References

Broderick, B., & Caverly, D. (1987). Techtalk: A system for choosing developmental education courseware. *Journal of Developmental Education*, 11(2), 28-29.

Broderick, B., & Caverly, D. (1992a). Techtalk: Another look at the computer as a tool. *Journal of Developmental Education*, 16(1), 36-37.

Broderick, B., & Caverly, D. (1992b). Techtalk: Another look at the computer as tutor. *Journal of Developmental Education*, 16(2), 34-35.

Caverly, D., & Broderick, B. (1993). Techtalk: Another look at the computer as tutee. *Journal of Developmental Education*, 16(3), 38-39.

Bill Broderick is Reading Professor and Director of the Reading Center at Cerritos College, Norwalk, CA 90650. David Caverly is Associate Professor of Curriculum and Instruction at Southwest Texas State University, San Marcos, TX 78666.

Techtalk: Another Look at the Computer as Tutor

By Bill Broderick and David C. Caverly

(From the *Journal of Developmental Education*, (Winter 1992), Volume 16, Number 2, 34-35. Reprinted by permission of Bill Broderick and David C. Caverly and the *Journal of Developmental Education*, Appalachian State University, Boone, NC 28608.)

One of the most important functions that a computer can play in developmental education is that of tutor. As a tutor, the computer interacts with students while they are either learning skills or reinforcing skills previously learned. Courseware designed to teach skills to students can be categorized as **interactive tutorial and simulation**. We defined tutorials as courseware "designed to provide direct instruction of skills" (Caverly & Broderick, 1988, p. 28). Simulations are courseware "transferring skills which have been learned in the classroom to 'real-life' situations where the student must predict what is going to take place, make decisions based on these predictions and generalize to other situations" (Caverly & Broderick, 1988, p. 28).

There are a number of tutorial and simulation programs that you may find of value for use in reading, writing, and math.

Primary Steps to Comprehension, Steps to Comprehension, High Steps to Comprehension, and *Urban Reader* (E.P.C.) are low-level reading programs that integrate comprehension and vocabulary. Each makes excellent use of graphics and student interaction.

*The Reading Realities At-Risk Serie*s (Teacher Support Software) is designed to help at-risk students develop as readers, writers, and thinkers. The program uses real-life situations and issues, and asks students to problem solve and make decisions on the realities of life. Reading, writing, speaking, and listening skills are intertwined with the text. Following each selection, there are different kinds of questions, including multiple choice, closed, discussion, and creative.

Figurative Language (Hartley, levels 7-8) features selections from literature and poetry. Hints guide students to the correct answer. Instructions and explanations of terms are provided and lessons are modifiable.

Intellectual Pursuits (Hartley, 11-college) is a game where two players or teams take turns answering questions. Questions cover 50 areas of English and American literature.

SEEN (Conduit) is a tutorial designed for critical reading. The computer imparts models for critical inquiry. The models ask questions that lead students to interpret artistic works. Students can use a bulletin board to give and receive comments about classwork.

Critical thinking is developed in interactive CD ROM programs such as *In the Holy Land* (Voyager) and *Desert Storm* (CD Gallery). These programs are also good for building background knowledge and for improving glossary, dictionary, and other reference skills.

Broderbund's *Where in Time is Carmen San Diego* and *Where in America is Carmen San Diego* are the latest in the Carmen San Diego series. These simulations use reading to solve geographical and historical problems and are excellent for improving reference skills.

Information Mapping (Tulane University) is a hypercard tutorial that teaches students how to create a semantic map while reading.

MORE (Symantec), *Learning Tool* (Intellimation), and *Inspiration* (Ceres) are powerful outliners that can be used as simulations to help students understand the relationship between main ideas and details in both reading and writing. Through the use of arrow keys, a student can indent or move ideas around an outline, thus representing subordination, coordination, and superordination between ideas. *Learning Tool* and *Inspiration* allow students to learn about structures such as time/order, cause/effect, and problem/solution. With a click on an icon, the program converts an outline into a semantic map, labeling the links created between subject nodes.

Brainstorming for engaging prior knowledge and developing critical and creative thinking can be simulated with *Mindlink* (Mindlink), *Idea Liner* (Intellimation), and *Idea Fisher* (Fisher Idea Systems). Students are guided through the brainstorming process by strategic and thought-provoking questions. As answers are entered, ideas are stored in a word processor for later use. *Idea Fisher* is particularly powerful for emulating those questions that should be asked.

Write This Way/LD (Interactive Learning Materials), is a word processor designed specifically for learning disabled students. Instructors can customize the programs to reflect a student's capability and understanding of grammar and spelling. Student work can be proofed at any time.

Language Experience Recorder + (Teacher Support Software) is a speech-synthesized word processor that enables disabled readers and ESL students to record their thoughts and then have them spoken.

Textra (Ann Arbor Software) is an inexpensive and easy to learn and use word-processor for developmental students with no knowledge of word processing.

Reading and Writing Connection I and II (Hartley, 7-8) helps students build writing skills by emphasizing the relationship between reading and good writing. Students can revise and combine sentences and create paragraphs. Feedback is given.

Research Paper Writer (Tom Snyder Productions) takes students through the process of writing a research paper. Students are assisted in picking a topic, writing a research question, and doing an online data search. They then read sources and take notes that are put on a Macintosh for organization into a final paper.

Writer's Helper (CONDUIT) is a highly adaptable package broken into three parts: prewriting, drafting and revising. The program is now available for Windows.

Collaborative Writer (Research Design Associated) simulates the stages of business writing, including reports and proposals. The program leads the user through the process by asking questions and providing models.

Nuts and HyperBolts (Sterling Software) is a hypercard tutorial stack for learning grammar, punctuation, and mechanics. Through the use of humor and relevant examples, students learn specific rules.

Algebra 1-6, Statistics 1-4, Precalculus 1-6, Calculus 1-6 (Professor Weissman) and *First Year Algebra* (CONDUIT) are low-cost tutorials that can be used for independent study or to reinforce concepts.

Another type of courseware is drill-and-practice defined as a "series of repetitive exercises providing the student an opportunity to practice a specific skill," (Caverly & Broderick, 1988, p. 28). Over the years, drill-and-practice courseware has changed. Much of it is now low level tutorial, with a brief explanation given at the beginning of a lesson or during a lesson when a student gives an incorrect answer. Following are some drill-and-practice programs worth considering.

Townsend Press has practice disks available for all of their reading and vocabulary books.

Queue Intellectual Software offers these programs: *Toward Better Reading Skills* (4-8) contains practice on a variety of comprehension and vocabulary skills. There are six disks, each containing a story divided into eight modules. Each module has four brief passages, with two questions following each module.

ADD (Adjusting Degrees of Difficulty) Reading Series (3-12) presents a 100- to 150-word passage that all students read. The level of difficulty of future selections is adjusted by the computer based on student performance on 12 questions following the selection.

Reading and Thinking I (2-3), *II* (4-6), *III* (6-8), and *IV* (9-12) stress inferential and critical reading with different question formats including multiple-choice, fill-in-the-blank, and close.

Lessons in Reading and Reasoning (9+) looks at critical thinking fallacies such as either-or, loaded words, and stereotyping.

Skills Bank II – Reading(Skills Bank Corp. 7-12) is designed to help students raise scores on standardized tests such as the California Achievement Test, Iowa Test of Basic Skills, and Stanford Achievement Test.

Comprehension Power (I/CT and Milliken, 1-12) provides practice on 25 specific reading comprehension areas from literal to analytical. A selection is presented in segments with each followed by comprehension and vocabulary-in-context questions.

Comprehension Connection (Milliken, 4-9) is designed for readers whose comprehension ability is behind their ability to identify words. A 150- to 300-word passage is followed by five questions. An on-line dictionary is always available.

Practical Grammar I, II, and *III* and *Practical Comprehension Package* (Queue) explain grammatical concepts, test student understanding, and provide exercises to reinforce understanding.

Essential Grammar and *Essential Punctuation* (Gamco Industries) combine drills in a variety of language skills. Sentences are randomly generated, and students must identify the line that contains an error. Students may see rules at any time. Students who score a certain percent are rewarded by playing an arcade-type game. Tests provide a "skill report" identifying strengths and weakness.

Algebra Drill and Practice I, II and *III* (CONDUIT) let students apply algebra to a variety of problems. Step-by-step solutions to problems are provided on request when a problem is answered incorrectly.

As in the case with most software, there have been major changes in tutor-based courseware over the last four years. Most programs are more powerful and user friendly. Further, almost all of them come with a built-in management system which allows you to keep track of how your students are performing. Software companies listen to educators, so that the next generation of courseware is likely to assist us even more than the programs we have mentioned.

Reference

Caverly, D., & Broderick, B. (1988). Techtalk: Types of courseware and how they can be used. *Journal of Developmental Education*, ii(3), 28-29.

For more information on any of the programs listed in this column, contact your local software distributor, the *Journal of Developmental Education*, Bill Broderick (Cerritos College, 11110 Alondra Blvd., Norwalk, CA 90650), or David Caverly (Southwest State University, Department of Curriculum and Instruction, San Marcos, TX 78666-4615).

Techtalk: Another Look at the Computer as Tutee

By David C. Caverly and Bill Broderick

(From the *Journal of Developmental Education*, (Spring 1993), Volume 16, Issue 3, 38-39. Reprinted by permission of David C. Caverly and Bill Broderick and the *Journal of Developmental Education*, Appalachian State University, Boone, NC 28608.)

One of the most powerful functions of the computer in developmental education is that as a tutee. This function empowers developmental students to explore language and number in a meaningful environment. Earlier, we introduced the computer as a tutee as the "user teaching the computer to perform certain tasks" (Caverly & Broderick, 1989, p. 30). Over the last four years, the world of tutee software has increased tremendously. In this column, we will review the growth in customizing courseware, authoring systems, authoring languages, hypermedia, and multimedia and discuss how it can be used to expand your students abilities.

Teaching the Computer

In **customizing courseware**, several programs allow you, or better yet, your students, to create drill-and-practice programs for vocabulary (*Word Attack Plus, Spellit*) or study cards for any test (*StudyMate*). Having students create drill-and-practice programs to teach vocabulary to their peers provides the multiple exposures students need to truly own the words (cf. Simpson & Dwyer, 1991).

New **authoring systems** simplify even more the process of creating your own courseware complete with text, pictures, sound, and even animation. For example, *Authorware Professional, Linx Lite, Linx Industrial*, and *MacroMind Director* guide you through the steps of creating tutorial software. *Authorware Professional* also allows you to create a program for either IBM or Mac. Rather than depending upon others to create tutorial courseware for your unique needs, you and/or your students can create sophisticated courseware with no more programming knowledge than the click of a button. Think of the possibilities of taking one of your successful lessons and converting it to tutorial courseware so the rest of us could benefit.

Even more flexible are **authoring languages**. Simple authoring languages (*Hypercard 2.1, Toolbook PLUS*) allow you or me, with little knowledge of programming, to create rather sophisticated programs including tutorials and simulations. These hypertext-based programs present information on screens called cards, and then allow the student to move between cards by clicking a button. Within Hypercard 2.1, for example, the cards, buttons, and connections between are created by selecting items from a menu.

The flexibility of authoring languages is revealed when they are used as "shells" serving as the opening, closing, and navigational tools for more complex programs. For example, you could use any of these authoring languages to introduce the concepts of main ideas and details via separate cards and buttons. Then, students could click a button and enter a presentation package (see following) to create a semantic map of a text read from one of their other courses. When students are finished, they could quit the presentation package and be immediately returned to the hypertext program which could then monitor their new-found understanding with a quiz. As you see, authoring languages expand the potential of other programs to provide the modeling, guided practice, and independent practice so necessary to our developmental students.

While *Hypercard 2.1* is platform specific to Macintosh, and *Toolbook* is platform specific to IBM, *PLUS* is available for both platforms. Also, there are means available to convert a program written in *PLUS* from one platform to another. This flexibility opens up whatever courseware you or your students develop to the rest of us.

Even more powerful is a new area called **presentation packages**. This tool software used as a tutee helps students create an outline of ideas garnered from reading or lectures and organizes the various authors' rhetorical structure ideas into cause/effect, comparison/contrast, sequence, or listing patterns. Constructing knowledge via exploration and organization of ideas is at the heart of the benefits of the computer as tutee.

Hypermedia

No doubt the largest growth in computer as tutee software has come in the area of multimedia and hypermedia. As we defined in an earlier column (Caverly & Broderick, 1990), multimedia uses more than one medium (e.g., text, audio, still pictures, animation, video) to direct the student through a lesson. Hypermedia, in contrast, is more comprehensive, incorporating multimedia, but controlled by the student.

Due to significant increases in memory and processing power of computers over the last several years, hypermedia has become a reality. Delivered on CD-ROM (compact disks with sound and pictures) or videodisks (laser disks with even more sound, pictures and/or video), students can learn about how Beethoven wrote his Ninth Symphony (*CD Companion*) while they explore word attack strategies in a content area. Students can learn about the strife in the Middle East (*In the Holy Land*) while they practice critical thinking strategies. Limited English proficient students can have everyday words pronounced and defined (*MacEnglish*).

A more powerful technology on the horizon is on-line compressions and expansion of audio and video. IBM and Intel have combined to create *Digital Video Interactive (DVI)* while Sony and Phillips have combined to create *Compact Disk Interactive (CDI)*. These two technologies will put full length movies on a compact disk and allow students to interact with the characters, rearrange the plot, or explore the setting as they come to understand narratives. Available today on *CDI*, for example, are tours of the Smithsonian Institute which developmental students can use to recreate world records like Chuck Yeager breaking the sound barrier. In so doing, they learn about fluid dynamics, aviation, and, more importantly for us, problem solving. This technology requires only a *DVI/CDI* player which has a built-in computer that connects to any TV.

The true power of hypermedia, however, will lie not in using courseware created by others, but in creating your own. Given a video capture board (e.g., *Video Spigot Pro* for Mac or *Video Blaster* for IBM), your developmental students can create their own multimedia/hypermedia presentation using a video camera. Think of the reading and writing strategies students would learn and practice if they created a hypermedia presentation about a campus issue.

Tutee software exists today for helping students create this type of presentation. At the low end is software that allows individuals to control CD disk (*Voyager, Video Stack*) by adding buttons to existing programs created either in *Hypercard 2.1* (for Mac) or *Linkway* (for IBM). In the middle is software that guides them through editing hypermedia much like an authoring system (e.g., *Adobe Premier*). At the high end are authoring systems for hypermedia that guide them through creating hypermedia for *Microsoft Window* environments on IBM PC's (*Quest* or interactive) or for Mac (*Linx Lite, Linx Industrial* or *Format*). *Format* is particularly powerful as it guides you through creating interactive learning modules, helps you to add questions to measure students' progress, allows you to have students skip or review information when right or wrong, and also tracks students' progress records, students' scores, and prints out performance reports. With little knowledge of programming, you could construct a hypermedia tutorial on any study skill.

In the end, the computer as tutee allows us each to teach developmental students using technology more in tune with their video literacy. In the age of MTV, the ability to create instructional lessons complete with hypermedia will motivate even the toughest challenge. Developmental students will be better prepared to use their new-found strategies in college and beyond.

References

Caverly, D. C., & Broderick, B. (1989). Techtalk: The computer as tutee. *Journal of Developmental Education*, 12(2), 30-31.

Caverly, D. C., & Broderick B. (1990). Techtalk: Hypermedia for developmental education. *Journal of Developmental Education*, 14(2), 32-22.

Simpson, M. L., & Dwyer, E. J. (1991). Vocabulary acquisition and the college student. In R. F. Flippo & D. C. Caverly (Eds.) *Teaching reading and study strategies at the college level* (p. 1-41). Newark, DE: International Reading Association.

For more information on any of the programs listed in this column, contact your local software distributor, the *Journal of Developmental Education*, Bill Broderick (Cerritos College, 11110 Alondra Blvd., Norwalk, CA 90650), or David Caverly (Southwest State University, Department of Curriculum and Instruction, San Marcos, TX 78666-4615).

Further Readings on CAI and Use of Technology

Askov, E. N., & Turner, T. C. (1989). Using computers for teaching basic skills to adults. *Lifelong learning: An omnibus of practice and research*, 9, 28-31.

Bailey, E. T. (1990, September). CAI and interactive video enhance students' scores on the college level academic skills test. *T. H. E. Journal*, 82-85.

Broderick, B., & Caverly, D. (1989). Techtalk: Starting up with computers. *Journal of Developmental Education*, 13(1), 28-29.

Caverly, D., & Broderick, B. (1991). Techtalk: A holistic or skills computer lab? *Journal of Developmental Education*, 15(1), 38-39.

Caverly, D., & Broderick, B. (1992). Techtalk: Another look at the computer as a tool. *Journal of Developmental Education*, 161(1), 36-37.

Caverly, D., and Broderick, B. (1993, Winter). Techtalk: Telecommunications for improving developmental education. *Journal of Developmental Education*, 17(2), 36-37.

> **Editor's note:** If you are interested in keeping up with the latest in educational technology for developmental education, read the Techtalk columns by Caverly and Broderick that appear regularly in the *Journal of Developmental Education.*

Christ, F. (1984). Computer competency for developmental educators. *Journal of Developmental Education*, 7(2) 26-27.

Christ, F. L. (1984). Managing information for developmental educators. *Journal of Developmental Education*, 7(3), 28-29.

Christ, F. L. (1979, January). An audio tour of a university learning assistance center. *Technological Horizons in Education*, 6(1), 50-51.

Kulik, J., & Kulik, C. C. (1987, February). Computer-based instruction: What 200 evaluations say. Washington, DC (ERIC Document Reproduction Service No. ED 263 890).

Kulik, C., & Kulik, J. (1991). Effectiveness of computer-based instruction: An update analysis. Computers in Human Behavior, 7, 75-94.

Rose, G. (1993, May). Strategies for addressing technophobia in nontraditional freshmen. Collegiate Microcomputer, 11(2), 120-122.

Smittle, P. (1990, Summer). Assessment's new wave: The Computerized/Placement Tests. *The College Board Review*, (156), 22-27.

Smittle, P. (1993, Fall). Computer adaptive testing: A new era. (Fall 1993). *Journal of Developmental Education*, (1), 8-12.

Turner, T. C. (1988). An overview of computers in adult literacy programs. *Lifelong learning: An omnibus of practice and research*, 11 (8), 9-12.

Wangberg, E. G. (1986). An interactive language experience based microcomputer approach to reduce adult illiteracy. *Lifelong learning: An omnibus of practice and research*, 9, 8-12.

Wepner, S. B., Feeley, J. T., & Wilde, S. (1989, September). Using computers in college reading courses. *Journal of Developmental Education*, 13(1), 6-8, 24.

> **Editors Note:** You will find other articles on software, computers and telecommunications listed in Spann, M., & Durchman, L. K. (Eds.) (1991). *The Annotated Bibliography of Major Journals in Developmental Education,* Boone, NC: National Center for Developmental Education, Appalachian State University.

Part 9

Mathematics

The increasing numbers of students needing remedial instruction in mathematics at the college level reflect serious national problems in teaching and learning mathematics as do the low math scores of U.S. students in comparison with their peers from other countries.

Many U. S. students today leave high school convinced of one thing – that they can't learn math. Changing this attitude is the first challenge for college mathematics specialists. Teaching them how to learn mathematics is the second.

These articles explore some of the reasons for the current crisis and suggest strategies for overcoming college students' math deficiencies.

Teaching Mathematics Effectively

By Robert Hackworth

Unless we produce students who are active, thoughtful learners, we are simply pushing them up a greased pole.
   Curtis Miles

One of the procedures I was taught long ago is that a teacher needs to preview a lesson. That seems reasonable. Also, I was told that a presenter needs to set an agenda for the audience. That, too, seems reasonable. And when behavioral objectives came along, I was told of the teacher's obligation for stating specifically his/her purposes of instruction and communicating those objectives to the students. Again, this seemed most reasonable. All of these suggestions for "good" teaching procedures were logical deductions of commonly accepted views of teaching/learning. They seemed reasonable and they became deeply imbedded in our instruction systems because they matched our ideas of instruction as delivery systems. We were interested in delivering information from our heads to those of our students.

What was wrong? From a wisdom of hindsight, it seems our instruction tended to overemphasize skills or facts-about-mathematics while ignoring or underplaying other factors that are, in fact, more crucial to the development of mathematical knowledge. For example, the use of behavioral objectives may have actually interfered with our ability to teach mathematics. Two decades after accepting the practice of communicating our objectives with a degree of specificity, we have a majority of students who are limited to dealing with problems within those degrees of specificity. Deviate slightly from the wording or symbols of a problem and suffer the cries of "We haven't been taught this." Deviate slightly from the types of problems taught in the last unit, chapter, or course and suffer the cries of "We can't be responsible for that type of problem." Many students, when given our end objectives, have little interest in the development of processes for achieving those objectives and, consequently, never learn mathematics in a way which makes it likely that they will remember, apply, and learn further.

This is all prelude, of course, to the belief that teachers of mathematics need to question closely the ways we have been proceeding with our jobs. Old practices need a fresh look; instruction that seemed to have worked well with students twenty years ago cannot be justified by our experiences today. When quality instruction is equated with the excellence of delivery systems, attempts to improve mathematics instruction focus on better explanations in more logical sequences, more information available in print materials, mastery testing materials, and expanded use of video and computer materials. For many mathematics instructors these emphases continue; they look for the WONDER BOOK or WONDER COMPUTER PROGRAM that will miraculously change student achievement levels. In other words, the vast majority of mathematics professors still seek better delivery systems as the answer to their instructional failures.

But many students are not reacting to improved delivery programs in the ways that were originally expected. Excellent explanations are frequently ignored as useless ritual. The student waits for the rote procedure needed to get answers. Mathematics teachers see the explanations as the "true mathematics" and the procedures used to actually solve problems as following logically. Meanwhile, the students see the procedures as "true mathematics" and the explanations as unnecessary fluff. These students try to pass the course by memorization. Often, they make Herculean efforts and still fail because those efforts are so inappropriate for learning mathematics.

> *When minds are stuffed with knowledge they don't understand, their thinking becomes chaotic.*
> ***Kamii & DeVries, 1978***

Because current efforts to teach mathematics are resulting in large numbers of failures, an alarming rate of anxiety, and increasing public criticism, the leadership of the major mathematics associations have accepted responsibility for altering current practices in instruction. The National Council of Teachers of Mathematics (NCTM) has courageously attacked the teaching practices of its members. In 1991 NCTM published its *Professional Standards for Teaching Mathematics* that promotes a different vision of mathematics teaching. The *Standards* state in positive terms the nature of the subject and methods for teaching it appropriately and effectively. No reader of the *Standards* can avoid its underlying criticism of current mathematics instruction.

The Mathematics Association of America (MAA) is also promoting changes in the ways mathematics is taught and learned. In early 1993, the MAA published *Guidelines for Programs and Departments in Undergraduate Mathematical Sciences* and urged, "Departments should be aware of the results of research on the teaching and learning of mathematics, and should make use of those results in improving instruction." Mathematics professors were encouraged to try alternative teaching techniques such as cooperative learning methods or organized study groups. The message from both NCTM and MAA is clear: Rely less upon lecture and more upon methods that involve students in classroom learning activities.

Two recurrent themes dominate the efforts of both the NCTM and the MAA. First, mathematics cannot be taught well without a drastic change in the public perception of the nature of the subject. When students believe that learning mathematics requires memorization of rules and procedures without understanding, it is imperative that their teachers alter those beliefs. Second, mathematics cannot be taught well without classroom activities that involve students in the processes of investigating, communicating, hypothesizing, confirming (denying), and proving (disproving). Every effort needs to be made to limit the teacher time allotted to providing information while increasing the amount of student time actively engaged in confronting mathematical situations.

Although the nature of mathematics is impossible to describe correctly for all members of the mathematics community, the following two quotations offer good starting points for anyone wishing to emphasize the nature of the subject in their own teaching:

> *Mathematics is systematized thought, supported by a beautifully adapted language and notation. It is characterized by the recognition, discovery and creation of pattern, and by the establishing of subtle connections between its apparently very dissimilar parts. Contrary to traditional school practice, it is*

not a set of distinct subdisciplines, but a unity, drawing on a diverse but interrelated repertoire of concepts and techniques. Again contrary to popular belief, it is not a set of facts; and mathematical understanding is not to be measured by tests of knowledge and memory. Thus, for the student, what matters is that he or she learn to think mathematically and any significant part of mathematics can be used as the vehicle to convey the necessary understanding and thinking ability. Conversely, no part of mathematics, however seemingly appropriate, can prepare the student really to use mathematics intelligently and effectively, if it is taught simply as a set of isolated skills, to be retained by the exercise of undiscriminating memory.

> Peter Hilton, distinguished professor of
> mathematics at State University of
> New York, Binghampton

I want students to develop mathematical power, meaningful concepts, healthy beliefs about the nature and value of mathematics, confidence in their ability to learn and use mathematics, and useful problem solving strategies. Traditional teaching methods are not very effective for helping students achieve these goals; actually such methods often work against them.

> Joe Garofalo, professor of mathematics
> education, University of Virginia

To broaden the view of instruction as a delivery system, Claire Ellen Weinstein, professor of educational psychology at the University of Texas, states that learning has at least three facets that must be addressed by instruction:

1. Skill. The language, techniques, facts, etc., of a subject.
2. Will. The attitudes and motivations which drive efforts to learn.
3. Management. The ability to make appropriate decisions for engaging in learning activities.

Obviously, most traditional instruction devotes little time or effort to two of these facets. In fact, all planning is focused on content delivery. Course calendars are written in terms of content coverage and serious criticism is given the teacher who does not "cover the required curriculum."

Professor Weinstein has outlined four areas of concern for quality instruction which she claims are necessary and sufficient conditions for learning. That is strong language for a mathematician. It carries great promise for achieving teaching success, but it also places full obligation on the teacher for meeting the four necessary conditions which are described below.

1. Create Quality Learning Environments

Each of our students lives in two environments: an academic environment and a non-academic environment. Most students in community colleges spend the greater part of their waking hours in non-academic settings and many of the difficulties for those students are directly related to influences outside the campus boundaries. An awareness of off-campus environments is a necessity even though instructors are severely limited in their ability to affect or control those environments. Professors in institutions where most or all of the students live on campus are blessed by circumstances where the on-campus problems generally dominate.

> *Our premise is that what a student learns depends to a great degree on how he or she learned it.*
>
> *. . . for each individual, mathematical power involves the development of personal self-confidence.*
>
> > Curriculum and Evaluation Standards
> > for School Mathematics (NCTM)

In some institutions the campus has real academic character and those characteristics will beneficially effect the students who live there. Other institutions have campuses which were designed on a strictly utilitarian model; the architect used the same design for both colleges and prisons. Staff members on campuses with a factory-like environment should, to whatever degree possible, find ways to alter the physical environment. It isn't possible to grow ivy on the walls, put bell towers atop buildings, etc., but less drastic changes can accomplish positive improvements.

Changes that might be made are:
1. Hang plants in the room.
2. Play background music (preferably classical with slow beat).
3. Hang paintings from the college library.
4. Put flowers on the tables.
5. Carpet seating areas.

Students tend to transfer their memories of past mathematics learning environments to new situations. Often, the math classrooms in higher education appear similar to those in public schools. Students expect a blackboard at the front of the room with rows of desks directed at it. Make the environment different from what the student has experienced in the past. Encourage the student to approach this learning experience differently by changing the physical qualities around them. Classrooms with teachers that work from the center, fewer blackboards, group work tables instead of individual desks, etc., are likely to encourage students to behave differently.

All attempts to improve the environment will fail unless they address the most important factor which is the teacher. Students expect mathematicians to be cold and logical. Altering the environment re-quires that the professor be warm, friendly, and maybe illogical. Students often believe mathematicians have no other interests; professors can explode this myth by sharing parts of a life outside mathematics. For example,
1. Bring a novel to class.
2. Talk about a concert or play recently attended.
3. Mention characteristics of parents, friends, etc., that led directly to a career in mathematics.
4. Be personal.

Play down the role of education for making money. That idea is far oversold and the student already gets plenty of it. Instead, emphasize the historical, cultural, intellectual role of mathematics. All content makes good sense under that umbrella. Puzzles, ridiculous word problems, rationalizing denominators in the age of calculators, etc., are wonderful topics when we get past the argument of "How am I ever going to use this?"

Anxiety is a major problem for many mathematics students. The essential element for reducing anxiety is to provide the sufferer control over that part of the environment that is the anxiety source.

Seligman

Recognize student fears and anxieties. Avoid scare tactics, harsh rules, etc., because they will not work with students who are already afraid. Exude patience, confidence, and a belief that hard work will overcome. Emphasize that anxiety frequently interferes with properly budgeting time, persevering, asking questions, and taking responsibility for their own learning.

Most students in trouble are reactive rather than proactive. They may attend class religiously, take prodigious quantities of notes, and strenuously attempt to decipher those notes. These students deserve an A for effort and will probably earn a low grade in mathematics. To become proactive, students should be taught Benjamin Bloom's three factors for predicting success/failure. Bloom's first and major predictive factor is the amount the student knows before a topic is taught — cognitive entry skills or prior knowledge. Students who know the most (have the greatest prior knowledge) at the beginning of a course almost always know the most at the end. A deficiency in prior knowledge may seem like a prediction of failure for weak students. In fact, it is a strong indication of what needs to be done to be successful: Prepare for each new topic by studying the prior knowledge needed for that topic.

Bloom's second factor is affective entry skills. Affective domain factors such as motivation, beliefs, values, and attitudes invariably facilitate and/or debilitate thinking and learning. Occasionally these affective entry skills dominate all others. This is the case with students suffering severe anxiety or with those who are unable to accept a mathematician's view of the subject. In general, however, affective entry skills are of minor importance compared to prior knowledge. Another important aspect of affective domain factors is the fact that they often appear to be less under the control of the student. However, good students do improve their probabilities of success by their awareness of strengths or weaknesses in this area.

The last major factor listed by Bloom is teacher behavior, and the research can be most discouraging for teachers. It seems to indicate that we have a minor influence on success/failure. In many instances that is true, but the teacher who uses Bloom's research can reverse that negative outcome. The teacher that assesses prior knowledge and affective skills and then actually does something about them can use them to positively influence outcomes. For example, since prior knowledge is so immensely important, a teacher can assure more learning occurs by adequately addressing this issue.

Students who are aware of Bloom's factors can also see themselves as responsible for success/failure — an absolute necessity for any instruction to be effective. They can regulate their study to learn more effectively. When a student becomes actively involved in planning their own learning, their likelihood for success greatly improves.

2. Process Information Correctly

Mathematics information can be divided into two categories:

1. **Information that needs to be carefully memorized**. Examples are definitions, symbols, postulates, perhaps some formulas, and occasionally a rule that needs to be practiced before it can be understood.

2. **Information that needs to be figured out each time it is encountered**. Examples are procedures, rules, problems, etc.

Good mathematics students use these two categories correctly. Poor mathematics students practice them in exactly the opposite way. For example, good students will solve most problems involving percents by:
1. Applying the definition of percent, and
2. Figuring out how to determine the desired result.

Poor students will solve most problems involving percents by:

1. Trying to fit the numbers into one of the three cases of percent, and
2. Computing a result that cannot be verified because the meaning of percent is not clear.

There is a strong correlation between vocabulary and critical thinking. The better a student's vocabulary, the more likely they are to engage in critical thinking. It follows that the student who understands the meaning of "percent" will more readily attack a percent problem with critical thinking skills rather than rote manipulation of the numbers.

Mathematics journals and educators currently are excited about the psychological theory called Constructivism. The allure of Constructivism is that it emphasizes prior knowledge and making inferences. Mathematical knowledge under this interpretation is developed like a brick wall. The wall is made of bricks, but the integrity of the structure depends upon the positioning of the bricks and the quality of the mortar that connects them. The knowledge of mathematicians is organized like the bricks in a wall with each brick in the wall having a position and connection with respect to all other wall bricks. The knowledge of students having trouble with mathematics is more like the bricks in a pile where each brick represents a separate entity without a position or connection to the other bricks.

The word "understanding" is frequently used in describing a desirable learning achievement. For example, most mathematics teachers have made a claim similar to "students demonstrated an **understanding** of linear equations." But when pressed for the meaning of "understanding," responses are often so vague that any teacher can claim quite honestly that they teach for "understanding." The constructivists have given us a better way for evaluating such statements. From the constructivist position a student demonstrates understanding by citing connections they have made. In other words, understanding requires an organization of the knowledge. This organization of knowledge into a structure may be unique for each individual.

One of the most valuable understandings that needs to be explicitly taught is the existence of three types of knowledge in mathematics.

1. Declarative Knowledge — The Whats of Learning
2. Procedural Knowledge — The Hows of Learning
3. Conditional Knowledge — The Whys and Whens of Learning

Good mathematics students treat the three types of knowledge as equals or, if not, they treat #1 and #3 as the most important. Poor students generally are unaware of the different types and, when they are, place great emphasis on #2. This means, of course, that they are making learning more difficult and less enjoyable. Teachers can help their students with these forms by constantly modeling the asking of good questions such as:

"What" questions that seek declarative knowledge:
1. What do I know about this?
2. What am I trying to find?
3. What can I do to present the problem another way?
4. What part of this problem can I solve?
5. What steps/strategies will I use?
6. What does this problem mean?
7. What sort of answer might I anticipate?

"Why" questions that seek conditional knowledge:
1. Why is this answer reasonable?

2. Why does this work?
3. Can I explain my strategy to someone else?
4. Is there another way to solve this problem?
5. Why is this the best approach on this problem?
6. Why would someone make errors on this type of problem?
7. Why would anyone want to solve this type of problem?

3. Maintain an Active Mind

Research consistently demonstrates that we use and retain very little of what we are told, what we read, or what we watch. Learners learn because they are engaged in creating, processing, and interpreting experience, both real and simulated.
> ISETA Newsletter (exploring teaching alternatives) Winter 1989

A mind that wanders is normal. Most of us can be reading a very interesting novel and suddenly find we don't know what has happened on the last few pages. Our reaction is to return to those pages and begin again where we need the review. Students frequently experience a similar experience when studying mathematics, but often they try to continue when they have no understanding of the preceding material. In mathematics this is like building a two-story house and then trying to dig out the basement. An active mind is a necessity for learning, and students need to be taught to maintain the mind's activity.

Two types of strategies should be applied on any problem. A cognitive strategy is an identifiable and reproducible thought process directed at a particular type of task (the quadratic formula for solving equations). A heuristics strategy is the use of a smorgasbord of thinking tools when reacting to a situation (solving non-routine problems). Some students want every problem reduced to a cognitive strategy, but that is neither possible nor desirable.

Since low-achieving students are not likely to develop effective cognitive and metacognitive strategies spontaneously, it is important to provide learning situations enhanced by explicit strategy instruction. On the other hand, if the students already have an efficient strategy for learning a skill or a given type of content, explicit strategy instruction may actually hinder achievement.
> Strategic Thinking and Learning, ASCD

Wherever possible use heuristics. The best way to do this is through the use of non-routine problems — that is, problems where no cognitive strategy has been developed or where the cognitive strategies are more difficult to apply than heuristics.

Keeping an active mind may be translated as "THINKING," but a major problem with the translation is the meaning of the word. Every teacher aspires to teach "thinking," but most descriptions of how that is accomplished are vague and difficult to replicate. One technique for teaching thinking is to consider it to be a search for meaning. Mathematics teachers can constantly stress a search for meaning by asking questions such as:

What does $3 + 5$ mean?
What does "Find the least common multiple of 21 and 35" mean?
What does 7% of 832 mean?
What does $x + 5 = 12$ mean?
What does $(x - 5)^2 = 49$ mean?

Examples of other questions which search for meaning are:

Write a simpler problem.
What does the answer to this problem look like?

If you had the answer, what would you do
to check it?
Find the last problem you could do correctly.
What is different about this problem from
others you have done?
If you could change something about this
problem to make it easier, what would
you select?

Teachers of mathematics need to primarily ask "W"
questions (What, Where, Why, When, Who). They
need to avoid asking "How" questions because these
frequently encourage the replication of some known
process.

Teacher questions are rarely as good as student questions. And the very best questions are those that a
student asks of him/herself. When a student questions her/himself it requires: (1) active processing,
(2) thinking about their own thinking processes,
and (3) the recall of prior knowledge.

4. Monitor Comprehension

*The skilled learner strives to reach two goals:
to understand the meaning of the tasks at hand,
and to regulate his or her own learning.*
Strategic Teaching and Learning, ASCD

Self-evaluation is a crucial, on-going process. Just
as prior knowledge is crucial to beginning successful study, so too is review crucial for integrating
and consolidating it. The students who pass one
test and immediately forget its content have never
learned that constant review and assimilation of
knowledge is a necessity in mathematics.

Teach students to treat evaluation and review as
important aspects of their study. To begin this
process take some time to teach your own version

of some learning theory. Any explanation of the
learning process will assist students to monitor their
own learning.

A simple example of a learning process for
mathematics is:
1. Awareness of the new learning intended.
   a. Background check
      (prior knowledge needed)
   b. Focus (put attention directly on the
      new learning)
2. Active response to some question or problem
   intended to illustrate acquisition of the new
   learning.
3. Feedback on the degree to which the active
   response was appropriate or correct.

Students also will benefit by evaluating their instruction. Making a conscious effort to judge their
instruction is part of the process for a student becoming responsible for their own success/failure.
Benjamin Bloom's criteria for quality instruction
provides a simple four-phase method for evaluation:
1. Does the instruction provide clear cues or
   directions?
2. Does the instruction include an appropriate
   learning activity?
3. Does the instruction provide feedback?
4. When difficulties are encountered, does the
   instruction provide corrective recycling?

At the heart of comprehension monitoring are
those skills which are labeled metacognitive.
Metacognitive skills are the thoughts (knowledge
and skills) used to plan, monitor, and evaluate an
individual's cognition. If cognition were thinking,
then metacognition would be thinking about thinking. The monitoring and evaluating functions of
metacognition are important when a student has

only a vague idea of how well or poorly they are learning. Many students are unaware of what they know and what they do not know. These students are having trouble monitoring and evaluating their comprehension. Successful students learn efficiently by utilizing the feedback they receive from the monitoring and evaluating functions to improve their future performance.

An interesting way to encourage students to engage in more metacognition is to tell them that all learning of mathematics comprises two components. The first is learning the content of the subject. The second is learning to what degree that content has been learned. The permutations of these two components are:

1. The student who knows the subject and knows he/she knows the subject. This is the student who is probably working towards an A.

2. The student who knows the subject, but doesn't know whether he/she knows the subject. This is frequently the student with anxiety, and anxiety reduction techniques may bring a dramatic improvement in performance.

3. The student who doesn't know the subject, and also knows he/she doesn't know the subject. This student has the knowledge to improve performance. The question here is if the student has the will and management skills.

4. The student who doesn't know the subject, and doesn't know he/she doesn't know the subject. This student suffers from "double ignorance." All is not lost, however, because awareness of the situation may move this student to take advantage of the plethora of materials now available to evaluate the degree of knowledge. If so, this student can become a #3 just with that knowledge. Again, does the student have the will and management?

Students today present new, more difficult challenges for their mathematics teachers. Explicit teaching of the nature of mathematics rather than solving routine problems can best overcome the mindblocks of those students that are real or marginal failures.

Robert Hackworth is currently President of H&H Publishing Company. He is a recently retired Mathematics Professor from St. Petersburg Jr. College, Clearwater, Florida.

Confidence in their own ability to learn mathematics makes the difference in whether students pass a college remedial mathematics course.

Factors Affecting Mathematics Achievement in High Risk College Students

By Charlee B. Goolsy, Patricia L. Dwinell, Jeanne L. Higbee, and Ann S. Bretscher

(Condensed from *Research and Teaching in Developmental Education*, 4(2), 18-27, Spring 1988. Reprinted by permission of Charlee B. Goolsy, Patricia L. Dwinell, Jeane L. Highbee, and Ann S. Bretscher and *Research and Teaching in Developmental Education*, a publication of the New York College Learning Association.)

Abstract. This study examined attitudinal variables, i.e., mathematics anxiety, confidence in learning mathematics, attitude toward success, perception of teacher's attitude toward the student as a learner of mathematics, and locus of control as predictors of first quarter grades in a developmental studies mathematics course for both male and female students. The regression analyses also included high school grade point average (HSGPA) and Scholastic Aptitude Test-Quantitative score (SATQ) as predictors. The dependent variable was course grades in a developmental studies mathematics course. The result of the regression analyses was that only confidence in one's ability to learn mathematics, HSGPA, and SATQ contributed significantly. For the total group the three variables accounted for 17% of the variance, for the male subgroup 14%, and for the female subgroup 25%.

In recent years mathematics educators and researchers increasingly have expressed an interest in the relationship between affective variables and achievement in mathematics. However, despite considerable research in this area during the last two decades, the results are inconclusive. Reyes (1984, p. 558) defines affective variables as "students' feelings about mathematics, aspects of the classroom, or about themselves as learners of mathematics." Among affective variables identified in the literature for study in relation to mathematics achievement are factors such as student's attitude toward success in mathematics, confidence in learning mathematics, mathematics anxiety, effective motivation and mathematics usefulness (Aiken, 1970a, 1970b, 1976; Butler, M. & Austin Martin, G., 1981; Fennema, E. & Sherman, J., 1976a, 1976b, 1977, 1978; Fox, L. H., Fennema, E., & Sherman, J., 1977; Richardson & Suinn, 1972). The stereotype of mathematics as a male domain has been identified as a factor which may influence the attitudes of females toward learning mathematics (Tobias, 1978). Additional mediating variables include teacher attitudes toward mathematics, parental attitudes toward mathematics and toward their children as learners of mathematics, and peer attitudes (Aiken, 1970; Fennema & Sherman, 1976, 1977). Locus of control or causal attributions may also serve as mediating variables which affect achievement in mathematics (Shea, K. A., & Llabre, M. M., 1985; Wolleat, P., Pedro, J. D., Becker, A. D., & Fennema, E., 1980).

Results of research related to the significance of mathematics anxiety as a predictor of performance on mathematical tasks or in college level courses have been contradictory. Fulkerson, Galassi, and Galassi (1984) scrutinized the cognitions of high and low mathematics anxious college graduates for sex and anxiety related differences by asking the students to "think aloud" while responding to items from the quantitative subtest of the Scholastic Aptitude Test (SATQ). Verbalizations were classified according to eleven categories of cognitions. No anxiety-related differences were found in mathematics performance or in the categorized cognitions.

In a study of achievement of both males and females in a beginning college algebra course the results indicated that mathematics anxiety, as measured by the Revised Mathematics Anxiety Rating Scale (RMARS), did not contribute significantly beyond the 10% explained by SATQ to the variance in grades (Llabre & Suarez, 1985). Similar results were reported by Resnick, Viehe, and Segal (1982) and Dew, Galassi, and Galassi (1984). Siegel, Galassi, and Ware (1985) found that mathematics anxiety was not as successful as a predictor of performance on the final examination of an introductory college mathematics course as were other variables, specifically incentives and self-efficacy.

Gourgey (1984) asserts that self-assessments made by mathematics anxious students are not necessarily realistic indicators of ability, yet these students perpetuate their low self-concepts by failing to recognize their mathematical accomplishments. Hackett (1985) determined that mathematics self-efficacy, as influenced by sex role socialization, amount of mathematics preparation, and mathematics achievement, is predictive of both mathematics anxiety and choice of college major. Several studies reported significant negative relationships between mathematics achievement and both previous number of mathematics courses taken and mathematics anxiety (Austin-Martin, Waddell & Kincaid, 1980; Buckley & Ribordy, 1982; and Alexander & Cobb, 1984). Wright and Miller (1981) found a lower mean on the MARS (Mathematics Anxiety Rating Scale) for the developmental mathematics subgroup than for students enrolled in the basic college algebra courses. In other studies, no significant differences were reported in locus of control between developmental students and other freshmen (Cartledge & Walls, 1985) nor between locus of control and mathematics achievement (Biaggio & Pelofski, 1984). No significant gender differences in locus of control were reported by Cartledge and Walls or by Blustein and Lester (1979).

It would appear that there are a number of inconsistencies in the findings pertaining to affective variables and gender, as related to mathematics performance and/or achievement of college students. This study examined attitudinal variables (mathematics anxiety, confidence in learning mathematics, attitude toward success, perception of teacher's attitude toward one as a learner of mathematics) and locus of control as predictors of first quarter mathematics grades for both male and female students enrolled in a developmental studies mathematics course. High school grade point average (HSGPA) and scores on the quantitative subtest of the Scholastic Aptitude Test (SATQ) were also included in the regression analyses.

Method

Sample
The sample consisted of 118 students who enrolled in a developmental algebra course in the Division of Developmental Studies at a large southern state university (enrollment over 20,000 students) during

the fall quarter of the 1985-1986 academic year. To be eligible for enrollment in Developmental Studies, students were denied regular admission because they did not meet minimum admission requirements. The progress of all students in the mathematics program is measured by standardized criteria created by the Division of Developmental Studies and approved by the university system Board of Regents.

Instruments were administered to students within the first two weeks of classes. The sample included 59 males and 59 females, of whom 96 were Caucasians and 22 minority group members. For the total group the mean HSGPA was 2.58 and the mean score on the SATQ was 408.

Instruments

Four Mathematics Attitude Scales (Fennema & Sherman, 1976a) were administered — Confidence in Learning Mathematics, Mathematics Anxiety, Attitude Toward Success in Mathematics, and Students' Perception of Teachers' Attitudes Toward Them as Learners of Mathematics. The splithalf reliability coefficients for the mathematics attitude scales used in this study range from .87 to .93 (Fennema & Sherman, 1976a). Items selected for inclusion in the scales were judged according to the following criteria: "(a) Items which correlated highest with the total score for each sex; (b) Items with higher standard deviations for each sex; (c) Items which yielded results consistent with the theoretical construct of a scale; (d) Items which differentiated mathematics and non-mathematics students," (Fennema & Sherman, 1976a). Each of the scales consisted of 12 items; the item scores were added to obtain the overall scale scores. A high score on the Mathematics Anxiety Scale indicated a low level of anxiety towards mathematics.

Locus of Control was measured by Rotter's Internal-External Scale (1966). The instrument consists of 29 forced choice items, including six items serving as fillers. Scores range from zero (highly internal) to 23 (highly external).

The first quarter course grade in mathematics (MGRADE), the SATQ score and the HSGPA were taken from student records.

Analyses

Multiple regression analyses (SAS, 1985) were used to assess the contributions of the independent variables to the dependent variable of academic performance in the first quarter mathematics course. All analyses were run on the total sample and separately for males and females.

Results

There were no significant differences between males and females on the mathematics attitude variables nor on locus of control; however, significant differences at the .01 level existed between males and females for the SATQ and HSGPA. Females had a higher HSGPA, $t(116) = 2.83$, $p < .01$. Males had a higher score on the SATQ, $t(116) = -4.43$, $p < .01$.

For the total group, male subgroup and female subgroup, the affective variables of student perceptions of teacher attitudes, anxiety toward mathematics, and level of confidence, were significantly related to first quarter grades in mathematics. However, the relationships of attitude toward success and locus of control to MGRADE were not significant. For the total group and the male subgroup mathematics anxiety was significantly related to the SATQ. For the total group and the female subgroup HSGPA was significantly related to the first quarter mathematics grade.

The correlation between HSGPA and SATQ score, which was significant for the total group and the female subgroup was negative, most likely due to the selection policy of the university's Admissions Committee. The result of this policy is that students who are rejected for admission to the university are subsequently referred for admission to the institution's Developmental Studies program. Typically, these students have an adequate HSGPA and a low SAT score or an adequate SAT score and a low HSGPA. These findings correspond with other studies conducted in this developmental program (Dwinell, 1985; Ervin, Hogrebe, Dwinell, & Newman, 1984; Hogrebe, Dwinell, & Ervin, 1985; and McFadden, 1985).

Intercorrelations among teacher attitudes, level of confidence, and anxiety toward mathematics suggested a moderate to high degree of overlap ranging from .66 to .71 for males to .52 to .62 for females. However, the correlations between the Confidence in Learning Mathematics Scale and Mathematics Anxiety Scale were very high, ranging from .83 to .87. These correlations are similar to those found by Fennema and Sherman (1976a).

The high correlation suggests that the two scales are measuring the same concept. Since the scale of confidence in learning mathematics measures a more positive attitude toward mathematics, it was included in the regression analyses and the anxiety scale was deleted.

The results of stepwise regression analyses indicated that only the confidence score significantly contributed to the proportion of first variances in mathematics grade. Teacher attitudes, attitude toward success, and locus of control did not account for significant variance in predicting MGRADE over and above the level of confidence, and were not included in further analyses. However, it should be noted that this finding may be partially explained by the high correlations between the attitudinal variables. The academic variables of SATQ and HSGPA were added to the final equation because they are already utilized in this developmental program as predictors.

> Confidence in one's ability to learn mathematics is the only affective variable included in this study which contributes significantly to prediction of performance in a first quarter developmental mathematics course (assuming the elimination of anxiety as a variable due to the high correlation between the anxiety and confidence scales).

For the total group, confidence and the academic variables of HSGPA and SATQ accounted for 17 percent of the variance in first quarter mathematics grade $F(3,114) = 7.82$, $p < .0001$. When the total sample was divided into two groups on the basis of gender, the three variables of confidence, HSGPA, and SATQ accounted for 14 percent of the total variance for males. Only confidence contributed significantly to the variance over and above HSGPA and SATQ. For the female subgroup, each of the three variables of confidence, SATQ, and HSGPA contributed significantly in accounting for 25 percent of the variance in estimating first quarter mathematics grade.

> Because few students in remedial mathematics classes have enjoyed previous success in mathematics, these students in particular can benefit by a less threatening mathematics classroom environment and a commitment to excellence in teaching.

Implications

The findings indicate that confidence in one's ability to learn mathematics is the only affective variable included in this study which contributes significantly to prediction of performance in a first quarter developmental mathematics course (assuming the elimination of anxiety as a variable due to the high correlation between the anxiety and confidence scales). Inferences drawn from this research are limited by the sample size and the highly selective Developmental Studies population. However, it would appear that students in similar programs would benefit from strategies designed to increase confidence and reduce the level of anxiety toward mathematics because few students in remedial mathematics classes have enjoyed previous success in mathematics; these students in particular can benefit by a less threatening mathematics classroom environment and a commitment to excellence in teaching. An effective instructor in developmental mathematics must not limit the instructional process to concerns of cognition; it is imperative that instructors focus attention on both the affective and cognitive domains. The instructors of Developmental Studies mathematics at this institution are available to provide considerable extra help outside the classroom. They frequently use individual tutoring and mathematics journals to teach study skills, analyze student progress, and understand the affective domain of students. A course required of all students in the Developmental Studies program which is taught by the counseling faculty assists students with goal setting (motivation), communication skills, study strategies, and anxiety reduction. Through techniques such as systematic desensitization and/or cognitive restructuring, students may develop more positive attitude toward learning mathematics and thus reduce mathematics anxiety. Assertiveness skills are taught to assist students in learning to ask for clarification or extra help.

Comparing mean differences in males and females, this study found females to have higher HSGPA's whereas males had higher SATQ scores. It is interesting to note, however, that males and females were equally successful in their first quarter mathematics course. It appears likely that intervention strategies used by the mathematics instructors and counselors may assist students in overcoming their entry level deficiencies in this content area. The strategies which are presented to students in this university's Developmental Studies program may help mitigate motivational barriers and skill deficiencies. Thus, individualized instruction provided by this program should be noted when comparing results of this study with findings concerning populations of students in other entry level university mathematics classes.

A significant limitation of this research is reflected in the 83% of the total variance which is not explained in the regression analysis. Among the variables which might account for this variance are number of high school mathematics courses completed, number of intervening years since a mathematics course was last taken, and the general motivation of the student, including reasons for pursuing a college degree. Further research incorporating these variables is indicated.

> For students participating in a developmental mathematics program, anxiety or lack of confidence in one's ability to learn mathematics may serve as a more viable predictor of success than such standard measures as HSGPA and SATQ scores.

The findings of this study have implications for admission personnel as well as mathematics instructors and counselors. The SATQ score, which generally has been perceived to be an excellent predictor of success, is perhaps less accurate when utilized in relation to high risk students. Further research focusing on developmental mathematics students is needed to confirm these findings. Meanwhile, the possibility that high school grade point average may be a more significant factor in assessing aptitude and/or motivation for female students than for male students in developmental mathematics programs merits further scrutiny.

Discrepancies among previous studies regarding the relationship of affective variables to mathematics achievement may be explained by a closer examination of the populations studied. For students participating in a developmental mathematics program, anxiety or lack of confidence in one's ability to learn mathematics may serve as a more viable predictor of success than such standard measures as SATQ scores and HSGPA.

References

Aiken, L. R., Jr. (1970a). Attitudes toward mathematics. *Review of Educational Research*, 40, 551-596.

Aiken, L. R., Jr. (1970b). Nonintellective variables and mathematics achievement: Directions for research. *Journal of School Psychology*, 8, 28-36.

Aiken, L. R., Jr. (1976). Update on attitudes and other affective variables in learning mathematics. *Review of Educational Research*, 46, 293-311.

Alexander, L., & Cobb, R. (1984). Identification of the dimensions and predictors of math anxiety among college students. Paper presented at the Mid-South Educational Research Association, New Orleans, LA.

Austin-Martin, G., Waddell, L., & Kincaid, M. B. (1980). Correlates of math anxiety in female college freshmen. Paper presented at Rocky Mountain Educational Research Association, Las Cruces, NM.

Biaggio, M. K., & Pelofski, D. D. (1984). Achievement in mathematics as a function of sex, sex role identity, self-esteem, and locus of control. Paper presented at the American Psychological Association, Toronto, Canada.

Blustein, J., & Lester, D. (1979) Locus of control and remedial students. *Psychological Reports*, 44, 54.

Buckley, P. A., & Ribordy, S. C. (1982). Mathematics anxiety and the effects of evaluative instructions on math performance. Paper presented at the Midwestern Psychological Association, Minneapolis, MN.

Butler, M., & Austin-Martin, G. (1981). High math anxious female college freshmen: What do they have in common? Paper presented at the American Psychological Association, Los Angeles, CA.

Cartledge, C. M., & Walls, D. G. (1985). Locus of control: A comparison of developmental studies, undergraduate, and graduate students. Paper presented at the Tenth Annual University System of Georgia Developmental Studies Conference, Jekyll Island, GA.

Dew, K. M. H., Galassi, J. P., & Galassi, M. D. (1984). Math anxiety: Relation with situational test anxiety performance, physiological arousal, and math avoidance behavior. *Journal of Counseling Psychology*, 31, 580-583.

Dwinell, P. L. (1985). The validation of variables used in the placement and prediction of academic performance of developmental students. (ERIC Document Reproduction Service No. ED 260 109).

Ervin, L., Hogrebe, M. C., Dwinell, P. L., & Newman, I. (1984). Comparison of the prediction of academic performance for college developmental students and regularly admitted students. *Psychological Reports*, 54, 319-327.

Fennema, E., & Sherman, J. A. (1976a). Fennema-Sherman Mathematics Scales: Instruments designed to measure attitudes toward the learning of mathematics by females and males. *JSAS: Catalog of Selected Documents in Psychology*, 6, 31.

Fennema, E., & Sherman, J. (1976b). Sex related differences in mathematics learning: Myths, realities, and related factors. Paper presented at American Association for the Advancement of Science, Boston, MA.

Fennema, E., & Sherman, J. (1977). Sex related differences in mathematics achievement, spatial visualization and affective factors. *American Educational Research Journal*, 14, 51-71.

Fennema, E., & Sherman, J. (1978). Sex-related differences in mathematics achievement and related factors: A further study. *Journal for Research in Mathematics Education*, 9, 189-203.

Fox, L. H., Fennema, E., & Sherman, J. (1977). *Women and mathematics: Research perspectives for change*, Washington, DC: National Institute of Education.

Fulkerson, K. F., Galassi, J. P., & Galassi, M. D. (1984). Relation between cognitions and performance in math anxious students: A failure of cognitive theory? *Journal of Counseling Psychology*, 31, 376-382.

Gourgey, A. F. (1984). The relationship of misconceptions about math and mathematical self-concept to math anxiety and statistics performance. Paper presented at the American Educational Research Association, New Orleans, LA.

Hackett, G. (1985). Rate of mathematics self-efficacy in the choice of mathematics-related majors of college women and men: A path analysis. *Journal of Counseling Psychology*, 32, 47-56.

Hogrebe, M. C., Dwinell, P. L., & Ervin, L. (1985). Student perceptions as predictors of academic performance in college developmental studies, *Educational and Psychological Measurement*, 45, 639-645.

Llabre, M. M., & Suarez, E. (1985). Predicting math anxiety and course performance in college women and men. *Journal of Counseling Psychology*, 32, 283-287.

McFadden, M. S. (1986). The prediction of college course grades in a developmental studies program using pre-enrollment academic and demographic variables. Unpublished doctoral dissertation, University of Georgia, Athens, GA.

Resnick, H., Viehe, J., & Segal, S. (1982). Is math anxiety a local phenomenon? A study of prevalence and dimensionality. *Journal of Counseling Psychology*, 29, 39-47.

Reyes, L. H. (1984). Affective variables and mathematics education. *Elementary School Journal*, 84, 558-581.

Richardson, F. C., & Suinn, R. M. (1972). The Mathematics Anxiety Rating Scale: Psychometric Data. *Journal of Counseling Psychology*, 19, 551-554.

Rotter, J. B. (1966). Generalized expectancies for internal versus external control of reinforcement. *Psychological Monographs*, 80, (1, Whole No. 609).

SAS user's guide (1982). Cary, NC: SAS Institute.

Shea, K. A., & Llabre, M. M. (1985). Gender differences in college students' attributions for success in two subject areas. Paper read at American Educational Research Association, Chicago, IL.

Siegel, R. G., Galassi J. P., & Ware, W. B. (1985). A comparison of two models for predicting mathematics performance: Social learning versus math aptitude anxiety. *Journal of Counseling Psychology*, 32, 531-538.

Tobias, S. (1978). *Overcoming math anxiety*. Boston, MA. Houghton Mifflin.

Wolleat, P., Pedro, J. D., Becker, A. D., & Fennema, E. (1980). Sex differences in high school students, causal attributions of performance in mathematics. *Journal for Research in Mathematics Education*, 11, 356-366.

Wright, D. E., & Miller, L. D. (1981). Math anxiety: A research report. Paper presented at the Mid-South Educational Research Association, Lexington, KY.

Charlee B. Goolsy is Chairperson of the Mathematics Component, Patricia L. Dwinell is Assistant to the Director for Research and Evaluation, Jeanne L. Higbee is Assistant Professor of Counseling, and Ann S. Bretscher is Assistant Professor of Mathematics, all in the Division of Developmental Studies at the University of Georgia, Athens, GA 30602.

Darken explains that years of failure have led to impoverished impressions of mathematics as a subject in which the primary aim is to get answers by following rules that make no internal sense.

Arithmetic + Calculators + College Students = ?

By Betsy Darken

(From Darken, B. (Winter 1991). Arithmetic + calculators + college students = ? *Journal of Developmental Education*, 15 (2), 6-10, 12, 35. Reprinted by permission of Betsy Darken and the *Journal of Developmental Education*, Appalachian State University, Boone, NC 28608.)

Abstract. Studies indicate that many postsecondary students are deficient in understanding of arithmetic concepts, especially in their ability to apply these concepts in problem-solving situations. Unfortunately, in attempting to combat this problem most developmental programs use curriculum which has become anachronistic, especially in light of technological developments. This article summarizes new standards set by the National Council of Teachers of Mathematics for the K-12 curriculum and recommends that developmental educators engage in similar reform efforts. Specific suggestions are made regarding the effect of calculators on the curriculum, methods of emphasizing applications which require critical thinking, and the balance between use of calculators and mental arithmetic.

A very disturbing situation exists in developmental mathematics today. As many developmental educators are only too well aware, some college students are not only unprepared for college-level mathematics but are also seriously deficient in arithmetic. While this in itself is a matter of grave concern, it is compounded by another problem over which developmental educators have direct responsibility. Specifically, the typical arithmetic curriculum used in most college-level developmental programs is outmoded. It is patterned after an elementary/secondary curriculum which is now the target of major reform by the National Council of Teachers of Mathematics (NCTM). The NCTM as well as a host of other reformers argue that this curriculum, with its emphasis on lower level skills, often fails to accomplish its main purpose: It does not lead many of our students to an understanding of numbers and comprehension of mathematical concepts so that ultimately they can use mathematics intelligently. These reformers also argue that this curriculum has become particularly anachronistic because of technological advances, especially in calculators (Commission on Standards for School Mathematics, 1989).

These charges apply doubly to the arithmetic curriculum at the postsecondary level. Our traditional curriculum focuses on rote work and increased proficiency with paper-and-pencil algorithms rather than conceptual understanding, problem-solving, or calculator skills. It is high time for change. The parameters of mathematics education have shifted so dramatically that the need for revision can no longer be ignored. The following sections will first present evidence of the need for change and then examine the key issues related to reform.

The Crisis in Mathematics Education

Over the last decade a flurry of reports have documented that American mathematics education is in serious trouble. Test results indicate that a major problem exists with higher level cognitive skills. According to the 1986 National Assessment of Educational Progress (NAEP), American students are relatively good at lower level skills, but "few students in their latter years of high school have mastered the fundamentals needed to perform more advanced mathematical operations" (Dossey, Mullis, Lindquist, & Chambers, 1988, p. 431). This conclusion is based on students' extremely poor performance on multistep problem solving and algebra. Only 6% of the 17-year-olds in their study demonstrated the capacity to solve problems like the sample given below.

> Christine borrowed $850 for one year from the Friendly Finance Company. If she paid 12% simple interest on the loan, what was the total amount she repaid? (Dossey et al., 1988, p. 43).

The same pattern occurred on international mathematics tests. Crosswhite and Dossey (1987) reported that achievement of American eighth graders on computational arithmetic was slightly above the mean in the Second International Mathematics Study of two dozen countries but below the mean for items involving comprehension and the ability to solve problems.

At the postsecondary level, the Conference Board of the Mathematical Sciences (CBMS) reported in 1985 that the need for remediation was the problem most commonly listed by mathematics departments at public colleges (Albers, Anderson, & Loftsgaarden, 1987). In the same survey, the CBMS also reported that 20% of public 4-year colleges and 47% of 2-year college mathematics enrollments were in developmental mathematics. Specific information about arithmetic deficiencies, available from states which conduct systematic placement testing, reveals an even more disturbing picture. The New Jersey Basic Skills Council reported in 1988 that 33% of full-time students and 47% of part-time students needed remedial work in computation. In 1988 the Tennessee State Board of Regents, which tests students with ACT scores below 16 (almost half of its first-time freshmen), reported that 47% of these students placed into arithmetic.

These statistics confirm what most developmental mathematics educators know firsthand. Around the country we are faced with the very difficult task of educating large numbers of college students at low levels of mathematical development. In specific regard to arithmetic, many of our students not only have tremendous difficulty with conceptual understanding and problem solving at this level, but also have severe deficiencies with regard to basic facts and algorithmic skills. The next section will examine the typical curriculum used by most postsecondary institutions to deal with this situation.

The College Arithmetic Curriculum

What curricula do colleges use if they choose to confront this problem? A thorough survey of college-level textbooks covering arithmetic indicates that the content is usually very traditional. Almost all of these textbooks consistently emphasize the teaching of algorithms and present large numbers of problems for drill, including many involving tedious computations. While several textbooks also stress applications, these problems are usually single step and arranged in typical textbook style. For instance, most, if not all, problems in a section on multiplication are solved by multiplication. This is characteristic of so many elementary mathematics texts that most students have learned not to bother to read the problem!

Another characteristic of most textbooks is their minimal reference to calculators. With one or two rare exceptions, the most attention given to this subject is to include optional sections providing a small amount of calculator instruction and then problem sets containing such problems as 2362 x 347. A more common practice is to mark problems containing large numbers with calculator symbols. Related to this low-level treatment of calculators is the small amount of space given to estimation, mental arithmetic, and other skills related to "number sense." At best these topics are mere appendages to the traditional curriculum.

> The widespread availability of the calculator has lulled some people into believing that arithmetic is no longer essential.

Surveys have indicated that the peripheral treatment of calculators in textbooks reflects common practice. Akst and Ryzewic (1985) reported that only 7% of college arithmetic instructors permitted students to use calculators in class and only 3% permitted use of calculators on exams. Times are changing slowly: McDonald (1988) reported that calculators were permitted on tests in 27% of 15 arithmetic classes and 31% of 54 arithmetic/algebra classes surveyed. While several innovative approaches to arithmetic have been reported in the literature (Akst, LaChica, & Sher, 1981; Chisko, 1985; Hoban, 1982), these seem to be exceptions that prove the rule.

These facts suggest that most developmental arithmetic programs are emphasizing paper-and-pencil algorithms and utilizing primarily single-step word problems and thus failing to come to terms with higher order cognitive skills or with the implications of calculators for school mathematics. While this curriculum may be effective in improving success rates on tests of lower level skills, it is very doubtful that students are being prepared to use mathematics competently in the modern world.

Characteristics of College Arithmetic Students

Any discussion of curriculum reform needs to take into account the academic problems of many developmental students. What Lochhead (1981) has said about secondary school remedial students certainly applies to our students as well: Years of failure have led to impoverished impressions of mathematics as a subject in which the primary aim is to get answers by following rules that make no internal sense. The poor learning skills identified by Lochhead as generating this vicious cycle can be observed in typical characteristics of college arithmetic students:

a. lack of knowledge about basic arithmetic facts (e.g., 7 x 8, $\frac{1}{2} = 0.5$);

b. lack of facility with arithmetic algorithms (e.g., 0.2 + 0.04, $\frac{1}{2} + \frac{1}{3}$);

c. lack of number sense and knowledge of basic concepts, especially in regard to fractions, decimals, and percents (e.g., not knowing that $\frac{6}{7}$ is close to 1 or that 0.40 = .4);

d. poor organization of work, including sloppy collection of information and disorganized written work;

e. proneness toward "careless mistakes" combined with heavy resistance toward checking work;

f. little facility with estimating answers or using mental arithmetic;

g. limited vocabulary and difficulty with reading comprehension (e.g., failure to recognize the principal in the phrase "Peter invested $1200");

h. difficulty with almost all levels of applications, typified by the question, "How do I know when to multiply and when to divide?"; and

i. a strong tendency to rely on rote memorization rather than understanding.

It is important to note that lack of computational skills of the sort listed in characteristics (a) and (b) is only a part of students' difficulties at this level. As NAEP researchers verified, "even when computation is removed as an obstacle, most teenagers cannot think sensibly about mathematics word problems" (Driscoll, 1987, p. 95). Yet computational skills pose a major dilemma for many developmental educators. We spend a great deal of time and effort working on lower level skills for the simple reason that many of our students have grave deficiencies in basic computation skills and number concepts. In spite of this problem, Lochhead states that successful remedial programs must shake students ". . . out of the memorize-regurgitate cycle," and ". . . place major emphasis on getting students to think actively" (Lochhead, 1981, p. 14). This is indeed a major challenge. We must focus on raising students' level of comprehension and accuracy of implementation even in the face of severe obstacles.

Reform Efforts

In 1989 the National Council of Teachers of Mathematics launched a major project aimed at reforming the curriculum of the elementary and secondary schools with the publication of standards for curriculum and evaluation and has continued to pursue change through publications and conferences. In addition, discussions by the American Mathematical Association of Two Year Colleges (AMATYC) regarding minimal competencies for college-level arithmetic are focusing on the ubiquitous presence of calculators and the importance of problem solv-

ing and number sense. In fact curricular reform emphasizing greater understanding and increased use of technology has become a major topic of discussion at mathematics conferences of all levels.

All who are involved in curricular reform are faced with challenging and complicated problems. However, educators working with the arithmetic curriculum have a special problem which is addressed in the following remark:

> *One of the dangers of the impact of the calculator is that we infer that arithmetic is no longer an important mathematical subject. Although the emphasis of arithmetic must change, the subject itself still has great import for students* (Luttrell, 1989, p. 2).

This raises a central point. The widespread availability of the calculator has lulled some people into believing that arithmetic is no longer essential. However, competence at arithmetic involves far more than attainment of a certain level of computational skill. The problems of students who fail to comprehend such basic concepts as the location of two-thirds on the number line are not going to be solved by simply making calculators available. While we have many questions to discuss regarding appropriate curricula and effective instruction for these students, we do not need to justify our insistence on conceptual understanding of mathematics at this level.

NCTM Recommendations for Change

The NCTM has recommended specific guidelines for the K-12 curriculum in its *Curriculum and Evaluation Standards for School Mathematics* (Commission on Standards for School Mathematics, 1989). For the K-4 curriculum the guidelines emphasize conceptual understanding, active involvement in doing mathematics, the development of mathematical thinking and reasoning abilities, applications, and thoughtful and appropriate use of calculators and computers. The following statement is made with regard to calculators:

> Calculators do not replace the need to learn basic facts, to compute mentally, or to do reasonable paper- and-pencil computations. The availability of calculators means, however, that educators must develop a broader view of the various ways computation can be carried out and must place less emphasis on complex paper-and-pencil computation (p. 19).

It is highly inappropriate to use an outmoded curriculum for college level developmental programs even as it is being updated at lower levels.

The recommendations for the 5th-8th grade curriculum include increased attention to open-ended problem solving, number and operation sense, estimation, and a broader range of topics including statistics and probability. Decreased attention is advised for routine, one-step problems, tedious paper-and-pencil computations, and formula memorization. Again this report states that the traditional stress on complex paper-and-pencil computation proficiency has become obsolete. It also suggests that the practice of prohibiting students in grades 5-8 from studying a broader curriculum until they have mastered basic computational skills is counterproductive. This raises an interesting question with regard to college students who have not mastered these skills.

I believe that these NCTM guidelines for revising the mathematics curriculum are extremely valuable not only to K-12 teachers but also to college developmental educators. Change is imperative. It is highly inappropriate to continue to use an outmoded

curriculum for college-level developmental programs even as it is being updated at lower levels.

Reform in College Level Developmental Mathematics

Even though the NCTM Standards Commission on Standards for School Mathematics (1989), provides valuable direction, developmental educators must deal with many issues regarding reform of the college arithmetic curriculum. First of all, K-12 curricular standards are undoubtedly not completely applicable to developmental programs. Secondly, the Standards is not intended to be a detailed curricular guide. The process of devising specific methods of teaching mathematical literacy and making nitty-gritty decisions about such matters as appropriate uses of calculators must be the main business of educators interested in change. Thirdly, the Standards discusses the problem of remediation in only the briefest fashion. Advocating that all students be guaranteed equal access to the same curricular topics, the NCTM bases its standards for grades 9-12 on the assumption that standards for previous grades have been implemented. While it is implied that some students may not have reached the desired level of computational proficiency by this time, the only comment made about this possibility is that "no student will be denied access to the study of mathematics in grades 9-12 because of a lack of computational facility" (p. 124).

Unfortunately, such assumptions about prior successful performance are so far removed from the current reality of American mathematics education as to threaten the entire reform movement. The failure of the NCTM to address the issue of unsuccessful students means that remedial/developmental educators at all levels must take prime responsibility for this inevitable problem, addressing not only general questions about standards for weaker students but also specific questions regarding the relative importance of curricular objectives for students with reduced time to learn.

In college-level developmental programs we need to discuss such questions as what level of paper-and-pencil or mental computational skill to expect of students with long histories of failure, how to use the calculator effectively in our classrooms, and how to deal with the special problems of learning disabled students. In addition, we need to continue to test ways of teaching arithmetic concepts more effectively, including innovative ideas about integrating arithmetic with algebra or using writing exercises in the classroom. It is important at this stage to share ideas on these matters, and to this end the rest of this article focuses on a few of the key issues related to reform.

It is worth mentioning here that, as we wrestle with the problem of exactly what adjustments to make, it would be wise to accept the fact that we are going to make mistakes. As with most other human endeavors into uncharted territory, we are best advised to avoid becoming entrenched in fixed positions and instead to learn as much as possible from our attempts to make progress, even if we sometimes wander into cul de sacs.

Issues Related to Calculator Usage

Opinion is divided over the appropriate use of calculators in developmental mathematics classes. The NCTM has recommended widespread use of the calculator after the fourth grade, a position supported by research indicating that such use does not have a deleterious effect on student performance. At the college level calculators are in common use except for courses in which they trivialize tests. In heated reaction to this situation, some say that such tests are completely irrelevant; others say that cal-culators are totally inappropriate. I suggest that before taking a position we first need to give a great deal of thought to the questions of what students need to understand about numbers and what we as teachers need to teach to promote this understanding.

As a starting point, consider these multiplication problems: (1) 3421 x 389 (2) 26 x 47 (3) 20 x 50 (4) 3 x 6. My current opinion is that skillful paper-and-pencil computation of problems like #1 is no longer a necessary skill, while the ability to mentally compute problems like #3 and #4 has become especially useful. As for #2 (which has thousands of prototypes in our developmental arithmetic texts), I believe that it is more important for college students who have not acquired this proficiency to spend their time learning how to apply mathematics rather than being drilled on multiplication algorithms.

As the above example illustrates, curricular reform must focus on questions about the value of each part of our curriculum. For each topic we need to ask, "Why do our students need to know how to do this?" This can be a very unnerving process since many of the traditional reasons for learning certain topics in arithmetic no longer apply. Yet I urge caution about taking extreme positions on this issue. On one hand, the fact that an inexpensive machine can perform an operation does not necessarily negate the usefulness of learning how to do it without a machine. For one thing, the human brain is faster for shorter calculations. In addition, because the process by which people gain an understanding of mathematics is not well understood, teachers have every right to be concerned that the premature use of machines may curtail understanding.

On the other hand, we must also be attuned to the power of tradition. It is very tempting to assume that a topic is important for our students because it was important for us or simply because it has been in the curriculum for a long time. Times change. It used to be valuable to memorize tremendous amounts of information and entire stories word for word; the invention of the printing press changed the situation dramatically. Likewise, calculators and computers have changed our world. Undoubtedly we must make some adjustments in our curriculum to take account of this reality.

> By removing much of the drudgery connected to checking answers, the calculator is a great aid in encouraging this habit.

Recommendations Regarding Mental Arithmetic

Let us return to the nitty-gritty question of when students should be permitted to use calculators. Actually, this may be the wrong question. The correct question may be: What types of problems should college students be expected to perform mentally? If our goal is to teach students to use mathematics intelligently in the real world of advanced technology, this shift in emphasis is appropriate. With this criterion, I argue that it is important for students to acquire "number sense," to understand basic arithmetic concepts, to acquire facility in certain basic operations, and to do mental arithmetic. It is also important for students to be taught how to use calculators, to check calculator work, and to combine calculator work with paper-and-pencil and mental arithmetic to become efficient users of mathematics.

Based on these criteria, the following is a list of suggestions regarding topics which students should master without recourse to calculators:

a. basic number facts, mainly for single digit numbers (e.g., 7 x 8);
b. operations with powers of ten (e.g., 30 x 5000);
c. the definition of exponents (e.g., 2^3);
d. conversions between percents, decimals, and fractions (e.g., 2% = 0.02);
e. order of operations (e.g., 4 + 2 x 3);
f. operations with simple rational numbers (e.g., $\frac{1}{2} + \frac{1}{3}$); and
g. operations with integers and signed numbers (e.g., (-3) − (-4)).

On the other hand, I suggest that calculator use is appropriate for most applications, for problems involving larger numbers, and for many exploratory learning situations. In the latter case, there are many NCTM journal articles and publications on how to use calculators to help students see patterns and make other discoveries.

Unfortunately the issue of calculator usage is compounded at some postsecondary institutions by required standardized paper-and-pencil computational tests. In these cases developmental educators not only need to make decisions about appropriate calculator usage but must also persuade higher authorities to revise tests accordingly.

Applications, Calculators, and "Looking Back"

As described earlier, "word problems" are our students' great nemesis. Recall that on the 1986 NAEP test, only 6% of 17-year-olds showed competence in two step problems. It is particularly appropriate to emphasize problem solving to students hoping to graduate from college. Hence I strongly recommend that developmental arithmetic programs include applications which are based on real world situations and require thoughtful analysis. This will usually mean supplementing textbook problems with many mixed multistep problems. Calculators do not play the central role in problem solving, but they can help to facilitate the process. With the availability of calculators, applications can be more realistic, students' attention can be focused on comprehension of the problem rather than on the drudgery of doing arithmetic, and answers can be checked more readily.

This last point is worth stressing. Polya's last step in his famous five-step approach to problem solving was to "look back." While this process of looking back can involve a great deal more than checking the accuracy of an answer, the development of this single habit would be a gigantic step forward for most developmental students. It is very effective in changing habits of carelessness. Students can be taught to determine if an answer is "in the right ballpark" and can learn various procedures for checking answers, including techniques other than simply working a problem twice by the same method. Such activities not only improve accuracy but often lead to deeper understanding, particularly for problems involving reverse operations like division. By removing much of the drudgery connected to checking answers, the calculator is a great aid in encouraging this.

Balancing Calculators with Mental Arithmetic

Many educators are concerned that some students will become too dependent on their calculators. We wince for good reason when students reach for their calculators for problems like 136 x 10. Lack of ability to do such problems mentally indicates lack of understanding of a basic concept. As the NCTM stresses, the ability to do mental arithmetic, to estimate answers, and to judge whether a calculator's answer is in the right ballpark are directly connected to students' understanding of numbers. "Number sense" which is even less common than common sense, can and should be taught directly in the classroom. It is particularly important to emphasize number sense in college-level arithmetic because it is conspicuously lacking among many students at this level.

It has been said that students tend to take an efficient common-sense approach in deciding whether to use calculators, paper-and-pencil, or mental arithmetic to solve problems. While this may be true of some students, my experience with weaker developmental students suggests otherwise. I have observed that students who do not learn rules easily tend to rely too heavily on calculators. For example, many students who were permitted to use calculators without restriction while learning integer arithmetic had enormous difficulty later on solving linear equations and simplifying polynomial expressions because they had developed no facility with sign rules. Teachers need to give students more direction in these matters to avoid such pitfalls.

Conclusion

The 21st century is almost upon us. It is high time that college-level arithmetic programs concentrate on mathematical reasoning and precise thinking, not on arithmetic proficiency. The calculator can be a great aid in this endeavor. It is time to use it.

References

Akst, G., LaChica, G., & Sher, L. (1981). The calculator in the college mathematics classroom. *Journal of the CUNY Mathematics Discussion Group*, Issue #8, 1-6.

Akst, G., & Ryzewic, S. R. (1985). *Methods of evaluating college remedial mathematics programs: Results of a national survey.* New York: City University of New York.

Albers, D., Anderson, R., & Loftsgaarden, D. (1987). *Undergraduate programs in the mathematical and computer sciences: The 1985-86 Survey.* Washington, DC: The Mathematical Association of America.

Chisko, A. M. (1985). Developmental math: Problem solving and survival. *Mathematics Teacher*, 78, 592-596.

Commission on Standards for School Mathematics (1989). *Curriculum and evaluation standards for school mathematics.* Reston, VA: National Council of Teachers of Mathematics.

Crosswhite, F. J., & Dossey, J. A. (1987). The second international mathematics study: A look at U. S. classrooms. In I. Wirszup & R. Streit (Eds.), *Developments in mathematics around the world.* Reston, VA: National Council of Teachers of Mathematics.

Dossey, J., Mullis, I., Lindquist, M., & Chambers, D. (1988). *The mathematics report card: Are we measuring up?* Princeton, NJ: Educational Testing Service.

Driscoll, M. (1987). *Research within reach: Secondary school mathematics.* Reston, VA: National Council of Teachers of Mathematics.

Eloban, M. (1982). Developmental studies: A model program. *Journal of Developmental and Remedial Education*, 6(13), 6-9.

Lochhead, J. (1981). *Problem solving for rote learners.* Unpublished manuscript.

Luttrell, C. (1989). *The philosophy of arithmetic.* Unpublished manuscript submitted by the Developmental Mathematics Committee to the American Mathematical Association of Two Year Colleges.

McDonald, A. (1988). Developmental mathematics instruction: Results of a national survey. *Journal of Developmental Education*, 12 (11), 8-15.

New Jersey Basic Skills Council (1988). *Effectiveness of remedial programs in public colleges and universities: Fall 1984 - Spring 1986.* Trenton, NJ: New Jersey Department of Higher Education.

Tennessee State Board of Regents. (1988). *Report #1: Remedial/developmental.* Nashville, TN: Author.

Betsy Darken is Director of Developmental Mathematics and Associate Professor of Mathematics at The University of Tennessee at Chattanooga, TN 37403-2598.

This article summarizes strategies for learning mathematical problem solving cooperatively and discusses the advantages and limitations of this approach.

Cooperative Learning Approaches to Mathematical Problem Solving

By Hope J. Hartman

(Excerpts from Hartman, H. J. (1993). Cooperative learning approaches to mathematical problem solving. In A. S. Posamentier (Ed.) *The Art of Problem Solving: A Resource for the Mathematics Teacher*. Kraus International Publications, 1993. Reprinted by permission of Hope J. Hartman and Kraus International Publications.)

Reciprocal peer tutoring (RPT) is for students learning mathematical computation. In this approach two or more students work together cooperatively and follow a structured format in which they teach, prompt, monitor and evaluate each other. Students alternate between teacher and student roles and engage in peer teaching, peer choice of rewards, and peer management (Fantuzzo & others, 1992).

6PQ Method of Discovery Learning

The 6PQ Method is a six-step question process, developed at Chemeketa Community College, designed to guide student thinking in the right direction while avoiding telling answers and lecturing. Its purpose is for students to be active, independent thinkers and learners. Each of the six question types starts with the letter "P." The tutor frequently paraphrases student's responses to questions within and between each step. Students can be grouped in pairs who take turns solving problems, either alternating roles as tutor and student or with stronger students tutoring weaker students. The entire class gets trained in this learning method so that all understand what was happening and why. This method can not only help students become active learners and independent problem solvers, it also develops students' questioning, communication, and leadership skills while simultaneously building their self-esteem and mathematics self-concepts. The six steps to use for problem solving are:

1. Preface. Establish rapport and identify the problem to be solved.
2. Pace. Determine what the student already knows about this problem and how to solve it. If the student knows how to solve the problem, observe the solution process and go to step 6.
3. Probe. Investigate the limits of the student's knowledge by seeking more detailed information. If the student solves the problem, ask her to make an educated guess about how to solve it, or ask how the student feels (rather than thinks) it might be done. If the student solves the problem, go to step 6.
4. Prod. If the student still has not solved the problem, move to step 6.
5. Prompt. If the student is stuck and all prior attempts have failed, give a hint, suggestion or show the student how to start the process. If this works, move to step 6.
6. Process. Have the student apply the same problem solving process to a similar problem.

Pair Problem Solving

Thinker and Listener Pairs working on problems and rotating roles has been a popular way of helping students think about their own problem solving. Students take turns serving as thinkers (problem solvers) who externalize their thought processes by thinking aloud, while analytical listeners track and guide the problem solving process as needed. It is a higher-level (metacognitive) self monitoring strategy that gives students feedback on what is understood and what is not (Whimbey & Lochhead,1982).

To make sure listeners really do their job, periodically teachers should ask listeners to summarize the steps the problem solvers used. The following activities were suggested by Larcombe to help student pairs learn to externalize their mathematical thought process:

1. Students take turns describing the rules they use;
2. Students describe to each other how the parts fit together when doing a construction task;
3. Working with concrete objects at first, students can describe operations used when calculating; and
4. One student must question an object, mathematical representation or graphic based on another student's description.

In a peer or cross-age tutoring situation the tutor is the questioner and the person being tutored is the problem solver. In a pair learning situation or cooperative learning context students take turns performing roles of questioner and problem solver.

What is the Teacher's Role in Cooperative Mathematics Problem Solving Lessons?

One of the key features about cooperative learning is that the teacher delegates considerable responsibility to the students. Both teachers and students must adopt roles that are quite different from whole class instruction. "The essence of good problem solving is self-correction. . . . teachers should become facilitators of learning, not sole dispensers of truth. . . . teachers must relinquish the safe seat of authority and step into the classroom" (Johnson & Johnson, 1990).

An important task in making cooperative learning successful is attitude change. The teacher's own attitude has to shift from teacher as transmitter of knowledge and center of attention and authority to teacher as manager and facilitator of learning. Attitudes toward noise in the classroom sometimes must be changed. Many people equate "a noisy classroom" with disruption, chaos and learning not taking place. In cooperative learning, noise in the classroom can reflect high level thinking and learning about mathematics! Several student attitudes must change so students show: interest in finding solutions, confidence to take risks and try various strategies, willingness to be wrong, accepting frustrations from not knowing, persevering when solutions are not immediate, and understanding the difference between not having found an answer yet and not knowing it. Students must shift from depending on teachers for the answers to becoming independent thinkers and learners (Johnson & Johnson, 1990). Teachers as role models must emphasize to students the importance of being problems solvers, active learners and seekers who are willing to take risks and make errors. Mistakes should be treated as learning opportunities and students must understand that important aspects of problem solving lie beyond the correct answer. Teachers and students alike must learn to value the process — not just its products.

A "Pretty Good List" of nine steps for teachers to follow in implementing cooperative learning is:

(1) Ensure a successful experience the first time, (2) Decide what to watch for, (3) Decide on a grouping strategy, (4) Prepare the materials, (5) Prepare yourself, (6) Explain the rules and expected behaviors, (7) Do it! (8) Debrief the class, and (9) Debrief yourself (Erickson, 1989).

Planning for Cooperative Learning in Mathematics

Training students for cooperation

Although many everyday life activities require cooperation, seldom are students taught how to work together cooperatively. Some educators recommend giving specific training in the skills needed for cooperative learning including: careful observations, reasoning, asking key questions, being supportive and helpful to others, explaining clearly, thinking visually, reasoning spatially, recording data, exploring new solution strategies, understanding the problem, being persistent and using ideas of other students.

What are Potential Pitfalls of Cooperative Learning for Teaching Mathematical Problem Solving?

Like other teaching methods, cooperative learning can be ineffective if it is not handled right. Not all group work is cooperative learning. Students can sit side by side in a group and do their work independently without cooperating. Potential problems implementing cooperative learning (in mathematics classes) may be student oriented or teacher oriented. Student oriented problems include: a group of students may become bored with each other, there may be inadequate leadership within a group, students may feel abandoned by the teacher, difficult problems may cause feelings of defeat while easy problems may be boring, and students may need a change of pace or more praise. Teacher oriented problems include: teachers may feel uncomfortable not being the center of the classroom, they may not have explained the task adequately and they may get mixed feedback about what students have learned.

Although many students prefer working cooperatively to working independently, some students would rather work alone so group participation should be optional. Such students can inhibit effective group interaction. The teacher's role as observer and supervisor is important in this type of situation. Depending upon the particular class and curriculum, teachers may decide to use cooperative learning as an option for students, rather than as a requirement.

Another problem is that one or two students can do all the work solving problems while the others do not participate. To prevent this, individual accountability is essential. Groups must be structured to foster cooperation between students. Assigning roles, sharing materials, requiring a group product and using group incentives can be used to structure effective cooperation.

Time can be a problem when implementing cooperative learning and sometimes lessons end without summarizing what was learned and assessing the group process. One way of handling this is to assign roles of summarizer and leader of group processing. Or the teacher can lead the summarizing and group processing at the end of each set of lessons.

Cooperative learning in mathematics can lead to incoherent presentation and interruptions while working so that students need more time reviewing and practicing. If initial training of students to work cooperatively is not adequate for some students or some groups, follow-up training may be needed. Sometimes problems arise if teachers set only academic goals rather than specifying both academic and social goals in advance.

Cooperative learning has many advantages for teaching mathematical problem solving. It improves mathematics achievement and higher level mathematical thinking. Working in pairs or small groups is highly motivating for most students and improves students' attitudes about themselves as learners and problem solvers. Improved interpersonal relations between students of different ethnic/cultural backgrounds is another benefit of cooperative learning.

There are many different approaches to using cooperative learning for teaching mathematical problem solving. Some methods involve small groups of 3-5 students learning together; others involve pairs of students working together.

The teacher's role in cooperative learning is different from whole class instruction. In cooperative learning, the teacher is more of a manager and facilitator of learning, or a coach, than a transmitter of knowledge. Major teacher responsibilities include: training students for cooperation, structuring groups, deciding whether/how to assign roles, selecting and preparing instructional materials (planning) and monitoring and evaluating student performance. Resources are available for cooperative math problem solving lessons.

There are some potential pitfalls to using cooperative learning for teaching mathematical problem solving. Some problems are student oriented, others are teacher oriented. However, overall the benefits outweigh the limitations.

Teachers can develop personal action plans to design cooperative learning lessons that meet the needs of their specific students and curriculum.

Cooperative learning is not just a fad. It has over a twenty year history of success as a technique for developing students mathematical problem solving skills. The benefits of using cooperative learning as a technique for teaching mathematical problem solving have been well documented. The advantages far outweigh the disadvantages. There is not a "right" way of using cooperative learning to teach mathematics; there are numerous options. Cooperative learning can make problem solving more lively and fun for both teachers and students.

References

Erickson, T. (1989) *Get it Together: Math Problems for Groups Grades 4-12.* Tucson, AZ: Zephyr Press, Addison-Wesley.

Fantuzzo, J., King, J., & Heller, L. (1992). Effects of reciprocal peer tutoring on mathematics and school adjustment. *Journal of Educational Psychology*, 84(3), 331-339.

Johnson, D., & Johnson, R. (1990). Using cooperative learning in mathematics. In Davidson, N. (Ed.) *Cooperative Learning in Mathematics*. Tucson, AZ: Zephyr Press, Addison-Wesley.

Whimbey, A., & Lochhead, J. (1982). *Problem Solving and Comprehension: A Short Course in Analytical Reasoning.* Philadelphia: Franklin Institute Press.

Hope J. Hartman is Associate Professor and Director of Tutoring and Cooperative Learning Program, City College of City University of New York.

Although this article appeared years ago, for many people it represents the ideal individualized mathematics course. Today's individualized programs can offer many more alternatives as a result of the vastly improved technology including multimedia, computer based interactive video programs, and other innovations although the basic course format can remain the same.

Math X: Variable for Student Progress

By C. W. Stine, Eugenie M. Trow, & Brendan Brown

(From the *Journal of Developmental & Remedial Education*, 1979, 3(1), 12-13. Reprinted by permission of Eugenie M. Trow and the *Journal of Developmental Education*, Appalachian State University, Boone, North Carolina 28608.)

Do students in the registration line tell you they want to take some math course, but the last one they had was eight years ago in high school and they are not sure how much they remember? Enroll them in Math X.

On the first day of your trig class, does a student tell you his work schedule is changing, and although he needs trig, the class hours probably won't work out for him a month from now and so he must drop? Send him to Math X.

Math X is an open-entry, limited open-exit, self-paced, self-instructional program offered at Antelope Valley College in Lancaster, California. AVC is a public, tuition-free community college with an enrollment of 5400, with 1000 students taking math classes. The courses are conducted in a self-contained laboratory with specialized assistance and major emphasis on student learning problems.

The Plan

Under the format of Math X, students may take arithmetic, the metric system, elementary algebra, geometry, trigonometry and college algebra, a total of seven sequential math classes during which a student may accumulate up to 22 units of math credits. Since many different courses may be taken in this format, and many students enter the program not knowing which class to take, the name "Math X" indicates an undesignated math class. The "X" in "Math X" may be thought of as a variable which takes on the value for each student of whatever course number that student chooses. As students earn course credit, a regular course code and course designation is recorded on the permanent record. These classes are also offered in the traditional lecture-discussion mode, and with the same textbooks that are used in Math X. The use of identical textbooks facilitates students' changing from one instructional mode to the other during a semester and helps to minimize differences between the same material learned under self-instruction as compared with lecture-discussion.

Some of the reasons students enter the Math X programs are (1) a desire to review quickly in order to move on to new material; (2) uncertainty as to which level to begin study; (3) the inability to stay at the same speed as a lecture-discussion class in a certain course; and (4) a need to review basic math before beginning study in other areas such as drugs and solutions — a unit required by the nursing department. Also in the nursing curriculum, students are tested by their nursing instructor in arithmetic and the metric system. Any student whose test results show a need for improvement is directed to the Math X program to make up such deficiencies.

There are four sections of Math X offered, each meeting for two hours twice a week for a 17.5 week semester. Table 1 indicates the course code, description, and units for each course.

Each section is staffed by two instructors and two student aides or one instructor and three student aides. During the first class period of the semester, the program is explained to entering students in a large group. Students entering any other time during the semester listen to an audiotape description of the program. This general explanation is followed by diagnostic testing using a standardized test battery. An instructor uses exam results to establish, during a personal interview, which course the student is ready to take and how long the student wishes to take in completing the course. Information gathered during this induction process is recorded in an individual folder established for each student. A "Line of Progress" is drawn on a chart for each student. The line connects the entry date and level of the student with the desired exit date and level. The line thus drawn gives a linear approximation of which unit in the course the student should be studying at any time during the semester in order to reach the desired goal.

TABLE 1

Course Code	Course Description	Semester Units
Math 50	Basic Arithmetic	3
Math 16	Metric System	1
Math A	Elementary Algebra	4
Math B	Geometry	3
Math C	Intermediate Algebra	4
Math D	Trigonometry	3
Math E\6	College Algebra	4

Chapter or unit tests are required in each course. Tests have two alternate forms, each of which may be taken once, and the better of the two scores is used in computing grades. Test results are recorded in the student folders. Each test is also kept in the folder until the student reviews it with an instructor or an aide. Most unit tests have been furnished by the textbook companies — a few are instructor made. After completing all unit tests, the student takes the standardized final which also has two forms, each of which may be taken once. The better score is used in computing final grades. Unit tests count 5/6 and the final exam 1/6 of the course grade.

Program Development

Math X at Antelope Valley College began in 1966 with a visit by three members of our mathematics department to Chabot College in northern California. Chabot College had three levels of algebra taught in a self-paced setting using programmed tests. A similar program was then instituted at Antelope Valley College.

The latest revisions in Math X began with ideas gathered at the 1976 American Mathematical Association of Two-Year Colleges Conference. These revisions took two distinct, complementary paths — the improvement of individualized instruction and the opening of a Math Lab at AVC.

To improve instruction, the department has adopted the texts *Essential Arithmetic, Essential Algebra, and Intermediate Algebra*, authored by Johnston and Willis (Wadsworth Publishing Company). These texts are used in arithmetic, beginning algebra, and intermediate algebra by all students.

Beginning in the fall of 1978, variable unit credit was granted to students who did not complete a full course. Previously students either received the full unit credit for completion of a course or they received nothing, even though they may have finished 75% of the work in a course. A student now receives unit credit for the work completed during the semester, e.g., a student who completes half of elementary algebra (a four unit course) will receive two units of credit with a grade that is the average of his/her grades. The student will return the following semester and complete the course. At that point, the remaining two units of credit are granted.

The opening of our Math lab greatly complemented the Math X program. Math X uses the lab for testing and as an audiovisual resource center. Math X students work at their own pace in classrooms adjoining the lab with a student aide always available. They come into the lab to take and review tests. For our lab, a math classroom was used with many of the desks replaced with tables. The key to the operation of the Math Lab is the student aides who are recruited from the better math students. An ability to communicate well with others is essential for these aides. Many aides have math skills through calculus, but we have often hired students with only algebra background since most of our Math X students and those who drop in to use the lab are enrolled in arithmetic or the algebra sequence.

In addition to the aides, it was determined that a professional was needed in the lab. Lacking the finances to hire someone, members of the department decided to volunteer a portion of their office hours for lab supervision. Initially, four instructors spent four of their five weekly office hours in the lab. This has been reduced to three hours per week because many students feel the need to consult with instructors in the privacy of their offices. The lab is in operation 17 hours per week in addition to the 15 hours per week that Math X is in session in the lab. All students at the college, Math X or non-Math X, are welcome in the lab during these 32 hours. The existence of the Math Lab allows all Math X students the opportunity to take a test whenever the student is ready and does not restrict testing to scheduled class hours alone. Students are asked to sign in when they use the lab, and last year approximately 3000 student contacts were made.

Student Success Rate

The rate of student success appears in Table 2.

TABLE 2

Semester	Enrollment		Course Credit		% of Success	
	Day	Evening	Day	Evening	Day	Evening
Spring 1976	174	70	75	41	43%	59%
Fall 1976	129	141	79	74	61%	52%
Spring 1977*	125	102	51	42	41%	41%
Fall 1977	148	94	76	48	51%	51%
Spring 1978	140	90	51	36	36%	40%
Fall 1978**	95	105	58	79	60%	75%

*Unit tests required in addition to final exam; Math Lab opened; Line of Progress used.

**Variable unit credit awarded for less than full course credit.

It is apparent that success rates have responded to the installation of variable unit credit more than any other single program development. The writers do not believe that Math X type programs should be used as the only method of math instruction. Some students can learn effectively only in the lecture type, formal class setting. On the other hand, many students have overcome math resistance in the Math X program and in the Math Lab. Our research indicates that average and below average students do exceptionally well in Math X. Math X and the Math Lab are tailored for students with changeable schedules and those who resist the traditional lecture classroom.

C. W. Stine was President and Eugenie M. Trow and Brendan Brown were Math Instructors at Antelope Valley College, CA 93536.

Further Readings on Mathematics

Akst, G., & Hirsch, L. (1991). Selected studies on math placement. *Review of Research in Developmental Education*, 8(4), 1-4.

Akst, G. (1986). Reflections on evaluating remedial mathematics programs. *Journal of Developmental Education*, 10(1), 12-15.

Forman, S. (1992, Fall-Winter). Is cooperative learning for you? Mathematics in College, 3-14.

Garland, M. (1993). The mathematics workshop model: An interview with Uri Treisman. *Journal of Developmental Education*, 16(3), 14-22.

Gourgey, A. (1992). Tutoring developmental mathematics: Overcoming anxiety and fostering independent learning. *Journal of Developmental Education*, 14(2), 2-6.

Gray, S. S. (1991, Spring). Ideas in practice: Metacognition and mathematical problem solving. *Journal of Developmental Education*, 14(3), 24-28.

Grossman, F. J., Smith, B., & Miller C. (1993, Fall). *Journal of Developmental Education*, 17(1), 2-7.

Hartman, H. J. (In press). Cooperative learning approaches to mathematical problem solving. In A. S. Posamentier (Ed.) *The Art of Problem Solving: A Resource for the Mathematics Teacher*. Kraus International Publications.

Hashway, R. M., & Hashway, S. E. (1991-1992). Solving mathematical word problems, integrating two different world models. Innovative Learning Strategies, Tenth Yearbook. 3-7.

MacLeod, S. (1992, Winter). Ideas in Practice: Writing the book on fractions. *Journal of Developmental Education*, 16(2), 26-28, 38.

McDonald, Anita D. (1988, September). Developmental Mathematics Instruction: Results of a national survey. *Journal of Developmental Education*, 12(1), 8-15.

Patricig, M. (1988). Combining individualized instruction with the traditional lecture method in a college algebra course. *Mathematics Teacher*, 81(5), 385-387.

Powell, A. B., Pierre, E., & Ramos, C. (1993, Fall). Researching, reading, and writing about writing to learn mathematics: Pedagogy and Product. *Research & Teaching in Developmental Education*. 10(1), 95-110. (Editor's Note: This is an annotated bibliography of studies about writing to learn mathematics and a new research paradigm.)

Sandberg, K. E. (1989). Affective and cognitive features of collaborative learning. *Research in Developmental Education*, VI(4).

Waits, B., & Leitzel, J. (1984, Fall). Early university placement testing of high school juniors. *Mathematics in College*.

Watkins, A. E., Albers, D. J., & Loftsgaarden, D. O. (1993, Spring). A survey of two-year college mathematics programs: The boom continues. *The AMATYC Review* (American Mathematical Association of Two-Year Colleges), 14(2), 55-66.

Wepner, G. (1987, September). Evaluation of a postsecondary remedial mathematics program. *Journal of Developmental Education*, 11(1), 6-9.

Math Anxiety

Hackworth, R. (1992). *Math Anxiety Reduction*. Clearwater, FL: H&H Publishing Company.

Tobias, S. (1978). *Overcoming Math Anxiety*. Boston, MA. Houghton Mifflin. (Note: a new edition of this book is in press.)

Wilding, S., and Shearn, E. (1991). *Building Self-Confidence in Math: A Student Workbook*, Second Edition. Dubuque, Iowa: Kendall Hunt Publishing Company. (Audio-tapes are available from the publisher to accompany this workbook.)

Part 10

Evaluation and Outcome Research

Striving For Excellence:
Program Evaluation Through National Standards

By Susan Clark Thayer and Martha Maxwell

Why have standards?

In the past several years there has been a groundswell of interest and commitment to the concept of self-assessment and program evaluation guided by the development of professional standards in the field of learning assistance. Seasoned professionals, as well as those new to the field, seem to be equally invested in the development of standards. One reason for this interest is the grim economic realities we are facing in so many of our institutions as they wrestle with accountability in tight budget situations. Maxwell (1991, p. 2) points out: "With so many institutions of higher education in deep financial difficulties, . . . on the one hand there is pressure to minimize student support, but on the other hand there is a demand to raise academic standards in response to public insistence on accountability."

Many learning assistance programs, originally developed by their institutions as an expedient way to handle a problem that was believed to be temporary, are now being viewed more seriously as student retention becomes a fiscal necessity. While declining general enrollments mean less tuition revenue, students who need intensive help have not disappeared from college classrooms. Keeping students in school has become more than a moral imperative; it is now necessary for the survival of colleges themselves. This need puts new pressure on retention programs. Higher education institutions now must go beyond the "political correctness" of merely assuring accrediting bodies, state or federal boards and potential constituencies that they HAVE a learning assistance program, now they must show that they have an EFFECTIVE program.

Considerable effort has already been directed toward developing standards for learning assistance programs. Materniak and Williams (1987), representing Commission XVII of the American College Personnel Association, drafted standards and guidelines for learning assistance programs that were approved by the Council for the Advancement of Standards for Student Services/Developmental Programs (CAS) (recently renamed Council for Advancement of Standards in Higher Education). Founded in the early 1980's, at present CAS is a consortium of 28 professional associations concerned with evaluating, approving and publishing standards in student affairs and support services areas. The goal of the CAS standards was to ". . . proffer a guiding vision of substance and integrity and stable and permanent criteria against which to measure out-of-class education, involvement, and learning pertaining to student development. They enable the student affairs practice to become more significant, valid, and credible in its quest to graduate from service programs of convenience to programs that reflect conviction, purpose, and persuasion" (Mable, 1991, p. 16).

The CAS Standards and Guidelines for Learning Assistance Programs are comprised of statements in ten areas: mission, program, leadership and management organization, human resources (including staff competence), funding, facilities, legal responsibilities (including affirmative action), ethics and evaluation. Within each of these general areas specific guidelines delineate the responsibilities of the learning assistance program. For example, one of the many requirements under legal responsibilities is that the learning assistance program should provide the academic community with current information about the unique characteristics and special needs of the learning assistance program's clientele as well as about available learning assistance programs and activities.

One of the CAS guidelines specifies that the facilities should provide private, sound-proofed areas for affective skills programming, testing, counseling, and other activities that require confidentiality or intense conversations. Standards for evaluation state that there must be systematic and regular research and evaluation of each functional area and that methods of evaluation "must include both quantitative and qualitative measures." Guidelines under evaluation specify that programs should be evaluated by users, including students, staff, and faculty. These are examples of what is contained in the lengthy document.

A Self Assessment Guide was also developed to accompany the CAS Standards and Guidelines. Self-study is the first step in credentialing and/or certifying academic programs in any discipline and provides the basis for internal peer reviews and reviews by panels of outside experts. Most public institutions whose programs are periodically evaluated by regional examining boards begin the process by requiring that each department complete a self-study.

NADE's Response to CAS

Following the publication of the CAS Standards and Guidelines for Learning Assistance Programs and Self Assessment Guide, the National Association of Developmental Education (NADE) became actively involved in standards work and appointed a committee to consider changes that would reflect the special roles and needs of developmental educators. In general, the committee agreed that the quality and comprehensiveness of the original CAS documents are impressive and represent a huge step forward for professionals in the field. However, while embracing their philosophy and intent, many colleagues in the developmental education field who reviewed the documents had serious concerns about their functional application.

The concerns about the CAS documents most frequently expressed by developmental educators fell into four areas: (1) GENERALITY — the CAS general standards and guides were not always easily applied uniformly to the diversity of activities found within learning centers. Certain commonalties provided an important overview but the general standards were hard to operationalize within diverse specific programs. (Example, the statement, "Learning assistance programs are purposeful," is appropriate to all programs, but the statement that, "The program promotes student development by encouraging appropriate personal and occupational choices," is not relevant to adjunct skills programs). (2) VAGUE/CONFUSING TERMINOLOGY — the meaning of some terms was not clear (Example: "The institution recognizes that the educational experience of students consists of both academic efforts in the classroom and *developmental opportunities through learning assistance programs*." Since some developmental education programs offer remedial courses as well as learning assistance services, this might be confusing). (3) The standards reflected a STUDENT SERVICES PERSPECTIVE — i.e., they contain many terms more appropriate for counseling services than for academic support programs. This exacerbated the terminology confusion. (4) LACK OF STRONG ACADEMIC/ PEDAGOGICAL COMPONENT — this was the most serious concern. Developmental education is essentially an academically related endeavor. There was nothing in the CAS documents to reflect this central feature of learning assistance.

NADE became a catalyst for other learning assistance organizations in addressing standards through using the CAS documents as a guide for developing specific standards for program components. To address the generality issue, self assessment guides were designed for each separate major learning assistance service (i.e., Tutor Program, Adjunct Skills Programs [including Supplemental Instruction], and Developmental Courses). The terminology problem was addressed through a standardized dictionary of terms developed by a College Reading and Learning Association (CRLA) committee (Rubin, 1991) that is appended to each self assessment guide. A self assessment guide on the teaching/learning process was developed to provide an academic/pedagogical component reflecting the philosophy of learning assistance programs. For example, the teaching/learning process guide includes items on instructor behavior, (instructors show awareness of each student's learning style), the teaching process, (instructors model processes and expected performances for students), as well as items on instructor's style, evaluation methods, and the other categories suggested by the CAS Standards (e.g., mission, legal responsibilities, ethics, evaluation, etc.). After NADE component standards are developed, they are field-tested, reviewed and revised. Also the endorsement of other professional groups such as the CRLA Board is sought.

People using the self-assessment documents are expected to make their own decisions about what is appropriate for their programs in the context of their own institutions in order to meet the criterion they set. After each section there is a Scoring Guide enabling the program director to total scores and list "strengths," "rationale for not meeting a criterion totally," and "actions feasible and recommended." The goal of the statements is to help program directors consider what components are necessary for a high quality program.

Clearly specified standards and guidelines can be useful for many purposes — establishing programs, evaluating existing programs, improving programs and as a guide to future changes. Reviewers indicate that standards are also beneficial in stimulating the decision-making process. They state that the NADE Self-Assessment Guides are useful in guiding program development, identifying and prioritizing areas needing improvement and encouraging directors to take a more comprehensive perspective of their programs.

For example, a standards document for establishing quality learning assistance programs can be invaluable to practitioners entering the field. This is especially true in a field where higher education administrators often assign someone who lacks developmental education experience to start a tutor program or administer a learning center or head a developmental education program.

When used to assess existing programs, national standards can provide program directors ammunition in budget discussions. Additional funds can be requested based on a desire to meet criteria established in published national standards. "I have compared my program with the national standards and find I am weak in this area. I need more resources so I can meet the national standards." Or, proposed cuts can be fought when they result in a lowering of program quality according to the national standards set by the profession. "I can cut that program, but if I do, you should know that I will no longer meet the national standards."

Maxwell (1991, p. 2) observes that, ". . . pressures from professional organizations that services meet professional standards and adhere to certification guidelines influence all of our programs." It is true that many professional organizations have been assertive in encouraging members to embrace national standards. In part, these efforts were originally motivated by the desire for increased professionalism and credibility for a discipline that deserved to achieve that status. "Professional standards establish the norms for a profession. Members of the profession have an ethical obligation to follow those standards as rigorously as possible or to systematically amend the standards to better assure the profession, the public, and the students that the end result of the educational process reflects the high-quality practice to the betterment of all concerned" (Miller, 1991, p. 60).

Finally, the best reason of all for established professional standards is the shared desire for excellence by professionals in the field of learning assistance. Miller points out ". . . the quality of a student's educational experience is directly related to the quality of the student services and development programs available as resources for students" (Miller, 1984, p. 413). Our ultimate goal is the successful college experience of the students we serve. Professional standards should be embraced to the extent that they help us meet that goal.

Conclusion

Boylan (1981, p.14) concluded in his discussion of the issues, needs, and realities of program evaluation: "Perhaps it is time for those involved with learning assistance programs to accept the reality of their environment and to respond aggressively to the challenge it presents." The interests of learning assistance programs will not be served by refusing to "determine or fix the value of" their services. They will be served by assessing what learning assistance programs do, determining how well it is done, and describing the benefits that result from having done it. If learning assistance is to have any relevance at all, its value must be determined, measured, and reported. That sentiment was written over ten years ago but continues to be true today.

We need the benchmark guide to excellence that national standards can give us as we assess current activities, develop new programs, guide budget discussions, demonstrate our professionalism, and meet our mission of helping students succeed in college. The CAS Standards and Guidelines for Learning Assistance Programs and the NADE Self-Study Guides for Tutor Programs, Adjunct Instructional Programs, Developmental Skills Courses, and the Teaching/Learning Process are valuable tools to help us achieve these goals.

References

Boylan, H. R. (1981). Program evaluation: issues, needs, and realities. In C. C. Walvekar (Ed.). *Assessment of Learning Assistance Services*, San Francisco: Jossey-Bass Inc., Publishers, 3-17.

CAS Standards and Guidelines for Learning Assistance Programs (1988). College Park, MD: Council for the Advancement of Standards, University of Maryland Office of Student Affairs.

Mable, P. (1991). Professional standards: An introduction and historical perspective. In Bryan, W. A., Winston, R. B., Jr., & Miller, T. K. (Eds.), *Using Professional Standards in Student Affairs*, 53, San Francisco: Jossey-Bass Inc., 5-18.

Materniak G., & Williams, A. (1987, September). CAS standards and guidelines for learning assistance programs. *Journal of Developmental Education*, 11(1), 12-18.

Maxwell, M. (1991). *Evaluating Academic Skills Programs: A Sourcebook*. Kensington, MD: M. M. Associates.

Miller, T. K. (1984, September) Professional standards: whither thou goes. *Journal of College Student Personnel*, 413-416.

Miller, T. K. (1991) Using standards in professional preparation. In W. A. Bryan, Winston, R. B., Jr., & Miller, T. K. (Eds.), *Using Professional Standards in Student Affairs*, 53, San Francisco: Jossey-Bass Publishers, 45-62.

Rubin, M. (1991, Spring). A glossary of developmental education terms compiled by the CRLA Task Force on Professional Language for College Reading and Learning. *Journal of College Reading & Learning*, XXIII(2), 1-13.

Copies of the CAS Standards and Guidelines for Learning Assistance Programs and The Learning Assistance Programs Self-Assessment Guide can be ordered from the Council for the Advancement of Standards, Office of Student Affairs, 2108 North Administration Building, University of Maryland, College Park, MD 21742.

Copies of the NADE Self-Assessment Guides for Tutor Programs, Adjunct Skills Programs, Teaching and Learning, and Developmental Studies Courses can be ordered from H&H Publishing Co., 1231 Kapp Drive, Clearwater, FL 34625 (1-800-366-4079).

Susan Clark Thayer is Chairperson of the NADE Committee on Standards and Ethics, CAS Representative from NADE, as well as Associate Professor of Education and Human Services and Director of the Geno A. Ballotti Learning Center at Suffolk University, 41 Temple Street, Boston, Massachusetts 02114-4280.

Martha Maxwell is an educational evaluator and consultant and CAS Representative from CRLA.

This paper lays out some of the many problems and biases that reduce the accuracy of attempts to measure the outcomes of remedial instruction.

Program Evaluation

By Geoffrey Akst and Miriam Hecht

(From Alice Trillin & Associates (1980). *Teaching Basic Skills in College*, San Francisco: Jossey-Bass, 261-296. Reprinted by permission of Geoffrey Akst and Miriam Hecht and Jossey-Bass Publishers.)

The literature on evaluating college remedial programs leaves the reader with two strong impressions: the first is that current evaluation procedures are enormously diverse; the second is that there has been little effort to systematize that diversity. Moreover, in most studies it is not clear whether procedures were chosen on the basis of intrinsic merit, expediency, or ignorance of the alternatives. The last possibility cannot be dismissed, if only because there is no single source which describes and compares the alternative methodologies. General texts on evaluation, even educational evaluation, are useful but unfocused. Published evaluative studies of individual remedial programs are not uncommon, but they usually employ specific approaches rather than exploring the range of possibilities. Moreover, most studies on remedial evaluation deal with a particular discipline, so that a study of methodological weaknesses in the evaluation of reading programs, for example, may escape the attention of the researcher in remedial writing or mathematics.

The discussion which follows presents an overview of the interests, constraints, pitfalls, and opportunities confronting the evaluator of any college remedial program. After considering the role and importance of remedial evaluation, we survey a variety of evaluative designs, and conclude with suggestions for implementing an evaluative study.

The Role of Remedial Evaluation

In an age of shrinking budgets and growing demands for accountability, the evaluation of academic programs hardly requires justification. However, the need for evaluation is particularly acute in college remedial programs. Such programs are apt to be large and expensive; it has been estimated that the City University of New York (CUNY) spent some $35 million a year on remediation in the 1970s. Programs that obtain funds from government or foundation grants may be required to submit evaluations. Often, the programs employ innovative teaching strategies which invite comparison with more traditional instruction. And perhaps most important, the viability of the entire curriculum may be determined by the effectiveness of the remedial program; only if the student body is properly prepared in basic skills can standards be maintained in later courses.

Despite these factors, relatively few remedial programs have been carefully evaluated. In mathematics, a national survey showed that three quarters of the responding colleges had never formally evaluated their remedial programs (Baldwin and others, 1975), and this may well be the case in reading and writing as well. Such studies as have been attempted vary widely in quality; while some appear to be thorough and objective, others are oversimplified or consist of little more than unfounded reassurances.

Why have so many colleges skirted the evaluation of their remedial programs? There are several explanations. For one thing, remedial staffs, often overworked and pressed for resources, may feel that time and effort spent on evaluation could be put to better use. For another, the idea of deliberately withholding remediation from a group of weak students to permit comparison with the remediated population has been widely opposed (Cross, 1976). And to assess any college program by systematic empirical research appears alien to the thinking of many academics; many faculty feel that learning is a slow and subtle process, more readily revealed through sympathetic interaction with students than by the application of yardsticks. Nonetheless, there is little doubt that on some campuses faculty avoid evaluation for a less laudable reason: they themselves have misgivings about the outcome. Roueche (1973, p. 26) reports charges that "community college leaders deliberately did not evaluate remedial programs because they knew beforehand how disastrous the results of such an evaluation might be." And in fact, the results of some remedial evaluative studies have been so negative that programs have been curtailed or in some cases entirely abolished (Cross, 1976; Sharon, 1970).

Before considering this type of comprehensive or "summative" evaluation, let us say a few words about "formative" evaluation, which is typically more modest in its goals (Scriven, 1967). The purpose of formative evaluation is to identify those elements of the instructional program which contribute to its effectiveness and those which need improvement. Formative studies are particularly valuable near the beginning of a program, while it is still taking shape. By contrast, summative evaluation sums up the worth of an ongoing program, not with reference to the separate components but to the value of the program as a whole; it often serves as a basis for deciding whether to continue or drop the program. In practice, the difference between formative and summative evaluation is sometimes blurred, but the activities appropriate to the two types differ sufficiently to justify the distinction.

Some evaluators believe that in terms of practical consequences, formative evaluation far outweighs summative (Gordon, 1970). Thus, Worthen and Sanders (1973, p. 47) observe, "The greatest service evaluation can perform is to identify aspects of the course where revision is possible." Several examples of formative evaluation show the wide range of possibilities. Middleton (1977) examined the relation between section size and success in remedial English and math classes; he found that large sections were at least as effective as smaller ones. A study of reading classes by Kingsborough Community College (1973) showed that classes in which tutors worked along with instructors were more successful than those in which instructors worked alone. Lachica and Brookes (1976) found that in an English as a Second Language (ESL) program, students taking ESL for the first time had a higher passing rate than those repeating the course. Akst (1976) examined a self paced remedial mathematics program to determine whether reading ability was a factor in mathematical achievement; he found that the two were unrelated.

Studies like these are quick, simple, and informative. They may be designed to examine any aspect of a remedial program, from texts to methods of instruction, from testing procedures to exit criteria, from which of the students are learning the content to what content is being learned. Such studies may not lend themselves to generalization nor be intended for publication. However, if judiciously planned and executed, they are invaluable in putting the remedial program on the right track.

Summative evaluation — our major concern — is usually more elaborate. Properly done, it calls for careful planning and implementation, possibly over a period of years, and may best be carried out by an external evaluator. Summative evaluation may cover a number of areas, such as:

1. Appropriateness of objectives: One may take the position that program objectives are not open to question, since they are presumably the premises on which the rest of the program is based. Occasionally, however, an evaluator may take exception to objectives that appear to be misguided or unrealistic (for example, the objective in a writing program of having foreign students attain the same proficiency level as native speakers).

2. Appropriateness of content to program objectives: At the inception of a remedial program, faculty determine the appropriate content and proficiency level, using their experience to guide them. Thus, reading faculty decide that students entering social science courses should be able to read texts at a certain indicated level of comprehension; mathematics instructors teach compound interest in the belief that it will help students in later life. In some cases — by no means all — such curricular decisions can subsequently be evaluated on empirical grounds. For example, if we can identify two groups of students, differing only in

the extent to which they have mastered reading skills, we can compare their performance in subsequent social science courses. However, it may he virtually impossible to follow the math students beyond graduation to determine whether an understanding of compound interest has in fact been useful.

3. Appropriateness of placement procedure: Whatever the basis of the placement procedure — high school record, interviews, a battery of tests, or self-selection — the procedure itself should be subject to careful scrutiny (Zwick, 1965). Issues meriting investigation include content and cut-off score of a test, and reliability of interview ratings, essay scores, and high school grades. Both judgment and empirical research play a role in addressing these concerns.

4. Effectiveness of instruction: The question here is whether students are in fact learning the remedial content and if so, whether their learning is the result of remedial instruction or extraneous factors.

5. Efficiency of instruction: Can the same learning be provided at a smaller investment of time or money? Alternatively, can more learning be obtained for the same investment? (Carman, 1971; Cosby, 1975).

Few evaluative studies consider all the above areas of inquiry. Colleges may not seek out an evaluator's views on the appropriateness of objectives — a question which is, in any event, a matter of judgment rather than empirical research. The investigation of content or placement is often precluded by the difficulty of longterm follow-up studies. And questions of efficiency or cost effectiveness may well be considered the province of a financial specialist rather than the academic evaluation. In practice, therefore, most remedial evaluations have focused on the effectiveness of instruction: whether students are learning the remedial content, and whether their performance in subsequent coursework is improved as a result. Even within these bounds, however, the summative evaluation of remedial programs is far more complex than one might expect.

Collecting Data

No matter how great the expertise of the program evaluator, an objective evaluation must be based, in part at least, on empirical data. Particularly important are the preprogram and postprogram measures — indexes of what remedial students know before and after participation in the program. The preprogram measure is used in several ways: as a base line for later comparisons, a device for sorting out groups to be compared, and a gauge of whether groups were equivalent before the start of remedial instruction. Often, it serves more than one of these functions in the same study.

In most remedial evaluations, a test score is used as the preprogram measure. One reason for this choice is obvious. Often, an appropriate test is already being administered for purposes of remedial placement; by using the same score as a preprogram measure, the test is made to do double duty. But a single test score provides a convenient preprogram measure even when placement is based on other factors (for example, the student's high school record).

Alternatively, the student's college grade-point average (GPA) may serve as the preprogram measure, but this is feasible only if placement occurs after the first semester (Entwistle, 1960).

When we turn to postprogram measures used to gauge knowledge after remedial instruction, we find a far greater variety of indicators. These may be classified as short- or long-range. Short-range measures describe the students' behavior while they are still in the course; examples are grades on final examinations and average quiz grades. Long-range measures are concerned with students' performance after they leave the remedial program; they include grade in the next course, GPA after a specified number of semester, verbal GPA (for reading, writing, and ESL remediation), quantitative GPA (for mathematics remediation), credits earned, and persistence in college. Tests administered after the student leaves the remedial program, or measures involving follow-up studies after college, are seldom practical and are not considered here.

The choice of postprogram measure is a matter of lively debate. Proponents of long-range measures argue that if the goal of the remedial program is to prepare students for college-level coursework, then the program has met this goal only to the extent that students subsequently perform better than they would have otherwise. Robinson (1950, p. 83) has characterized short-range measures as "specious, ill-considered or clearly superficial." The opposing camp, defending short-range measures, points out that the remedial instructor can do no more than improve students' skills while they are in the program; whether students retain these skills over succeeding semesters is not the instructor's responsibility. Moreover, in nonremedial courses it is common practice to measure learning no later than the end of the semester; holding remedial staff to more stringent standards would therefore be unfair. The choice of measure is particularly important because results based on short-range measures are usually positive whereas those based on long-range measures are more likely to be equivocal (Piesco, 1978; Santeusanio, 1974).

Of course, the same evaluative study can use several postprogram measures, some short-range and some long-range. Indeed, some studies have used as many as a half dozen. Roueche and Snow (1977, p. 107) conclude that ". . . the most successful developmental education programs are generally those that use a number of indices on which to evaluate their efforts."

After choosing the preprogram and postprogram measures, the evaluator must extract from data collected about individual students a single quantity – a number — that provides information about the entire group. This number, which we refer to as the **grouping statistic**, can be obtained in either of two ways. In the first, the evaluator is concerned only with the proportion of students who succeed — where success in defined, as, say, passing the course (however poorly) or scoring above a certain cutoff on a posttest. For each student the question is only, "Did he succeed?"; no attempt is made to quantify the result by asking, "How well did he succeed?" In the second, the evaluator is concerned with averages (average test score or average GPA), which actually measure the extent of the student's knowledge instead of merely separating the wheat from the chaff. The choice of grouping statistic — proportion or average — can have a significant effect on the outcome of an evaluation (Akst, 1976) and warrants careful consideration.

Although preprogram and postprogram measures comprise the most essential data in remedial evaluation, other types of information may also be needed. In particular, it is important to document in detail the actual implementation of the program; this information can be obtained from faculty and student interviews, syllabi, texts, departmental memoranda, and, of course, from direct observation. Other data of possible interest include peripheral effects of the program, costs, and attitudes of students, faculty, or other concerned groups.

Finally, the evaluator must decide which students should participate. In sufficiently small remedial programs the entire remedial population can serve. However, when a population is large, this is not only unwieldy but unnecessary; in such cases a randomly selected subset, representative of the larger groups may serve quite as well. Another strategy for controlling the volume of data is the statistical technique known as **multiple matrix sampling**. This newly developed procedure permits the evaluator to administer only a few test items to each participant in the study and then, by extrapolation, estimate how the entire population would perform on the complete test. For details of this technique, the interested reader should consult Wolf (1979) or Shoemaker (1973).

Measuring Learning

Clearly a critical component of program evaluation is measuring how well the content has been learned. Novices usually see this as a fairly straightforward matter. "There's nothing to it," they will say. "Just give all the students a test at the beginning, another at the end, and see how much they've improved." This procedure is in fact the first of the eight evaluative designs which we will consider.

The Single-Group Pretest-Posttest Comparison
Of all the designs to be discussed here, the single-group pretest-posttest design is undoubtedly the simplest. It is concerned only with the remedial population — hence the term single-group — and uses as preprogram and postprogram measures two equivalent forms of the same test. Often this test is the one originally used for remedial placement, so that by definition everyone in the study will ini-

tially have fallen below the cutoff. If the grouping statistic is an average, then the pretest and posttest scores are averaged separately, and the difference between the two results is taken to be the measure of learning. If, on the other hand, the grouping statistic is a proportion, then the effectiveness of the program is gauged by the proportion of students who score above the cutoff on the posttest.

The single-group pretest-posttest comparison can be represented by the diagram shown below:

(Remedial)

M1 – – – – Remediation – – – – M2

Here M1 stands for the preprogram measure (pretest) and M2 for the postprogram measure (posttest). The broken time line and the word *Remediation* signify that remedial instruction has taken place between administration of the two tests, and the word *Remedial* in parentheses indicates that all the students in the evaluative study belong to the population originally placed into remediation.

The single-group pretest-posttest comparison is probably the design most commonly used in the evaluation of remedial programs. The main reason for this popularity is that the design is so easy to implement. In contrast to other evaluative designs, it avoids such difficulties as withholding remediation from students who need it, rounding up exempted students for posttesting, and waiting a semester or more to investigate GPA or grade in the next course.

Unfortunately, while it is the design most convenient to implement, it is also the one of least value. Even if postprogram scores are significantly higher than preprogram scores — and as we will see, they usually are — the evaluator cannot automatically attribute the gain to the effectiveness of the reme-

dial program. This problem is so serious that Wolf (1979, p. 143) notes, "Specialists in research design generally dismiss the single-group pretest-posttest as useless. The evaluation worker may not because the alternative — no study at all — is unacceptable."

Here the novice is apt to become defensive. Eager for quick, positive results, he challenges such objections with questions like, "Why shouldn't test gains be attributed to the effectiveness of the program? How else can they possibly be explained?"

One reason that the gains cannot be attributed solely to the remedial course is that the favorable results may have been obtained by chance. Fortunately, there are reliable, statistical techniques (t-test, chi-square test, and others) for indicating when a result is merely accidental and when it is statistically significant. These techniques are discussed in any standard text on inferential statistics and the evaluator should certainly be familiar with them.

Far more serious is the fact that the single-group pretest-posttest comparison is particularly vulnerable to a host of extraneous factors, known as biases, which distort results and cloud interpretations. In fact, Wolf (1979, p. 143), having already warned against the design, later makes the point, "If used — no matter how reluctantly — the only course open to the evaluation worker is to systematically eliminate each competing alternative explanation so that the presumptive conclusion of a treatment effect is tenable." It is to these "competing alternative explanations," or biases, that we now turn.

Evaluative Biases

The following biases described are of two types. Some relate to (the fact that) learning does in fact take place but is not attributable to the remedial program. Others relate to spurious gains resulting not from any learning at all but from peculiarities of tests and testing procedures.

Test Administration Bias

If, in an educational study, the administration of the pretest differs in a significant way from that of the posttest, gains may result merely from this difference and not from any actual learning. Test administration bias is of particular concern in remedial evaluation; often the pretest is part of a large battery of tests, given in a poorly-lit auditorium over a period of hours, while posttests are given separately in the relative comfort of the remedial classroom. Here the pretest scores may be artificially lowered by the students' discomfort or fatigue. To compound the difficulty, posttests are often administered by the remedial teachers themselves; for reasons altruistic and otherwise, these teachers may answer leading questions, allow extra time, and otherwise contribute to exaggerated gains.

Student Attitude Bias

Scores on tests may be affected by the student's attitude. Students frequently underestimate the importance of the pretests and do less than their best work, thereby contributing to an illusory gain later on. However, students who are overly anxious on the posttest (which may also serve as the final examination) sometimes perform poorly, so that program effectiveness is underestimated.

Teaching to the Test

Often the remedial instructor is familiar with the content of the posttest. As a result, he may perhaps unconsciously stress topics he knows are included, at the expense of other equally important material. Thus, an instructor may emphasize one type of algebra problem over another because he knows the former appears on the test. The outcome, of course, is an artificial increase in scores.

The Practice Effect

The mere experience of taking the pretest may prepare students to do better later on. They will be informed about the format of the test, the use of the answer sheet, the allocation of their time, and so on. If the same form is used twice, they may simply remember answers. In any event, the outcome is again an artificially high posttest score.

Instrument Bias

If the pretest and posttest are to reflect relevant learning, they must be both valid (that is, the content and minimum proficiency level must be appropriate) and reliable (the results must be consistent). Otherwise, any indicated changes, whether gains or losses, may be either irrelevant or simply a matter of chance.

The Hawthorne Effect

It has often been noted that students' performance is apt to improve merely because they realize that they are receiving special attention. This phenomenon, known as the Hawthorne Effect (after a classic study conducted in Hawthorne, Illinois) results in gains which, while genuine for the experimental population, may not be sustained for subsequent groups.

Dropout (Mortality Bias)

It is all but inevitable that more students will start an educational program than finish it. This is particularly serious in evaluating remedial courses, not only because dropout rates are commonly high but because it is apt to be the weaker students who drop out; in effect, the bottom of the class is sifted out rather than taught. Posttest scores for these dropouts are seldom included in the statistical analysis; hence a comparison of pretest and posttest scores may suggest an exaggerated gain.

Regression Toward the Mean

Regression toward the mean is a surprising but well-documented statistical phenomenon: if a group of students is given a test and then retested, those who initially scored at the extremes (whether very high or very low) will, when retested, tend to move toward the middle of the distribution. This shift will probably take place regardless of any learning or forgetting, and, in fact, tends to occur even if the second test is given immediately after the first.

Many people find the regression phenomenon difficult to accept; perhaps the following analogy will help. Suppose that each member of a group rolls a die twice. Those who initially rolled a one, the lowest possible score, will very likely go up toward the group mean on their second roll, while those who initially rolled a six will go probably down. Similarly, all chance events (and every test score incorporates an element of chance) exhibit regression toward the mean, so that extreme scores tend to be moderated on a second try.

This bias is particularly relevant to the evaluation of remedial programs, since frequently remedial students are those who have scored low on a pretest (placement test). Their scores tend to rise on retesting because of regression, whether learning has taken place or not. It should be noted, however, that when the remedial population includes the vast majority of entering freshmen — and instances have been reported as high as 98 percent (Anderson and Grady, 1977) — the effect of regression is minimal.

External Learning Bias

Students often improve their basic skills for reasons having little or nothing to do with remedial instruction. Thus, their arithmetic may improve through self-study; their reading may become more proficient as a result of assignments in nonremedial courses. The sheer excitement of being in college provides some students with the impetus to sharpen their skills. For example, Robinson (1950) found that college students improved their reading skills even when given no remedial instruction at all.

History Bias

This bias concerns the possible impact of accidental, often unpredictable, external events on the program under evaluation. Thus, a one-year grant may result in small classes and exceptional performance; a crippling snowstorm or strike may have the effect of reducing achievement. The longer the duration of the evaluative study, the greater the risk of such atypical events.

Maturation Bias

A posttest-over-pretest gain may simply reflect the student's normal maturation or mental growth. However, among students of college age this is probably a minor factor.

Controlling Biases

When the remedial evaluator uses a pretest-posttest comparison, this formidable array of biases may seriously distort results. The problem is compounded by the fact that of the eleven biases described, eight tend to operate toward making the remedial program appear more effective than it actually is. The remaining three — attitude, instrument, and history — may either exaggerate or underestimate the apparent effectiveness of the program, depending on circumstances (see Table 1). This may explain why Piesco (1978, p. 20), in her review of research on CUNY remedial programs, found that, "One-group pretest-posttest designs demonstrated without exception, that students who completed remedial courses showed some improvement in basic skills." By the same token, Cross (1976, p. 33), reviewing remedial evaluations of the 1940s and 1950s, notes, "It is significant that generally speaking, the better designed studies showed less glowingly positive results than the simpler but less adequate research studies." In short, the cumulative effect of these biases may be to represent as very successful a program which is in fact of questionable value.

Table 1
Single-Group Pretest-Posttest Comparison: Probable Direction of Biases

Bias	Probable Direction of Bias
Test administration bias	up
Student attitude bias	?
Teaching to the test	up
Practice effect	up
Instrument bias	?
Hawthorne effect	up
Dropout bias	up
Regression toward the mean	up
External learning bias	up
History bias	?
Maturation bias	up

If an evaluative study is to produce justifiable conclusions, the effect of the above biases must be minimized. In some cases, the very recognition of the bias suggests appropriate remedies; in others, remedies may be relatively technical or obscure. Examples of steps that may reduce the influence of each bias, if not eliminate it altogether, include the following:

Test administration bias: Avoid having classroom instructors administer posttests.

Student attitude bias: Persuade students of the importance of doing well on the placement examination.

Teaching to the test: Use a "secure" posttest, unfamiliar to the instructional staff.

Practice effect: Use alternate rather than identical forms for pretest and posttest.

Instrument bias: Use tests of established validity.

Hawthorne effect: Conceal from the remedial population (if not from the instructions themselves) the fact that the program is being formally evaluated.

Dropout bias: Average pretest scores for only those students who also take the posttest; analyze separately the pretest scores of students who do not complete the course.

Regression toward the mean: Use instruments of established reliability. A more complex technique is to use a separate pretest for the purpose of program evaluation, distinct from the placement examination originally given (Sparks and Davis, 1977). Although students placed into remediation perforce score near the low end of the **placement test** distribution, this may not be true of the separate pretest. Thus, regression is not operative.

Three biases are absent from the previous list: external learning, history, and maturation. These three may be described as **biases of false attribution**; that is, they are associated with learning gains which, while real, are not attributable to remedial instruction. To compensate for these and other biases, a number of remedial studies have abandoned the basic single-group pretest-posttest design in favor of alternatives using a control group.

The Control Group

A control group, in this context, is a population of students who, while initially comparable to those entering the remedial program, are nevertheless excluded from the program. The term may refer either to a group of students receiving no remedial instruction or to one receiving an alternate form of remedial instruction.

In the single-group design just described, the success of the remedial **population** does not necessarily imply the success of the remedial **program**. As we have seen, improvement may be entirely illusory; even if real, it may be due to one or more of the three false-attribution biases mentioned above. When the remedial group is compared to a control group, however, we can assume that the biases affect both groups equally and can therefore be disregarded. Having thus neutralized the effect of the biases, we are free to attribute any difference between post-program measures for the two groups to the effectiveness of the program itself. Thus, the use of a control group is a strategy for "turning back the clock" and determining how remediated students would have fared had they received alternate remedial assistance or none at all.

We will begin our discussion of control-group designs with two in which the controls receive no remediation at all: the remediated-unremediated comparison and the marginally-remedial, and the marginally-exempted comparison.

The Remediated-Unremediated Comparison

The remediated-unremediated comparison requires the division of the remedial population into two comparable groups, one of which receives remedial instruction while the other does not. Assignment to the two groups should be random in order to increase the likelihood that the groups are initially equivalent. As indicated here, the unremediated group (Remedial 2) serves as a control group for the remediated group (Remedial I).

(Remedial 1)   M1 ----- Remediation ----- M2

(Remedial 2)   M1 ---- No Remediation ---- M2

The average preprogram measures (M1) for the two groups are compared to check initial equivalence. The extent to which the postprogram measures (M2) differ is the gauge of program effectiveness.

The major disadvantage of the remediated-unremediated comparison is that the deliberate withholding of remediation is ethically questionable. Arguments on this score often become very heated, replete with allusions to open doors becoming revolving doors, essential medications being withheld from the sick and dying, and sheep being led to slaughter. However, none of these metaphors addresses the very cogent argument that until the effectiveness of the remedial program is clearly demonstrated, any ethical questions are somewhat premature; the program may in fact be an outright waste of time. Thus, Piesco (1978, p. 4) writes, "Although no evidence exists regarding effectiveness . . . colleges offering remedial programs have been generally reluctant to randomly exempt from remedial work a proportion of those students identified as being in need of remediation. This reluctance has prevented the conduct of the experimental research which might enable educators to determine which remedial techniques are effective, for whom, and under what conditions."

While a number of evaluative studies have employed unremediated control groups (for example, Losak, 1968; Sharon, 1970), they are certainly in the minority. Frequently, various strategies are introduced to circumvent the ethical issues. One such strategy, used when remedial placement is voluntary, is to consider as a control group those students who test into remediation but elect not to participate. Another practice, employed when placement is purportedly mandatory, is to identify and use as controls those students who nonetheless manage to evade it (Berger, 1972). A third approach is to use as a control group students who, having been among the last to register, are closed out of the requisite remedial classes. Unfortunately, in each of these cases, the two groups are apt to differ with respect to such traits as motivation, self-image, attitude toward mathematics, and so on, thus biasing the results. Perhaps preferable is the strategy of randomly choosing a control group and then postponing, rather than eliminating, their remedial obligation. This approach may moderate, if not completely resolve, the ethical issues.

The Marginally-Remedial, Marginally-Exempted Comparison

The marginally-remedial, marginally-exempted design involves a comparison between a remediated population and an exempted control group. However, the participants in the study are chosen in a special way. The marginally remedial students are those who narrowly fail the pretest and therefore receive remediation; the marginally exempted students are those who narrowly pass. The premise is that since the two groups are separated by only a few points, they start off so similar as to be considered equivalent. As before, the difference in postprogram measures serves as an indication of program effectiveness.

Cutoff Pretest Scores

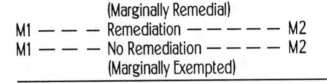

Figure I. Comparing Marginal Students

(Marginally Remedial)
M1 — — — Remediation — — — — — M2
M1 — — — No Remediation — — — — M2
(Marginally Exempted)

While this design avoids the moral dilemma posed by the remediated-unremediated comparison, it poses its own problems. One is that it measures the program's effectiveness only for the best of the remedial students; but the performance of these students is not necessarily representative of the entire remedial population. Another problem is that since the two groups are only approximately comparable at the outset, the postprogram measures may be difficult to interpret. If the remedial group surpasses the exempted one, there is some evidence of the remedial program's success. However, if the exempted group surpasses the remedial one, we are hard-pressed to decide whether the program has some value (although perhaps not enough), or whether it is altogether useless. This design might thus be called **inequitable**; results can be interpreted if they go in one direction, but not if they go in the other. The problem of inequitable designs will be considered again later in the discussion.

Biases in Cross-Group Designs

Apart from the eleven biases presented earlier, the two control-group designs just considered introduce biases of their own. These new cross-group biases are **differential biases and initial differences**.

Differential Biases

In introducing a control group, we proceeded on the assumption that even if the original biases continued to operate, they would operate equally on the two groups and could therefore be discounted. If this is not the case — that is, if the biases affect the two groups to different degrees — our assumption is unwarranted, and the results are again distorted. For example, in a remediated-unremediated comparison, the dropout bias may favor one group over the other; in a marginally-remedial, marginally-exempted study, regression toward the mean will usually favor the remedial group. In such cases, postprogram measures may be difficult to interpret. A good strategy for controlling any differential bias is to follow the earlier recommendation for the corresponding single-group bias.

Initial Differences

In comparing groups on postprogram measures, we would like to associate the superior performance of one group with a superior instructional experience. Such a conclusion is invalid if the higher-scoring group was superior even prior to instruction. This problem arose in considering the marginally-remedial, marginally-exempted comparison. It also arises in connection with the remediated-unremediated comparison if, one way or another, students place themselves into the two groups instead of being randomly assigned. Reed (1956) and Santeusanio (1974) have found that overlooking the initial difference bias produced by such self-selection has weakened a large number of studies.

While the best way to control the initial difference bias is by random assignment, this is not always feasible. In such cases, other approaches must be found. A number of early studies tried to equate remedial and control groups by matching students across groups on variables believed to be educationally significant; for example, age, sex, IQ and the like (Entwistle, 1960; Gordon, 1970). This procedure had the obvious disadvantage of restricting the evaluative study to students who might in no way have been representative of the populations from which they were drawn, and has been generally abandoned. Recent remedial evaluations have employed complex statistical techniques, notably analysis of covariance.

Editor's note: The chapter goes on to discuss how more complex designs can be applied to evaluating remedial programs.

References

Akst, G. R. (1976). A study of the effect on learning of pacing and testing procedures in a two-year college remedial mathematics course. Unpublished doctoral dissertation, Teachers College. *Dissertation Abstracts International*, 37, 2035A.

Anderson, H., & Grady, M. (1977). *A Study of 1775 Students Who Entered El Paso Community College in the Fall of 1973*. Educational Resources Information Center, ED 137 323. Colorado Springs, CO: El Paso Community College.

Baldwin, J., & others. (1975). *Survey of Developmental Mathematics Courses at Colleges in the United States*. Educational Resources Information Center, ED 125 688. Garden City, NY.

Berger, D. (1972). *Effectiveness of College Skills and Basic Writing Courses in Preparing Students for Regular College Classes*. New York: Office of Research and Testing.

Brookes, G., & Withrow, J. (1974). *10 Steps: Controlled Composition for Beginning and Intermediate ESL Students*. New York: Language Innovations.

Carmen, R. A. (1971). *A Cost-Effectiveness Analysis of Various methods of Instruction in Developmental Mathematics*. Educational Resources Information Center, ED 057 793. Santa Barbara, CA: Santa Barbara City College.

Cosby, J. P. (1975). *Remedial Education: Is It Worth It?* Educational Resources Information Center, ED 099 067. Fort Lauderdale, FL: Nova University.

Cross, K. P. (1976). *Accent on Learning: Improving Instruction and Reshaping the Curriculum*. San Francisco: Jossey-Bass.

Entwistle, D. (1960). Evaluations of study skills courses: A review. *Journal of Educational Research*, 53,117-125.

Gordon, E. W. (1977). Compensatory education evaluation in perspective. *IRCD Bulletin*. New York: Columbia University Press.

Losak, J. G. (1968). *An Evaluation of Selected Aspects of a Junior College Remedial Reading-Writing Program*. Educational Resources Information Center ED 027 021. Miami: Miami Dade Junior College.

Middleton, J. R. (1977). Successful outcomes and class size in remedial programs: Intensive writing and reading skills, Spring 1974 to Fall 1975. Unpublished report of Instructional Testing and Research, Borough of Manhatten Community College.

Piesco, J., Shrier, I., & Podell, L. (1978). Review of the evaluative literature in open admissions at CUNY. Unpublished report, office of Program and Policy Research, City University of New York.

Reed, J. C. (1956). Some effects of short-term training in reading under conditions of controlled motivation. *Journal of Educational Psychology*, 26, 257-261.

Robinson, H. A. (1950). A note on the evaluation of college remedial reading courses. *Journal of Educational Psychology*, 41, 83-96.

Roueche, J. E. (1973). Accommodating individual differences. *Community College Review*, 1, 24-29.

Roueche, J. E. & Snow, J. J. *Overcoming Learning Problems: A Guide to Developmental Education in College*. San Francisco: Jossey-Bass.

Santeusanio, R. P. (1974). Do college reading programs serve their purpose? *Reading World*, 14(4), 259-271.

Scriven, M. (1967). The methodology of evaluation. In R. E. Stahe (Ed.) *Curriculum Evaluation*. AERA Monograph Series on Evaluation, No. 1. Chicago: Rand McNally.

Sharon, A. T. (1970). *Effectiveness of Remediation in Junior College*. College Entrance Examination Board Research and Development Report RDR-70-71, No. 2. Princeton, NJ: Educational Testing Service.

Shoemaker, D. M. (1973). *Principles and Procedures of Multiple Matrix Sampling*. Cambridge, MA: Ballinger.

Sparks, J., & Davis, O. (1977, April). A systems analysis and evaluation of a junior college developmental studies program. Paper presented at the annual meeting of the American Educational Research Association, New York.

Wolf, R. M. (1979). *Evaluation in Education*. New York: Praeger.

Worthen, B., & Sanders, J. *Educational Evaluation: Theory and Practice*. Worthington, Ohio: C. A. Jones.

Zwick, E. J. (1965). An evaluation of the effectiveness of the remedial mathematics program at the Ohio State University. Unpublished doctoral dissertation, Ohio State University. *Dissertation Abstracts*, 25, 6323.

Geoffrey Akst is Professor of Mathematics, Manhatten Community College, New York City, NY, and Miriam Hecht is Assistant Professor of Mathematics Emrita at Hunter College, New York City, NY 10021.

What can an open admission college do to insure that it has a developmental education program of the highest quality? In a case study of Miami-Dade Community College, Roueche and Baker discovered institutional leadership, policies, and procedures that support the excellence of Miami-Dade's developmental skills program.

A Case Study on an Exemplary Developmental Studies Program

By John E. Roueche and George A. Baker

(Condensed from John E. Roueche and George A. Baker, (1987). *Access and Excellence: The Open Door College*. San Francisco: Jossey-Bass (ERIC Document Reproduction Service No. ED 274 391), and John E. Roueche and George A. Baker (1986), *Access with excellence*. In G. H. Vogel (Ed.), New Directions for Community College Students, San Francisco: Jossey-Bass. Summary approved by J. E. Roueche.)

The case study of Miami-Dade Community College by Roueche and Baker (1986, 1987) is an example of a large-scale qualitative review of a developmental program in its institutional context. Miami-Dade Community College has long been regarded as the top two-year college in the nation and has the largest foreign-born student population of any U.S. community college as well as the greatest student diversity. Although its entering freshmen make the lowest basic skills scores of those in any public college on the Florida state mandated placement tests, the college's results are impressive. Florida requires students completing their AA Degree or advancing to junior standing in a four-year institution to pass all four sub-tests of the College Level Academic Skills Tests (CLAST – sometimes referred to as the rising junior test). Miami-Dade students who take the advanced basic-skills test score in the upper 10-percent of those taking the test in the state of Florida. For example in the spring of 1985, 85% of the Miami-Dade students passed all four of the subtests. This was a better passing rate than sophomores from the local university earned.

In the case study, the authors examined college leadership, organizational climate and teaching excellence, as well as policies and faculty expectations for students, curriculum changes, and student services.

To understand the organizational climate of the campus, the investigators surveyed a sample of faculty, administrators, and classes. They reported that administrative leadership was characterized as having confidence in staff, being approachable, actively seeking ideas, encouraging faculty to develop their ideas and supporting their efforts and having a clear sense of administrative direction. Open ended questions were used to determine teaching excellence, and the researchers found strong and powerful relationships among organizational climate, administrative leadership, and teaching excellence.

The administration focused on eight areas of reform including a basic required curriculum of courses in five areas — communication, humanities, social environment, industrial growth and development, and physical education.

In addition, a special honors program was offered for accelerated students, and a computerized advisement and graduation information system was developed. Also every faculty member was required to qualify to teach, even part-time faculty.

How did the college create a cultural milieu to nurture effective teaching and learning?

Certainly a major part of this was the president's administrative style and acumen and his dedication to providing a quality education for a predominantly minority student body. The president motivated faculty members by giving latitude to individual autonomous instructors and involving them directly in instructional decisions and in many other ways.

That teachers and advisors provide intensive monitoring of students' work was another factor underlying the program's success. An academic alarm system notified students and advisors by letter, informing them of their status and impending problems. Also Miami-Dade Community College developed its own mid-level CLAST Test to give students practice and to identify areas where they need to improve. Special services for the second-language students were also provided.

Other factors that seem to make a difference are the tightly controlled testing-counseling-placement program, a responsive and dedicated faculty, and a policy of limiting the number of courses students who work may take. Students who work full-time are limited to one three-credit course. Other reasonable policies are rigidly enforced such as prohibiting students from starting classes after the first day of class.

The administration and faculty attempt to raise expectations for students by letting them know that they are expected to attend class regularly and work hard enough to meet the requirements of each course. Realizing that giving students financial aid is not enough, administrators and faculty agreed that students be given more direction, fewer choices of curriculum, more information about college requirements, and closer follow-up by advisers and counselors. Acknowledging that underprepared students will take longer to graduate, the college established a clear point where students must show evidence of academic progress or leave the college.

As mentioned earlier, Miami-Dade Community College has the highest percentage of minority students of any college in Florida and 58% of the Hispanic students in Florida who took the CLAST were from Miami-Dade. In the Spring of 1985, 85% of Miami Dade students passed all sub tests on the CLAST — a better rate than that of local university students and 63% passed three of four subtests.

The improvement in student retention rates is also impressive. Comparative follow-up studies showed that in 1977, 46% had graduated or were still in school, 53% in 1981, compared with 74.5% in 1983-84.

Students do take longer to complete the program, but when they finish, they are able to demonstrate their competence. One of the best pieces of evidence for the value of mandatory assessment is that students who took Miami-Dade's developmental courses had a nine times better chance of graduating than those who needed but did not take the courses.

John E. Roueche is Sid W. Richardson Regents Professor in the Education Department at the University of Texas, Austin, TX 78712.

The Impact of Developmental Education Programs

by Hunter R. Boylan and Barbara S. Bonham

(Reprinted from the *Review of Research in Developmental Education Programs*, Volume 9, Issue 5, 1992. Reprinted by permission of Hunter R. Boylan and Barbara S. Bonham and the *Review of Research in Developmental Education*, Appalachian State University, Boone, NC 28608.)

Although programs designed to assist underprepared college students have been a fixture in American higher education since 1849 (Brier, 1985), relatively little empirical research exists to describe the impact of these programs. Most of the information supporting the effectiveness of these programs (currently called "developmental education programs") comes from individual efforts to evaluate the success of program activities.

Boylan (1983) reviewed over 60 of these evaluation reports and determined that developmental programs tended to improve student GPA and short-term persistence. Kulik, Kulik, and Schwalb (1983) conducted a major meta-analysis of reports from more than 300 programs and also found that participation in developmental programs was associated with improved GPA and increased short-term persistence.

Little information has been accumulated, however, on the effects of developmental programs on cumulative GPA, long term retention, or subsequent student performance in regular college courses. These issues were explored as part of a comprehensive national study of the efficacy of developmental education. The study was supported by the Exxon Education Foundation and conducted by the National Center for Developmental Education.

The study involved 150 institutions representative of all colleges and universities in the United States. These institutions were selected using a circular systematic random sampling process. This process insured that institutional types would be represented in the sample consistent with their representation in American higher education. The types of institutions represented included four-year public, four-year private, research universities, two-year community colleges and two-year technical colleges. Of the 150 institutions selected through this process, 108 have, at this writing, provided sufficient data to participate in the study.

Students enrolled in programs at each of the participating institutions were then randomly selected for inclusion in the study. Of these students (N = 5,166) 62.5% were white, 26.6% were African-American, 6.6% were Hispanic, 2.6% were Asian, and 1.6% were American or Alaskan Indian. Information was not available for a fraction of a percent of participating students. Males represented 46.6% of the sample, and females represented 53.1% with gender data being unavailable for .3% of the students.

As part of a larger project, admissions information, financial aid data, and transcripts were collected for the sample of students participating in these programs. For four-year institutions this information was collected for students entering during Fall of 1984 and continuing through Spring of 1990. For two-year institutions the information was collected for students entering during Fall of 1986 and continuing through Spring of 1990. Students at two-year institutions were, therefore, tracked for 3 1/2 years, and students at four-year institutions were tracked for 5 1/2 years.

Transcripts were analyzed to determine: (a) persistence rates, (b) individual term and cumulative GPA, and (c) the relationship between participation in developmental courses and grades in regular college courses. The results are presented here. It should be noted that these results represent only a small portion of the total study. They represent, in effect, the initial and the least complex aspects of the study. Nevertheless, even these results provide information that has previously been unavailable for a national sample of developmental students.

Persistence and Graduation Rates

The persistence rates for developmental students differed widely depending upon institutional type (see Table 1). Research universities had the highest persistence rates; 48% of their developmental students have either graduated or were still enrolled as of the Fall of 1990. Private, four-year institutions had the next highest rates of retention with 40.2% of their developmental students having graduated or having remained enrolled as of the Fall of 1990.

Table 1
Persistence/Graduation Rates for Developmental Students

Institutional Type	Persistence/Graduation Rates
Two-year Community colleges	24.0%
Two-year Technical colleges	33.7%
Four-year Public Institutions	28.4%
Four-year Private Institutions	40.2%
Research Universities	48.3%

Grade Point Averages

High school grade point average varied widely for developmental students (See Table 2). Not surprisingly, developmental students enrolled in research universities had the highest high school grade point averages (GPA): 2.83. The next highest GPAs for developmental students were those enrolled at four-year public (2.58) and four-year private (2.52) colleges and universities. Among two-year institutions, developmental students enrolled at community colleges had high school GPAs of 2.44 while those enrolled at technical colleges had high school GPAs of 2.27. The difference in high school GPAs between developmental students at community college and those at four-year public and private institutions was not significant.

Table 2
High School and College GPA By Institutional Type for Developmental Students

Institutional Type	High School GPA	First-Term College GPA	Cumulative College GPA
Two-Year Community Colleges	2.44	2.46	2.27
Two-Year Technical Colleges	2.27	2.57	2.33
Four-Year Public Colleges	2.53	2.21	2.03
Four-Year Private Colleges	2.52	2.19	2.18
Research Universities	2.83	2.09	2.10

It is interesting to note that for developmental students enrolled at community colleges there was no significant difference between high school GPAs and first-term GPAs. The mean first-term GPA for community college developmental students was 2.46. At technical colleges the mean first-term GPA for developmental students was 2.57.

Among four-year institutions the highest first-term mean for developmental students was found at four-year public institutions: 2.21. At four-year private institutions the mean first-term GPA was 2.19. At research universities it was 2.09.

Cumulative GPAs for developmental students declined from first-term GPAs at all institutions. At two-year community colleges, the cumulative GPA for developmental students was 2.27. At two-year technical colleges the cumulative GPA for developmental students was 2.33. The decline from first-term GPA for developmental students was about 1/5th of a letter grade at two-year institutions.

There was no significant difference between the first-term GPA and the cumulative GPA for developmental students enrolled in research universities or four-year private institutions. At four-year private institutions cumulative GPA for developmental students was 2.18. Cumulative GPA for developmental students at research universities was 2.10. At four-year public institutions cumulative GPA for developmental students was 2.03, thus representing a decline of almost 1/5th of a letter grade from first-term GPA.

Grades in Developmental and Regular Courses

One measure of the success of a developmental program is the extent to which it prepares students to succeed in regular college courses (see Table 3). If the developmental courses are effective, students who pass developmental courses should also pass regular curriculum courses in the same or related disciplines.

Table 3

Percentage of Students Passing Developmental Courses Who Also Passed First College-Level Courses in Same Subject

Subject	Percentage Passing Developmental Courses
Developmental Math/ College Math	77.2%
Developmental English/ College English	91.1%
Developmental Reading/ College Social Science	83.0%

An analysis of transcripts revealed that among those students who took and passed developmental mathematics with a grade of C or better, 77.2% also passed the regular college mathematics course with a grade of C or better. For those students who passed developmental English with a grade of C or better, 91.1% passed the regular English course with a grade of C or better.

Among the institutions sampled, there was usually no regular curriculum college course equivalent to developmental reading. Comparison was made, therefore, between developmental reading courses and introductory social science courses. Among those who passed the developmental reading course with a grade of C or better, 83% passed their first social science course with a grade of C or better.

Discussion

One finding of this study which already contradicts conventional wisdom has to do with the racial composition of developmental programs. It has been suggested that, "Many people probably believe that remedial/developmental work began as a response to the Civil Rights movement or the equal opportunity legislation of the 1960's and 1970's" (Abraham, 1991, p.1), "and consequently, students participating in these programs were likely to come from minority backgrounds." However, the data concerning ethnic backgrounds of students have shown that the majority (62.5%) of those students participating in developmental programs were white.

For purposes of this study, "developmental students" were defined as those judged by local institutional criteria to be underprepared for college work. In most cases, local institutional criteria were based on scores from standardized achievement or placement tests. Those students placed in developmental programs, therefore, were considered by their institutions to have the least chance of success as measured by grades and retention.

For the most part, the grades of developmental students lagged somewhat behind the grades of other students throughout their academic careers. At most institutions, the first-term and the cumulative GPAs of developmental students were lower than the average GPAs for that institution. That is not surprising since these students were judged to be underprepared in the first place.

Retention and graduation rates for developmental students however, were higher than might be expected. This is particularly true of community colleges, technical colleges, private 4-year institutions and research universities.

According to Tinto (1987), for instance, "Over an extended period, roughly 27 percent of the entering two-year cohort can be expected to complete their . . . programs in the institution in which they first enrolled" (p.17). The persistence and graduation rate of community and technical college developmental students compare favorably with the national average. The percentage of developmental students graduating or still enrolled after four years was 24% at community colleges and 33.7% at technical colleges.

According to the U. S. Office of Education (1983) about 45% of all students entering 4-year institutions will complete a bachelor's degree. Consequently developmental students should not be expected to graduate at rates comparable to their better prepared colleagues. Nevertheless, at research universities and private four-year institutions, those who participate in developmental programs persist and graduate at rates of 48.3% and 40.2% respectively. This compares favorably with the national rate of 45% for four-year institutions.

Only at four-year public institutions were the persistence and graduation rates of developmental students lower than the national average for all students. At these institutions, only 28.4% of the developmental students had graduated or were still in school at the end of 5 1/2 years.

It is clear from the data that those who participated in a developmental program were about as likely to persist and graduate as those students who were judged to be better prepared for college. Perhaps this should not be surprising. The fact that developmental students were judged to be underprepared also means that they were targeted for special intervention. The purpose of this intervention was to reduce the likelihood that their underpreparedness would keep them from being successful or to reduce the differences between the poorly prepared and better prepared students. The data suggest that developmental programs were successful in this effort.

This is true for all types of institutions except four-year public institutions.

Although participation in developmental programs appears to be associated with retention and graduation for underprepared students, increasing retention is not the primary purpose of developmental education. Among programs participating in this study, the most frequently cited purpose was to prepare their students for success in later college courses.

If this is a major criterion to be used in judging the effectiveness of developmental programs, they are certainly successful. As noted earlier, 77.2% of those passing developmental mathematics passed their first college mathematics course, 83% of those passing developmental reading passed their first social science course, and 91.1% passed their first college-level English course. Apparently, developmental programs do a good job of accomplishing their primary purpose since those placed in developmental courses were originally judged to have little or no chance of passing regular college courses without developmental intervention.

Conclusion

The basic message from this portion of the study is that, on the whole, developmental education programs do seem to work. While they generally do not have a strong impact on cumulative GPA, it should be noted that cumulative GPA for those participating in developmental programs was consistently above 2.00 at all institutions. This, in itself, is significant since 2.00 is generally the minimum GPA required for graduation.

Developmental programs also have a positive impact on retention and success in later courses. Apparently students who participate in developmental education programs are much more likely to pass their initial courses in the regular curriculum and are far more likely to graduate than might be expected given their entry characteristics. The evidence suggest, therefore, that across the nation and across varying types of institutions, developmental education programs are successful in accomplishing the objective of improving student academic performance. Furthermore, participation in these programs also appears to increase the likelihood that underprepared students will persist and graduate.

References

Abraham, A. A. (1991). *They came to College? A remedial/developmental profile of first-time freshmen in SREB states.* (Issues in Higher Education Report No. 25). Atlanta, GA: Southern Regional Education Board.

Boylan, H. (1983). *Is developmental education working: An Analysis of the research* (Research Report 2. National Association of Remedial/Developmental Studies in Postsecondary Education). Chicago: NARDSPE.

Brier, E. (1985). Bridging the academic preparation gap: An historical view. *Journal of Developmental Education*, 8(1), 2-6.

Kulik, J., Kulik C., & Schwalb, B. (1983). College programs for high risk and disadvantaged students: A meta-analysis of findings. *Review of Educational Research*, 53, 397-414.

Tinto, V. (1987). *Leaving college.* Chicago: University of Chicago Press.

U. S. Office of Education (1983). *Digest of educational statistics.* Washington, DC: U. S. Government Printing Office.

Hunter R. Boylan is Director of the National Center for Developmental Education and the Principle Investigator for the Exxon Education Foundation Research Project; Barbara S. Bonham is an Associate Professor of Higher Education and a Research Associate with the National Center for Developmental Education at Appalachian State University, Boone, NC 28608.

The Performance of Minority Students in Developmental Education

By Hunter R. Boylan, Leonard B. Bliss, and Barbara S. Bonham

(From *Research in Developmental Education*, 10(2), 1993. Reprinted by permission of Hunter R. Boylan, Leonard B. Bliss, and Barbara S. Bonham and *Research in Developmental Education*, Appalachian State University, Boone, NC 28608.)

Some advocates of educational opportunity for minorities claim that participation in developmental education has a negative impact on the retention of students of color in higher education. They argue that since standardized achievement tests are often poor measures of minorities' ability, students of color may sometimes be misplaced in remedial/developmental courses. As a result, placement in such courses represents an unnecessary roadblock to the completion of a college degree and contributes to minority attrition.

Miller (1990) further argues that minority retention is more a function of the extent to which institutions are willing or able to take a comprehensive approach to serving the needs of students of color. Placement in existing developmental education courses is simply not sufficient to insure the success of underprepared minority students. One problem with these arguments is that no comprehensive research has actually been done to determine the extent to which minority students in developmental programs are retained. Although a substantial body of research exists on the retention of minority groups in higher education, none of this has yet focused on the retention of minorities who participate in developmental programs.

This paper attempts to explore the extent of minority retention (specifically that of African-American and Latino students in developmental programs). Using data from the National Study of Developmental Education (funded by the Exxon Education Foundation and conducted by the National Center for Developmental Education), it will describe the retention of minority students participating in developmental programs at various types of institutions. This study will not consider whether minority students are accurately placed in remedial/developmental courses. It will, however, address the degree to which they are retained following placement in such courses at various types of institutions. It will also look at the retention of students of color compared to that of white students participating in developmental programs.

Methods

Design
Data for this study were drawn from a systematic circular sample of 150 different colleges and universities. This procedure provided for random selection on the basis of institutional type and the proportion in which these types are represented in American higher education. Institutional types selected for inclusion in the study included community colleges, technical colleges, four-year public colleges and universities, four-year private colleges and universities, and research universities.

From each of the institutions included in this sample, a sample of students participating in developmental programs at these institutions was also selected. Participation was defined as being enrolled in one or more remedial/developmental courses. There were more than 5,000 students selected for this sample. Of these, data on ethnic background were available for 4,625 students.

Procedure

For each of these students, transcripts were obtained and data from them entered into a computer data base. The data were then analyzed by institutional type to determine the extent to which minority students participating in developmental programs were retained. These retention rates were then compared with those of non-minority (i.e., white) students participating in these programs.

For purposes of this study, retention was defined at a two-year institution as students having graduated or remained continually enrolled at the end of 3.5 years. At four-year institutions retention was calculated at the end of 5.5 years.

Results

Among students participating in developmental programs, whites consistently were retained at higher levels than either African-American or Latino students. A major exception to this finding was that African-American students in developmental programs were retained at higher levels than either whites or Latinos at private, four-year institutions. The differences in retention rates among ethnic groups varied substantially according to institutional type (see Table 1).

Community Colleges

The greatest disparity in retention rates was between white students and African-American students participating in community college programs. After 3.5 years, 30.1% of the white students had graduated or were still in school. Only 10% of the Afro-American students had graduated or were still in school at the end of this period. Latino students participating in community colleges were retained at a rate of 22.2%.

The difference between white and African-American developmental students attending community colleges is not only statistically significant, but it suggests that white students are three times more likely to be retained than African-American students. A disparity of this magnitude was not found at any other type of institution.

Table 1
Comparative Retention Rates of Developmental Students

Total students Number Retained Percentage Retained	Whites	African- Americans	Latinos
Community Colleges	970 291 30.1%	248 25 10.0%	99 25 22.2%
Four-year Private	781 320 41.0%	177 93 46.9%	35 12 34.3%
Four-year Public	556 182 32.7%	469 112 23.8%	117 34 29.1%
Two-year Technical	315 111 35.3%	189 51 26.9%	17 4 23.5%
Research Universities	245 135 55.1%	163 71 43.6%	45 14 31.1%
Total Students at all Institutional Types	2867	1248	513

Four-year Private Colleges and Universities

As noted earlier, African-American students had the highest retention of any group of students participating in developmental programs at four-year private colleges and universities. Among African-American students at four-year private institutions, 46.9% had graduated or were still enrolled after 5.5 years. Among white students, this figure was 41%. A total of 34.2% of the Latino students enrolled in developmental programs at this type of institution had graduated or were still in school after 5.5 years.

Four-year private colleges and universities and research universities had the highest rates of developmental student retention of any type of institution in this study. A review of SAT scores, however, indicated that there were no significant differences between developmental students enrolled at community colleges and four-year private institutions.

Four-year Public Colleges and Universities

There were no statistically significant differences between the retention rates of white students and Latino students at four-year public colleges and universities. White students participating in developmental programs at these institutions had retention rates of 32.7%. These were followed closely by Latino students who were retained at the rate of 29.1%. African-American students had slightly lower retention rates. After 5.5 years, 23.8% had either graduated or were still enrolled.

It is also worth noting that the number of African-American students participating in developmental programs was highest at the four-year public universities. Apparently a larger number of underprepared African-American students from this sample attended four-year public institutions than any other institutional type.

Two-year Technical Colleges

White students participating in developmental programs had higher rates of retention at two-year technical colleges than either African-American or Latino students. The retention rate for white students was 35.3% after 3.5 years. For African-American students, the retention rate was 26.9% after 3.5 years. The retention rate for Latino students attending technical colleges was 23.5%.

There were no significant differences between the retention rates for African-American and Latino students enrolled in developmental programs at two-year technical colleges. It should be noted, however, that the sample size for Latino students attending two-year colleges was small.

Research Universities

White students participating in developmental programs at research universities had the highest rates of retention of any group at any type of institution. After 5.5 years, 55.1% of them had either graduated or were still in school. For Latino students, the rate of retention was 31.1%.

Among all students participating in developmental programs, the SAT scores and high school grades were, as might be expected, highest at research universities. This was true for students of color as well as for white students.

Discussion

The data presented here suggest that, in general, minority students participating in developmental programs are retained at lower rates than white students. The differences in retention rates, however, are not consistent in all cases. Whites are retained more often than African-American students at two-year colleges but African-Americans are retained more often than whites in private four-year colleges. Latino students are retained more often than African-Americans at community colleges but less often at research universities. African-Americans attending research universities are retained in greater numbers than whites at four-year public universities.

It is true that, with the exception of four-year private colleges, white students participating in developmental education are generally retained at higher rates than nonwhite students. This, however, is true throughout higher education. According to Tinto (1986), the retention of minorities in higher education generally lags behind that of nonminorities.

Data from the National Longitudinal Survey of High School Class of 1972 (Eckland & Henderson, 1981), for instance, indicate that of all African-American students entering college only 27.5% graduate on time (i.e., after four years) as compared to a 37.8% graduation rate for whites. For Latinos, the on-time graduation rate is only 13.4%. Nationally there is about a 10% difference in the overall retention rates of white and African-American developmental college students. This is based on all students, not just those participating in developmental education programs.

With the exception of those participating in developmental programs in community colleges, the difference in retention rates for white and African-American developmental students is similar to the national population: about 10%. In other words, there are differences in the retention rates of white students and minority students, but these differences are not necessarily due to their participation in developmental programs. Such differences apparently appear in the nondevelopmental population as well. There may be a variety of factors endemic to higher education that have a negative impact upon the success of minority students whether they are enrolled in developmental programs or not.

Data are not currently available to determine if differences in retention rates for minority and nonminority students in higher education are the same for those who participate in developmental programs within the same institutions and those who do not. An examination of such data would certainly cast light on whether participation in developmental programs represents a barrier to minority success.

At the moment, we can only say that while there are differences in the retention rates of white and minority developmental students, these differences cannot be said to result from their participation in developmental programs. At four-year private institutions, participation in developmental programs obviously does not serve as a barrier to retention. African-American students participating in developmental programs at these institutions are not only retained at higher levels than white students, their retention rates are also higher than the national norms for retention.

At community colleges, however, the disparity in retention between white students and African-American students participating in developmental programs is certainly a cause for concern. There are probably many reasons for this finding and, as a guide to further research and to policy makers at community colleges, some speculation regarding these reasons may be in order.

It should be noted that, unlike four-year institutions, community colleges rarely have residential populations. Furthermore, students attending community colleges are more likely to have adult responsibilities, to have families, to work part-time or full-time, and to attend the institution on a part-time basis. As a consequence, students attending community colleges are seldom involved in the academic or non-academic environment of the college. Yet as Astin (1975) and Turnbull (1986) suggest, involvement is a key to retention. It may be that the lack of opportunities for involvement resulting from the nature of community colleges and community college students has more of a negative impact on minorities than on whites.

Furthermore, there is a great deal of evidence suggesting that developmental and psycho-social factors have an important impact on the success of minorities in college (Higher Education Extension

Service, 1992a). Factors such as identity development, self-efficacy, and internal versus external locus of control all contribute to the success of students, yet these factors are often different for white and minority students. Those attending the community college have fewer opportunities to participate in counseling, advising, social experiences, mentoring, and other activities that might contribute to identity development, self-efficacy, and an internal locus of control. Yet all of these factors are known to be associated with the success of students of color, particularly those attending predominantly white institutions (Allen, Epps, & Haniff, 1991; Higher Education Extension Service, 1992b).

Few community colleges are able to provide systematic counseling and intervention designed to promote student development for any students, let alone specifically for students of color. Yet, these activities, available in abundance at private four-year colleges (where minorities in developmental education fare well) may be essential in promoting minority retention.

Furthermore, most community colleges are unlikely to have financial and personnel resources suggested by Miller (1990) and Fleming (1985) as necessary for a comprehensive approach to minority retention. As Shirley Chisholm notes in her interview with Larry Keeter (1987), minority students bring strengths as well as weaknesses to the academic environment. It is up to institutional administrators to provide environments where students of color can capitalize on their strengths and overcome their weaknesses.

Conclusion

For community colleges the retention rates of African-American developmental students are particularly low compared to those of white students. The retention rates of Latino developmental students were uniformly lower at all types of institutions compared to the retention rates of white developmental students.

Since the retention of minorities consistently lags behind that of white students, the differences in retention of white students and students of color may not be attributed exclusively to the latter's participation in developmental education programs. The fact that such differences exist, however, should be a cause for concern among all segments of higher education.

This is particularly true since our analysis suggests that there were few statistically significant differences in the admission credentials of white students and students of color participating in developmental programs at the same type of institution. The differences in performance cannot be explained simply by differences in entry characteristics between white students and students of color.

Evidence from the research suggests that differences in retention are the results of some combination of institutional characteristics and the developmental and/or psycho-social attributes of students of color (Higher Education Extension Service, 1992b). The interaction between minority students' attitudes and personalities and the experience of institutional and/or individual racism may also be contributing factors (Abraham & Jacobs, 1990; Boyer, 1990), particularly at community colleges.

This is not to say that institutional or individual racism is found more often at community colleges than at other types of institutions. This is most unlikely to be the case. It may be, however, that fewer support mechanisms are available at community colleges to assist minority students in overcoming the effects of racism.

These factors and their interactions require further research if minority retention is to be improved in American higher education. In addition, greater efforts by community colleges in particular, as well as higher education institutions in general, should be made to provide systematic intervention on behalf of students of color. Furthermore, these efforts should be supported by institutional policies and procedures which recognize that the retention of students of color will not be accomplished by "business as usual."

It should also be noted that the findings from this study do not support the notion that the community college is the best vehicle for underprepared minorities to attain a higher education. Most community college developmental programs apparently do not provide the same benefits for students of color

as they do for white students. Until serious efforts are made to enhance the retention of the most poorly prepared minority students at community colleges, they may not be the best choice for promoting educational opportunity for students of color. Nevertheless, the findings of this study support those of others (Fleming, 1985; Tinto, 1986; Abraham & Jacobs, 1990; Allen, Epps, & Haniff, 1991) in suggesting that much work remains to be done at all types of institutions before underprepared minority students have an equal chance to succeed in American higher education.

Note: The authors wish to express their thanks to Dr. Alexander Erwin, Assistant Dean of the Reich College of Education, for his help in reviewing and critiquing this article.

References

Abraham, A., & Jacobs W. (1990). *Black and white students' perceptions of their college campuses*. Atlanta: Southern Regional Education Board.

Allen, W., Epps, E., & Haniff, N. (1991). *Colleges in black and white*. Albany: State University of New York Press.

Astin, A. (1975). *Preventing students from dropping out*. San Francisco: Jossey-Bass.

Boyer, E. (1990). *Campus life: In search of community*. The Carnegie Foundation for the Advancement of Teaching, Princeton, NJ: Princeton University Press.

Eckland, B., & Henderson, L. (1981). *College attainment four years after high school*. Report prepared for the National Center for Educational Statistics, Office of Research and Improvement, U. S. Department of Education, Research Triangle Park, NC: Research Triangle Institute.

Fleming, J. (1985). *Blacks in college*. San Francisco: Jossey-Bass.

Higher Education Extension Service. (1992a). The influence of developmental and emotional factors on success in college. *Higher Education Extension Service Review*, 3(2), 1-10.

Higher Education Extension Service. (1992b). *The academic performance of college students: A handbook on research, exemplary programming, policies and practices*. New York: HEES, Teacher's College, Columbia University.

Keeter, L. (1987). Minority students at risk: An interview with Shirley Chisholm. *Journal of Developmental Education*, 13(3), 6-11.

Miller, C. (1990). Minority student achievement: A comprehensive perspective. *Journal of Developmental Education*, 13(3), 6-11.

Tinto, V. (1986). *Leaving college: Rethinking [the] cures of student attrition*. Chicago: Universi[ty] Press.

Turnbull. W. (1986). Involvement: The key to reten[tion]. *[Jour]nal of Developmental Education*, 10(2), 6-11.

Further Readings on Evaluation

Abraham, A. A., Jr. *A Report on College Level Remedial/ Developmental programs in SREB States*. Atlanta, GA: The Southern Regional Education Board, 1987.

Akst, G. (1986). Reflections on evaluating remedial mathematics programs. *Journal of Developmental Education*, 10 (1), 12-15.

Akst, G., and Hecht, M. (1980). Program evaluation. In A. Trillin & Assoc., *Teaching Basic Skills in College*. San Francisco: Jossey-Bass Publishers.

Black, M., Mansfield, W., and Farris, E. (1991, May). *College Level Remedial Education in the Fall of 1989, Survey Report*. Washington DC: Department of Education, National Center for Education Statistics.

Boylan, G., George A., & Bonham, B. (1991) Program evaluation. In R. Flippo & D. Caverly (Eds.) *College Reading and Study Strategy Programs*, Newark, DE: International Reading Association.

Clowes, D. A. (1993). Remediation in American Higher Education. In Smart, J. C. (Ed.) *Higher Education: Handbook of Theory and Practice Volume VIII*, Bronx, NY: Agathon Press, 1992, (462-465).

Clowes, D. A. (1984). The evaluation of remedial/developmental programs: A stage model. *Journal of Developmental Education*, 8(1), 14-15, 27-30.

Materniak, G., & Williams, A. (1987, September). CAS standards and guidelines for learning assistance programs. *Journal of Developmental Education*, 11(1), 12-18.

Maxwell, M. (1993). *Evaluating academic skills programs: A sourcebook*. Kensington, MD: MM Associates.

Morante, E. A. (1976). The effectiveness of developmental programs: A two-year follow-up study. *Journal of Developmental Education*, 9(3), 13-15.

New Jersey Basic Skills Council (1991). *Effectiveness of Remedial Programs in Public Colleges and Universities – Fall 1987–Spring 1989*. Trenton, NJ: New Jersey State Board of Higher Education.

Wiener, H. S. (1989). Evaluating assessment programs in basic skills. *Journal of Developmental Education*, 13 (2), 24-26.